T0353949

Mother State

Mother State

A Political History of Motherhood

HELEN CHARMAN

ALLEN LANE
an imprint of
PENGUIN BOOKS

ALLEN LANE

UK | USA | Canada | Ireland | Australia
India | New Zealand | South Africa

Penguin Books is part of the Penguin Random House group of companies
whose addresses can be found at global.penguinrandomhouse.com.

First published in Great Britain by Allen Lane 2024

001

Set in 12/14.75pt Dante MT Std
Typeset by Jouve (UK), Milton Keynes
Printed and bound in Great Britain by Clays Ltd, Elcograf S.p.A.

The authorized representative in the EEA is Penguin Random House Ireland,
Morrison Chambers, 32 Nassau Street, Dublin D02 YH68

A CIP catalogue record for this book is available from the British Library

ISBN: 978–0–241–51282–1

www.greenpenguin.co.uk

Penguin Random House is committed to a
sustainable future for our business, our readers
and our planet. This book is made from Forest
Stewardship Council® certified paper.

It's more parasitic,
as Weil said of divine love, another mother's
eggs laid in you so you have to keep coming back
to feed them, and that's how we all get vicariously
fed.

Daisy Lafarge, 'How to Leave a Marriage'

Contents

Preface

I am worried about my mother's knees. Recently I went to stay with her while she recovered from the second of two knee operations. The first, a knee replacement, didn't work; it left her unable to fully use her leg and trapped a nerve in her spine which prevented her from easily using her right arm. The second operation, a manipulation under anaesthetic, didn't go very well either: while I was there, she could barely sleep, was reliant on heavy pain relief, and was suffering a lot. Born in 1957, in a very small coal-mining town on the west coast of the South Island of New Zealand where it rains almost constantly, my mother has given her knees, as she would say, 'a hell of a beating'. Working from the age of thirteen cycling long distances delivering mail to neighbouring villages, she eventually trained as a physiotherapist, a profession which requires constant bending, lifting, kneeling and crouching, actions she performed for the National Health Service from her move to England in 1980 until her retirement almost four decades later.

Our bodies are the document of our circumstances, but of all the tales that the body tells, motherhood is at once the most central and the most conspicuously absent. Whether or not you yourself have given birth to a child, your very existence reveals that you were given birth *to*. What it can't tell us is who it was that fed you, who held you, who wore away their own bodies working elsewhere to provide for you. (It also can't tell us how you felt about your needs, or how you felt about having them met.) Not all maternal stories begin in the womb: 'mother' is not a category limited only to those who have given birth to a child, and even for those who have, the attention afforded to this particular organ is hysterically overdetermined. It seems to me that it is my mother's knees that are the true record of mine and my brother's existence: yes, we began our lives in her uterus, but nine months pales in comparison to the long years her care for us was performed through those complicated joints.

The movements that are traditionally associated with motherhood are, after all, not easily distinguishable from those of domestic labour – in many accounts, motherhood simply *is* domestic labour – and for part of my childhood, my mother supplemented her work as a physio with work as a cleaner. Just as some of those fragments of worn-away bone are from carrying me and my brother inside her body for nine months – pregnancy, like cleaning, fucks up your knees – and some are from forty years of helping other people's bodies move more freely through hospital wards and care homes, some are from scrubbing the wine stains out of someone else's carpets. My mother has always been someone with a truly unbelievable, sometimes intolerable, amount of energy, getting by on little sleep and, until she remarried after I had left home, making do with little money. Now, her knees are holding her accountable: refusing to function, they are making her body's history manifest in its present.

Inside them are political as well as personal stories. One is of migration and industry: she was born in the settler colony of New Zealand because her father moved there as a child with his family, who were in search of a more lucrative life than they had in a mining community in County Durham; she moved to England because the NHS was a friend to healthcare workers from the Commonwealth. There is a story in there, too, about the dismantling of the British welfare state: by the time she retired, overworked and overwrought in a newly stealth-privatized community care trust run by Richard Branson's Virgin Care, the NHS was so overstretched that she spent years on the waiting list for the operation that would alleviate some of the knee damage she accrued in its service.

The maternal story held inside her knees, punctuated by all that carrying, rocking, bending and crouching, is also a political one. As a child I both knew my mother wanted and loved me and knew that her life, which was structured around making a series of sacrifices – money, time, peace of mind, sleep – in order to support us, was often a difficult one to live. If her ruined knee represents both the care she gave us (unwaged labour) and the care she gave others (waged labour), then connecting both of them is an absence: the care that wasn't given to her, the missing support that would have eased some of her burdens. I don't mean that she was entirely without: she had and still has many friends and family members, and we were entitled to some government welfare payments, but, on the whole, her mothering was a solitary pursuit. And yet the third party in my relationship with my mother has always been the welfare state, or rather a specific rose-tinted conception of it, intertwined with my deeply felt perception of myself as a New Labour baby, the child of a holistic social contract that was already well on its way out by the time I was born in 1993. We lived within a fantasy of the post-war commitment to nurture.

'I love the state,' the historian Carolyn Steedman writes in a 2017 essay called 'Middle-Class Hair', 'because it has loved me.'[1] This particular piece is about the 1963 Robbins Report, which recommended the foundation of six new universities and a significant increase in the number of students able to pursue higher education in Britain, changing Steedman's life in the process. It could just as easily be about another government report, the one compiled in 1942 by the Liberal economist William Beveridge and his wife Janet, which recommended the basis of what became the British welfare state. Steedman wrote about that one thirty years earlier, in *Landscape for a Good Woman*, a book which recounts her own 1950s childhood in south London alongside her mother's in Burnley, Lancashire, in the 1920s. 'I think,' she writes, 'I would be a very different person now if orange juice and milk and dinners at school hadn't told me, in a covert way, that I had a right to exist, was worth something.'[2] When I first read these words, I experienced a feeling of total recognition, despite the fact that most of the things she is describing – the universal free provision of milk, juice, school dinners and higher education – had been abolished long before I ever crossed the threshold of my primary school. (One thing I did still have was the public library: if childcare couldn't be found, I would get dropped off there in the morning and picked up at closing time. I took a packed lunch, the librarians were all really nice to me, and I read every book about vampires and every book by Jilly Cooper I could find, leaving me with the clear sense that whatever sex was, it had equal parts to do with exsanguination and horse riding.)

My anachronistic conviction that I lived within the shelter of a nurturing state was encouraged by my mother who, I think, wanted to bolster our sense of worth by showing us that we were valued not just by her, a single entity, but by the government, no, by the *country* itself. I didn't look too hard at anything: I didn't ask why, if the NHS was indeed such an organ of love, she got home from work so many hours later than she should every night, why she was so unbelievably stressed, or why she had to take on other work for extra money. As New Labour were replaced first by the coalition government and then by the undiluted Tories, as the culture calcified around the shaming of benefits and those who claimed them, and as the health service itself was reshaped around bitter notions of scarcity and deservingness, I was busy living inside an alternate reality, perhaps inherited from my mother's own youthful dreams of a different life and certainly constructed from my own belief that if only I could be enveloped by the obliterating equality of universal care, nobody would bother to stop and count how many parents lived in my house. I was a complete fantasist: choosing love, I persisted.

During my time staying with my mother after her operation, increasingly frustrated by my failure to make her feel better and by her non-linear recovery (sometimes she'd wake up feeling much better; the next day, she was unable to move), I went for a long run wearing old shoes, a beaten-up pair of pink trainers I'd had since I was a teenager. Within sight of her house, I mis-stepped, and – thanks to the relics on my feet – strained a ligament. I spent the rest of my stay walking at her pace, limping beside her. I started to suspect I had, unconsciously, done it on purpose: unsettled, perhaps, by the inversion of our usual dynamic, her the pragmatic reassurer, me the operatic hypochondriac. In needing something from her I became again, to borrow the Freudian term I find the funniest, Her Majesty the Baby. This was very relaxing. In obsessing about my own body, I could concentrate on something other than my mother's, which, in its failings, was an unwelcome reminder that we are all held captive by time.

I've always been terrified of the idea of losing my mother. ('If you ever die,' I have said to her on more than one occasion, 'I will be so angry with you.') In my early teenage years, well prepared by the intensive vampires-and-erotica reading list I'd constructed for myself in Dorking library, I became obsessed with the American television programme *Buffy the Vampire Slayer*. My secret, feverish viewings of the show left me with persistent night terrors and one overwhelming and foundational visual memory. In the sixteenth episode of the fifth season of the show Buffy's mother, Joyce Summers, dies of a cerebral aneurysm. At first, nobody can really accept it. Buffy, her little sister Dawn and her group of friends, well used by now to fighting supernatural monsters – by this point Buffy herself has already died and been resurrected once – find it almost impossible to understand that Joyce has died of natural causes and cannot be revived; that this is how things are. Mothers get sick, and mothers die.

The episode is very famous, among fans and television scholars alike, and it is called 'The Body': Joyce's corpse is the central focus, dragging the transfixed viewer from the sofa where it's discovered to a table in the Sunnydale morgue and recurring over and over again in flashback. Departing from the gothic visual conventions of the show, the episode uses natural light and diegetic sound, eschewing its usual crucifixes, guitar music and leather jackets, generating a very pure kind of horror. Even when Buffy slays a vampire, it happens in the hospital morgue, not in cemetery shadow but in clinical lowlight, a sideshow distraction from the real object of the drama: Joyce's body, covered by a sheet, on the neighbouring steel slab. Although it is this episode that is remembered as the moment we lose Joyce, in actual fact her lifeless form is discovered at the end of the previous episode, a really stupid one about an abandoned sex robot, with the awful moment of confrontation repeated at the beginning of 'The Body': the reality of Joyce's corpse, in an awkward pose on the sofa, eyes open and unseeing, stretches across the narrative gap, filling the space between the two instalments. It exceeds the story. For many years, I would wake up in the middle of the night drenched in sweat, chased by nightmarish visions of Joyce's lifeless body back into consciousness, screaming for my own mother, asleep down the hall.

The maternal body is perhaps the most psychically freighted cultural object: as a point of convergence between life and death, the womb is hard to separate from the tomb. One of the tasks of feminism has been to interrogate and challenge the unease and repulsion generated by the birthing body, which have often been understood as the buried feelings at the root of patriarchy: the need to violently expel the spectre of birth–death that so disturbingly reminds us of the limits of our own lives.[3] In order to become adult subjects, we have to establish our separation from our origins. What about when that body, the one that contains both our beginning and our end, dies? In her 1964 memoir *A Very Easy Death* – a text which Steedman also discusses – Simone de Beauvoir recounts her inability to look at her mother's naked body in the final weeks of her life. Her mother declared herself to be without shame, but for her daughter, the 'sight of my mother's nakedness had jarred me. No body existed less for me: none existed more.' She knows, it even seems 'reasonable' to her, that the body 'should retain its dual nature, that it should be both repugnant and holy – a taboo'. But when the chips are down, she is disassembled, 'astonished' at the violence of her own distress.[4]

Grieving children – of any age – often describe the experience of losing their mother as one of violent dissociation: they lose a part of themselves, and they lose their grip on something both historical and personal. Many new mothers speak of their experiences of childbirth similarly: an experience of total obliteration, of being swallowed up or erased by the totalizing force of maternal identity. In memoirs of children grieving their mothers, or caring for them as they die, an explicit inversion often occurs: the child becomes the mother, or the mother becomes a child. This is a reversal of what we usually think of as history: the easy chronology of generation, of daughters begetting daughters begetting daughters begetting daughters. In death as in birth, maternity has the terrifying potential to turn the order of things upside down. At the centre of this equation we find the body, not in the sense of full physical reversal – burial is not pregnancy – but rather in the embodied manifestation of care: its repetitive tasks, whatever form they may take. The essence of mothering is transferred in recognizing need and trying to meet it, and in recognizing vulnerability and trying to offer protection.

Still, the state also governs how we live and how we die. I was born in a nationalized hospital and so was my brother, and my mother's first knee operation was done in one, and done badly. (It was hard to come to terms with that, not least because of its irony: an NHS physio walks her exhausted joints into an operating theatre . . .) Today, as the British government continues its assault on the welfare state, care for both children and the elderly is being pushed from the sphere of public responsibility to the private. Without the financial resources to outsource either, love becomes compulsion.

The passage from *A Very Easy Death* that Steedman quotes in *Landscape for a Good Woman* is de Beauvoir's description of the immediate aftermath of her mother's death, from which the book takes its title. A nurse tells de Beauvoir that the death, in a private Parisian hospital, was an easy one: an upper-class death. 'Outside,' Steedman contests, 'for the poor, dying is a different matter', before adding a description of her own mother's death as a comparison: 'she lived alone, she died alone: a working-class life, a working-class death.'[5] De Beauvoir's point, of course, is the irony: the 'very easy' death of her mother in Paris is still almost unbearably painful, still generates that shocking, violent distress. Dying is never easy. But Steedman is reminding us that, for many people and by varying degrees, living isn't either.

I can't get all these mothers out of my head. If it's true that the mark of becoming a self-sufficient adult subject is successfully banishing the spectre of infancy, I've failed on two counts, because I can't get the state – my fantasy state, the one that loves me – out of my head, either. I don't know, though, if I agree with this idea that our very personhood depends on banishment and separation. The maternal body as a symbol, after all, is not so different from the most naively fantastical idea of a welfare system: a blueprint for a politics of reciprocity and sustenance that links us together, within which a successful life is defined by connection, not competition. There's violence in this closeness too, of course, and all the murky psychic hardships that social life engenders. But the achievement is managing the difficult work of living – and dying – together: of simply going on, going through.

The seventh episode of season six of *Buffy the Vampire Slayer* is a musical one. Cursed by a demon, the show's protagonists are compelled to reveal their inner feelings through bursting embarrassingly into song, making the subtext of all their interactions the text. Dawn Summers – in the middle of the melodramatic, hysterical turbulence of puberty – ends one musical performance with the line 'the hardest thing in this world is to live in it.' This has always struck me as being very wise. It's an observation which, for all the melodrama of its delivery, is rooted in something small, something daily, something repetitive. Within this contradiction sits maternal politics: the drama of life and the mundane practicalities of its sustenance. It's not an acapella performance. We have to help each other with the difficult work of living that is yet to come.

Introduction

Hysterical History

I have been tempted to write a chapter headed 'Politics',
so that it could be skipped by people who find the whole
subject boring, but politics permeated everything.

Doris Lessing, *Walking in the Shade*

Motherhood is a political state. Nurture, care, the creation of human life – all immediate associations with mothering – have more to do with power, status and the distribution of resources, both by mothers and for them, than we like to admit. For raising children is the foundational work of society, and, from gestation onward, it is unequally shared. Political maternity has two parts: first, the social and cultural contexts that mothers exist within and are constrained by – the way things are – and, second, the expansive possibilities of reorganizing these structures: the way things could be. Acknowledging that motherhood is inherently political helps us identify precisely who benefits from the status quo: a government and an economy reliant on the denial of collective responsibility. It is also the first concrete step towards liberating mothers from their current position, where so much is expected of them and so little provided.

There is a crucial difference between the recognition that all motherhood is political and the politicization of motherhood for particular ends. The former is an emancipatory tool; the latter reduces the mother to a weapon to be deployed in someone else's argument. Motherhood has been put to work, over the course of the last fifty years and before them, by many conservative ideologies, in headlines, in policymaking and in cultural representation: bad mothers are too poor, the wrong race, the wrong sexuality, the wrong gender; they have the wrong politics, the wrong housing, the wrong reasons for being mothers at all. The good mother, on the other hand, is a conveniently wholesome container: she brings a certain sympathetic quality – that feminine touch! – to whatever doctrine is poured into her, but she exists firmly outside the realm of the political itself.

There have been recent attempts to make motherhood visible as a political issue. As the popularization of liberal feminism reshaped the mainstream in the 2010s, mothering became something of a zeitgeist topic, though this has mostly been limited to a very particular set of concerns relating to middle-class mothers who work, whether through the frequent positioning of motherhood as an opposite to the creative vocation of being a writer or an artist, or simply a concern with making capitalism function better for such women.[1] To fight for fair employment practices for mothers is, of course, fundamentally political; motherhood has long been the leading factor in gendered inequality in the workplace. This operates at both a literal and a conceptual level: whatever your personal circumstances, if you are perceived by your boss to be a woman of childbearing age, the risk of discrimination applies to you, too.[2] Yet to focus on isolated politicized moments – when childcare becomes difficult to balance with work commitments, for example, or when breastfeeding is understood as a public faux pas – falls short of understanding motherhood in its entirety. Such isolated campaigns, however worthwhile, still position the public and the private as separate spheres, connected via the experiences of individuals who have children, suggesting that motherhood becomes political only at these moments of contact with civil society: this became particularly clear during the COVID-19 pandemic, when lockdown, in contracting all public life to the home, temporarily dissolved the boundaries between the two. The dominant view of mothering in contemporary discourse, both culturally and politically, is that it belongs to the domestic realm, where it can be conveniently ignored. This both seriously limits the imaginative possibilities of what mothers can be and obscures the real, complex history of public maternity in the twentieth and twenty-first centuries. The mothering that happens in these chapters, from the 1970s to the 2010s, takes place in comfortable homes, in glossy magazines and reality TV shows, in prisons, in protest camps, in squats, on picket lines, in hospitals and on public transport.

To declare motherhood an entirely political state is to claim back territory for ourselves. To do so, we have to confront its relationship with *the* state: which, for my purposes, is the governing body of Britain and Northern Ireland, the sixth largest economy in the world, where one in four children are living in poverty.[3] (I use the disputed term 'Northern Ireland' because it is the state that goes by that name – its impositions and its illegitimacies – that I am dealing with.) In her 2020 book *Feminism, Interrupted*, Lola Olufemi writes that women's lives have always been 'intimately linked to the state': earning, on average, less than men, 'they disproportionately depend on the state for a range of services such as child maintenance, legal aid, and housing provision.' If you add to this the fact that 90 per cent of lone parents are working mothers who, although historically characterized as leeching off the state, are more often than not in work that does not pay them enough to provide for their families, we can begin to see the scale of the problem.[4]

The title of this book is *Mother State*, inspired, in part, by Olufemi's words. Its project is to bring together elements that are usually considered distinct and separate: the state of being a mother itself, including but not limited to the physical experiences of pregnancy and birth; the relationship between mothers and the state; the uses the state puts mothering to – its politicization, in other words – and, finally, the conception of the welfare state as some kind of maternal entity in and of itself. Within it, too, are the echoes of the pejorative 'nanny state', the accusation levelled at government policies by critics of welfare, economic interventionism, and public health and safety initiatives. The nanny, of course, is a substitute figure for the mother: the fear of replacement, the fear of abandonment and uneasy divisions of labour haunt the term. There are other ghostly phrases inhabiting the title: motherland, mother country, even Mother Earth. It is difficult, in the third decade of the twenty-first century, to preserve the plenty in these phrases against the shadows of misogynist reduction, imperial nostalgia and resurgent fascism that flock around them; I'd still like to try.

One of the primary insights of feminism has been that things previously understood as private, intimate and natural are actually public, cultural and socially constructed. I want to consider how we can rectify the current state of affairs, in which maternity is constantly *politicized* – manipulated to specific ends – without being understood as *political*, without either denying the importance of individual subjectivity – the deeply personal feelings mothering generates, muddies and destabilizes – or submitting to the weaponization of such feelings in the service of the status quo. There is a more personal reminder in the title, too: to reckon with my own blind spots, the false memory I cultivated as a child of a kind of welfare state I never really knew.

Although many who grew up in the 1950s, like Carolyn Steedman, felt that the 'good things' provided by the state were a 'birthright' to be taken for granted, 'just as we took for granted our right to be in the world', for others – who weren't white, or weren't able-bodied, or didn't have the right passport – the state was far from a nurturing guarantor. Back in 1985, in their landmark work of Black feminism *The Heart of the Race*, Beverley Bryan, Stella Dadzie and Suzanne Scafe wrote of the 'uncaring arm of the state', underlining the role played by social work and healthcare in policing and surveilling Black communities: 'legislation designed to protect the NHS from "abuse" by foreigners means that hospitals now record our medical history *and* our immigration status.'[5] Over thirty years later, Jacqueline Rose opened her book *Mothers* with the story of Bimbo Ayelabola, a Nigerian woman who had delivered quintuplets by caesarean section in an NHS hospital in 2011 and was subsequently hounded by the press with the intent of whipping up outrage that the births had cost 'us' – the taxpayer – money. Mothers like Ayelabola, Rose writes, are 'held accountable for the ills of the world, the breakdown in the social fabric, the threat to welfare, to the health of the nation'.[6] Never understood to be deserving recipients of the nurture that by rights belongs to all, their bodies are the places where distinctions between 'us' and 'them' are plotted.

Before we meet this book's many mothers, I want to set out the ideas it builds on. An expansive, political understanding of motherhood has room within in it for a variety of relationships and identities, for men and women, and it can be a powerful metaphor for a politics that centres interconnectedness in its understanding of liberation. In this way, it is opposed to any attempt to use motherhood to limit definitions of womanhood itself. 'Mother', like 'woman', is a vexed category, one embedded at the heart of contemporary moral panics about gender and sexuality.[7] It is not difficult to see, in the 'gender critical' movement, that that positions biology at the centre of identity, a deeply reactionary understanding of how gender is defined and how people are described and valued.

This kind of essentialist thinking – a woman is a woman because of her reproductive organs, her experience of menstruation, and her ability to bear children – has far more in common with the conservative movements throughout history that have categorized women as caregivers, domestic agents, worth only what their reproductive capacities can offer, than any feminist movement worth its name. Judith Butler wrote in 2020 that 'When laws and social policies represent women, they make tacit decisions about who counts as a woman, and very often make presuppositions about what a woman is.'[8] They make presuppositions about what a mother is, too. Think of the intense transphobic abuse faced by the mother and Trades Union Congress policy officer Mika Minio-Paluello, who went on national television in the summer of 2023 to speak about the cost-of-living crisis and its impact on mothers in particular: Minio-Paluello's point – that mothers need adequate resources to support their children – was, for those querying her right to speak as a mother, far less important than her identity.

Despite this contemporary uterine fixation, it is a myth that giving birth has ever been enough to guarantee the social, legal or political status of motherhood or even the female gender itself.[9] Such histories of inequality are made manifest in maternity care. In the UK, Black mothers are four times more likely than their white counterparts to die in childbirth; the same 2021 report found that mothers in the most economically deprived areas of the country are three times more likely to die than those in affluent areas.[10] Just as there is no universal maternal experience, the care and support afforded to mothers today is far from evenly provided. To advocate for the rights and needs of mothers, we have to refuse the forces that try to paint maternity as one easily digestible, easily definable state of being, and in doing so try to individualize its responsibilities. We all have a stake in the social future.

Homework

Imagine a day in the life of a mother with a small child or a baby. It's not a workday, or maybe she doesn't have paid work. It is shaped by a series of repetitive tasks, trying to provide for the child and keep it safe. Labour, in other words. The great trick of patriarchal capitalism has been to designate certain kinds of work as inherent to maternity and, therefore, not really work at all. In Kate Briggs's novel *The Long Form*, which depicts a single day in the life of Helen and her baby daughter, Rose, a section entitled 'MOTHERING' declares it to be

> one historical name for the category of human (and not only human) work that, for as long as there are children, must be undertaken by *someone*. An individual or partnership or group, taking over from whomever it was that left the baby here, fed and wrapped, seemingly safe and asleep – taking up from where their life-preserving work stopped and *continuing* it. For a baby on its own doesn't exist. It can't.

Briggs builds up the thought, bringing in the expert witness, the paediatrician and psychoanalyst Donald Winnicott:

Show me a baby, Winnicott wrote, and I will show you the person (or people) living near it, next to it. There can be no reality of a baby, no proper understanding of what a baby is – as well as, in real terms, no continued lifetime of a baby – outside of its relation with/to someone else ('the great responsibility it must be to someone'). But – who will do it? A 'mother'? The 'mother'?[11]

What's the difference between 'a mother' and 'the mother'? Does one have more rights over this baby than the other? Or is it simply that more is expected of her? Perhaps, though, they're two sides of the same coin. Later in the novel, Helen considers the fiction of the unified maternal self. 'Helen', to herself, 'was a gathering, a little group' of selves: 'mobile, tense with types and energies; some bolder, capable and confident, others more nervy and difficult. But among them there was no "mother".' This is a cause of some consternation to Helen, who has been expecting the appearance of this capable character, who would 'take over' the ragtag bundle of other, earlier selves inside her: 'The mother-character. A person not just physically capable of doing the care-taking work that a baby requires but fully and uncomplicatedly embracing it'. Her arrival will make Helen a better, steadier, more coherent version of herself. When this never happens, it provokes a realization: there is no 'immediate, radical, inner change'. Instead, there is just the 'doing of it': the small tasks of care, which add up to the serious work of life preservation, done by someone who is still nervy, unsure, difficult.

The idea that motherhood somehow marks a decisive break with an earlier self is related to the idealization of mothering as a form of self-sacrifice. Virginia Woolf's declaration in *A Room of One's Own* that 'we think back through our mothers if we are women' is one of the most frequently quoted lines of all her work. After thinking back through this maternal line herself, she came to the conclusion that, in order to write, women had to kill their mothers, or, at least, 'the angel in the house'. Woolf elaborated on the characteristics of her victim in 1931: she was 'intensely sympathetic', 'immensely charming' and, crucially, 'utterly unselfish'. In particular, she 'sacrificed herself daily': if there was chicken, she took the leg; if there was a draught she sat in it.'[12] The relationship between mothers and daughters has often been understood to be particularly difficult because of the weight of such sacrificial expectations. If the parameters of permissible maternity are kept narrow, and mothering is inscribed as a necessarily female duty, then the mother can represent, to the daughter, a curtailment of freedom that is yet to come, an obliteration of the self and all its pleasures and complexities. My lodestar Carolyn Steedman describes a letter she wrote to a friend during a university vacation 'in which I describe my sitting in the evenings with my mother, refusing to go out, holding tight to my guilt and duty, knowing that I was her, and I must keep her company'. In my own teenage diaries I can find pages and pages of diatribe against my mother's expectations I might help her with the endless housework that I could see was always threatening to swallow her whole. I was *never*, I swore with fervent vitriol, going to allow such mundane stuff to overwhelm my life when I was older.[13]

The angel in the house is a legacy of the Victorian period: the phrase originates in a poem by Coventry Patmore, first published in 1854. (Woolf's own mother's life spanned almost exactly the second half of the nineteenth century.) By the middle of that century, as industrialization and the bedding-in of capitalism moved production from the household to the factory, the structure of the family itself had begun to change, and an idealized mother figure emerged who was removed from the field of labour: her tasks of care were, rather, understood as acts of self-sacrifice proper to the female character. An embodiment of domestic, private virtue, the image relies on a particular middle-class white sensibility: it's a figure of exclusion, disguised as a universal idea. The angel was ideologically useful to the state, both in foreign policy – the 'British home' was a primary export to colonized countries – and at home, where it offered a useful means of controlling the serious threat of female sexuality which, prized and feared in equal measure, could only be properly controlled through marriage and legitimate maternity. Mothering, performed correctly, replaced the process of reproduction (sexuality) with its product (gentle, selfless infant care).[14]

The post-war reorganization of British society, beginning in most accounts with the founding of the welfare state, is often credited with a total rewiring of so-called Victorian attitudes. This is attributed first to the fact that so many women had joined the workforce for the first time during the war effort, many of whom were mothers, and second to the headily liberatory social and sexual politics of the 1960s, as well as the educational opportunities newly offered to young women.[15] It wasn't that simple (it never is). After the Second World War, in response to the low birth rate which had been a concern since the 1930s, there was widespread, state-endorsed encouragement for women to have children. In Denise Riley's *War in the Nursery*, a landmark 1983 study of the relationship between the role theories of infant development played in the formation of the welfare state, she identifies within this pro-natalism a targeted attack on the very idea of the working mother, a reinforcement of the old divisions of labour along gendered lines. The state nurseries which had been set up during wartime to provide childcare for the children of working women closed down rapidly once the war had ended: the government 'repeatedly emphasized', Riley notes, that they had been 'intended as aids to war production and not social services in themselves'.[16] As wartime industries ceased production and men returned in 1945, women left the workforce: the woman's place became once again within a marriage, staying at home with her child. Motherhood was positioned as another kind of national service, a woman's duty and a replacement for professional work.

Salvation for mothers came not from the welfare state, then, but from feminism. Riley was very active in the British Women's Liberation Movement, to which she attributed the general social origin of the challenge to the 'transparently conservative account of motherhood' that had taken hold after 1945.[17] The WLM's existence is generally dated to the first National Women's Liberation Movement Conference held at Ruskin College in Oxford, between 27 February and 1 March 1970, gathering together groups that had been meeting regionally across the country. (I use British here intentionally: although there was significant feminist organizing occurring in Northern Ireland, there were complaints from Irish feminists that the movement was frequently Anglocentric in the extreme.) The relationship of mothers to the state was a principal problem for the WLM from the very beginning. Its first four demands, decided at the Ruskin conference, were for equal pay, equal educational and job opportunities, free contraception and abortion on demand, and free twenty-four-hour nurseries. These demands, alongside a further three that came later, are engaged with a reform of the state, working with it and implying some faith in its ability to deliver more liberatory conditions. The best way, I think, of understanding this perhaps contradictory position – asking for things from a system understood as unsalvageable at worst and oppressive at best – is via the political theorist Katrina Forrester's description of feminism in this period as working 'in and against the state' to disentangle state support, like social security payments, from state control, like the restrictions placed on how those claiming benefits could live. Forrester's work discusses a central conflict within feminism in the rapidly de-industrializing United Kingdom: 'resources we need involve us in relations we don't'. The question was whether it was possible to redistribute such resources without becoming ensnared in their traps.[18]

Mothering is often held to be synonymous with domestic labour. Marxist and socialist feminists – who made up a sizeable proportion of the WLM and were advocating for an engagement with the state rather than a wholesale rejection of it – understood the tasks that constitute the everyday work of mothering through the concept of social reproduction: unpaid work that allows capitalist society to reproduce both itself and the inequalities of gender, race and class embedded within it. This encompasses more general care, including for the unwell and the elderly, an extension, in other words, of Kate Briggs's 'life-preserving work': in 2017, the Conservative MP David Mowat said that the solution to the social care crisis faced by the country was for people to simply accept that they themselves had a 'duty' to care for their elderly parents, just as they have to look after 'their own children'.[19] Whenever I'm thinking about the history of social reproduction, especially if I'm talking about it with students, I turn to a print by See Red Women's Workshop, a feminist collective active between 1974 and 1990: it shows a factory production line featuring scenes of care, with the slogan 'CAPITALISM ALSO DEPENDS UPON DOMESTIC LABOUR'. Another shows a woman's day from 6 a.m. when the baby wakes to the evening when she knits after preparing and washing up dinner, alongside her husband's declaration to a colleague over a coffee break that 'MY WIFE DOESN'T WORK'. Around the same time that See Red were making their prints, a network of feminist groups were organizing under the banner of 'Wages for Housework', arguing that reproductive labour was entirely central to both society and the economy, and that, as such, it was unpaid work, not a natural byproduct of love.

The historian Tithi Bhattacharya describes social reproduction theory as something which restores the 'messy, sensuous, gendered, raced, and unruly component' of living human beings to the economic process.[20] Part of this unruly mess is the fact that, particularly when it comes to maternal relationships, love remains a stubborn cog in the wheel. There's a danger, as feminist scholars like Lisa Baraitser and Stella Sandford have warned, of a 'swallowing up' of maternal labour into the broader category of social reproduction, the erasure of its specificities.[21] When it comes to specifically maternal work, the assumed 'naturalness' of feminized labour has a double edge: not only does it allow for the synthesization of childbearing and purpose – this is what your body is for – but it also erases more complex histories of delegation. Consider, for example, the lullaby, that paradigmatically maternal sound. In the words of the poet and writer Holly Pester:

Who is the traditional singer of lullabies? The mother, the sister, the maidservant, the nanny, the wet nurse and colonized bodies of imperial systems; commoning women, those whose work is turned into capitalized care and that in turn supports work outside the home and global economies.[22]

Maternal work has, historically, been outsourced by mothers as much as performed by them: working-class women are present in every link of the chain of feeding and clothing and cleaning that can be traced through households and workplaces and out into the broader expanse of history. The social changes that have altered the landscape of work and family life since the Wages for Housework Campaign was officially launched at the 1972 International Feminist Conference have rendered the housewife a perplexing category: rather than a figure of banal familiarity, the word today is more readily associated with the glamorous women of reality-television franchises and the wives of the super-rich, whose households are run by staff and whose children, more often than not, are dispatched to elite boarding schools.

The Personal is Political

In the 1970s, long before the Real Housewives of Orange County erupted into our cultural consciousness, feminists began to focus on the isolation and alienation experienced by women within the traditional family: the angel in the house needed attention. Although the genteel history of this figure didn't help with the WLM's image problem – Beatrix Campbell made fun of those who attended the Ruskin conference in the *Morning Star* for being 'middle-class mothers' who were horrified to find themselves in 'servantless homes' – many feminists in the WLM were drawing on family abolition, a concept central to Karl Marx and Friedrich Engels's *Communist Manifesto*, which has experienced a resurgence in popularity in recent years, thanks in particular to the work of theorists like Sophie Lewis and M. E. O'Brien.[23] The aim, repeated again and again in the literature of the movement, was a transformation of every form of relation. As Sheila Rowbotham, a socialist feminist and a pivotal figure in the wider movement, asked in 1979: 'How do we conceive and imagine a completely different society, involving not only change in the external structures but an inner transformation of our consciousness and our feelings?'[24] One answer, it was hoped, was by talking about these feelings. Feminists engaged in the practice of consciousness-raising, or CR: groups met and discussed aspects of their lives – housework, marriage, sex, birth, abortion, post-partum depression – and, together, moved towards understanding and naming these things as political. The phrase 'the personal is political', most often attributed to the American radical feminists Shulamith Firestone and Anne Koedt, became a defining slogan of the second-wave feminist movement.[25] Simply put (ha ha), the phrase has come to refer to the fact that the isolated individual experiences of loneliness, distress, horror and ennui experienced by women are not, in fact, isolated but rather produced and sustained by systemic, structural inequalities. Motherhood is central to this idea, both for mothers themselves and for their children: the cages we make for ourselves and each other out of obligation and expectation, which we call duty or love.

There were dissenting voices from the notion that looking inward was a route to outward transformation, particularly from groups like the Brixton Black Women's Group, the Organisation for Women of Asian and African Descent, and anticolonial groups with an internationalist focus, who felt that these discussions were a distraction from the urgency of resistance.[26] In his collection of writings on Black struggles for socialism, *Communities of Resistance*, the writer, organizer and former director of the Institute for Race Relations in London A. Sivanandan takes a dim view of 'the personal is the political' as a mantra for change. In practice, he writes, it has tended 'to personalize and fragment and close down struggles'. He suggests an inversion: 'the political is personal', a phrase concerned with 'what is owed to society by one', rather than 'what is owed to one by society'. The former produces 'radical individualism', while the latter produces 'a radical society'.[27] Sivanandan is advancing a critique of identity politics: to understand that the political is personal is to accept that identification is not a totalizing force. This is a helpful framework within which we can place the vastness of mothering. The fact that women *in general* and mothers *in general* have been the victims of oppressive political systems throughout history does not erase distinctions of time and place, race and class. If even the most powerful women have suffered, how much more can the stories of those with less power tell us? And in which ways has motherhood itself been weaponized by those with the interests of the most powerful in mind?

Yet I do not think, as Sivanandan does, that a concern with 'what is owed to one by society' is incompatible with the radical collective potential of 'the political is personal'. Quite the opposite: the isolation and poverty experienced by many mothers and children over the past five decades, a number increasing with each passing month, is overwhelmingly due to the fact that society is not giving them what they are owed: the fulfilment of their needs. The historical period that this book covers encompasses the demolition of the welfare state by successive governments, culminating in the post-2010 programme of austerity, an anchor for its final chapters and the defining political feature of my own lifetime, shrivelling and warping the social fabric at devastating speed. In 2017, the House of Commons Library reported that women had borne 86 per cent of its burden. Enfolded within that percentage are other figures, too: women of colour have higher unemployment rates than white women, and austerity reinforced and increased the inequalities reproduced in British society before the 2008 financial crisis, when the poverty rate among minority ethnic groups – 40 per cent – was double that of the white population.[28] In her book *Crippled*, Frances Ryan details how austerity administered the double blow of dramatically reducing the support received by disabled people and launching a media campaign of demonization that categorized them as 'scroungers' whom the state simply cannot afford.[29]

If living by the understanding that the political is personal produces 'a radical society', what place does motherhood have in its construction? Riley concludes *The War in the Nursery* like this:

There can be no version of motherhood *as such* which can be deployed to construct a radical politics. [. . .] Great intricacies are wrapped up in the bland package labelled 'motherhood'; stubborn and delicate histories, wants and attributions are concealed in it.[30]

We might add to this Jacqueline Rose's warning that 'feminism has nothing to gain from a validation of motherhood in the name of creativity or power.'[31] I'm certainly wary of the word 'radical', one which has been used with such wild profligacy over the past ten years – often in relation to female 'power' – that it no longer retains, for me, anything of its essential meaning. Aspects of mothering have been heralded as radical with increasing regularity, in fact, in recent years, almost always within a particular individual context: an MP bringing their baby to the House of Commons, or a famous actress using a double breast pump while wearing expensive lingerie. In these images, the links between the mother and social democracy – where the raising of children is in some sense a burden shared by the state and its inhabitants – have been replaced by the neoliberal ideal of the professional middle-class mother, 'doing it all'.[32] Radical, used in this way, becomes something merely aspirational: a means of escaping the political reality rather than mounting a serious challenge to the status quo.

Cultural myths last a long time, and the housebound angel has been particularly resilient, as illustrated by the eerily perfect – and, as Candice Brathwaite's work shows, overwhelmingly white – images transmitted from the world of Instagram mothering, the 'mumfluencers' (some of whom, as I write this, are cosplaying nineteenth-century domestic tableaus, based, apparently, on the 'best mothers in literature').[33] In January 1983, Margaret Thatcher gave an interview to the London Weekend Television programme *Weekend World* during which, describing her plan for a more 'self-reliant' society in which 'people are more independent' rather than expecting their 'standard of living to be guaranteed by the State', she expressed her desire for a return to the 'Victorian values' on which 'our country became great', a fantasy of 'independence and initiative' rather than 'compulsion by the State'.[34] To whatever extent the post-war consensus did manage to banish the ghost of the Victorians, it was a short-lived exorcism.

Hysterical History

In *Women in Dark Times*, Jacqueline Rose observes that 'the personal is political' has become 'a well-worn feminist claim'. 'In the beginning,' she continues, it drew attention to the way that women's private lives were 'soaked in the ugliest realities of patriarchal power. But if the claim has faded somewhat, it might be because it shied away from the most disturbing component of its own insight – which is that once you open the door to what is personal, intimate, you never know what you are going to find.'[35] One serious question that we need to ask in order to build a feminist understanding of motherhood as an expanded term is how to accommodate both the work of mothering and the feeling of it, without falling back on the old rigid categories, the private/public divide by another name. To do so, we have to consider the murky legacies of our psyches, too.

There is no single unifying maternal feeling, and motherhood can be a deeply ambivalent experience, as much as a joyful or liberatory one. This insight comes partly from object-relations psychoanalysis – a school of analysis focusing, very broadly speaking, on the development of the ego during childhood – which came to prominence in Britain in the twentieth century through the work of practitioners like Winnicott and Melanie Klein. Ambivalence is the term they use for the enmeshing of love and hate, care and resentment, that sits at the heart of the mother–child relationship. One of the major accomplishments of psychoanalysis has been to emphasize the importance of these mixed feelings: to 'mother' is a much more expansive verb than it is often assumed to be. Not all care is performed virtuously, altruistically, or even well: it can cause harm as much as it prevents or alleviates it.

Many feminist projects of the 1970s and 80s centred on the ambivalence of daughters, thinking back, as if following Woolf's directive, through the lives of their mothers and grandmothers and great-grandmothers. In *Dutiful Daughters*, a collection of personal histories edited by Sheila Rowbotham and Jean McCrindle which was published in 1977 with the subtitle 'Women Talk about Their Lives', older women describe their difficulties reconciling reproduction with their political and emotional lives. Contraception, communism, illness, the post-war tenants' movement, socialist Sunday schools, factories and strikes all feature heavily, knitted right into the heart of maternal and grandmaternal memory and experience.[36] Almost every account begins with the interviewee's fierce response to being asked about their relationship with their mother, something the historian Margaretta Jolly echoes in her account of compiling an oral history archive of the WLM itself forty years later: the 'intake of breath almost all took when an interviewer asked about their mothers – and indeed, my own, when I was asked'.[37]

In my years of researching motherhood (before this book, I wrote a PhD thesis about maternal sacrifice in mid-to-late Victorian fiction) I have learned the most from those who refuse to shy away from the personal, who confront the emotional specificity of experiences – closeness and separation, both at times unbearable; the pain and the tedium of love – while never losing sight of the structures that surround them. Lauren Berlant, for instance, writing that their mother, through cigarettes-as-weight-reduction and a high-heel-induced spinal injury, 'died of femininity', or Hazel Carby drawing her family history as a fault line in a cracking empire, in the process disrupting the narrative of Black feminism as an explicitly maternal lineage.[38] Lorna Sage, in her memoir *Bad Blood*, describes her teenage pregnancy in a household haunted by the spectre of her maternal grandfather's amorous disgrace, her father's rigid conformity and her mother's neurotic fear of bodies, as something she has *done to her mother*, rather than something that has happened and indeed is happening to her: 'I've done it now,' she writes. 'I've made my mother pregnant.'[39] Texts like these are attentive to the way things bleed into each other and, in doing so, alter: how do the bodies of mothers and children impress themselves on each other, and what gets reproduced in them both?

Any reckoning with the oppressive aspects of family history in which the mother is solely understood as a repressive or conventional presence, an obstruction to feminist self-realization, is a castigation of the gaoler that lacks an analysis of who gave them the keys. (I often think of, and am deeply unsettled by, Simone de Beauvoir recalling her difficult mother, approaching the end of her life, telling her difficult daughter that 'I know you don't think me intelligent; but still, you get your vitality from me. The idea makes me happy.')[40] Some of these projects are intended as a redress for the fact that the lineage of women's writing is disrupted both by exclusion from the canon and by the practical impossibilities of writing when you're wielding a duster or feeding a baby.[41] In *Silences*, first published in 1978, the American writer, communist and union organizer Tillie Olsen maps these absences in literary history and contextualizes them within exactly this bind. Olsen, who spent her entire life battling to find space and time to write while raising four daughters on the money she made as (variously and not only) a waitress, a factory labourer, a meat trimmer and a domestic worker, writes that, 'In the twenty years I bore and reared my children, and usually had to work on a paid job as well, *the simplest circumstances for creation did not exist.*' 'More than any other human relationship, overwhelmingly more,' she elaborates, 'motherhood means being instantly interruptible, responsive, responsible.' In a journal entry written in the 1950s, she describes herself as continually being 'pushed by the most elementary force – money – further more possibly away from writing'.[42]

In this context, we have to ask where the gaps are in historical testimony: who is able to express what they feel and what has happened to them? For whom does the vocabulary most easily bend? Roland Barthes, writing in 1981 in *Camera Lucida*, an elegy for his mother masquerading as a book about photography, declares: 'History is hysterical: it is constituted only if we consider it, only if we look at it – and in order to look at it, we must be excluded from it.'[43] This exclusion, for Barthes, is something to be lamented: hysteria is the manifestation of a yearning for a lost, unfragmented past. But what if hysterical history could be an aspirational concept? A process in which the repetition, ill feeling, dead-ends, confusion, falsehood and misreadings which make up real life were counted? The psychoanalytic term, after all, refers to the past rearing its head in the present. It was commonly understood as a specifically female disease, originating linguistically in *hystera*, the Greek word for uterus, and rooted in the case studies of the female hysterics whose lost voices, fainting fits, paralysis, disturbed vision and imaginary pregnancies were the manifestations of repressed events from their own pasts: 'Hysterics', Freud and Breuer tell us in 1895's *Studies on Hysteria*, 'suffer mainly from reminiscences.'[44]

Canonically, the hysteric is an unreasonable, overly emotional, irrational woman, familiar in so many iterations of the stock mother character. In a feminist reading, however, she is simply a woman who can no longer bear the conditions of her life: in response to the unliveable demands imposed upon her, her body rebels. In *Studies on Hysteria*, Freud ventriloquizes her complaint: 'Why, you tell me yourself that my illness is probably connected with my circumstances and the events in my life. You cannot alter these in any way. How do you propose to help me, then?' It's a good question.[45] Within our unhappy maternal associations, is there a way to reassess the damage that gets done to us, as well as by us? If hysteria is personal, doesn't it stand to reason that it is political, too?

The only way out is through, but we have to go through it *together*. Writing in 1970, the radical feminist Shulamith Firestone decried the 'blackout of feminist history' between the so-called first and second waves of feminism that kept 'women hysterically circling through a maze of false solutions': unable to see the past clearly, and unable, therefore, to build on a legacy of collective action, their old pains kept returning in new guises.[46] Amid the new, overtly socialist forms of history-writing that emerged in Britain in the 1960s, particularly those related or adjacent to Raphael Samuel and the History

Workshop movement, feminist historians struggled to advance the study of women's lives not just as one kind of history-from-below but specifically a history from within: 'Why open up history to the unconscious?' asks Sally Alexander, before answering her own question: 'Historians are as familiar as the analyst, poet, philosopher, everyone in their daily lives, with the power of the imaginary: dreams, phantasy, desire, fear, envy.' (A little earlier in the same book, Alexander recalls the 'gust of masculine laughter' that greeted the suggestion made by a group of women present at the 1969 Ruskin History Workshop that a meeting could be convened of those interested in working on 'Women's History'.)[47] Here, it's the boundaries of history itself that need to change: to become more malleable, more flexible, admit the impossibility of objectivity, reconsider the kinds of documents that count.

Denise Riley, who is my favourite slippery poet as well as the influential theorist of gender and motherhood we've already encountered here, writes in her book *The Words of Selves* 'What am I up to, when I depict myself?'[48] The appropriate question in this context, perhaps, is what am I up to when I don't? As a post-feminist child in a strictly chronological sense, it is very easy to make my own daughterhood politically legible: I know that I inherited my understanding of politics from my mother. I don't mean that she and I share an exact set of opinions, although there are certain common things upon which we agree; I don't mean, either, that she was particularly didactic in the way she spoke about political parties, although she was always an outspoken Labour voter. I mean that, growing up in the way I grew up, with the mother I had, who had grown up in the way she had, I would never have been able to understand the world around me as anything other than fatally material: there was no line in our house between the political and personal, between the inside and the outside. I make no claims for this book as an exhaustive account of mothering; rather, it is an attempt at writing, in all senses, a hysterical history. I've started with where I came from – the worn-out cartilage in my mother's knee, her NHS uniform going endlessly round and round in the washing machine – before beginning to work my way out, to the state of affairs we face today.

Mother State is divided into three parts. The first deals with the body: birth, abortion, conception. The second turns to mothers organizing within the state, up until the seismic changes to its structure that were implemented by Margaret Thatcher, who is in many ways this book's own bad mother. The third part confronts this head on, considering the legacies birthed by her administration in the first decades of the new millennium. Clearly, the forward march of chronology does not always equal progress. But we are all historical subjects who, at our very best, draw strength from what has come before: we are ambivalent mothers, giving birth to each other.

PART ONE

The Body

I.

Suffering

To let the baby out, you have to be willing to go to pieces.

Maggie Nelson, *The Argonauts*

At the very beginning of 2012, a year particularly thick with nostalgia for Britain's imagined past, the BBC premiered a new television show in the traditional Sunday-night period-drama slot: *Call the Midwife*. The series, which is still on air, is phenomenally popular. A fictionalized version of the bestselling memoirs of Jennifer Worth, it follows young midwives nursing alongside an order of Anglican nuns in London's East End from 1957 until, at the time of writing, the late 1960s. Each individual birth story is enveloped within a broader historical and local narrative, documenting the long slow decline of shipbuilding and the still-recent devastation of the Blitz: as Vanessa Redgrave's narration intones in the very first episode, this is an area plagued by 'poverty, appalling housing, lice, filth, families sleeping four to a bed', a state of affairs the new(ish) welfare state was trying to ameliorate. Like Danny Boyle's Olympic opening ceremony of the same year, which included a sequence in which 'NHS' was spelt out in enormous, illuminated letters, *Call the Midwife* was read by many as an interjection against the defunding of the health service by the coalition government: indeed, in the first episode, during a difficult delivery, a physician literally says, almost breaking the fourth wall in the process, 'credit should go to the National Health'.

To be unusually liberal for heritage programming is not the same as having a coherent political message, and commentators who praised the politics of *Call the Midwife* were often reluctant to address the specific contemporary assaults that threatened nationalized healthcare in the here and now. The show is a prime example of the nostalgia that, in recent years, has dominated contemporary representations of national history: Helen George, who has played the central character Trixie in the show since its conception, sang 'The White Cliffs of Dover' at Buckingham Palace in a BBC special that marked the 75th anniversary of VE Day in May 2020. Despite its overt investment in uncovering hidden aspects of the past, it mostly eschews the radical local histories of the East End, which, having seen rapid housing expansion in the nineteenth century and then slum clearances in the twentieth, was an area shaped by large-scale immigration and the resettlement of refugees, two factors which, alongside its industrial hubs, made it a political melting pot and a locus of anti-fascist and anti-colonial organizing.[1] By the same token, the show engages only superficially with race and class. Poverty is represented primarily through the lens of the midwives' philanthropic ministrations, understood as a personal misfortune rather than a structural issue, and, despite the intertwined histories of the NHS and the migration of workers from the Commonwealth to the UK, all the characters in its main cast are white until the seventh series, which aired in 2018.[2]

Still, almost immediately upon *Call the Midwife*'s release it became apparent that its particular aesthetic – think steadfast midwives bicycling through London and interminable jokes about cake – was an excellent pairing for the concurrent resurgence of liberal feminism: Keep Calm and Advocate for Reproductive Rights. Caitlin Moran, who had published her bestselling *How to be a Woman* the previous year, declared in the *Sunday Times* that the 'lovely Christmas specialy, cover-of-the-*Radio-Times* sensation *Call the Midwife* is actually the most radical piece of Marxist-feminist dialectic to ever be broadcast on prime-time television'.[3] There is certainly a feminist dimension to the representation of birth in a working-class community on Sunday-night television, and the show has been rightly praised for its representation of issues including tuberculosis, cystic fibrosis, puerperal psychosis and female genital mutilation, but here Moran is making a far more conservative point, albeit in a joking tone. Rather than consider what feminist theory might bring to television, or vice versa, she is pitting what she casts as the academic pretentions of contemporary feminist thought against the hard-hitting, recognizable realism of the show's representation of 1950s London: the 'Marxist-feminist dialectic' as a concept is simultaneously called upon and mocked for the benefit of *Sunday Times* readers.[4] The implications of this are twofold: Moran's twee framing tries to shut down in advance the relevance that Marxist feminism might have for the way viewers actually watch *Call the Midwife*, while papering over the superficiality of the show's maternal politics, which remain laughably far from the lived complexities that Marxist feminists have long tried to articulate.

One such complexity is the question of why the most popular primetime show of the austerity era was a nostalgic drama about nationalized midwifery. If the maternal body occupies a particularly significant position on the permeable boundary between the public and private, then childbirth, which now mostly takes place in Britain and Northern Ireland within the public healthcare system, connects the body and the state. As the figure of the midwife became newly ubiquitous in mainstream British culture, it also became representative of the beneficences of the state itself, and celebrated as such. At a moment when people's experiences of birth within the NHS were rapidly worsening, and care more generally was being pushed back into the domain of private responsibility, *Call the Midwife* made a myth of progress, which it identified it as this movement of birth into the public sphere. And yet the chronic underfunding of the health service that has characterized the late twentieth and early twenty-first century has resulted in serious disparities in experiences of childbirth that divide along racial and economic lines. In 2018, in response to calls to act on the dangerous overstretching of the NHS, the Conservative government announced a ten-year plan for the health service that included an expansion of maternity services and recruitment in order to, according to the then Health Secretary Matt Hancock, make Britain 'the best place in the world to give birth'.[5] The plan focused on a 'continuity of care', with the goal being that pregnant people would have the same midwife throughout their pregnancy. Since then, swathes of midwife-led birthing centres and Neighbourhood Midwives services across the country have been closed, often with very little notice, severely limiting choices for place and mode of birth. These closures were, at least in part, due to serious staffing shortages in hospital maternity units. In April 2021, reports suggested that up to 8,000 'demoralized' midwives were planning to leave the profession after the unprecedented stress of the pandemic.[6] Every aspect of pregnancy and early motherhood is shaped by socio-economic factors: working conditions (your own and those of those who are caring for you); the state of repair or disrepair of the hospital facilities; the leave you can afford to take; your immigration status. The suffering of labour is coloured by these things, too.

As a mainstream cultural product that centres on childbirth – the series begins with Redgrave announcing that midwifery is 'the very stuff of life' – *Call the Midwife* is a marker of a broader cultural sea change. In 2013, Lisa Baraitser and Imogen Tyler diagnosed the 'cacophony of maternal publicity' that dominated British television after the turn of the millennium, including 2006's *Birth Night Live* – broadcast from a maternity unit – and Channel Four's ongoing *One Born Every Minute* as programming that breaks the 'taboo aesthetics' of childbirth, removing it from the domestic sphere and breaking the privacy of institutionalized healthcare.[7] But, unlike these shows, *Call the Midwife* draws on a historical document – Worth's memoirs – and as such it dramatizes not just the individual births it features but the history of birth in Britain. In doing so, it performs the debates that stalk contemporary understandings of childbirth and, like any attempt to tell the stories of our medical past, it is profoundly concerned with the values of the present. As an index of progress, the show is particularly aware of the two simultaneous timelines of its setting and its broadcast: it teaches the viewer to understand the medicalization of birth as something which perpetuates and incorporates women's knowledge. The East End community it documents is allowed to exist nostalgically, a token of a past that we should be happy to have left behind. (In a Comic Relief sketch from 2013, a woman in a contemporary labour room 'calls the midwife' and gets the show's cast. When the real midwife arrives, the punchline is that she is mistaken for a man: in response to her protests that she is, in fact, a woman, Trixie says, 'You can't be, you get paid and you're wearing trousers.')

What 'public birth' might mean is still, in the show's timeline, at a moment of transition. The midwives mostly attend home births; until 1939, most births occurred at home, and well into the sixties one third of births in England and Wales still took place in a domestic rather than institutional space. The drama of labour in *Call the Midwife* is domestic and female, with male characters, including the medical practitioners, supplementary to the driving force of the plot: the enclave of women who, from within the maternal structure of Nonnatus House, draw reproductive history into view. For the academic Louise Fitzgerald, the feminist power of the show resides in its 'rescue' of the figure of the midwife from the 'margins', creating a space for the stories of working-class pregnancies.[8] This space is often literal, with the midwives and the formidable older nuns creating a sanctuary around the birthing person and keeping children, husbands and neighbours at bay during the delivery. The births are often surprisingly graphic, and labour itself is represented as a state of extremity, but not hysteria: instincts are trusted, and agonies are attended to with respect. The affective power of the show relies upon the relationships it builds between patients and midwives: the midwife, standing in for the viewer, experiences the heartbreak and joy of each situation dramatized in the episode. This conflation, however, also aligns the viewer with the bigger structures that govern the conditions of birth: those of the medical and religious institutions the midwifes and nuns are agents of. The show makes each birth count, but it also, in personalizing the NHS and the Anglican Church, ignores the cruelties that such systems can perpetuate.

In the second episode of the show's third series, which takes place at the beginning of 1959, a conflict is staged between two ideologies of childbirth. The young Nurse Miller and the indomitable Sister Evangelina disagree over a lecture given by the visiting Dr Latham about modern 'natural' childbirth techniques, including upright positions and breathing exercises, replete with a slideshow of images of 'primitive childbirth'. (The opening narration leans into this colonial language, asserting that 'our work was birth, the primal act of a woman's life'.) Sister Evangelina is sceptical of such 'huffing and puffing', until Miller successfully calms down a woman in the throes of a difficult labour, advocating for her right to try to give birth in the way she wants to, rather than be taken to the hospital or attended by a (male) doctor. The anxious, very young woman has recently lost her mother, a loss which inflects her entire feeling towards labour: 'My mother always said I'd be a natural,' she says, 'but how can you be?' Latham, who has a particular interest in 'matriarchal societies', encourages Miller to teach his techniques herself: the women trust her, he says. Midwives, it is implied, are part of the matriarchal structure of Poplar: in helping the mother-less woman to relax and give birth, Miller fulfils part of the work of mothering.

Nuns, of course, are often understood matriarchally: governed as they are by the Mother Superior and residing as they do in the 'mother house'. Yet the Anglican Church more generally has historically operated as a patriarchal system of control. In their opposition to new techniques for 'natural' childbirth – and it's not just Sister Evangelina who is sceptical – the nuns are not only resisting a perceived assault on their professional expertise but also defending the religious under-standing that the suffering of women in labour is purposive: in the book of Genesis, pain in childbirth is God's reward to Eve for her transgression. Sister Monica Joan, the eldest nun and the only surviv-ing founder of Nonnatus House, rebuffs the enthusiastic Dr Latham with the dry assertion that 'Women's suffering is not confined to birth alone. I hope you have a solution for that as well.' This line seems, to me, to be a central thesis of the show, the steel beneath its blousy exter-ior. Despite the incorporation of birth into public health, childbirth will always be a site of pain and suffering, and this pain is, by definition, an individual experience: it is the private within the public. The extent to which that pain can or should be alleviated, however, is central to historical and ideological disagreements about virtue and value, and to the punitive ideas that shore up the violence that public institutions, like Churches and hospitals, are capable of inflicting. In relation to maternity, these are centred around sacrifice: the titillating closeness of birth and death, the sense of a duty to be paid.

The Burden of Eve

In one of the most famous feminist texts about motherhood, 1976's *Of Woman Born*, Adrienne Rich asks, 'How have women given birth, who has helped them, and how, and why?', before continuing: 'These are not simply questions of midwifery and obstetrics: they are political questions.'[9] Every choice made in pregnancy and childbirth is a choice delimited by medical, legal and religious structures, essential to Rich's project of distinguishing between 'two meanings of motherhood, one superimposed on the other: the *potential relationship* of any woman to her powers of reproduction and to children; and the *institution*, which aims at ensuring that that potential – and all women – shall remain under male control'.[10] The history of midwifery is, from a feminist perspective, one of the usurpation and demonization of women's knowledge, and the wresting of control over reproduction from women themselves. Until the late seventeenth century, childbirth was almost exclusively assisted by women: midwives were part of communities, and birth would typically occur in an enclosed, domestic space. In 1773, the surgeon and 'man-midwife' Edward Chapman published the design for the Chamberlen forceps, the famously vicious 'hands of iron' that replaced the midwife's 'hands of flesh' in difficult labours. The advent of the forceps is often taken to be the origin point for a bitter public dispute between midwives and surgeons, which eventually ended with the primacy of the latter: lying-in hospitals were opened where women could give birth attended by doctors. An epidemic of puerperal fever – a post-birth infection that caused blood poisoning – followed, which dominated such hospitals for much of the eighteenth and nineteenth centuries: although neither midwives nor surgeons knew to wash their hands to prevent the spread of bacteria and lethal infection, midwives were likely to be less invasive and to stay with just one patient for the duration of labour.

Despite strident efforts to curtail their practice, culminating in the criminalization of 'unqualified' midwifery at the beginning of the twentieth century, midwifes – historically known by other names like handywomen, gossips and, in Scotland, howdies – continued to assist births, particularly in rural areas: they were trusted members of their communities, something particularly relevant in parts of Ireland where the official district nurses were Anglican, middle-class and urban.[11] The relationship between the rise of the (male) medical profession and the persecution of women as witches became a focal point of the feminist movement in the 1970s, with texts like Barbara Ehrenreich and Deirdre English's 1973 pamphlet *Witches, Midwives and Nurses: A History of Women Healers* becoming touchstones of the second wave, something which would later prove crucial to Silvia Federici's alternative reading of the transition from feudalism to capitalism, 2004's influential *Caliban and the Witch*. In such readings, the female subject was a threat to the development of capitalism as a system, with control over her reproductive system a central object of financial as well as social control: resistance to it, then, could also be found in the woman's body.[12]

To understand childbirth as a generative site for feminist struggle in Britain in particular relies on an understanding of the history of the idea of the maternal body as a public good, a utility to be taken advantage of. Throughout the nineteenth century, the effectiveness of lying-in hospitals, forceps and wet nursing was fiercely debated, and the discourse – particularly in publications like the *British Medical Journal* and the *Lancet* – was suffused with anxiety about the health of the mother in a national context: a vital producer of citizens.[13] These discussions cared little for the experience of the mother: how it actually *felt* to give birth was not a consideration. 'Even in a place and time where maternal mortality is low,' Rich writes in *Of Woman Born*, 'a woman's fantasies of her own death in childbirth have the accuracy of metaphor. Typically, under patriarchy, the mother's life is exchanged for the child; her autonomy as a separate being seems fated to conflict with the infant she will bear.'[14] This framing of motherhood and sacrifice as being near-synonymous, a straight swap, expects the submission of a mother's 'previous' self in order to satisfy the needs of her child, but it also has its roots in the theological tradition that figures labour pain as the 'burden of Eve'. This is the 'women's suffering' referred to by *Call the Midwife*'s Sister Monica Joan: the pain is necessary to the production of the child, and – in the biblical tradition at least – the price women should expect to pay for their ancestral misbehaviour.

When the Scottish doctor James Simpson discovered in 1847 that the contractions of the uterus did not rely upon the consciousness of the labouring mother and began to experiment with the use of chloroform as pain relief, there was an enormous backlash. It wasn't until Queen Victoria herself accepted chloroform during the birth of her seventh child in 1853 that the use of anaesthetic in childbirth gradually became accepted practice. (Rich describes this as the only truly radical act of her reign). The question of the morality of alleviating pain brought into the open anxieties about the changing position of a maternal body in relation to the public sphere: did she belong to man, who could administer anaesthetic, or to nature and its attendant miseries? The entry of men into the lying-in chamber had introduced questions about women's modesty and privacy, and the narrative constructed around anaesthesia used the figure of the passive, unconscious body – midwives had traditionally used the upright obstetrical chair, in which it is easier to push – to cement prevailing ideologies of gender. Anaesthesia, of course, was one way to ensure mastery: an unconscious woman, as Simpson wrote, cannot resist 'the introduction of the hand into the maternal passages'. This didn't go unnoticed by those worried about propriety: the cultural historian Mary Poovey has written about the extensive repercussions of an infamous case in which a surgeon was accused of taking advantage of his labouring patient. These concerns were mostly expressed through the semi-apocryphal figure of the husband, cuckolded by the multiple surgeons 'attending' to his wife's promiscuous needs: it was primarily understood as a property violation.[15]

Today, although general anaesthetic would be administered during childbirth only in very rare cases, the use of some form of pain relief is common. Yet if the anaesthesia debate of the mid-nineteenth century (insofar as it *was* a debate) shows the challenge to patriarchal control posed by the reproductive body, it also complicates the popular construction of maternal sacrifice. If the good mother's role was to suffer, and perhaps even die, in the service of producing her child, a mother whose pain was alleviated was suspect: not only could she have 'lost her virtue' while unconscious and unguarded, but a less painful labour was not a satisfactorily arduous process. Motherhood was both a site of self-renouncing feminine virtue, and a debt owed by women to society. As Denise Riley argues in *War in the Nursery*, the Victorian ideology of sacrifice evolved into an understanding, in the next century, of mothering as a *job*: the metaphor of the mother as worker came to dominate popular discourse after the Second World War, building on the huge increase in women in employment and attempting to even out the relationship between 'man's work' and 'women's work'. In Riley's words, this metaphor was harmful 'not because mothers aren't workers in the obvious sense – far from it' but because instilling a separation between mothers, who are 'always at home', and women, who are 'always at work' is artificial and dangerous: 'it asserts "motherhood" as a self-evident value, but at the same time works directly against any admission of the real needs of women with children.'[16] If reproduction is both a woman's duty and a replacement for paid work, then childbirth is literally a kind of labour. ('Every miscarriage is a workplace accident.') Yet the actual processes of birth are still, for the most part, kept secret, meaning the pain and violence that can characterize that process is a price to be both willingly and privately paid.

The Factory

Pro-natalism was intimately tied up with the establishment of the NHS, which came into being in the summer of 1948. Spearheaded by Aneurin Bevan, Health Minister in Clement Attlee's Labour government, the National Health Service Act effectively nationalized volunteer-run and municipal hospitals and aimed to establish a uniform standard of care, including maternity services. Babies born in Britain were now 'national babies', as the writer Sarah Campion described it in her 1950 book of that name, which begins with her receiving a positive pregnancy test result five days after Bevan's launch: in her womb, she realizes, was one of the first beings entrusted to the NHS not only from cradle to grave but throughout their gestation, too.[17]

In the newly established service, the anaesthetist was given the same status as other specialist practitioners, and responsibility for maternity care was divided between hospitals, general-practice surgeries and local authorities. Women and children, according to the historian Angela Davis, benefited the most from this new system, as they had been less eligible for pre-war health insurance schemes, and maternal mortality continued the steady decline that had begun at the end of the 1930s.[18] Correspondingly – predictably – childbirth became increasingly medicalized, with government committees directly advocating hospital birth: the 1959 Report of the Maternity Services Committee, known as the Cranbrook report, introduced the target of 70 per cent of births to take place in hospitals. By 1971, the Peel report, named after the consultant obstetrician who chaired the committee (he was also, at the time, Surgeon-Gynaecologist to the Queen), recommended that the aim should be increased to 100 per cent, a controversial direction that was criticized for its lack of evidence and its limitation of maternal choice.[19] From 1975 onwards, the number of births that took place at home was never more than 5 per cent.

This move into the public space of the hospital had its opponents. In 1933, the obstetrician Grantly Dick-Read – the inspiration for *Call the Midwife*'s Dr Latham – had published *Natural Childbirth*, coining the term in the process, in which he argued against intervention of any kind. Dick-Read blamed the declining birth rate on women's 'fear' of birth, arguing that the tension produced by this fear was responsible for labour pain. His second book, *Childbirth without Fear* (originally published as *Revelation of Childbirth* in 1942), became an international bestseller: in it, he elaborated on his beliefs that 'primitive' women did not experience fear or pain during labour, blaming it instead on 'civilization', and stated that women were 'primarily made' to fulfil their reproductive duty. (As well as being offensively colonialist, these analogies were also untrue: as the doctor and writer Annabel Sowemimo observes, for example, caesareans were practised in Uganda in the nineteenth century with the use of banana wine as pain relief.)[20]

Rather than positioning mothers as workers, Dick-Read imagines the reproductive body as a workplace itself: 'The mother is the factory, and by education and care she can be made more efficient in the art of motherhood.' If the mother is a factory, a specifically industrial place, then Dick-Read's 'naturalness' sets itself in opposition to medical intervention as interrupting the processes that occur inside the body, rather than celebrating the 'natural' powers of the labouring person herself. What's more, if the mother is the factory, she isn't the worker, or even a person at all, and her body becomes a particular form of fixed capital: a private property, whose profits are reinvested to increase the 'efficiency' of its output. This, in turn, raises questions about who both the factory and its output belong to. The anthropologist Emily Martin, writing about the dominant imagery used in representations of menopause and infertility, observes that it inspires a 'horror' of a '*lack* of production: the disused factory, the failed business, the idle machine'; she goes on to ask what position the doctor occupies in this metaphor: a mechanic who fixes the machines, a factory supervisor, or 'even an owner'?[21]

Discourses of the natural and the unnatural have historically been more oppressive than liberatory. If one choice is a 'natural' one, then there must by definition be an opposite number: an unnatural decision, one that divides mother and child and prioritizes the former's needs. (We can see this in the repetitive popular panic over pregnant people being 'too posh to push' and choosing caesarean sections without a medical reason.[22]) Inspired by Dick-Read's ideas and by her own experiences of traumatic childbirth and baby loss, Prunella Briance founded the Natural Childbirth Association in 1956, which was renamed The National Childbirth Trust in 1961, and is today a charity with some 300 branches, overseeing drop-in events, antenatal groups, birthing classes, nearly new sales and first-aid courses. Despite this rebranding, and although it provides for a crucial support through the first thousand days of their child's life, many mothers who have used the NCT's services have identified its focus on natural birth as an impediment to their own wellbeing: epidurals and caesareans are considered to be less of a 'genuine experience' of labour, often with the implicit suggestion that the mother and the baby will struggle to bond if they haven't fully lived the experience of birth. The classes are also expensive, entrenching inequalities in birth support as cuts reduce the number of NHS alternatives available.

Of course, the medical establishment also has its agendas: pregnant people who want to have a home birth are often frustrated in their ambitions, and C-section rates have been rising enough in the UK to cause concern from medical professionals and the World Health Organization. As childbirth has modernized, its processes have certainly become more efficient, but who does this efficiency benefit? The right to choose, in the context of birth, means both that a pregnant person should not be prevented from choosing surgery, *and* that they should not be pressured into operations unnecessarily, either. In my own experience, working as a voluntary birth companion in Glasgow, I have seen first-hand the ways in which pregnancies deemed to be high risk – often simply because the pregnant person is seeking or has recently been granted asylum – are targeted for the medical induction of labour as soon as the expected due date arrives, despite the twin facts that due dates are far from an exact science and inducing labour makes it far more likely that further medical intervention will be required down the line. In 2021, the National Institute for Care and Excellence (NICE), released controversial draft guidelines proposing that induction should be considered at thirty-nine weeks for all women from an ethnic minority background. Spokespeople from the medical profession and human rights in childbirth organizations noted that this heavy-handed attempt to address racial inequalities in maternity care would only risk increasing them; when the official guidelines were published that November, the recommendation had vanished, but the questions about the uneven use of induction remain.

At the same time, pregnant people who request C-sections are often ignored. In 2022, a five-year investigation into Shrewsbury and Telford Hospital Trust concluded that 300 babies died or were left brain-damaged due to inadequate care and an alleged preoccupation with hitting targets for 'normal' (vaginal) births.[23] Central to such tragedies is not a binary distinction between good and bad births, or normal or abnormal ones, but a failure in the provision of flexible care based on informed consent. If birth exists in the area between the public and the private, how can we construct a model of support that reflects, rather than flattens, its complexities? The answer does not lie in the efficient factory, but rather in a publicly funded system that is secure enough to allow for the greatest possible expression of private desires and needs – individual autonomy, in other words. This is the opposite of what we have at present: an increasingly privatized system, which, because of its lack of funding and structural support, is so concerned with battling to provide the bare minimum service safely that it cannot meet the diverse and complicated needs of those who use it.

Impossible Nature

Historically, challenging the medicalization of childbirth has been a feminist fight, coloured by the suspicion of the state that characterized the feminisms of the 'second wave'. In 1976, the Association of Radical Midwives was founded. Their name was an ironic nod to the artificial rupture of membranes: also known as an amniotomy, this obstetric procedure requires that a hook be inserted into the vagina to puncture the amniotic sac containing the 'waters' which protect the foetus during gestation. The ARM were opposed to the proliferation of all such unnecessarily invasive procedures, including another very common one, the episiotomy. This procedure, in which a cut is made in the skin that separates the vagina and the anus to widen the opening, is often used as a shortcut in cases where the physician thinks the skin is going to naturally tear: during the 1970s, over half of all hospital deliveries included it. The first research into its effects was carried out for the NCT by ARM member Sheila Kitzinger and published in 1962 in *The Experience of Childbirth*: the procedure was extremely uncomfortable, increased recovery time, and was often experienced as an unnecessarily traumatic intervention. It was also haunted by the spectre of the 'husband stitch', a truly horrific name for a common occurrence in which the medical practitioner would sew up the perineum opening more tightly than it had previously been, in order to artificially create more sexual pleasure for the male partner.

Kitzinger was an influential figure both within the NCT and beyond it: a 'forebear' of the WLM, she was a social anthropologist and natural-birth activist known, among many other things, 'for her irreverent re-enactments of giving birth at conferences'.[24] Kitzinger believed that 'natural' birth taught pregnant people 'how to take control of their bodies ... trusting them, living through them, expressing themselves. And that affects sex of course, and our feelings about our sexuality, whatever it is, as well as childbirth.'[25] Natural birth, in this feminist framing, brought the sexual body back to childbirth. Sexuality was key to the movement in more practical ways, too. The American midwife Ina May Gaskin is known in some circles as the 'mother' of the natural-birth movement: although she has no formal medical training, she has delivered thousands of babies at The Farm, a former commune in Nashville, Tennessee. (A manoeuvre for delivering babies with shoulder dystocia, a dangerous complication in which the child's shoulders get stuck in the birth canal, is named after Gaskin, though she herself says the technique originates in Guatemala.) Her book *Spiritual Midwifery*, first published in 1977, advocates for home birth as a euphoric and even psychedelic experience: in pain, it finds a possibility for transcendence, pleasure and orgasm, something not unrelated to the second-wave feminist work to reclaim the clitoris as a source of pleasure. (In *I Am Not Your Baby Mother*, Candice Brathwaite describes Gaskin's work as a useful antidote to the institutional whiteness of British maternity care: 'although her books were completely devoid of any description of pregnancy or birth for black women, I took heart from the images and words that depicted birth as an almost spiritual experience.'[26])

In 2008, Gaskin took part in *Orgasmic Birth: The Best-Kept Secret*, a documentary which follows eleven women through labour. Although orgasms feature, it's primarily a film that advocates for all 'natural' techniques and criticizes the medicalization of birth in the United States. Orgasmic birth – also called ecstatic childbirth – is a controversial topic. According to the film's director Debra Pascali-Bonaro, anecdotal research suggests that more women experience the phenomenon than are recorded in official statistics: they feel compelled to keep it to themselves. Clitoral stimulation, which can also be used to induce labour, is taboo enough when being used as a replacement for pain relief; the idea that orgasmic birth might be induced for pleasure alone is almost unthinkable, and absent even from most studies into the subject.[27]

Although we are still a long way from a full reconciliation of the maternal with the sexual, a path can be glimpsed ahead. After all, midwives, in their earliest form, also assisted desire, providing both aphrodisiacs and abortifacients. In Audre Lorde's 1982 'biomythography' *Zami: A New Spelling of My Name*, she describes the Erotic Mother: a conceptual figure who is transformed from a repository of love and labour for others into a powerful and generative resource for the self. The eroticism central to Lorde's theorization of the maternal is not solely sexual, but rather a way of weaving together her adult self, her relationship with her own mother and her childhood experiences; in *Uses of the Erotic*, published two years later, she describes it as something which 'flows through and colors my life with a kind of energy that heightens and sensitizes and strengthens all my experience'.[28] In *The Argonauts*, Maggie Nelson writes that motherhood 'isn't like a love affair. It *is* a love affair. Or rather, it is romantic, erotic and consuming.'[29] (The fact that this book became an unlikely sleeper hit when it was published in 2015 suggests that general readers were ready for a text that refuses to separate the maternal from the explicitly sexual: it opens with a description of anal sex.)

In recent decades, as celebrity culture and social media have rendered the dramatization and publication of the domestic both increasingly possible and financially fruitful, sexualized images of pregnant women have become familiar parts of the cultural landscape – think of Annie Leibowitz's iconic photograph of a nude, pregnant Demi Moore for *Vanity Fair* in August 1991 – and these images are conventionally understood to be 'empowering' in their affirmation of pregnant women's ability to remain conventionally sexy.[30] This is not the same thing as a loosening of the hold of the cultural taboo around orgasmic birth, however. Ecstasy means, literally, removal or displacement: a kind of rapture that temporarily expels the mind from the body; a transcendence of the physical, achieved, in the case of sexual climax, by a thoroughly embodied experience. In ecstatic birth, then, the sexual exists not in the way the body appears or is observed but in the way it *feels*: it is a highly personal experience, resistant to external control, and is therefore far more threatening to existing norms than any number of aestheticized Instagram posts or magazine shoots. Part of its unsettling potential, of course, comes from the proximity of the child, or, rather, its closeness to the moment the child actually *becomes* a child, entering the world as a separate being from the mother. The fact that most pregnancies arise from heterosexual intercourse doesn't seem to alleviate the discomfort that orgasmic birth provokes: at conception, the child is still nine months away, an abstract notion, a bunch of cells shifting on a sonogram screen. (And, of course, you can get pregnant without having an orgasm.) But this doesn't account for all of it. The discomfort produced by orgasm also comes from its release, its surrender: it gives the birthing person something that they don't have to share. This is key to understanding birth as an experience, rather than simply a productive process: one in which the labouring subject is neither the worker nor the factory. What happens to you through that experience? How do you change? And what happens if your labour brings nothing forth? This, culturally, is a much more difficult story to tell.

Acts of Liberty

In February 2020, the actor Vanessa Kirby was nominated for an Academy Award for her role in *Pieces of a Woman*. The film was directed by Kornél Mundruczó and written by Kata Wéber, adapted from their 2018 play of the same name. It follows Kirby's character, Martha Weiss, through a home birth that goes tragically wrong when the baby, deprived of oxygen, dies shortly after she is born. The film opens with a confrontationally long depiction of labour, in a single take that lasts twenty-four minutes. *Pieces of a Woman* is not, in my or in most critics' opinions, a brilliant film. Yet Mundruczó and Wéber made a powerful case for the urgency of their project. The film was partly based on their own experience of miscarriage, but its second half, which documents the trial of the midwife present at the birth, was inspired by the legal case brought against the obstetrician and midwife Ágnes Geréb in Hungary in 2010. Geréb, who graduated as an obstetrician in 1977, began her career at the

Szeged Women's Clinic, where she was promptly disbarred for allowing the non-birthing parent into the labour room for support and encouragement (when the clinic formally began allowing this now-standard practice, in 1984, she did not receive a pardon). In 1989, Geréb began practising as an independent midwife and founded the first birthing centre in the country, influenced by international figures like Gaskin and Kitzinger. Until its legalization in 2011, home birth in Hungary existed in a liminal legislative space: it was not explicitly criminalized (EU countries have to accept the right of pregnant people to give birth where they choose), but medical assistance at home births was not permitted. Geréb's repeated appeals for a professional licence were denied and, from the mid-1990s onwards, if a home-birth midwife called an ambulance to respond to a complication that required hospitalization, a police car would arrive, too.

Geréb's arrest in 2010, which was condemned by midwifery organizations internationally, followed the death of a baby in 2007 who suffered from shoulder dystocia. The parents pressed charges against her – it would not have been tried as a criminal case had it happened in a hospital – and the national press depicted her, and the midwives on trial with her, as complicit in child murder. Geréb was held in pre-trial custody for three months, wore leg shackles and handcuffs in court, was strip-searched and denied regular visitors.[31] (She was eventually sentenced to two years in prison; she received an official pardon in 2018.) In an interview about *Pieces of a Woman*, Mundruczó said the case was 'about the question of who owns your child's body: the state or you as the woman? And can you decide where you want to give birth or not?' During one of several meetings they had with Geréb during their creative process, she told them, 'The newborn has to decide when she wants to be born', something Wéber describes as 'the first act of liberty that you can give to your child. That he or she decides when they want to be born.'[32]

Geréb's story is dramatic, but it is not unique. In 1999, Britain's 'best-known midwife', Caroline Flint, the former president of the Royal College of Midwives, who had published several books and delivered babies for celebrities including Thandiwe Newton and Davina McCall, had to face a disciplinary committee following the death of a child, Alicia Wright, who had been born in the breech position; her mother, Nyree, was a recently qualified midwife herself. An outspoken advocate for less medically interventionist midwifery, Flint had opened the first natural birth centre in London and privately attended many home births. Despite her exoneration – she was reprimanded only for inadequate note-taking and some observational failures – the tragedy inspired a flurry of headlines that asked if this was 'the end' for home birth.[33]

A decade later, the Albany Midwifery Practice in south-east London was closed by the King's College Hospital Foundation Trust, and its longest-practising midwife, Becky Reed, was suspended from practice. Between 1997 and 2009, the pathbreaking self-managed partnership had offered highly successful care that was frequently cited as excellent both nationally and internationally: it had a lower rate of perinatal mortality than the country as a whole, a consistently low C-section rate, a very high number of new parents breast or chest feeding immediately after birth, a high number of successful home births and a continuity of care that enabled pregnant people to develop a relationship with one or two midwives who saw them through the entire process of pregnancy, birth and post-partum care. Based in Peckham, 57 per cent of those served by the Albany were from Black, Asian and Minority Ethnic Communities and a third were single parents, with a significant majority of the patients coming from low-income households: precisely the demographic who experience worse than average care in the NHS as a whole.

The closure of the Albany, then, made no sense in a health service which had been recommending precisely this model of midwifery since 1993, and it occurred so abruptly that pregnant people using the service were suddenly left without their midwives. The seven midwives who worked there, meanwhile, were, in the words of the ARM, left 'bereft and barred from practice'. In response to this shock closure, there were demonstrations organized by 'Albany Mums' past and present, supported by high-profile figures like Kitzinger, who all concurred that the practice had been targeted because it was seen as a threat. Independent midwives did not want to work in NHS 'baby factory' conditions; one 'Albany Mum' observed that this might cause tensions with professionals who remained within the health service: 'I can't imagine an obstetrician taking kindly to giving advice to a patient only to have her turn round and say, "Well, actually, my midwife says this and that's what I'm going to do."' Sarah Davies, a Senior Lecturer in Midwifery at the University of Salford, agreed: 'Empowered women threaten all kinds of professions. Albany empowers women. That was the problem.'[34] The Albany model, understood as a challenge to the established way of doing things and related to that supremely twenty-first century word, empowerment, is yet another example of the use of childbirth as a staging ground for other, more diffuse, debates: who exactly benefits from the reduction of choice in childbirth? Is it simply a case of the mismanaged policing of scarce resources? Or is, in a culture still haunted by the image of Eve and of the body-as-factory, the notion of an 'empowering' birth too difficult to stomach?

Going to Pieces

History lives in the processes of birth. I am not just referring to the history of medicine. In *Pieces of a Woman*, the protagonist Martha is a second-generation Hungarian Jewish immigrant; her mother, Elizabeth, escaped the Holocaust in infancy. Wéber, describing her own experience as 'a member of a Holocaust survival family and within a certain generation in that family', observes that 'Holocaust survivors tend to feel that survival is the ultimate and only knowledge you have to pass on to your daughter. But there are certain situations where this just doesn't help, right? Being the best survivor doesn't help if you are in the midst of this kind of tragedy.'[35]

Transgenerational trauma, often called historic trauma, is a complex and disputed field of study or, rather, several interlinking fields of study, documenting the ways in which traumatic experiences engender a kind of inherited PTSD. Gestational stress experienced by a foetus during pregnancy is a key but not an exclusive factor in this complicated inheritance. Accounts of the reproduction of intergenerational trauma can be partially traced back to the work of the Hungarian-French psychoanalysts Nicolas Abraham and Mária Török and to Helen Epstein's 1979 *Children of the Holocaust*, the first non-medical book to interrogate the impact on what Epstein calls '2G' – the second generation – of their parents' experiences in concentration camps. (Epstein continued her project with *Where She Came From: A Daughter's Search for Her Mother's History*, a history of three generations of Czech Jewish women.) In *Pieces of a Woman* it is Elizabeth who wants the legal case to go to trial, not Martha: she desires some kind of justice for the loss of the next daughter in a fraught, threatened lineage. In this film, resistance and survival are both rooted in the actual process of labour, that twenty-four-minute scene that grounds the entire narrative in the struggle to emerge into life.

In Sheila Heti's *Motherhood*, a novel published in 2018 and partly structured around the different stages of a menstrual cycle ('Ovulating', 'Bleeding', 'PMS'), the central question of the book – whether or not its narrator should have a child – is positioned at crucial points as a question about what to do with the pain her mother inherited from *her* mother, a Hungarian who lived through Auschwitz. 'Someone cursed me,' the narrator writes, 'and my mother, and my mother's mother before me . . . I have taken on the curse as my own.' Earlier in the novel, a tarot reader tells her 'something's stopping you', concluding that this something is grief: 'It may be,' she muses, 'that you're porous and the grief isn't yours. Does your mother have a grief?' Reproduction, for Heti's narrator, is intertwined with duty, with redress for unspeakable wrong: '*If you don't have children, the Nazis will have won.* I have felt this. *They wanted to wipe us from the earth, and we must never let them.* Then how can I imagine *not* having children, and selfishly contribute to our dying out?' But she can imagine it: the book is not resolved with the decision to have a child, and writing becomes a kind of reproductive act, recognized by the protagonist's mother as one that will keep her grandmother 'alive forever'.[36]

Childbirth itself, whatever the exact circumstances of the bodies involved, is a moment of dangerous volatility: there are no guarantees. An acceptance of the proximity of death to birth, for all its complex psychoanalytic implications, is also a potentially transformative feminist weapon that extends beyond parturition: Kitzinger, interviewed three years before she died and reflecting on a lifetime of advocacy, compared the hurdles faced during the 'transition *into* life' to those that we need to deal with as we 'move towards death'.[37] It also restores some of the sheer physicality of labour, which, in *The Argonauts*, Nelson writes of as something which 'does' you, rather than the other way round:

> If all goes well, the baby will make it out alive, and so will you. Nonetheless, you will have touched death along the way. You will have realized that death will do you too, without fail and without mercy. It will do you even if you don't believe it will do you, and it will do you in its own way.

Later, the description of birth itself that forms the book's denouement is interspersed with her partner Harry Dodge's recollections of the night his mother died: the breathing sounds, the jerking movements, the labours of her body as it bridged the 'doorway' between life and death.[38]

This passage always brings to my mind lines from the song 'Divers' by the American musician Joanna Newsom, in which she asks why the agony of birth is 'lighter borne' than that of death. Immediately beforehand, Newsom refers to the philosophical concept of infinite regress, which revolves around a recursive principle that determines the way each subsequent part of a series depends upon or is produced by its predecessor. In my mind's eye, it is a hall of mirrors. I'm like this because my mother was like this because her mother was like this because her mother . . . (Jacqueline Rose, at the end of her book *Mothers*, writes of her shock when she discovered she shared a psychological symptom with her father, who was held as a prisoner of war in Japan during the Second World

25

War: 'I had always assumed, as daughters often do, that any suffering of body or mind I had inherited, in fact pretty much everything I had inherited, must have come from my mother.')[39]

This maternal inheritance is often represented as something processed or transmitted through physical suffering (labour pains), in touching death to bring forth life. And if death sits at the centre of the metaphorical or conceptual power of birth, trauma has its place, too. In 'An Uncommon Language', a lyric essay that takes a miscarriage as its subject matter, the poet Sandeep Parmar writes of a transgenerational haunting that combines reproductive loss with other forms of violence both institutional and historical. At first, she describes the experience of preparing for pregnancy as someone othered by her educational 'privileges', which manifest in her decision to opt for a consultant-led birth, as well as her status as being 'not quite English': 'The NHS leaflets piled thick in your palm. The hostile posters on the wards threatening those without legal status. This woman of the State is disappointed in you.' Visited by ghosts in the hospital, the fluorescently lit realities of the setting begin to recede, replaced by inherited memories of other places and other systems: her 'grandmother, who died giving birth' explains 'what makes carnelian so red'; used by the Romans, it is the 'pulse of empire'. This miscarriage in a British hospital, with its smooth plastic and pastel leaflets and hostile-environment posters on the walls, brings to mind a different place: 'A village and its farms and its wells', the historical 'smell of blood and panic'.[40]

If, for a daughter, part of the struggle to live freely is to establish a self outside of the mother, the monumental challenge of childbirth is to accept that you have to let that hard-won self go. The Russian psychoanalyst Sabina Spielrein, whose 'Destruction as a cause of coming into being' was a key influence on Freud's *Beyond the Pleasure Principle*, believed that it was necessary to destroy the self completely in order to give birth. (In the same essay, she references cases in which patients who wish to have children see themselves being transformed *into* children in their dreams).[41] As

Nelson puts it in *The Argonauts*, 'It's easy enough to stand on the outside and say, "You just have to let go and let the baby out." But to let the baby out, you have to be willing to go to pieces.'[42] In *A Life's Work*, the writer Rachel Cusk's experience of a C-section is one which robs her, temporarily, of her status as a living being itself: her voice 'sounds preternatural coming out of my dead body'. In this momentary death, 'Some transfer of significance has occurred: I feel it, feel the air move, feel time begin to pour down a new tributary.' Later, this fluidity is replicated when, feeding her daughter, she imagines antibodies flowing from her body into her baby 'like a river of light'. She begins to dissolve: 'I imagine my solidity transferring itself to her, leaving me unbodied, a mere force, a miasma of nurture that surrounds her like a halo'.[43] Birth, then, is simultaneously a process of separation and consolidation (for the child) and of disintegration (for the mother). In this logic, we can again see the roots of the discontent expressed by mothers throughout history: the poet Alice Notley, writing in 'A Baby is Born Out of a White Owl's Forehead – 1972', characterizes the decision to have a second child as the decision to 'obliterate myself again'; the poem ends with the line 'but first, for two years, there's no me here.'[44] Adrienne Rich, meanwhile, argues that a woman's fantasies of death in childbirth have the accuracy of metaphor: that pregnancy, even when longed for, 'may be experienced as the extinguishing of an earlier self'.

And yet. Obliteration, disintegration, a loss of distinction, going to pieces: within all of these concepts there is awe as well as horror. Essential to the reclamation of birth as a site of agency, even of 'empowerment', might be the project of recasting it as an experience of the sublime. This, generally speaking, describes something – an experience, a place, a text, an artwork – that pushes us beyond our selves, that exceeds our boundaries, our limits. The sublime is, traditionally, a masculine concept, and feminist theorists have worked to identify its gendered economy: Barbara Claire Freeman, for example, argues that canonical theories that 'seem merely to explain the sublime' actually place it in opposition to an otherness that is almost exclusively 'gendered as feminine'.[45] This excluded otherness could be figured as specifically reproductive: the unclassifiable private extremity of birth. Sheila Lintott offers another corrective, repositioning childbirth as not only abject or beautiful but a moment of 'potentially feminist sublimity'. Lintott quotes from Edmund Burke's 1757 *A Philosophical Enquiry into the Origin of Our Ideas of the Sublime and Beautiful*, in which pain and terror become something approaching joy:

> If the pain and terror are so modified as not to be actually noxious; if the pain is not carried to violence, and the terror is not conversant about the present destruction of the person, as these emotions clear the parts, whether fine, or gross, of a dangerous and troublesome incumbrance, they are capable of producing delight; not pleasure, but a sort of delightful horror, a sort of tranquillity tinged with terror; which as it belongs to self-preservation is one of the strongest of all the passions. Its object is the sublime.[46]

Gestation can produce this delightful horror, although Lintott notes that in the mainstream cultural representations of birth, pain and terror are, as we have already seen, not often openly discussed: the apprehension and fear that many pregnant people feel as the birth approaches is repressed, banished from official accounts. (Cusk, in *A Life's Work*, compares it to standing at the top of a ski slope, knowing the only way is down.) This fear is related to the unknown that lies beyond: if the willing acceptance of this pain is a kind of self-obliteration, how do you begin to pick up the pieces of your identity afterwards? Maternal terror never, it seems, fully goes away: Zadie Smith, writing of the distinction between pleasure and joy, recasts early motherhood as a perpetually sublime experience:

> Occasionally the child, too, is a pleasure, though mostly she is a joy, which means in fact she gives us not much pleasure at all, but rather that strange admixture of terror, pain, and delight that I have come to recognize as joy, and now must find some way to live with daily.[47]

When I stretch to consider the conceptual strangeness of childbirth, this indescribable and singular experience by which pregnant people cleave another living being from within themselves, it is not the sublime that strikes me but another disputed philosophical term: catharsis. Originally theorized by the Greek philosopher Aristotle in the *Poetics*, it relates to the social function of art: for a spectator, a tragedy is a dramatization of events that arouse 'pity and fear, wherewith to accomplish its catharsis of such emotions'. Aristotle offers no clarification of what this precisely means, and so the term now has a variety of definitions: purgation, purification, release, enlightenment, expulsion, etcetera. Nelson, in *The Art of Cruelty*, observes as many others have before her that 'the phrasing of Aristotle's original sentence leaves it unclear whether "catharsis" applies to *incidents* or *emotions* – that is, whether the action takes place inside an individual, outside of her, or somewhere in between.'[48] This 'somewhere in between', a third space where expulsion is experienced as a release that clarifies or alters the mind, is a parallel for the indescribability of childbirth: this line between living and dying, where the intersubjectivity of the pregnant body – where one person contains two subjects, one life system supporting and producing another – splits and the second subject is released, and, at that very moment, *becomes* a person.

The thick untranslatability of catharsis and its association with tragedy – an art form which defies consolation and therefore provides it, that grapples with the impossibility of bearing suffering and therefore makes it in some way bearable or at least intelligible – seems to me appropriate for an experience that is still denied its full weight in the culture. Why is birth taken more lightly than death? In Attic tragedy, it isn't, and many classicists have noted that this is perhaps in part due to the fact that giving birth marked a civic role for mothers, a parallel to participating in military and political life for men: Medea, Jocasta, Clytemnestra and Hecuba are all primary actors in the conflicts and horrors that unfold on their stages. Catharsis is central to the maternal experience in psychoanalysis, too: although Freud moved away from his work on hysteria that conceptualized catharsis-as-cure, it was only by locating the source of the symptoms that the 'truth' about what was causing the hysteria could be articulated. The repressed trauma is realized, set free, purging its bodily manifestations.[49] Hysteria, as I've already discussed, has become a feminist shorthand for the fact that a woman's body has always been a site of medical, legal and social anxiety, characterized, too, by the fear of a certain female doubleness: the bad body inside the good body.

It is also, in part, a question about what women *produce*. Catharsis blurs the boundary between the public and private: the release of emotion at the theatre is an individual experience which, according to Aristotle anyway, cements social bonds. Peter Wollen, in his *Alphabet of Cinema*, offers a reading of catharsis as something which was educative as much as purgative, and

> enabled us to learn about history and how it works, even – especially – in its most frightening and overwhelming aspects: the fateful moment when hidden truths are revealed, when families and dynasties fall apart and the passions destroy public order.[50]

Childbirth, too, in its rules and taboos and habits and practices, enables us to learn about history and how it works. What do we gain by understanding it along traditionally masculine lines of existential pleasure and terror? In part, the ability to recuperate lost ground, a rebuttal of the dismissal of experiences related to maternity as a minority concern: a recovery of pain, fear, and ecstasy that reorients the story of life around, rather than away from, the bodies which produce it. We also forge for ourselves a vocabulary of maternal experience and emotion that draws on the sexual, the adult and the taboo. The moment of birth does not symbolize a woman crossing the nursery threshold and being banished from adult life. It takes strength to let yourself disperse, and even more, afterwards, to gather the pieces up again, work out how they might now fit together. At the end of 'A Baby is Born Out of a White Owl's Forehead – 1972', Notley's poem about maternal self-obliteration, she moves beyond the annihilation of subjectivity to something opaque about existence itself, both within a gendered identity and beyond it:

> having another child
> not to be a form of woman
> but in allegiance to the process I
> can't quite see.
> I have begun to be.

This becoming, this evolution outwards into a new kind of body, redefines inheritance. In its positioning on the very edge of the private, it can welcome in something communal. When I was training to be a birth companion, one of the most surprising lessons we were taught was about the permeability of personal boundaries. Part of the role, as well as advocacy and organization, is providing *maternal* care to the person who is on the very cusp of (usually) becoming a mother themselves. At the moment of transition between the first and second stage of labour, which is often a moment of extreme beauty and terror, you might, as a companion, find that you have to become the mother who isn't there. You touch them, you talk to them, you tell them you're staying. You won't leave them in the institutional space alone.

2.

Choosing

Emotions cannot be 'free' or 'true' in isolation: they are dependent
today on a social base that imprisons and determines them.

Juliet Mitchell, *Woman's Estate*

Even as the supportive pro-natalist state recedes, we're still held
hostage at the shrine of the national baby: the reproductive body is
policed, invaded and made public property. Abortion in particular
has been a battleground for most of the twentieth century. I am
writing this in 2023, in the wake of the defeat in the US Supreme
Court of Roe v. Wade, and as a conservative alliance that includes
the Scottish Family Party protests outside abortion clinics in Glasgow, the city where I live. Abortion makes pregnancy if not the
property of the commons then of its carnival-mirror inverse: the
responsibilities of reproduction – from conception to financial
support – are firmly within the purview of the individual, but the
possibility of termination is a responsibility decided upon by committee. The slogan 'my body, my choice' is, in this context, a utopian
ideal. Yet the notion of choice is central to the way our understandings of reproduction have been constructed, so much so, in fact,
that for myself and many of my peers who grew up in a UK obsessed
with the spectre of teenage pregnancy, we found ourselves surprised when, in our mid-twenties, the script abruptly switched to
one about *trying* to get pregnant, not making selfish choices, not
leaving it 'too late'. (All these conversations, of course, immediately
assume that your body works in tandem with your gender, and that

your organs are pleasant, functional and amenable. That your uterus, in other words, is a *good girl*.)

In the final episode of Joey Soloway's 2017 television adaptation of Chris Kraus's cult 1997 novel *I Love Dick*, Chris (played by Kathryn Hahn) floats uninvited in the pool outside the eponymous Dick's mansion in the Marfa desert. As she begins to drift off into sleep, two handsome naked men, oilfield workers who made a brief appearance earlier in the episode, appear in the pool. 'I'm your miscarriage,' says one of them. 'I'm your abortion,' says the other. 'Did you get to do everything you wanted?'[1] Chris is a woman whom we have witnessed push herself to the limits of shame: in the grip of an infatuation with Dick, who represents a particular kind of detached masculine power that appears impervious to emotion, she has written literally hundreds of agonized, explicit, unanswered love letters. Chris is a figure of total un-consummation. She hasn't got *anything* that she wanted. In this sense, she embodies the problem with reproductive choice as a concept. The notion that a terminated pregnancy (and, here, a miscarriage) is a transactional agreement you broker with your future self suggests that the only way to atone for a non-reproductive life is to have a very productive one: in the case of women artists like Chris, there is a historically confirmed dichotomy between making babies and making art.

There is a feminist point to be made about the inaccessibility of creative practice and professional fulfilment for those with caring responsibilities: Linda Nochlin, in her influential 1971 essay 'Why Have There Been No Great Women Artists?', stresses the '*institutional* – i.e. the public – rather than the *individual*, or private, pre-conditions for achievement or the lack of it in the arts'.[2] Yet the cultural fascination with the perceived incompatibility of motherhood per se with artistic endeavours persists. In the current maternal zeitgeist, the focus is on a middle-class, white, cis woman in the Global North, writing from a personal perspective, tries to reconcile having a child with the 'vocation' of being a writer or an artist. Once again, Virginia Woolf tends to dominate this discourse. Rebecca Solnit designates her in *The Mother of All Questions* (2017) as a blueprint for eschewing motherhood in the pursuit of genius. 'After all,' Solnit writes, 'many people make babies; only one made *To the Lighthouse* and *Three Guineas*.' 'Brains,' she continues, 'are individual phenomena producing wildly varying products; uteruses bring forth one kind of creation.'[3] Leaving aside the assumption that every human being is 'one kind of creation' – where, in that case, do these amazing brains come from? – this argument both implicitly devalues the work of mothering and suggests that those who do not choose to have children should in some way compensate for it with a generation-defining work of art.

Under what conditions is choice possible, anyway? Adrienne Rich, in *Of Woman Born*, describes childbirth as 'a form of forced labour': without access to reliable and safe contraception or abortion, pregnancy and birth are rarely elective processes.[4] But even in a country where abortion is – within limits – legal, it is only a matter of choice if both options – having a baby and accessing a termination – are equally materially possible. It is not a coincidence that free contraception and abortion were part of the same demand at the inaugural conference of the WLM at Ruskin College in 1970, or that they were accompanied by a demand for free twenty-four-hour childcare. Conceptually central, here, is the distinction between reproductive rights and reproductive justice. The latter term was coined in 1994 in Chicago by Women of African Descent for Reproductive Justice, a group who recognized that focusing on abortion advocacy alone was not sufficient. Reproductive justice refuses to separate reproductive rights from healthcare more generally: in doing so, it acknowledges that rights are not guaranteed but can be withdrawn by a hostile state, that not everyone is equally able to afford to raise a child, and that multiple factors govern and delimit what choice actually means for each person. Economic precarity – itself unevenly spread across racial lines – is one of the most significant factors that govern reproductive decisions in twenty-first-century Britain: in 2020, the British Pregnancy Advisory Service reported that women from 'deprived' backgrounds were almost three times more likely than their wealthier counterparts to have an abortion. The previous year, it was reported that 40 per cent of abortions performed in the UK were 'repeat abortions', something often framed as the result of bad decision-making, or 'abortion as birth control': in reality, the reasons for these include intimate partner violence, coercive control, lack of birth-control provision and a lack of understanding of birth control or the menstrual cycle itself.[5] 'Choice' is not a neutral demand.

Abortion before the Abortion Act

In the UK, abortion or the assisting of abortion is technically a crime: the landmark 1967 Abortion Act did not legalize it per se but rather introduced a series of circumstances in which a pregnancy can be lawfully terminated, up to twenty-four weeks. These circumstances require the signatures of two doctors, agreeing that continuing the pregnancy would gravely injure the pregnant person's mental or physical health.[6] People are still prosecuted in the criminal courts for accessing abortion outside these limits: in 2022 a group of sixty-six organizations including the BPAS, Southall Black Sisters and the Royal College of Obstetricians and Gynaecologists, wrote a letter to the Director of Public Prosecutions calling for the dropping of charges against two women accused of illegally using abortion pills. In 2021, a fifteen-year-old was investigated by the police after a stillbirth at twenty-eight weeks, and subjected to a year-long investigation in which her phone and laptop were confiscated during her GCSE exams, and she was reportedly 'driven to self-harm'. (The case was subsequently dropped.) In 2023, a mother of three was sentenced to twenty-eight months in prison for taking abortion pills after the ten-week limit, despite the fact that she was unable to access maternal care, including the scans that would identify the gestational age of the foetus, because the UK was in lockdown to prevent the spread of COVID-19. In Northern Ireland, meanwhile, because it was an issue of 'sexual morality', the 1967 Act was never adopted, meaning that until 2019, when a law was 'smuggled' into being while Stormont was dissolved, abortion remained completely illegal, including in the case of rape and foetal abnormality.[7]

Despite the occasional interventions made in Northern Ireland by English politicians, abortion rights campaigners often feel abandoned by Westminster. Joanna Biggs, reporting from Belfast in 2017 for the *London Review of Books*, observed that throughout her visit she was frequently reminded that in 2008 Harriet Harman, widely heralded as a feminist MP, blocked a move to extend the 1967 Act to Northern Ireland in order to gain the DUP support necessary for the passing of a bill allowing for the 42-day detention of terrorism suspects. Pregnant people in the six counties seeking terminations have historically had to travel to England: figures suggest that over 6,000 such crossings have been made since 1968, though that statistic doesn't include those for whom the journey was prohibitively expensive. In the past two decades, it has also been possible to buy abortion pills online, an act for which a woman was given a suspended prison sentence in 2016 after her housemates reported her to the police: one, as Biggs notes, declared that she was not 'anti-abortion', and believed 'there are circumstances, like rape, where it should be a woman's choice.' She reported her housemate, she said, because of 'her attitude. It was as if she was getting rid of a piece of clothing.'[8]

While many people, or so I would like to believe, would think twice before reporting their housemate to the police, the idea that there are appropriate and inappropriate circumstances in which the right to choose should properly be exercised is common. This is the subject of Erica Millar's 2017 book *Happy Abortions*, which seeks to challenge the 'emotional script' that governs dominant representations of termination.[9] Nominally pro-choice, this script frames abortion as a necessarily negative or upsetting experience, for which women deserve sympathy rather than punishment. This, however unintentionally, in effect echoes the anti-abortion movement that has, from the 1980s onwards, centred the supposed emotional well-being of women – often white women – who come to regret their abortions after the fact as much as it has centred their belief in the right to foetal life.

This, in turn, has impacted the way other (non)reproductive experiences are approached within feminism. In *Pregnancy without Birth*, a book which advocates 'full-spectrum solidarity', Victoria Browne argues that paying attention to the feelings that miscarriage can entail, including grief, does not require it be set up as an oppositional experience to abortion. Such opposition hinges on choice: one is chosen, one is suffered. However much we might want to resist the co-option of regret by the anti-abortion movement, a reliance on a clear and enforceable distinction between the chosen and unchosen event simplifies the experience of abortion and miscarriage, which risks alienating those who have experienced both and risks ignoring the many structural inequalities that govern these choices, making a perceived moral distinction between the right and wrong kind of decision. It also ignores the fact that anti-abortion legislation frequently criminalizes those who miscarry, too.[10]

Like miscarriage, abortion is a physical process: it requires delivery. One way that we might get around the problem of choice and morality which has come to colour all representations of termination – each generation haunted by their own particular urban legends – is by thinking of it as a kind of work: a bodily labour, moving oneself away from a possible future. In Annie Ernaux's *Happening*, an extraordinary account of the illegal termination she procured in Rouen in 1963 – eight years before the likes of Simone de Beauvoir and Agnès Varda signed the iconic 'Manifeste des 343' and admitted to having had abortions – she describes the labour-intensive process of finding a method of termination: putting an end to the pregnancy busily progressing inside her becomes a full-time job. Much of her account is taken up by the laborious process of information-chasing, and its multiple dead-ends include approaching men who instead simply try to sleep with her instead of helping. (Her pregnant body is inscribed with a presumed promiscuity: she's already done it once, after all.) Once the termination, which requires her to walk around with a probe in her cervix for several days before delivering the foetus, has been secured, Ernaux experiences serious complications and is taken to hospital, where she is treated very badly until it is revealed that she is a student, an acceptable subject for a termination: bigger reasons, better things ahead. And yet, for Ernaux herself, the pregnancy enforces a return to her origins: unmarried and pregnant unexpectedly, she experiences a deeply felt 'connection between my social background and my present condition'. Born into a family of 'labourers and shopkeepers', her entry into higher education has steered her away from manual and retail work, but 'neither my baccalaureate nor my degree in literature' had 'waived that inescapable fatality of the working class': 'the legacy of poverty – embodied by both the pregnant girl and the alcoholic. Sex had caught up with me, and I saw the thing growing inside of me as a stigma of social failure.'[11] She has to borrow the money to pay the abortionist, whom she can only access because of university connections: her tenuous thread to the world of those who are permitted their clandestine mistakes in service of their bourgeois endeavours.

Abortion, as Ernaux almost discovers, can be fatally material. In Britain, the 1967 Act came about after decades of campaigning by the Abortion Law Reform Association, a slow generational change in attitudes, and increased support for abortion in the case of foetal abnormalities in the wake of the Thalidomide crisis. Before 1967, termination was regulated by two pieces of legislation, the 1861 Offences Against the Person Act and the 1929 Infant Life Preservation Act, both of which demonstrated the permeability of the boundaries between mental and physical, social and moral 'justifications' for abortion: the first made it illegal in any circumstances, while the second ruled it acceptable only in the case of the preservation of the life of the mother. 'Life' became a usefully ambiguous concept. In 1938, the gynaecologist Aleck Bourne was tried at the Central Criminal Court, London, for terminating the pregnancy of a fourteen-year-old girl who had been raped by five officers from the Royal Horse Guards (he didn't charge a fee). She had been sent away from St Thomas's Hospital without the procedure because, due to the military rank of those who assaulted her, she might be 'carrying a future prime minister'.[12] Bourne was acquitted, with his actions later commended by the *Lancet*, and this case set out, at least in theory, an argument for termination that did not depend solely on physical health, although the example was extreme and the decision did not reduce either backstreet abortion or its mortality rate. Bourne himself is no easy hero: as a retired physician, he opposed the 1967 Act, and campaigned on behalf of the Society for the Protection of the Unborn Child. The argument in favour of terminating the pregnancy of a fourteen-year-old rape victim is an easier one to make than the one that asserts the equal right to end the pregnancy of a happily promiscuous thirty-year-old with no health problems, or a married woman with two children and the means to provide for more.

Although it is often spoken of as if it has always been a crime, abortion only became illegal in the nineteenth century, and even then it was only criminal after 'quickening' (when a person begins to feel the child moving inside them, usually around eighteen weeks into a pregnancy). The history of law enforcement more generally is all surprisingly new: as Juno Mac and Molly Smith note in *Revolting Prostitutes*, the 'institutions of policing and borders may seem natural or inevitable, but they are recent inventions', with professionalized police forces emerging only in the nineteenth century, intended, in large part, to deal with the 'restive urban working class organizing against bad working and living conditions'.[13] Criminalizing both abortion and the procurement of instruments with intent to abort, as the 1861 Act did, extended the power of the law over troublesome bodies: it was followed three years later by the Contagious Diseases Act of 1864, legislation that effectively used the widespread panic about venereal disease to arrest women who appeared to be in some way threatening to the social fabric. The bodies of women of colour and working-class women were rendered particularly vulnerable, and the Act 'gave the police the power to subject any suspected prostitute to a forced pelvic exam with a speculum': the speculum, which is still used today, is a device with a history of extreme cruelty, invented as it was by James Marion Sims, who 'experimented' on enslaved Black women.[14] After 1861, prosecutions for abortionists were common: according to the historian Caroline M. de Costa, at any one time around fifty women convicted of this crime were incarcerated in London's Holloway Prison, sometimes sentenced to up to fourteen years.[15]

None of this curbed demand. By 1966 abortion was the 'leading cause of avoidable maternal death' in England and Wales.[16] Historians estimate that in the 1950s 100,000 illegal abortions were performed, with complications from these terminations accounting for 25 per cent of maternal deaths, estimates borne out by the significant drop in emergency abortion-related hospital admissions in 1968.[17] Backstreet abortionists are significant figures in the national cultural memory, fictionalized in, among others, Graham Swift's Booker Prize winning novel *Waterland* (1983), multiple episodes of *Call the Midwife* and Mike Leigh's acclaimed 2005 film *Vera Drake*. Perhaps their most influential twentieth-century representation, however, was in the 1965 BBC television film *Up the Junction*, directed by Ken Loach. Part of the Wednesday Play series which was later to premiere *Cathy Come Home* and other emerging classics of the kitchen-sink realism genre, the production attracted the opprobrium of the right, including the notorious conservative campaigner Mary Whitehouse. It intersperses harrowing footage of the protagonist Rube's abortion, who is shown howling in pain, with no doctor in attendance in case they try to save the baby, with clips of young women in Battersea talking about sex and relationships, and an interview with a doctor, who discusses the 'thirty-five deaths per year that we know are directly attributable to the backstreet abortions'. In his view, even when women survived, 'the most common and seriously disturbing result' of undergoing a termination is that, if complications occur, 'she may not be able to have any more babies.' Without diminishing the fact that sterility was and remains a serious potential side effect of unregulated abortion, this framing is both telling and troubling. The doctor is not concerned with the potential future in which the person who has

had the illegal abortion has equal possibility of choosing to reproduce or not reproduce, but one in which she is prevented from
following her body's natural course, once her circumstances are
more *appropriate*.

Up the Junction was adapted from a story by Nell Dunn, the daughter of a wealthy English family who, rebelling against her upbringing,
began living in Battersea and working in a sweets factory. In 1965,
Dunn published *Talking to Women*, a book of long interviews with
nine of her peers aged twenty-four to thirty-two (Dunn was twenty-
eight at the time). Though her interviewees, including the novelist
Edna O'Brien, came from a range of class backgrounds, they are
overwhelmingly concerned with perhaps the defining problem of
British feminism in the second half of the twentieth century: the
division between domestic labour and professional work. All the discussions of abortion in the book foreground the difficulty of
balancing a personal or creative life with the demands of mothering,
and the domestic sphere – especially marriage – is often figured as a
kind of trap. Having a child has different implications for each
woman, often within the same interview: sometimes a burden, now
a fear, now a pleasure (at one point Dunn herself refers to the experience of having a child as a 'rewarming' that returns you to the fire of
youth).

In the interviews that mention abortion, ambivalence – that
canonically maternal feeling – is far more prevalent than shame.
Antonia Simon, a 26-year-old photographer, speaks of her decision
to abort a pregnancy that originated in an extramarital relationship
as something held in painful balance with her deeply felt desire to
have a child with her husband: 'Yes, I wanted to have one terribly.
And yet I just couldn't bear that I was carrying that thing around
with me, I felt physically sick. And I didn't feel any guilt at having an
abortion, I just felt such a relief. It was so marvellous not to be
pregnant anymore.' The experimental novelist Ann Quin, aged
twenty-nine, describes the reasons behind her abortion as 'mainly
financial'. Asked whether she regretted it, she replies that 'I didn't
regret it because it was something that I'd chosen to do, and there

seemed no alternative, therefore I went ahead and did it.' She continues, analysing the experience in explicitly gendered terms: 'Obviously the whole feminine side of me got the upper hand as it were and the whole physical sense of losing something that was a part of me emotionally distracted me a lot and created a lot of emotional feeling for quite a time afterwards.'[18] This 'feminine side' seems to indicate both the traditional understanding of women as emotional beings, the counterpart to masculine rationality, and something inherently maternal: the desire to have a child is somehow foundational to femininity. Quin's language both centres choice and rejects it, or rather underlines its impossibility: 'it was something that I'd chosen to do', but there 'seemed no alternative'. She had nowhere to *put* a baby.

It is easier to change the law than change a culture. Even after the implementation of the 1967 Act, people seeking abortions were often treated very badly in medical contexts, especially if they were neither white nor wealthy. Gail Lewis recalls that when she terminated a pregnancy in 1969 at the age of seventeen she was 'treated abusively in the hospital, was not given painkillers, and was put next to a woman who had miscarried'.[19] Attitudes towards abortion were not permissive: the Thalidomide tragedy had influenced public opinion, but only in the case of births deemed not physically viable, underscoring the centrality of 'necessity'. And in the years after the passing of the Act there was a mania in sections of the British press for reporting that abortions were being used as a form of contraception, or that London was now 'Europe's abortion capital', with 'package' tours for foreign women that included one: there was no statistical evidence for either claim.[20] This is an almost laughably neat demonstration of certain aspects of the national character: abortions might be wrong, but they're *our* wrong (British abortions for British workers!).

In April 1968, just one year after the Act became operational, the Conservative MP Norman St John-Stevas tried to amend and restrict it through a private member's bill: this failed, but it set the stage for multiple similar attempts throughout the following decades. Organizations like the Abortion Law Reform Association and the

National Abortion Campaign, founded in 1975, found themselves tasked with simultaneously protecting the provisions of the 1967 Act and emphasizing its limitations. The NAC officially formed in response to the Abortion Amendment Bill proposed by James White, Labour MP for Glasgow Pollok, which sought to (further) restrict the circumstances in which abortion was permitted. It had a non-hierarchical structure, worked with feminist publications, crafted progressive legislation, organized demonstrations and drew attention to attendant issues, like the assumption in marital contracts of the husband's right to have a child. (After the defeat of White's bill, there were further amendments proposed by the Conservative MP William Benyon in 1977, and by the Scottish Conservative and Unionist Party's John Corrie in 1979.) By June 1975 the NAC was able to organize a demonstration attended by 20,000 people, and by 1976 there were 350 local affiliated groups. These groups liaised across Britain's internal borders, where there were significant geographical disparities to access: in Wales and Scotland, although the 1967 Act applied, it was often very difficult in practice for terminations to be obtained. In Cardiff, for example, where there was a very active branch of the NAC, it was especially hard: doctors would, according to accounts from women active in the movement, purposefully delay proceedings until the time limit was exceeded.[21] (The Cardiff Abortion Campaign organized demonstrations, film screenings and even fund-raising puppet shows. One member, Wendy Bourton, recalls being pelted with nails by a group of bored children who weren't enjoying an afternoon performance of the Cardiff Abortion Rights Puppet Theatre.[22])

In the west of Scotland, compounded by the ongoing legacy of religious sectarianism, the provision of abortion care was sporadic at best and actively hostile at worst. Doctors here would similarly employ the tactics of delay, and the long waiting times for NHS terminations essentially prevented many from accessing them at all. None of the charities that operated in England, including the British Pregnancy Advisory Service, had clinics in Scotland, and many, particularly from Glasgow and its environs, had no option but to travel south of the border. The Glasgow Family Planning Association stated that often 'the only way in which termination can be obtained is for the girl to be given the address of a pregnancy advisory centre in England.' Perhaps because of this, the Scottish Abortion Campaign was more radical than the NAC as a whole, focusing on not simply defending the 1967 Act but securing free abortion on demand, with no caveats: one of the points of their constitution was to 'work towards abortion being given a more positive place in existing sex education programmes'. As I write this, recent data has come to light showing that still, in 2022, pregnant people are being sent across the border to England to access abortions: there is no health board in Scotland that provides abortion care up to the legal limit of twenty-four weeks.[23]

In Northern Ireland, meanwhile, despite the belief in Westminster that the extension of the Act to include the six counties would, before the 1998 Good Friday agreement, further inflame ongoing conflicts of the Troubles and, after 1998, endanger the peace process, abortion was one of the few issues that stretched across sectarian divides. Many Irish organizations over the past half a century have campaigned for abortion reform: in the 70s, the Family Planning Association of Northern Ireland, the Ulster Pregnancy Advisory Association and the Northern Ireland Abortion Law Reform Association; in the 80s, the Northern Ireland Abortion Campaign (who sent 600 wire coat hangers to Westminster attached to fake British Airways tickets, with the declaration 'These are the two ways in which NI women get abortions'); and in the 90s, the Alliance for Choice, which is still active today. Cathy Harkin, who worked for Derry Women's Aid in the 1970s, described the six counties as an 'armed patriarchy', but, as one 2020 study of abortion-law reform demonstrated, anti-abortion politics in the north can't be reduced to gender difference. In one interview, Goretti Horgan, who was a founding member of the AfC and the Derry Women's Right to Choose Group, spoke of the disconnect in women's group meetings she attended with the idea that abortion was a feminist cause or even a common experience: 'they just didn't want to talk about it.'[24]

The taboo around abortion is difficult to dismantle, and heavily inscribed with prohibitions religious, cultural and social: it's understood by all sides, after all, as a matter of life and death. The question is: whose?

Abortion Work

Abortion is conceptually and practically related to production. In Loach's *Up the Junction*, the scenes which directly depict the termination of Rube's pregnancy are intercut with footage of her at work in the sweets factory: the speedy labouring hands are the same as those which later grip her face in agony and terror. The relationship between abortion-rights campaigns and what can be loosely termed the left-wing establishment – the Trades Union Congress and the Labour Party – was a complex one, coloured both by the indisputable fact that women were workers and the more controversial understanding of reproduction as a kind of work itself. Both the women's and gay-liberation movements were putting pressure on the default positions long held by the left in the UK, and Labour, in the 1960s and 70s, had serious problems with recruiting women, both as members and as potential candidates: in 1970, only ten elected Labour MPs were female, a third fewer than were elected as Conservative Members of Parliament. By the decade's end, Labour committed at its party conference to the protection of reproductive rights including abortion on demand, which, coming after the Labour government's passing of the 1970 Equal Pay Act and the 1975 Sex Discrimination Act, was a mark of the slow loosening of its own position on what were understood to be gendered – and therefore *women's* – issues.

The 1970s saw both substantial changes and substantial difficulties for women organizing within the traditionally masculine union structures of the United Kingdom. The Trades Union Congress, too, had been attempting to face up to the changing workforce. In 1959, only 1.5 million of the 8.5 million working women in the country were represented by affiliated unions: between 1964 and 1970, 70 per cent of the increase in union membership came from women. Abortion was, perhaps surprisingly, an essential part of this changing relationship. In 1974, women involved in the movement launched the 'Working Women's Charter', a landmark list of ten demands, explicitly address-ing contraception, abortion, childcare and maternity leave as well as more traditionally industrial issues of pay and training. Reproduction was a workers' issue, and, crucially, the Charter forged a connection between the personal and the industrial, locating the source of wom-en's oppression in their dual roles in the home and the workplace. Although it was supported by many unions, in 1975 the motion that it should be adopted by the TUC as a whole was defeated at conference because of two significant sticking points: its commitment to the national minimum wage and to abortion rights, the latter of which was understood to not be an 'appropriate' union matter.

'Within the next half hour,' however, as Ruth Elliott noted in her 1984 *Feminist Review* article 'How Far Have We Come?', which sur-veyed the relationship between feminism and the union movement, 'abortion was to become a trade union issue': a motion was carried opposing White's Abortion Amendment Bill and calling for 'the right of all women to adequate services for contraception and abortion on request available free of charge on the NHS'.[25] Those pushing for the left to take up a pro-abortion stance made explicit the link between reproductive justice and class: the NAC argued that the bill was anti-working-class legislation and that, for women without financial means, the dangerous backstreet abortionist would again become the only option. In her speech advocating the motion's passing, Terry Marsland, the Deputy Secretary of the Tobacco Workers' Union – which had a 60 per cent female workforce – reminded the TUC that they were 'responsible for the health and welfare of millions of women, both outside and inside our ranks'.[26]

The uneasy coalition between the TUC and abortion-rights cam-paigners remained for the rest of the decade and beyond. In 1979, when the Corrie Bill passed its second reading in the House of Commons, the NAC and the TUC co-organized a march that took place on Hallowe'en: 100,000 people took to the street in what was, according to *Spare Rib,* 'the largest trade union demonstration ever held for a cause which lay beyond the traditional scope of collective bargaining'. (It was also the biggest ever pro-abortion march.[27]) The relationship, however, was not entirely harmonious: angry at the fact that the march was mostly led by male TUC delegates, a group of women, including some marching under a *Spare Rib* banner, stormed the front. North of the border, relations were somewhat easier: as the historian Kristin Hay's research demonstrates, the Scottish Abortion Campaign, which had split from the NAC in the early 80s, worked and marched in tandem with the Scottish TUC, due in large part to the ferocity of the Scottish labour movement and a strong national class consciousness that understood abortion to be materially encoded.[28]

Ultimately, none of the campaigns of the 70s succeeded in the liberalization of the law, and during the 1980s there were several more attempts to restrict abortion access, meaning the NAC was frustrated by the necessity of maintaining a consistently defensive position. (Positive campaigns like the Labour MP Jo Richardson's 1981 Facilities Bill, which hoped to improve NHS abortion services, failed to get a second reading.) In 1985, almost twenty years after his violently racist 'rivers of blood' speech, Enoch Powell proposed the 'Unborn Child Protection Bill', which was on the face of it a proposal to drastically limit IVF research but was regarded by many as a covert attack on abortion rights.[29] In 1987, the Liberal MP David Alton introduced a bill that sought to reduce time limits: although this eventually failed, the supportive public response was concerning. The *Guardian,* in its leader comment, wrote that the 'Right to Choose lobby is now rather out of tune with the times. There is more of a recoil from "social" abortions', a term which indicates once again the belief in right and wrong abortion stories.[30] (Aren't all abortions, really, social abortions?) Eventually, in 1990, the Abortion Act of 1967 and the Infant Life Preservation Act of 1929 were amended via legislation that, like Powell's proposed bill three years earlier, primarily concerned fertility: the Human Fertilization and

Embryology Act restricted abortions to twenty-four rather than twenty-eight weeks.

The British public, when asked directly, has never been in favour of abortion on demand. In 1983, only 37 per cent of the adult population endorsed the 'right to choose'.[31] Yet wider political and social developments reframe questions of gender, sex and power all the time. By the mid-1970s, dramatic headlines about the horrors of backstreet abortion had mostly disappeared, and tabloids focused their anti-abortion coverage on graphic depictions of late-term terminations. (In 1974, the *News of the World* published a series of stories about aborted foetuses 'crying', later published in the book *Babies for Burning*, imagery that anti-abortion groups still use today.)[32] Although Margaret Thatcher was firmly anti-choice, she wasn't prepared to commit to the Corrie Bill in the first year of her premiership, and even the *Daily Mail* supported only the more modest parts of it, such as the right for doctors to 'conscientiously object' to performing the surgery themselves. As Margaretta Jolly writes in *Sisterhood and After*, 'perhaps the dissociation of sex from reproduction and marriage proved too useful to the leisure and consumer industry to be curbed, not to mention the sheer pleasure it offered to men, perhaps even more than women.' Abortion rights, she argues, are 'a very weak challenge' both to patriarchy and to the prevailing neoliberal order: 'the endurance of abortion rights in Britain lies not so much in the power and interests of men pursuing "free" sex, so much as a more comprehensive influence of New Right ideologies of liberalization and choice, combined with the need to push women into the workplace.'[33] Although the intensely complex feelings generated by abortion are crucial to the politicization of both maternity and sexuality more generally, the principle of choice alone cannot guarantee anything, including freedom.

Difficult Feelings and Diva Foetuses

In recent years, abortion has once again risen to the top of the national and international news agenda. In the Republic of Ireland in 2018, the campaign to repeal the eighth amendment to the Irish constitution was successful, with a landslide referendum result ruling in favour of technically legalizing abortion. The amendment was introduced by spooked anti-choice fundamentalists in 1983, in the wake of the Roe v. Wade ruling in the United States, and it recognized the 'right to life of the unborn'. Constitutionally, this enshrined the 'equal' right to life of the pregnant person and the foetus: it exercised the power of the state (and the Church), to 'defend and vindicate' pregnancy. Much of the coverage of the 2018 referendum focused on campaigning efforts that crossed generational divides as well as stories from previous decades that were being brought back out into the light. The *Irish Times* published new interviews with people who knew Ann Lovett, a fifteen-year-old who died giving birth alone beside a grotto in County Longford in 1984, emphasizing the complicity of the Church and the Gardaí in the culture of silence that prevented her from accessing help; flowers were laid at the mural in Portobello, south of Dublin, of Savita Halappanavar, who died of sepsis at University Hospital Galway after being denied an abortion, and crowds chanted 'Savita, Savita, Savita' outside Dublin Castle. Ana Kinsella, writing immediately after the referendum in *n+1*, noted the relative reserve of the Church in the run-up to the vote. After the multiple sex abuse scandals it has been beset by and the recent revelations about the Mother and Baby Home in Tuam, County Galway, where children had died and were left without proper burial, Kinsella writes, 'it is increasingly hard for the Church to preach on babies and bodies when we know what we do now about what it did in the recent past.'[34]

In advance of the referendum, the novelist Sally Rooney wrote of the unique position of the foetus in relation to the care it can demand:

Pregnancy, entered into willingly, is an act of generosity, a commitment to share the resources of life with another incipient being. Such generosity is in no other circumstances required by law. No matter how much you need a kidney donation, the law will not force another person to give you one. Consent, in the form of a donor card, is required even to remove organs from a dead body. If the foetus is a person, it is a person with a vastly expanded set of legal rights, rights available to no other class of citizen: the foetus may make free, non-consensual use of another living person's uterus and blood supply, and cause permanent, unwanted changes to another person's body. In the relationship between foetus and woman, the woman is granted fewer rights than a corpse.

This, Rooney continues, whatever framework it's couched within, have 'less to do with the rights of the unborn child than with the threat to social order represented by women in control of their reproductive lives'.[35] Such fear of this unbearably embodied threat to the social order is also visible in the idea that abortion is in some way being used incorrectly, that there is some platonic ideal of the perfect termination, and moral citizens are tasked with the regulation of it. Yes, we gave you freedom, these voices seem to say, but we didn't intend for you to use it so freely. (Think again, of the woman in Belfast who reported her flatmate to the police because she didn't like her 'attitude'.) On the fortieth anniversary of the 1967 Act, Lord Steel himself called for greater 'sexual responsibility', believing abortions were being taken 'too lightly'; in the same news cycle, the then Archbishop of Canterbury Rowan Williams called for review of the twenty-four-week limit, which had, in his words, 'normalized' abortions. Always, the rights of the foetus were invoked, often juxtaposed with a stereotype of a 'bad' mother, deserving of judgement: 'The pregnant woman who smokes or drinks heavily,' Williams writes, 'is widely regarded as guilty of infringing the rights of her unborn child, yet at the same time, with no apparent sense of incongruity, there is discussion of the possibility of the liberty of the pregnant woman herself to perform the actions that will terminate a pregnancy.'[36]

In 1994, the theorist Lauren Berlant diagnosed the United States with 'a culture of national fetality'. Discussing the use of foetal imaging in anti-abortion propaganda, Berlant argues that technological advances in medical imaging which allow a foetus to be visualized in utero have also encouraged people to identify with it, enabling the construction of a foetal personhood that composes 'a magical and horrifying spectacle of amazing vulnerability'.[37] Images of foetuses provoke extreme feelings: to force a woman to carry a pregnancy to term becomes an act motivated not by control but *justice*, protection of the defenceless being flickering in black and white on the ultrasound machine. (In one of the films Berlant discusses, *Eclipse of Reason*, which premiered in 1984, the images of 'mute and innocent victims' of abortion are likened to footage from Hiroshima, a famine-struck Ethiopia and Nazi concentration camps.) The foetus, Berlant argues, has become a celebrity: a diva, moving through the world with a particular claim to adoration and universality.

None of this is to say that difficult feelings about abortion are solely the prerogative of those who have the least to lose in the regulation of the uterus. A significant point of tension within feminist organizing in the 70s and 80s was the perceived dissonance between the language of choice, especially of abortion on demand, and the diversity of abortion's attendant emotional experience. In 1979, in a *Spare Rib* article called 'The Feelings behind the Slogans', Eileen Fairweather lamented that during campaigns 'the complexity of abortion and its emotional significance for women somehow got lost'; Sheila Rowbotham, meanwhile, wrote in the same year that 'we found it difficult to carry over the experience of the women's movement in discussing abortion in relation to our personal experience of our sexuality, our relationships, our attitudes to having children or childcare.'[38] Although many of those involved in the NAC had decided to join precisely because of their own experiences – its national co-ordinator Jan McKenley said her abortion was the event that awakened her to feminism as a whole – there was a general feeling that the campaign offered a limited perspective on what abortion meant for those who had experienced it.[39]

In 1979, the year of the Corrie Bill, a public meeting was held that became, as many recall, startlingly emotional: attendees were 'testifying to sadness, guilt, loss and shame, as well as relief'. By offering space for the personal ambivalence or even trauma associated with abortion, it also allowed sections of the activist community to emphasize the blind spots in a campaign that centred reproductive rights rather than reproductive justice. The NAC, which would eventually split entirely into two separate groups in 1983, was challenged for its failure to consider that 'abortion on demand' glossed over the complexity of choice, especially the fact that some pregnancies were considered less 'valuable' than others due to prevailing assumptions about race and ability. Gail Lewis, reflecting on these conversations several decades later, writes movingly about her knowledge that her mother, who was white, had seven illegal abortions because she did not want another mixed-race child.[40] Public opinion was openly prejudiced in favour of the 'rightness' of terminating a pregnancy if the foetus indicated potential disability.

Discussions of ableism in the abortion-rights movement continued into the early 1980s, particularly after the founding of Sisters Against Disablement, an organization that challenged the inaccessibility of the women's movement as a whole, as well as prevailing assumptions about disability. (In 1983, they picketed the inaccessible venue chosen by the Lesbian Sex and Sexuality Conference.) Kirsten Hearn, one of SAD's founding members, recalled in her *Sisterhood and After* interview that feminist demands for abortion on demand 'took for granted' the idea that a disabled child was more likely to be 'unwanted': in the end, Hearn said, she would 'find myself standing up at National Abortion Campaign meetings and going, "You're talking about killing babies, or killing foetuses or ending foetuses who might grow up to be someone like me." '[41] The relevance of these arguments only increased as medical technology advanced, particularly the use of amniocentesis to diagnose chromosomal abnormalities in utero.

Choice, again, was problematized: in *The Tentative Pregnancy*, published in 1993, the sociologist Barbara Katz Rothman wrote that the
decision 'to abort a foetus with spina bifida when you live in a
fourth-floor walkup in a city designed without access for wheel-
chairs is not really an exercise in free choice'.[42] Even the reactionary
right-wing Society for the Protection of Unborn Children had its
unlikely feminist supporters. In a 1975 issue of *Red Rag,* a letter was
published from a P. Shiels in Leamington Spa, who emphasizes the
'socialist demands' of the SPUC manifesto, which included single-
parent family allowances, educational and maternity grants, and an
increase in childcare services.[43]

Feelings, especially the focus on them through the practice of
consciousness-raising, had long been a point of conflict in feminist
organizing. In 1971, the Black Women's Action Committee of the
Marxist-Maoist Black Unity and Freedom Party published a statement arguing that, while consciousness-raising practices 'must
inevitably give the black woman a new "self image"', it is of 'even
greater importance' to consider what it can contribute to the
'black movement in particular and the revolutionary movement in
general'.[44] This isn't a rejection of feelings as such – although it
has often been read as one – but rather a rejection of individualism, or the prioritization of a specific affective disclosure over
revolutionary objectives. Margaretta Jolly writes that the statement from the Action Committee, as well as the discussions that
divided the movement more generally, especially those related to
abortion, 'defined consciousness as something to be attained
through new institutions and common struggles, far from feelings'.[45] I don't think that this is true or, at least, I don't think that
it's so simple. Common struggles and political movements are not
'far from feelings' but in the deepest felicity with them: they draw
on the emotions that offer strength, and confront and try to understand the ones that retreat from justice and from solidarity. (This
conflict is a form of love.) Here's the psychoanalyst Juliet Mitchell,
writing in the same year that the Action Committee released their
statement:

In the ideology of capitalist society *women* have always been the chief repository of feelings. They are thus among the first to gain from the radical 'capture' of emotionality from capitalist ideology for political protest movements. But the elevation of this quality ignores its really oppressive side within our society. Emotions cannot be 'free' or 'true' in isolation: they are dependent today on a social base that imprisons and determines them.[46]

Feelings isolated from socioeconomic structures are feelings out of time, removed from both their history and their possible future, which could be, in Mitchell's terms, 'radical'.

Of course, it is true that choice is materially determined, and that decisions made by individuals reflect and reinscribe the inequalities they experience and enact in their daily lives. Organizing to change these societal conditions is a necessity, and to do so the myopia of a movement which focuses on reproductive rights alone must be challenged. But for me, the slogan 'abortion on demand' acknowledges that there cannot be a compromise on the first principle: access to abortion itself. We cannot concede ground to the ideologically easier path of the much-lamented, difficult decision: that takes us back to an inverted version of maternal sacrifice. As Rooney observed in 2018, the 'vastly expanded' legal rights of the foetus come at the direct expense of the person who carries it; think once again of Rich's account of the 'fantasies of death in childbirth' that have 'the accuracy of metaphor'. When I say maternal sacrifice here, I don't mean the daily challenges of caring for a child, but the imperative to inhabit a maternal existence that you *do not want*, that you *cannot afford*, that can be deadly. The legal scholar Drucilla Cornell sees total bodily autonomy and control over what those choices mean as a prerequisite for personhood itself:

If a woman's personhood is truly to be respected by the law, then she must also be the ultimate source of both the decision to abort and the meaning given to that decision. It is the woman, not the state, that should have the narrative power over her decision. The narrative power is as important for her personhood as the decision itself since the chance to become a whole person is dependent on the imagined projection of one's self as a whole.[47]

The difference between a political position – abortion free on demand – and a matter of personal feeling is where choice actually lies: as should be obvious from the never-ending moral panics over what kind of abortions get performed, anything less than total accessibility invites a distinction between those who deserve to have an abortion and those who deserve to suffer an unwanted pregnancy, authorized and audited by the law.

Everyone deserves an abortion. In *Happening*, Ernaux paints a vivid picture of the tyranny of having no choice: her unwanted pregnancy performs an 'erasure of the future'.[48] In her account of her struggle to exercise bodily autonomy, the abortion itself is, as well as a logistical triumph, both exactly the right decision and a site of deeply complex feeling. What is interesting about these feelings in particular is that they are entirely related to the abortion as a discrete and contained experience: at no time is the possibility of the pregnancy continuing ever understood to be an option. The termination therefore takes on a symbolic significance as the threshold of adult life: it is the means by which she comes into her adult subjectivity. Rather than a separation from the body of her actual mother, the classic psychoanalytic formula, for Ernaux the abortionist *becomes* her mother. During the procedure, 'I feel that the woman who is busying herself between my legs, inserting the speculum, is giving birth to me. At that point I killed my own mother inside me.' Later, she tells the reader that, though she never saw her again, 'I have never stopped thinking about her. Involuntarily, this avaricious woman – whose flat was nonetheless poorly furnished – wrenched me away from my mother and into the world.' Before she is rushed to hospital, Ernaux delivers her aborted foetus in her college dorm room. As she struggles, trying, with the help of a friend, to cut the cord, the scene becomes the boundary between existence and oblivion: 'It's an indescribable scene, life and death in the same breath.

A sacrificial scene.' But what, here, is being sacrificed? It would be too obvious to say it is simply the bundle of cells in her hand, however familiar the narrative of child sacrifice might be to her readers. I think Ernaux is describing a transaction in which a part of herself is expelled to make room for what comes after: for her, the abortion was the process through which she became a woman. I don't mean, and I don't believe Ernaux means, that this is the only way of becoming a woman, nor that a reproductive experience in general is distinctly female: rather, this is what was true for her. This was her assertion of her own personhood.

Like Sheila Heti's account in *Motherhood* of the decision not to have children as being a way of preserving relationships with her maternal forebears, this anti-reproductive act situates Ernaux in a generational lineage: 'For the first time I felt caught up in a line of women, future generations would pass through us.' Later, she writes that this 'ordeal and this sacrifice were necessary for me to want to have children. To accept the turmoil of reproduction inside my body and, in turn, to let the coming generations pass through me.'[49] Abortion, truly, is central to maternity: like day and night, we cannot understand one without the clarifying contrast of the other. As Sophie Lewis writes in 'Antiwork Abortion', at present we live in a society in which we are compelled to care – 'our care is ripped from us' – and forced gestation, which is the consequence of restricted abortion, is simply the most invasive form of this coercion.[50] We can only defeat the 'pro-life' movement by demonstrating how little value they place on life itself: forced care, life 'as default', comes at the expense of other lives. My life. Yours, too, if you have a uterus. Abortion on demand treats life as something consciously chosen, and therefore as something very sacred. It can, as Ernaux writes, put us into contact with our own reproductive desires: this may not necessarily end, as it did in her case, with having children willingly and joyfully further down the line, but it might. The point is, we get to choose.

3.

Family Planning

Whose desire might qualify as the desire of the state?

Judith Butler, 'Is Kinship Always
Already Heterosexual?'

Choice has other mechanisms besides abortion. When I was thirteen years old, I was prescribed the combination oral contraceptive pill by a gynaecologist who looked exactly like a character from the Happy Families card game I'd had as a child. For several years, I had been experiencing agonizing and sometimes completely debilitating period pain, technically called dysmenorrhoea, as well as fainting, vomiting and insomnia. The pill I was prescribed to treat this was Microgynon 30, the cheapest available on the market and therefore the first port of call in the beleaguered NHS. After experiencing terrible side effects, as many who are prescribed Microgynon do, I tried Yasmin and Marvelon, each intolerable in their own specific ways, before moving on to Cerazette, a progesterone-only pill that I continued to take for many years. I didn't have penetrative sex with a man – the kind that could have resulted in an accidental pregnancy – until a few months after I had stopped taking it altogether.

Taking The Pill, its capitals reverently inscribed in my mind, felt like gaining access to a thrilling normality. It felt like an important milestone, a transgression sanctioned by the non-sexual reason for its prescription but containing within it the tantalizing possibility of sex, and with it the validation I desperately craved and comprehensively lacked as a young adult. As I continued to take it, the rhetoric of it being good and sensible to take the Pill 'just in case' felt like wish fulfilment, positive visualization: perhaps now I was regulating my painful body like a heterosexually active subject, the other parts of it would fall in line, too, become desirable. As well as the implication that my future certainly included straight sex by default, the way my body was spoken of by doctors always assumed a reproductive future, or at least a desire for one: even at thirteen, I was offered advice about assisted conception that was intended to shore up an eventual pregnancy as the fixed point ahead, the star by which I could orient my adult life. My womb and my ovaries were not simply organs in my body that were hurting me, but vessels for the future: they contained another potential citizen, someone else's time. The diva foetus, to borrow again from auren Berlant, was centre stage, even at a time when any conception inside my particular body would have been immaculate. (This is true of the technical workings of the Pill itself: a hormone-based contraceptive, it works by mimicking the conditions of pregnancy. The body prevents conception by being fooled into thinking it has already conceived.)

What does it mean to make normal choices? In being prescribed the Pill I was constructed as a compulsorily heterosexual and a compulsorily reproductive subject: with the benefit of hindsight, I can locate some personal struggles, particularly those to do with sexual identity, within this relentless exposure to the medicalized ideal of the normal female body from such a formative age. In the decades in which I have been trying to manage my chronic menstrual pain, I have experienced what Emma Heaney describes in her essay 'Is a Cervix Cis?' as 'social and historical feelings' of connection and solidarity with those who have experienced similar failures in the medical system, some of them women, some of them not, some of them with similar organs, some of them without.[1] My reproductive suffering has nothing to do with my gender: if you took it away, I wouldn't be less of a woman. Pain is not constitutive of womanhood, despite the fact that it has long been considered so. When I chose to stop taking the Pill, I made a decision that was completely within my rights, but one which has in practice essentially prevented me from seeking any further treatment: I go to the doctor, they suggest I take the Pill, I say no, and my refusal is understood to be a resistance to medicine, an abnormal decision. (This would not be the case if I were trying to conceive.)

Every now and again, a story will be published in the British media recounting how a young woman is being denied her request for a hysterectomy or an ovariectomy. Sometimes this is for the purpose of sterilization, though more often as treatment for debilitating menstrual pain which is frequently related to endometriosis, a condition that affects an estimated one and a half million people in the UK and has, on average, an eight-year-long wait for diagnosis. The reasoning is that these women may wish to get pregnant *in the future*: they might change their mind, make a normal choice. In my professional life, I have had several conversations with midwives and academics working in the field of midwifery studies who have told me with some assurance that women who know they don't want to have children always change their minds by the time they reach their early thirties. Yes, I often think to myself, in your professional experience, as *midwives*. The data set might be a little skewed.

Preventative States

Birth control and assisted conception are both reproductive technologies: those which aim to prevent pregnancy and those which aim to produce it are two sides of the same coin. Such technologies, of course, have been and continue to be liberatory for many people who have used them. It is still necessary, however, to question what they do, and how they reinforce the norms ascribed to 'feeling' or 'living' like a woman. What does the state consider to be a normal body? Who benefits from its control? Medically, as well as socially, motherhood is an essential part of what theorists like Judith Butler and Lauren Berlant have called the performance of the female gender: it frames, in Berlant's words, 'womanhood in a natural narrative movement of the body, starting at the moment a child is sexed female and moving to her inscription in public heterosexuality, her ascension to reproduction, and her commitment to performing the abstract values of instrumental empathy and service that have characterized norms of female fulfilment'.[2] Berlant is writing from a US-American perspective, but they could just as well be describing the British medical and educational terrain in which I grew up.

The contraceptive landscape as we know it emerged in England, Scotland and Wales, on the first day of April 1974 when, after the passing of the Reorganization of the NHS Act the previous year, contraception became available free of charge, regardless of the age or marital status of the person requesting it. Half a century earlier, the UK's first birth-control clinic had been founded in London by Marie Stopes, followed a decade later by the formation of the National Birth Control Council. But it wasn't until 1960 that contraceptive advice was available to unmarried women, and it was another decade after that before the National Birth Control Council, which was now called the Family Planning Association, began offering free treatment to all without restriction. The 1973 Act integrated these existing clinics into the NHS. (The anticipatory training of doctors and nurses in contraceptive techniques had started in 1969.) The term 'family planning' both includes within it a tacit dismissal of non-reproductive sexual activity and locates the responsibility for the family in the body of the mother: this incorporation of 'family planning provision' into the health service was simultaneously a victory for reproductive rights and further confirmation that women's bodies were state business.

The Pill was first made available on the NHS (to married women only) in 1961; six decades later, it remains a powerful symbol of the 'sexual revolution'. Unlike earlier barrier methods of contraception like condoms, pessaries and diaphragms, its long-lasting cyclical nature (taken correctly) effectively separated sex from reproduction for the first time. This, especially in the context of a taxpayer-funded public healthcare system, positioned it at the centre of long-running political and moral arguments. On the left, there has historically been a tendency towards the heralding of the Pill as a straightforwardly good thing, a magic dose of choice and power. It is certainly true that the Pill altered the fabric of British life profoundly and struck emancipatory blows against the normative nuclear family: fewer pregnancies contributed to the increased number of women entering the workplace, a decline in the marriage rate, which fell from 60 per cent in 1970 to just over 20 at the turn of the millennium, and a reduction in the number of children up for adoption. In 1974, the birth rate fell below Britain's 'replacement level' of 2.1 children per woman, where it still lies. Also indicative of its impact is the fact that it was subject to attacks from the right, although never in as sustained a manner as those waged against abortion. The most famous of these was a maternal one: in 1983, Victoria Gillick, a mother of ten, brought a landmark case against the High Court protesting the fact that medical practitioners could prescribe contraception to under-sixteens without their parents' knowledge or consent. This protracted legal battle resulted in the 1985 House of Lords ruling that established the 'Gillick competence' in England and Wales, which ensures the legal right to make decisions moves from the parent or guardian to the child themselves as they mature. At the heart of the Gillick furore was the relationship between the family and the state. Gillick believed, and vocally expressed at any opportunity, that the latter was usurping the former, resulting in 'sexual delinquency': 'instead of mother knows best, children now have "the Nanny State"-knows-best dictum.' (Beatrix Campbell described the case in 1987 as the 'stuff Thatcherism was made of'.[3]) In this image of the nanny usurping the mother we can find 'natural' maternal care being replaced by something artificial, but we can also find traces of the fear of the public usurping the private: a transfer of potentially reproductive bodies from the family to the state.

Still, there is no such thing as a straightforwardly liberatory technology. The Pill was a conundrum: on the one hand, birth control represented a troubling threat to the regulation and control of female sexuality through pregnancy and marriage, but, on the other, the possibility of curbing the reproduction of less desirable citizens was, to many, an attractive one, which could ensure the 'right' kind of families were created. This, by another name, is the philosophy of eugenics: the belief that the 'genetic quality' of a human population can be 'improved' by the exclusion of groups of people deemed to be inferior to a specific ideal. Two women, with the same initials, born within a year of each other on opposite sides of the Atlantic, are fundamental to understanding the relationship between eugenics and birth control: Marie Stopes and Margaret Sanger. Sanger was the founder of the American Birth Control League and Planned Parenthood, who organized the funding drive for the development of the Pill. They met at a Fabian Society meeting in 1913, where Sanger spoke about her efforts to provide birth control in New York state, despite a ban on its provision and distribution. Stopes, who was writing her first book, *Married Love*, asked Sanger's advice about the chapter on contraception. Although she was a scientist – she had a PhD in palaeobotany – Stopes had almost no functional knowledge of sex when she married her first husband, Reginald Ruggles Gates, in 1911 (she was thirty). After giving herself a crash course in sexual education in the reading room of the British Museum, she successfully managed to get the marriage annulled on the grounds of non-consummation in 1914. This, alongside a painful experience of stillbirth during her second marriage, inspired her interest in sexual education: she published *Married Love*, which included that Sanger-approved chapter on contraception alongside other writing about intercourse and orgasm, in 1918. It was swiftly followed by *Wise Parenthood: A Book for Married People* (exclusively focused on contraception, with a pamphlet version, 'Letter to Working Mothers' distributed for free in the slums of East London) and, in 1920, *Radiant Motherhood*, which dispensed advice about the health of pregnant women and their infants.

Stopes was an unabashed eugenicist; in her will she bequeathed her clinic to the British Eugenics Society, of which she was a Life Fellow, and she disinherited her son for marrying a woman who wore glasses. In 1918, she advocated the compulsory sterilization of people 'unfit' for reproduction. Yet, as the historian Deborah

A. Cohen has detailed, she made clinical decisions that were at odds with her beliefs.

Her Mothers' Clinics, which opened first in London in 1921 and then extended to Leeds, Aberdeen, Belfast and Cardiff, in tandem with two travelling rural 'Caravan Clinics', went out of their way to attract middle-class clients of the kind that 'positive' eugenicists wanted to reproduce, fitting them with cervical caps and diaphragms if they wished (condoms were provided if these didn't work).[4] The clinics also advised on fertility – an early example of birth control being folded into reproductive planning – and Cohen documents several instances of working-class women being helped to conceive. Other working-class women were fitted with contraceptives, which seems to partially fulfil Stopes's eugenicist ambitions, but personal letters attest that many women who accessed the clinic experienced this both as choice freely made and a welcome relief. Stopes employed midwives, prioritizing those who were older and had children of their own, and some of them were able to relate to their patients in a way that no other medical professional had: Nurse Rae, a mother of four employed in Aberdeen, described her work as her 'religion' and wrote to Stopes of the 'good of your Birth Control – I had a hard life – and I myself wish I had known of it'. The clinics also built on the work of more radical forebears: the Workers' Birth Control Group, set up by the socialist feminists Dora Russell and Stella Browne, gave free lectures on birth-control methods across the country, advocating them not just for practical purposes of family reduction but for a utopian society based on democratic, comradely, pleasure-based sexual relationships.[5]

Stopes, in official accounts, is given the benefit of the doubt: eugenicist views were widespread, and her motivation, in her own words at least, came from working with traumatic unwanted pregnancies and botched backstreet abortions. Yet she stressed in her writing and public speaking the danger unfettered reproduction posed to 'civilization'.[6] Damning, also, is her relationship with Sanger, who had in 1921 published an article in *Birth Control Review* titled 'The Eugenic Value of Birth Control Propaganda'. Sanger's was a pro-natalist eugenicism: 'every potential parent,' she writes, 'and especially every potential mother, must be brought to an acute realization of the primary and central importance of bringing children into this world.' Giving these 'potential mothers' control, she goes on to declare, is the only way both to 'improve the quality of the generations of the future, but even to maintain civilization even at its present level'. Sanger believed that the world had drifted into 'sexual and racial chaos', and between 1939 and 1942 she held a supervisory role on the Negro Project, a programme funded by the Birth Control Federation of America with the explicit purpose of 'delivering information' about birth control to economically disadvantaged black communities.[7] In a letter of 1939, Sanger wrote of the project that 'we do not want word to go out that we want to exterminate the Negro population.'[8] (I'd like to note here that neither Sanger nor Stopes was in favour of abortion: they advocated forced sterilization, but baulked at the prospect of choice after conception.)

Population 'control' was key to the development of oral contraceptives, and not just in Sanger's funding drive. In both the US and the UK, population growth in 'developing' countries caused significant anxiety to their former colonizers, whose own birth rates were declining.[9] As Angela Y. Davis writes in *Women, Race and Class*, the birth-control movement was 'robbed of its progressive potential': rather than provide liberation, it 'would be called upon to serve in an essential capacity in the execution of the US government's imperialist and racist population policy'.[10] Enovid, the first commercially available contraceptive pill, was developed in America by Dr Gregory Pincus: after a trial in Massachusetts, the next phase of testing moved to Puerto Rico. The island, an American territory, was one of the most densely populated areas in the world, with endemic poverty, and already at the centre of a programme of forced sterilization. Between 1930 and 1970, one third of Puerto Rican women of childbearing age were sterilized, with the operation presented as the only viable form of birth control. (The US government pursued this policy at home, too: by 1976, almost a third of women indigenous to America had undergone sterilization.) Those who took part in Pincus's trial were only informed they were being given a pill that prevented pregnancy, not that they were participating in a clinical experiment, and Pincus performed laparotomies – invasive abdominal surgery seeking evidence of ovulation in the ovaries – on women who did not speak English without obtaining informed consent. Three participants died, but no autopsies were performed. Although the trials successfully prevented ovulation, 17 per cent of the women involved experienced painful and debilitating side effects, which Pincus dismissed, believing they were being exaggerated or misreported, or that they were psychosomatic.[11]

Enovid was licensed for retail in the USA in 1960, and British clinical trials began in the same year, in Birmingham, London and Slough. The Birmingham programme proved disastrous: coordinated by the Family Planning Association and running low on funding, a low-hormone dosage regime was decided upon. After three months, fourteen of the forty-eight participants, each of whom had had to receive signed permission from their husbands to participate, were pregnant. In Slough, a higher dosage of oestrogen was used, and correspondingly only one of the thirty-eight subjects fell pregnant in the first few months; this was blamed on the woman herself, who had been lax taking the tablets. By most medical standards, these studies were inconclusive, and it was not possible to tell whether the Pill actually prevented ovulation. (Animal testing was useless: as most animals used in laboratory research don't tend to have sex for pleasure, any alteration in hormonal balance often leads to a lack of intercourse altogether.) The fact that the Ministry of Health approved the prescription of the Pill on the NHS despite this anticipates the lack of concern that is still displayed by the medical profession about the debilitating side effects the Pill has on a significant number of those who take it today. A common talking point in relation to the stalled development of the male contraceptive pill is that the side effects deemed too severe for men are the same as those experienced by women; often, it is suggested in a 'feminist' manner that men should have to take it anyway, as women have done for half a century. I personally think our standards for everyone should be higher.

In 1960, Birmingham was a city with a large industrial workforce and a rapidly increasing immigrant population, particularly from South Asia and the Caribbean. Following the failure of the first trials, participants were switched to a higher dosage of progesterone and oestrogen. This time, only one woman in the trial conceived. Glenys Bond, the medical officer for the Birmingham FPA, wrote that this 'could not be attributed to failure of the tablets, but to the patient's low IQ'. In a write-up of the trials from the year the Pill was first licensed for use, a professor in Social Policy at the University of Birmingham wrote that, as the class and race of the women who were involved in the trials showed, 'the present pill is likely for long to remain one of the contraceptives of an affluent and sophisticated society': for 'poor' and 'simple' women – like those who got pregnant – a cheaper and easier contraceptive method was necessary.[12]

By the time the NHS Reorganisation Act came into effect in 1974, making the Pill freely available to all who wanted it, the women's liberation movement had built a coalition who staged actions, organized demonstrations and ran small-scale support groups that tried to ensure contraception reached those who needed it. Yet when it came to the potential abuses of contraception by the medical establishment, the mainstream of the movement was blinkered: it was groups like the Organisation for Women of African and Asian Descent (OWAAD) who led the way on such misuses.[13] OWAAD, which had formed in 1978, frequently worked in collaboration with other groups including Afaaz, a South Asian women's organization: they were at the forefront of a 1979 sit-in at London Heathrow airport protesting the invasive 'virginity tests' that were performed by immigration officers on South Asian women who were entering the country intending to marry a British citizen. In *The Heart of the Race*, Beverley Bryan, Stella Dadzie and Suzanne Scafe document the ways in which the Pill was overprescribed to Black women in particular, with doctors often failing to explain other options. After detailing the painful side effects that came from taking two different kinds of Pill and the traumatic removal of an IUD, one woman interviewed in the book recalls that, at the end of her tether,

> my friend introduced me to one of the low oestrogen pills, and I went back to the clinic and asked if I could try it out. I really had to put up a fight to get them to prescribe it for me. You know why? Because it was a low-dosage pill and they didn't think I was responsible enough to take it regularly at the same time every day.

Black women were considered to be a 'high promiscuity risk' and encouraged to use contraceptive methods perceived as less risky: the health service, broadly speaking, was prioritizing pregnancy reduction rather than patient care, a course of treatment founded on racist assumptions.[14]

One of the least risky contraceptive methods, in these terms, was the contraceptive injection Depo-Provera: it needed to be administered only four times a year and had a high success rate of pregnancy prevention. With such ease came the potential for abuse. Often, the injection was administered without explanation of either its long-lasting effects or its potential side effects, and it was disproportionately prescribed to 'irresponsible women', including women who had had abortions, were unmarried, working class or had learning difficulties. Ideal candidates in the eyes of the state also included women of African and Asian descent; on this, the British medical establishment was in agreement with the National Front. The fascist perspective on birth control, as Vron Ware outlined in the 1978 pamphlet *Women and the National Front*, was that for white women abortion should be banned, but abortion and sterilization 'encouraged' for women of other racial backgrounds.[15] (Depo-Provera remains central to racist reproductive scandals: in 2013, the Israeli Deputy Health Minister admitted that it had been given to Ethiopian immigrants without their consent; the Ethiopian birth rate in Israel had dropped by almost 50 per cent.)[16]

OWAAD organized a protest outside a meeting of the government Committee on the Safety of Medicines and distributed flyers and information sheets about the injections, attempting to resist the pressure of the state and build support groups for those who needed advice. Slowly, awareness grew of the ways in which contraception traversed the intersecting boundaries of race, gender and class. Rowena Arshad, a member of the first Black women's group in Scotland, remembers visiting women who had been given Depo-Provera in Ferguslie Park in Paisley, one of the most deprived areas in Scotland, in the early 1980s, and thinking:

> hey, hang on a minute, women in India are being given this as well. Hm, this is very curious. And then realizing of course that the drug was being used to control women who society deemed to be irresponsible, shouldn't be having children, et cetera. So it was used as a population control mechanism. And often without the women knowing the full side-effects of it.

This realization led to solidarity across national borders. Arshad recalls that when the Ferguslie Park residents discovered what was happening, they were 'just angered, really angered to know this. But it was so good, because they were in solidarity with the women in India': nobody, they were adamant, should be 'treated like that'.[17] Such solidarity was built on discrimination: certain kinds of bodies were understood to be more disposable, more appropriate for such experiments.

Piss Prophecy

It's difficult to imagine, in an era when you can purchase three test strips for £1 in a high street chemist, that it wasn't always so easy to diagnose your own pregnancy. One relatively neglected aspect, historically speaking, of the WLM's reproductive politics is their provision of free pregnancy testing and post-test counselling. DIY testing allowed women to exercise control over their reproductive bodies both as patients (those accessing the tests) and as practitioners (those administering them). Although there were, as ever, ongoing discussions within the movement about the benefits of creating 'alternative structures' rather than pressurizing the state to provide what was needed, either way the tests were necessary, given the general state of pregnancy diagnosis in the UK at the time.[18] And there were reasons, too, not to trust the NHS when it came to testing: between 1950 and 1978 over 1.5 million women took Primodos, a pill for detecting pregnancy that was subsequently linked to birth defects and fatalities. Many who had taken it were never informed: one woman, for whom it had caused stillbirth, only realized what had happened when watching a Sky documentary about the scandal in 2017.[19]

Pregnancy, historically, has been the subject of self-diagnosis, based on an attunement to the body's clues: prophetic dreams, mood changes, swollen breasts, bellies and feet. A missed period is, of course, the most recognizable sign, though as not everyone who menstruates has a regular cycle, this is not as reliable as popular culture has led us to believe. Urine has always been central: from the Ancient Egyptian practice of urinating on seeds to see what would grow (wheat for a girl, barley for a boy, nothing for nothing) to the Persian tenth-century practice of pouring sulphur over urine to see if it produced worms, to the 'water doctors' (or 'piss prophets') of the early twentieth century. In the UK up until the mid-1960s, lab technicians injected urine into living mice, rabbits, frogs and toads and monitored what changes hCG, the 'pregnancy hormone', produced in them. (The use of the African clawed frog for this purpose had significant unintended consequences: it's believed international trade in them introduced a lethal fungus that has decimated frog populations worldwide, while some escapees 'colonised Wales'.)[20] Until the first commercially available self-testing kit came on to the British market, pregnancy diagnosis was the purview of professionals: although it was technically free on the NHS, this was only for medical reasons, and the historian Jesse Olszynko-Gryn's research into early testing documents many examples of women being turned away by their doctors as 'so-called curiosity cases'. DIY kits, which looked like chemistry tests, became more widely available in the early 70s, but they were still prohibitively expensive, and difficult to administer.

Free community testing, then, addressed several problems at once. By the middle of the decade, *Spare Rib* reported that women's groups were already 'doing pregnancy testing the way we want it done: with easy access, immediate results, and either free or for the cost of the test alone'. Moreover, the tests were performed by 'women who understand and are sympathetic to the feelings and needs of the women using the services'.[21] This sympathy was as significant as the practical aspects of the service. The emotional architecture of the free programme centred on the mixed feelings that the results engendered: those who administered the tests did not ask prying questions but directed people to resources that might be useful. In her memoir *Paper Houses*, Michèle Roberts recalls working as a testing volunteer and collapsing in tears, emotionally exhausted by giving out results and dealing with responses.[22] Many volunteers had their assumptions challenged, as, rather than mostly young women who did not want to be pregnant, relief at a negative result was spread across age brackets, as was disappointment. Sue Jones, who was involved with testing in Bolton, Lancashire, spoke of her surprise that many of those who came were married women who were finding it hard to conceive: here, long before 'we heard about test tube babies or infertility or anything', was an indication that infertility would go on to become a big 'industry'.[23]

The fact that a significant proportion of the women who received negative diagnoses were surprised by them demonstrates that, even within a feminist movement that resisted simplistic maternal narratives, many assumed that conception was their body's default: a natural process that it required effort to avoid, not to seek. The complicated logic of choice does not extend only to the prevention and termination of pregnancy, but also to its instigation. As the 1970s drew to their close, advances in reproductive technology accelerated at a breakneck speed: before the decade was out, Louise Brown of Oldham, Greater Manchester, was the first baby born who had been conceived by the new process of In Vitro Fertilization. IVF has six stages:

1. The menstrual cycle is medically supressed
2. Medication is taken to encourage an increased production of eggs by the ovaries
3. The maturation of the eggs is monitored via ultrasound, with more medication
4. The eggs are collected from the ovaries via a needle inserted through the vagina
5. The eggs are mixed with the sperm and left for several days to fertilize
6. The embryos are transferred into the womb

Two weeks after the transfer occurs, a pregnancy test is taken. Still a gruelling process by any standards, in 1978 the demands IVF placed on the bodies of those trying to conceive were even more substantial. Participants spent up to three weeks staying on the grounds of their clinic as inpatients, collecting all their urine and giving samples every three hours, including during the night: one participant recalled that 'We were in beds in ranks, six of us in each of the Portakabins. They'd come round and wake us up in the middle of the night and we'd all troop off and we had to wee in a bottle so they could monitor our hormones.'[24] If a urine sample indicated ovulation, then exactly twenty-six hours later the eggs would be harvested. Gravity was assumed to be helpful for implantation: crouching forward, bottom aloft, was the posture recommended for participants to hold for several hours afterwards.

The laborious processes of IVF change the body and mind in discomforting ways. Like the side effects of the Pill, this is medically understood to be of secondary importance compared to the goal of controlling fertility: if the reproductive body is a factory, this is simply the background hum of the spinning machines. The sociologist Sarah Franklin observes in her book *Biological Relatives* that the obvious comparison for the 'reproductive revolution' that Louise Brown's birth marked in the summer of 1978 is the Industrial Revolution that began, too, in the north-west of England. Franklin extends this comparison further, noting that, like the government interest in industrial manufacturing in the nineteenth century, new reproductive technologies have been at the centre of protracted public and legislative debate since Brown's birth. These debates were fuelled by the 1984 Warnock Inquiry, in which the human right to access embryos was deliberated on, culminating in the Human Fertilisation and Embryology Act 1990, which established the regulating body that became the Human Fertilisation and Embryology Authority: IVF became, as with Enoch Powell's stealth attack on abortion in 1985's Unborn Children (Protection) Bill, the sign under which the regulation of all reproductive bodies was discussed.[25]

In its earliest days, 'normality' was crucial to IVF's branding. Brown's birth was heralded as something both normal and national: one which *belonged* to the health service, and also to the concept of scientific advancement itself. In this, it also belonged to the nation. In the British press the birth was presented as a success for her parents Lesley and John, for consultant gynaecologist Patrick Steptoe and research scientist Robert Edwards – Jean Purdy, a nurse and embryologist involved from the beginning, was forgotten – and for the country: it became a story about 'Britishness winning out against the odds', with the *Manchester Evening News* describing it as an 'all-British miracle'. In Oldham, a local councillor was quoted in the *Evening Chronicle* saying that Steptoe and his colleagues had 'put Oldham on the map'. The front page of the *Evening News* on the day Louise was born emblazoned her image with the headline 'SUPERBABE'. A world first makes good copy, and it was easy to find human interest in this nice English family and their desire for a child, but Lesley Brown herself – inside whom this miracle had actually occurred – was curiously erased: the *Mirror* wrote before the birth that 'Mr Steptoe's miracle baby will be the envy of doctors around the world.' Her body, however, was still opened up to public scrutiny: the C-section was filmed, partly in order to demonstrate that Brown's fallopian tubes were damaged and the birth was not, therefore, a hoax. (In Steptoe and Edwards's 1980 book, *A Matter of Life*, a significant amount of time is spent discussing the logistical challenges of hiding Brown from the press.)[26] In an interview with

Time magazine in 2018, marking her fortieth birthday, Louise herself noted that the public nature of her arrival was not a choice but a necessity: 'Had there been anything at all wrong with me, it would have been the end of IVF.'[27] The burden of proof was on her, barely seconds old, to be a reassuringly ordinary baby, part of a recognizably normal family.

Dr Strangelove of Belgravia

It's tempting, although not particularly useful, to speculate on what would have happened had the Browns not been so certifiably normal: the decisions that led to their selection were not blind to context, appearance or to the British appetite for public outrage. Such speculation is anyway unnecessary: we have a counter-example from the very same year. At the beginning of 1978, the *London Evening News*, which had a reputation for manufacturing sex scandals, launched another salacious exposé. Headlined 'Dr Strangelove: The Belgravia man who helps lesbians have babies', it revealed that the gynaecologist Dr David Sopher, a member of many prestigious associations, had been artificially inseminating lesbians at his private practice in that affluent part of London.[28] The newspaper purposefully represented the secrecy of the process as a marker of shame or even of medical malpractice, falsely claiming that Sopher was working against the advice of the British Medical Association. The clandestine nature of the process was in fact necessitated, as the historian Rebecca Jennings has shown, by Sopher's desire to avoid being consumed by the broader cultural debate about sexuality and the family. This conversation had been growing particularly frenetic under the auspices of Mary Whitehouse and others who sought to connect the 'moral pollution' of permissiveness with economic difficulties and ongoing industrial action that dominated the news cycle: a threat to the family was a threat to the structure and success of the nation.[29]

Lesbians were less prominent targets of homophobic newspapers than gay men, but the slow increase in lesbian public figures was beginning to turn the tide: the Labour MP Maureen Colquhoun, who left her husband and came out in 1976, was frequently the butt of public 'jokes'.[30] As the gay and women's liberation movements expanded, coming out became both more possible and more overtly politicized: as well as aiming to change public attitudes and the legal reality for their communities, groups like the Gay Liberation Front encouraged pride rather than assimilation (the first UK Pride parade was held in London in 1972, with 2,000 attendees). Amid feminist calls for women to embrace independence outside the nuclear family, more people were identifying as lesbians at a younger age, before succumbing to the social expectation that they would get married: if they wanted to have children, they had to find a new way to do so. Lesbian motherhood, then, encompassed both those who had married and had children before having the opportunity to fully explore their sexuality – or who had married in the hope that it might reconcile them to heterosexuality – and those who were hoping to conceive for the first time. It was a central topic of the first National Lesbian Conference in Canterbury, Kent, in April 1974, where the resolution was formulated that would become the sixth (controversial) demand of the WLM: an end to discrimination against lesbians, and women's right to identify their own sexuality.

For those who had had children before coming out, the risks of publicly identifying yourself as a lesbian were phenomenally high, and risked a bitter custody battle that was almost certain not to rule in your favour. As lesbians across the country lost custody of their children, their rights became a principal activist concern: groups like Wages Due Lesbians, Action for Lesbian Parents, the Association of Lesbian Parents, the Rights of Women (a group of feminist lawyers) and women's centres more generally campaigned for their maternal rights to be recognized.[31] The first play produced by the women's company of the Gay Sweatshop Theatre Company, a collective aiming to raise awareness of homophobic oppression, was 1977's *Care and Control*, which linked the treatment of lesbian mothers to (straight) single mothers. According to its programme,

A woman is suspect in the eyes of the State when she asserts her right to live independently of men. She is seen as a direct challenge to family life and the traditional sexual roles which the court upholds. It is against these attitudes and assumptions, which deny all of us the right to decide the most basic and intimate matters of our lives, that women are organizing to fight the custody battle.[32]

The insemination scandal of 1978, then, emerged at the very point that lesbian motherhood was being recognized both as a concept and as a cause. When it comes to the latter, we mustn't succumb to the temptation of idealization: in defending the rights of women to parent together, some were quick to reinforce perceived ideas of 'good' and 'bad' mothers. Some campaigners argued, for example, that it was better for a child to be brought up by two women than by a single mother, or by middle-class lesbians rather than working-class women or sex workers: an article in the *Derby Evening Telegraph* asked its readers to weigh up a lesbian mother's 'strong maternal instincts' against those of the 'promiscuous typist, the prostitute who came unstuck, even the career woman who manages to fit in a quick pregnancy before going off again to pursue her career'.[33]

Artificial insemination was not Sopher's invention: it had been in use since the eighteenth century, mostly in the case of a husband's infertility, and eugenicists favoured it as a 'positive' strategy for population 'improvement'. There were significant religious objections, replete with comparisons to the sexual sins of infidelity and masturbation, from both the Vatican and the Church of England: in 1948 a report led by the Archbishop of Canterbury advised that it should be criminalized. These ethical debates were fairly muted by the time the *Evening News* ran its exposé of Sopher, capitalizing on the growing furore around Louise Brown's approaching birth. There was no governing central body, meaning that individual clinicians were free to decide whether they offered their services to single and lesbian women as well as traditional families who needed assistance conceiving. Although most medical professionals did not provide this service, some, like Sopher, were doing so throughout the 70s: Sopher himself had attended a meeting about motherhood held by the lesbian social club Sappho in 1972 and was sufficiently convinced by its necessity to begin practising. (Sappho also published an eponymous magazine where successful births were announced.) As well as performing the procedure, Sopher encouraged his patients to collect and refrigerate sperm samples themselves. Each insemination at Sopher's clinic cost twelve pounds, with half of that being paid to the donor, less than a tenth of what most private clinics charged.[34]

It was through Sappho meetings that the *Evening News* journalist Joanna Patyna infiltrated Sopher's clinic, pretending for two months to be Joanna Allison, a lesbian who wanted a child. Once the story had broken, it created a heightened climate of fear among its targets, not least that their children would be ostracized by their teachers or peers.[35] One significant reason custody cases discriminated so relentlessly against lesbians and, indeed, that public opinion was so easily manipulable, was that homosexuality was considered to be harmful to children. In response to the Artificial Insemination by Donor scandal, the innocence of the child was repeatedly weaponized. This required an inversion of the logic applied to anti-abortion positions: rather than fighting to preserve the unborn child's right to be conceived, regardless of circumstance, opponents of AID thought it better that a desired child should not exist than grow up in a lesbian household. After the publication of the *Evening News* story, the Conservative MP Jill Knight, a founding member of the Lords and Commons Family and Child Protection Group, which defined 'child protection' as preventing young people from accessing birth control, declared in Parliament:

> I am not concerned with the lifestyle of the lesbians, nor would I condemn them. But it is very worrying from the point of the children that this should be permitted. A child needs above all a normal and natural family environment. I cannot imagine that it is in the best interest of children to be born in such circumstances.

A 'normal and natural family environment' clearly means a hetero-sexual couple, regardless of the well-documented damage that these family set-ups frequently wreak on their members. Another Conservative MP, Rhodes Boyson, demanded that artificial insemi-nation for lesbians should be banned: 'To bring children into this world without a natural father is evil and selfish. This evil must stop for the sake of the potential children and society, which both have enough problems without the extension of this horrific practice.' This 'horrific practice' refers not only to insemination itself but to lesbian mothering more generally: its 'unnaturalness' was implicitly linked to the idea of same-sex desire as a perversion of the norm. The idea that children themselves might not be straight, or even that children had a sexuality of their own at all, was out of the ques-tion; the fact, too, that a heterosexual couple was exactly as 'sexualized' as a queer one was irrelevant. A lesbian mother was understood to be fundamentally more sexual than a straight (or closeted) one. Mothers were not permitted to have sexual desires and be good mothers; the only acceptable container for those desires was a het-erosexual marriage which produced children, sanctioned by a state that, as the next chapter will demonstrate, routinely forced children to remain in violent domestic situations and denied abused mothers divorces.

A few days after the *Evening News* article was published, a group of protestors affiliated with Action for Lesbian Parents, *Spare Rib* and the Gay Sweatshop Theatre Company staged a sit-in at the newspa-per's offices, chanting 'our bodies, our lives' and demanding the right to speak to Patyna and her editor, Louis Kirby; when a right to reply in print was granted, they stated that lesbians had the right to repro-duce, and that the exposé, as feminist coverage had also stated, was an attack on reproductive freedom in general. AID continued to be available to lesbians at the discretion of practitioners, and Sopher himself, despite what the *Evening News* had reported, was consist-ently supported by the BMA and the College of Obstetricians and Gynaecologists, who declared his conduct to be 'ethical and proper'.[36] Public disapproval proved difficult to dispel, however, and Janis

Hetherington, the first mother to have been successfully impregnated through AID in Britain, felt compelled to try and rectify this by telling her story. Janis, her partner Judy and their son, Nick, lived in north London with Judy's five-year-old daughter Lisa. Hetherington's interview with the *Observer* – 'My AID son – by a lesbian' – was published on the 8 January. Over thirty years later, in 2011, Hetherington, who had known she was a lesbian since childhood, recalled that: 'It was because of Lisa – being a mother to her, more than anything, reminded me that I could have a child and I didn't have to have a man.' Like Louise Brown, the infant Nick Hetherington was the subject of a significant amount of representational pressure. Janis made a point of saying that her son was 'perfectly normal, and very intelligent' – as if any perceived defect would be blamed on either the process or some deeper moral perversion, transmitted via osmosis – and was aware of the 'responsibility' she bore: 'if I blew it, I'd blow it for everyone else.' Nick, in the same interview, speaks of the pressure he felt on his own sexuality, feeling he had to be straight to prove something: they were, in his words, 'the spin-masters for this movement and community'. This famous and documented normality did not help when Judy died suddenly and tragically of a heart attack at thirty years old. Janis, with no legal claim on Lisa, engaged in a two-year-long custody battle in which she had to prove to a magistrate that she was a 'capable mother'. (She won.) Motherhood, she said in 2011, is 'fighting'; 'it's your most basic instinct.'[37]

Brothels and Bombs

What do reproductive technologies do to the maternal or potentially maternal body? One answer is that they can liberate it from the obligation to be a maternal body at all. It is easy to assume, bearing in mind the opposition from the Christian right and the oversimplified logic of choice, that IVF was considered a feminist project. In fact, reproductive technology was and remains a profoundly ambivalent site for feminism, even, in the words of the feminist researcher and nurse Margarete Sandelowski, creating 'fault lines' in the concept of sisterhood itself.[38] In 1970, Shulamith Firestone published *The Dialectic of Sex*, a text which, among other things, predicted the invention of artificial wombs, something Firestone believed would free women from 'barbaric' pregnancies; she also writes that 'to envision it [the artificial womb] in the hands of the present powers is to envision a nightmare.'[39] This barbarism is conceptual, but also literal, when it comes to the physical process of pregnancy. As the self-described 'critical Firestonian' Sophie Lewis has written in her work on surrogacy, 'it is a wonder' that we allow foetuses inside us at all; 'biophysically speaking, gestating is an unconscionably destructive business.'[40]

Resistance to technological advances crystallized in the 1980s around the extremely wordily named Feminist International Network of Resistance to Reproductive and Genetic Engineering (FINRRAGE), which was founded in the Netherlands in 1984 as the equally demanding FINNRET (Feminist International Network on New Reproductive Technologies). The five founding members, Robyn Rowland, Jalna Hanmer, Renate Klein, Gena Corea and Janice Raymond, as Lewis notes, were all 'white Euro-American scholars'. The stated intention of the network was to research and critique IVF, embryo transfer and surrogacy, with some members also opposed to hormonal contraception and amniocentesis. Medical and technological intervention in the female body, according to their inaugural manifesto, was variously exploitation, commodification, slavery, prostitution and a declaration of war, paving the way for the artificial production of human beings. FINRRAGE believed that technological intervention into reproduction fundamentally threatened *all* women's 'natural' existence: their goal was to 'resist becoming test tube women'.[41] Sarah Franklin, who attended FINRRAGE meetings from 1986 onwards, writes that, in her experience, members of the network had a far more diverse array of opinions on new reproductive technologies than its official stance encompassed, and were 'consistently equivocal across the so-called radical-feminist versus socialist-feminist divide' that split the movement(s) during the period. FINRRAGE, for Franklin, had a broad definition of collective action that included research, information sharing, workshops, conferences, organization, campaigning, writing and publishing. They would compile and circulate 'international packets' of policy documents and media clippings using Xerox machines and the postal service, hoping to develop analyses of new technologies that drew together women's rights and environmental and economic issues. In practice, this meant there was a network within the network which favoured caution, scepticism and analysis over the official position of total opposition to all new reproductive technologies. Barbara Katz Rothman, for example, writing in *Test-Tube Women: What Future for Motherhood*, a 1984 anthology, cautioned that 'we must not get caught into discussions of which reproductive technologies are "politically correct", which empower and which enslave women': they all had the potential to do either, and to be 'used for or against us'.[42]

This conflict, as well as others building within the group and within feminism as a whole, played a significant part in FINRRAGE's fragmentation at the close of the decade. Within the network there was a significant ideological kinship with the 'pornography wars' that raged within feminism in the 1980s, as well as the anti-sex-work stance that persists today, particularly in transphobic feminism's anxieties about the perceived capture or seizure of womanhood: anti-surrogacy positions are becoming mainstream again among 'gender-critical' feminists in the British media, who are also vocally opposed to recent medical breakthroughs in uterus transplants.[43] Contemporary critiques of surrogacy now extend to opposition to IVF when it helps gay men start a family. Julie Bindel and Germaine Greer have both written at length about IVF and surrogacy 'deconstructing' motherhood, targeting high-profile gay men like Elton John and the journalist Owen Jones. This is, in part, a scarcity myth, a fantasy of limited resources: reproduction is not a zero-sum game, and the ways in which other people make their families have nothing to do with your own ability to mother – or father – should you wish to. These critiques forget, too, the feminist achievement of identifying ambivalence as a fundamental part of motherhood. The positions taken by Bindel, Greer and others are rooted in a certainty about the 'right' way to reproduce that is surprisingly (to them, I imagine) close to the most fundamentally conservative understandings of femininity and the family. Surrogacy is unconscionable precisely because it separates the process of pregnancy from its product, transforming it into either financially rewarded labour or an act of kinship and non-biological love. To follow this logic is to see motherhood as inherent or essential to womanhood and IVF, therefore, only to be tolerated if performed by a woman who is unable to conceive a child 'naturally': a substitution process that helps her hang on to her status as a 'real' woman. In this context, IVF is a technology that reproduces prevailing structures as much as it does human beings.[44] Yet it also possesses the ability to change or adapt the traditional family, which is partly why it's construed as something that threatens the natural kind of maternity. In the case of Bindel, who campaigned for lesbian and gay adoption in the 80s, it also implies that the only permissible queer family is one made possible through adoption. (I am not suggesting here that adoption is a lesser option, but rather that to position this as the only acceptable way for non-heterosexual people to become parents is to suggest that these people 'owe' something to society through their parenthood in a way that straight people do not.)

Today IVF, which is difficult to access on the NHS, is primarily a consumer relationship defined by promise, loss, payment and guarantee. The late Lisa Jardine, in her final address as the Chair of the HFEA, stated that her chief regret had been her inability to fulfil her 'personal mission' of public engagement, educating the public on 'the benefits and disadvantages of all aspects of assisted reproduction' and managing expectations:

> This proved to be unexpectedly difficult to do. There is an extraordinarily high level of coverage of any story involving IVF in the media – celebrity births, tales of miracle babies after years of trying, and above all, breakthroughs in clinical practice which may bring hope to thousands wishing for their own child. This is a sector that

trades in hope, and the papers and women's magazines are full of encouragement.[45]

Throughout her speech, Jardine employs the vocabulary of economics, establishing that the 'market in hope' has a double edge: the trade-off comes when the hope is not fulfilled, and the procedure instead 'delivers' not the hoped-for baby but rather 'grief and a sense of failure'. It is hard, at a very basic level, to pay for something, in money and in pain, that you don't get.

One problem with describing infertility is that at its core is a non-event, something that links incomplete IVF procedures to the ontological stasis of miscarriage and stillbirth.[46] How can you talk about what hasn't happened to you? Advances in fertility treatment have made infertility newly experiential, an active state with its own narrative, its own attendant suffering and wisdom. It is often described as a kind of bereavement, its failure resulting in grief not only for the child, but for the parental self that might have been. In her HFEA address, Jardine mentions a 2013 article by Zoe Williams, titled 'Where's all that grief going?', in which she visits the Alternative Parenting Show – now, since its rechristening in 2017, called the 'My Future Family Fertility Show' – an event that advertises itself as a tool to make the 'dream of having a family a reality'. The entanglement of IVF in profit asks anew old questions about the productivity of the maternal body. Its language is the language of productivity – to ejaculate, even, is 'to produce' – and this is shadowed by the threat of failure. (This is not unique to IVF: Lucy van de Wiel in her work on egg freezing describes it as a process by which embryos are conceptually transformed into little persons, the manifestation of their future product.)[47] In Williams's article, Susan Bewley, a professor of Complex Obstetrics at King's College London, references, in her conversation with Williams, a study showing IVF to be 'as traumatic as chemotherapy'. 'It's a kind of death,' she states. 'We have our somatic deaths at the end of our lives, but we also have reproductive deaths.'[48]

Franklin, reflecting in 2013 on almost four decades of research into the experience of IVF, writes of the complex balance of losses and gains the process can produce:

> the choice to undertake IVF may be made on the basis of a kind of guarantee that at least if you fail, you will have the compensatory satisfaction of having tried everything, meaning you will at least not be worse off even if you do not succeed in bringing home the much-desired take-home baby, since you will have more, not less, than what you started with (having neither a baby nor the emotional closure of having left no stone unturned). What this equation leaves out, I learned, is the extent to which IVF changes the terms of this guarantee over time. By enabling a woman to begin to experience pregnancy, for example by seeing her own eggs, seeing them fertilized with her partner's sperm, and then having potentially viable embryos transferred back into her womb, IVF ironically intensifies the very deficit it is intended to mitigate. Often, once this proximity to pregnancy is physically and emotionally experienced, the more offered by simply knowing you have tried everything is no longer enough. Thus IVF may have taken away something you did not even realize you could lose.[49]

Perhaps the desire to conceive a child becomes an example of Lauren Berlant's 'cruel optimism': 'when something you desire is actually an obstacle to your flourishing'.[50] It is certainly one of the main avenues through which unrequited longing is made manifest. Often, the uncertainty of motherhood and pre- or potential motherhood – shall I, should I, will I, what if I – transforms into a pure and driven desire once the surprise of difficulty arrives: a commitment to realizing a future that you fear might not belong to you after all. The term 'family planning' incorporates a tacit appropriate chronology into the obligation on the female body to reproduce: first, you plan to not have a family, and you take your contraception; then, you plan to fulfil this duty within the tidy boundaries of a normal family. Medical advances serve, in this schema, to widen the possible margins of such normality.

If, as Janis Hetherington declared of her custody battle, mother-hood's 'most basic instinct' is the instinct to fight, what does this mean, in the context of infertility? And how can we hear our own instincts, faced with a range of technological possibilities designed to encourage choice in a social world that continually narrows and reduces it? How does state provision regulate, endorse and control as much as facilitate desire? What do you want? Why do you want it? How do you know? The fact that emotions are socially produced is not a comfort when you are experiencing the worst of them. Why we might desire what we desire is easy to lose sight of, but so is, from the removed vantage point of a critic, the feeling of that desire itself. You want a baby because you want a baby because you want a baby. You don't want a baby because you don't want a baby because you don't want a baby . . .

PART TWO

The State

4.

Making Claims

Secure the milk
and we'll talk about
'Marxism Leninism Mao-Tse Tung Thought'
which is milk thought
which is what I believe

Simone White, *Dear Angel of Death*

My mother worked for a long time as a paediatric physio. My brother and I would joke about how late she would get home from work after battling to see as many of her patients as possible, patients she referred to as 'my kids'. Everything, we could see, was connected via her body. We were her kids, and they were her kids too, and that made perfect sense. I realize now that I wasn't unique in conflating the universal care of the state (or, at least, its potential to provide it) with motherhood, both ideologically and practically. What I couldn't see at the time was how difficult it can prove to separate roots that have grown so densely together, and how the stronger partner, backed up as it is by the weight of consensus, of national finance and the status quo, can leach the nutrients from the other over time. What does motherhood lose in being conflated with the welfare state? What does the use of the maternal as a metaphor legitimize? And how can mothers who are engaged in resistance frame their specific struggles in opposition to its all-encompassing maternalism? In this second part, we're going to meet mothers who have organized both within and against the state, fighting to stake a claim to the meagre resources available to them, and, in a broader sense, to challenge prevailing notions about what a mother could be.

The maternal turn that characterized psychoanalysis between the wars in Britain – a move from Freudian analysis to what is now called object relations – had a significant impact on welfare policy at the very moment the welfare state itself was being constructed. The work of practitioners like Winnicott, John Bowlby and Klein had a relevance well beyond analysis itself: it was taken up by social policy makers, educationalists and medical professionals in the hope of defining what 'maternal' roles and qualities the British state could have. It was also incorporated into public education: Winnicott, for example, gave some fifty BBC broadcasts about mothering between 1943 and 1962. The sociologist Shaul Bar-Haim writes of the kernel of truth embedded within that contemporary right-wing bogeyman, the 'nanny state': one of the central objectives of the post-1945 welfare state was to allow the state to perform maternal duties if necessary, stepping in to support children whose own mothers were less able. 'Dismissing the welfare state,' he writes, 'by portraying it as a "nanny" is a refusal to imagine the state as a maternal entity that has some caring responsibilities toward its own children-citizens.'[1] But mothers themselves were also crucial cogs in the wheel of social democracy: by the end of the 1950s, they were the primary intermediaries between the child and agents of the state like teachers, doctors, social workers and psychiatrists.

In one sense, the idea of the nurturing maternal state is an attempt to hold motherhood up as a political model, a blueprint for a way of being in the world that resists individualism and separation. This kind of thinking upends the image of the upright, separate self – the rugged individual, the upstanding citizen, the reasonable man – that remains the default baseline for a person participating in public life. In the work of the feminist philosopher Adriana Cavarero, it is instead the 'inclined subject' that takes precedence. By defining it as a feminized stance, like that of a mother reaching towards her child, Cavarero recasts this posture of dependence as a state of mutual liberation. The idea of the inclined subject, crucially, finds motherhood in a physical but not necessarily biological relation, enacted and repeated in caring for others. It also, when taken to mean an emotional inclination as well as a physical one, allows for an understanding of care that doesn't automatically assume an able body, and troubles the very idea of who that body can belong to.[2] Nobody, the inclined subject's posture tells us, is self-sufficient. Nobody should want to be.

In the wake of the events of the past few years – a global pandemic and a perpetual economic crisis – left-wing advocates for total reform and expansion of the state have used similar maternal metaphors: in March 2020, the group of writers called the Care Collective (Andreas Chatzidakis, Jamie Hakim, Jo Littler, Catherine Rottenberg and Lynne Segal) declared the pandemic to be 'a crisis of care, the result of decades of neoliberal policies prioritizing profit over people'. This could have been, they suggested, an opportunity, a moment to build 'a politics that puts care front and centre of life' (it wasn't). The Collective advocated a 'caring state', one in which 'notions of belonging are based on recognition of mutual interdependencies rather than on ethno-cultural identity and racialized borders'.[3] These maternal metaphors of connection and reciprocity are certainly useful when criticizing existing patriarchal structures, but they risk, at times, forgetting that maternal feelings also include possessiveness, ownership and control.[4]

After all, the conception of the state as a mother figure meant that the government could both provide and withhold nurture. In the 1942 Beveridge Report, 'want, disease, ignorance, squalor and idleness' are identified as the obstacles to a reconstructed social democracy. Within these vaguely chastising terms, we can hear not just the diction of the period – it's all very Mary Poppins – but also the idea of the deserving and undeserving citizen that would persist: it's difficult to banish the spectre of the scammer once it has been invoked, no matter how much evidence is patiently compiled of its falsehood. For all that the welfare state is key to liberal notions of what British society is, it now appears most often in political life in the anxious policing of its resources and mothers who have claimed some form of benefits, welfare or social security from the state have been persistently shamed.[5] (Think of, for example, two frequently invoked figures: the teenage single mother who produces children in exchange for council housing, and the 'economic migrant' or 'illegal immigrant' who has come in search of the same.[6]) State provision, in its reliance on drawing divisions between those who deserve support and those who do not, is isolating, not communalizing, and we're very far from a society in which networks of mutual support like those advocated by the Care Collective can autonomously thrive. Still, the fact remains that state support can offer respite from the harm that can be perpetrated within the family unit: neglect, sexual abuse and domestic violence.[7]

Juliet Mitchell, writing in 1966 of the family as the 'universe of their own' that women were offered instead of participation in political and economic life, cautioned that, 'like woman herself', the family 'appears as a natural object, but it is actually a cultural creation'. Later in the same essay she writes of the 'trend' set by Bowlby and his peers, a shift away from 'the cult of the biological ordeal of maternity (the pain which makes the child precious, etc.)' – the burden of Eve, in other words – to 'a celebration of mother-care as a social act'.[8] In this reading, the move to understand mothering as essential labour for the building of society itself, rather than an individualized emotional and biological relation, is no radical shift outwards but rather another burden to be added to the idealized mother figure. Not only is she responsible for keeping her own child safe, but the fate of the social fabric itself lies within her care.

The relationship between feminism, family and the state is a dense and thorny one; it's hard, sometimes, to work out whose terms are whose. For decades, family abolitionists, socialist feminists and (some) Marxists have been advocating a politics that recognizes that care is not solely centred within the family, one that expands our definition of kinship. (Mitchell took a dim view of the 'slogan' of family abolition itself, which she believed to be 'maxi-malist in a bad sense'. 'The goal,' she wrote, 'is the liberation of women and the equality of the sexes, not the abolition of the family.'⁹) Recognizing that family roles are flexible, and stretch to include many people both related and not, can be a first step towards building interconnected networks of mutual dependence and sup-port within communities. Where does that leave motherhood? To a certain extent: where it has always been. The 'family' has never really been stable or nuclear. But the second question this raises is: where does that leave the state? And how can we make a claim on it ourselves?

Take the Pills, Love the Baby

The viability, both politically and practically, of making demands of the state is, as we have already seen, continually disputed by activists: to identify the domestic as integral to the wider economic and social conditions of the day was not the same thing as agreeing on a path forward beyond this state of affairs. At the end of that 1966 essay, which is called 'Women: The Longest Revolution', Mitchell dismisses the 'reformism' of the feminist movement and their 'limited ameliorative demands: equal pay for women, more nursery schools, better retraining facilities, etc.', as being 'wholly divorced' from real liberation.[10] Just over a decade later, Elizabeth Wilson, a prominent feminist activist, writer, editor and member of the Gay Liberation Front, published *Women and the Welfare State*, a book which first took form as a *Red Rag* pamphlet. In it, she declares that 'feminism and socialism meet in the arena of the Wel-fare State, and the manipulations of the Welfare State offer a unique demonstration of how the State can prescribe what a wom-an's consciousness should be.'[11] The welfare state, in Wilson's terms, is a 'conglomeration of legislation and services' that can only be understood with the tools that feminism provides, particu-larly in relation to motherhood:

Only feminism has made it possible for us to see how the State defines femininity and that this definition is not marginal but is central to the purposes of welfarism. Woman is above all Mother, and with this vocation go all the virtues of femininity: submission, nurturance, positivity. The 'feminine' client of the social services waits patiently at clinics, social security offices and housing departments, to be ministered to sometimes by the paternal authority figure, doctor, or civil servant, sometimes by the nurturant yet firm model of femininity provided by the nurse or social worker; in either case she goes away to do as she has been told – to take the pills, to love the baby.[12]

In locating the state's ideological repression in social workers in particular, whose work she sees as a form of community social control, Wilson hits on a complicating factor in ongoing debates about the state itself. 'The state' was both a local and a national structure: the municipal control exercised by local councils meant that one thing could be going on at a national level and quite another at a local one, with left-wing governing bodies like the Greater London Council under Ken Livingstone's socialist leadership from 1981 to 1986 meaning in some areas radical projects would be embarked upon and even publicly funded. (Some feminists like Sheila Rowbotham and Hilary Wainwright entered local government themselves in this period.) And yet, for many feminists, the state was simply a synonym for the patriarchy, and therefore was not to be engaged with. By the final national conference of the WLM, held in Birmingham in 1978, the splintering within the movement between socialist, radical and revolutionary feminists – including lesbian separatists – culminated in a group of revolutionary feminists submitting a proposal to cancel all previous demands: it was 'ridiculous', they felt, to 'demand anything from a patriarchal state – from men – who are the enemy'.[13]

It is difficult to believe that no demands are better than seven. In the wake of the 1979 Conservative election victory, the WLM, like the left, faced a difficult and bleak future. Rowbotham, Segal and Wainwright published *Beyond the Fragments: Feminism and the Making of Socialism* in the hope of forging a path forward amid the confusion, offering a summary of the WLM and its links with other movements: what Wainwright describes, rather glibly, in her introduction as 'the women's movement, the trade union movement, the black movement, etc.'.[14] The book suggests that the reason so many people voted Tory and so few Labour, despite the decade of industrial and social turmoil that preceded the election, was that Labour had become totally swallowed by and integrated into the capitalist state. There were dissenting voices on the left, and within feminism particularly: the Socialist Feminist Social Policy Group published a response in *Red Rag* in August 1980 that accused the book's authors of 'naïve simplification'. The state, they argue, does not act on women per se, or women as a class, but women in specific and diverse situations. The questions they propose, then, are 'Should socialist feminist policy be directed against the state? Or are demands to be made on the state? And how does this relate to the question of men as the oppressors of women?'[15]

As the worsening economic climate threw people on the mercy of the state, there was renewed emphasis on how 'affordable' the welfare state was and how 'deserving' its applicants. For many, it provided punishingly little support: Mary, a woman interviewed in *Spare Rib* in 1979, said, 'It's not "life" on Social Security (SS), it's "existence"', and, made to feel like she was 'begging', she was afraid to make too many claims.[16] Although for some, like Jackie, a single mother in Bristol interviewed by Nell Dunn in 1977, the state represented a way out of a different kind of dependent relationship with her husband, John, who:

> used to lay it on me – 'I keep you, therefore you will do the cleaning and that's what I keep you for.' So I decided, 'I don't want that laid on me so I won't take money from you', so, when I left for a few months, I got on Social Security – now the State keeps me and the kids because he doesn't.[17]

This equation, in which the state essentially replaces the father and takes on the paternalistic duty of 'keeping' the family, is exactly what many feminists had criticized about welfare provision: the replacement of one danger with another. (The information that has come to light over the past few years about the government's use of spycops to infiltrate political movements undercover, with policemen often having intimate relationships and even children with their targets, underlines this all the more heavily. Some women affected by this behaviour have described it as 'rape by the state'.[18]) Still, there was the practical question of need: how were those who needed support supposed to get it? If children were a collective responsibility, then how was that responsibility to be shared out and paid for?

On the Dole

Theoretical discussions about the role of the state often ignore the organizing work of those who had the closest relationship with its offices: welfare claimants themselves, many of whom were mothers. Mothers in Action, one of the first groups of this kind, was set up in 1967 by five single mothers who, according to one of their leaflets, were 'dissatisfied with the conditions under which they were forced to live'.[19] By 1969, the membership numbered over 1,000, and they ran two big campaigns: first, for an increase in day nursery places, and second, in 1970, for improvements in housing. That year – the year of the first WLM conference, where some of their aims were incorporated into the demands – the 'Organizing Committee composed entirely of unsupported mothers working from their homes' became overwhelmed. Formal membership was discontinued in 1972, although, with a grant from the Social Services Trust, they were able to secure secretarial help to set up smaller working groups and continue producing their publications.

Their baton was carried by the Claimants Unions. The first had been formed in Birmingham in 1968, and by the early 1970s there were almost a hundred similar unions across the UK. Each branch was self-governing and controlled by rank-and-file members, meaning that they understood themselves to be individual organizations that supported each other and differed from one another 'in character and tactic', rather than local branches of a national organization. By 1978, there were 'co-ordinating unions' who kept information about local organizations in Swansea, Manchester, Bristol, South Shields, Derry, Edinburgh, Glasgow and Deptford in south London: the latter, based in the old Albany building at 47 Creek Road, was partially burnt down in a presumed fascist arson attack in 1978.[20] For their members, the unions fought claims at Social Security offices, appeals tribunals and in court; organized demonstrations, conferences and publications; and led playgroups, food co-ops, trips, summer camps and squats.[21] When 400 women went on strike for equal pay at Salford Electrical Instruments factory in 1975, part of a nationwide strike against the multinational General Electric Company, Claimants Unions stepped in to support the large percentage of striking workers who were single mothers in trying to claim Social Security during the strike.[22] These groups were both ideological and practical: they prioritized the immediate needs of those who relied upon state funds in their advice and assistance, but they never lost sight of the overarching fact that the system needed total reform.

In *The Fight to Live ~ The Claimants Union Handbook for the Unemployed*, published by the National Federation of Claimants Unions in 1977, they describe themselves as 'groups of people on social security and unemployment benefit who have got together to help each other and to fight collectively around the four demands known as the Claimants Charter'. The charter was as follows:

1. The right to an adequate income without means test for all people
2. A socialist society in which all necessities are provided free and which is managed and controlled by the people

3. No secrets and the right to full information
4. No distinction between so-called 'deserving' and 'undeserving'

The Fight to Live is full of useful information, ranging from simple principles – 'Never meet the SS (Social Security) alone' and 'Don't let them grind you down' – to detailed guides to claiming different kinds of benefit, to astute analysis of why unemployment was rising. The federation published multiple books throughout the 1970s and 80s, each containing information about how to set up your own union, and many stating on the inside cover that it was not possible to 'live' on Social Security, but only to 'exist'.[23]

They campaigned for a Guaranteed Minimum Income from 1970, an unconditional, universal basic income, which was also called a Citizen's Income. Their campaign emphasized the gendered inequality embedded in the welfare system itself: married women who claimed benefits were prevented from receiving them in their own right, and council housing was only available in the husband's name. Welfare officers – or 'sex snoopers' – would frequently spy on and harass single claimants, meaning that any man they had a relationship with, even sometimes a friendship, would be assumed to be a source of financial support, resulting in the suspension of benefits. Many women who lost their jobs did not appear in unemployment statistics, because two thirds of married women and one third of single women would never sign on: often, they hadn't paid enough National Insurance to qualify for contributory benefit, which replaced earnings, and the pay gap between men's and women's wages prevented many from claiming earnings-related supplements, based on the previous tax year's earnings.[24] In 1977, at the penultimate WLM conference, a resolution endorsing a Guaranteed Minimum Income, proposed by women from Claimants Unions, passed with a majority vote.

A high proportion of the CU membership identified as single mothers, and the second text the unions collectively published was the *Unsupported Mothers Handbook* in 1970, republished as *Women and Social Security* in 1975.[25] In it, they argued that domestic work should be understood on the same terms as paid work: 'Caring for the elderly, the sick or children seems never ending. Our shift begins when we wake up in the morning, and ends when we go to sleep at night.' This prevents women from having any 'real choice' over what to do with their lives, how to spend their time. A reorganization of the entire structure of social life was necessary:

> We must each be free to decide what to do, and to obtain satisfaction out of our work. This means organizing playgroups and outings. It means babysitting rotas, housework and shopping rotas. It might even mean everyone in the home pooling her/his income and sharing it out equally. In turn this might mean the end of the nuclear family and the end of the household. This might mean liberation for millions of women. Liberation from the drudgery of housework and childcare.[26]

The 1978 *Guidebook* included key information for single parents, such as not to tell Social Security if you had to go into hospital unless you couldn't avoid it: if lone parents went into hospital, benefits would be stopped immediately apart from 'rent and pocket money' – you were getting fed in the hospital, after all – and there was a risk of your older children being taken into care. Instead, the guidebook reassures the reader that 'If you haven't any relatives or friends who will look after them your local Claimants Union will usually rally round.'[27] It also included information about when you could claim during pregnancy and what for, how to navigate the allowance when you needed a more nourishing diet, and how to deal with the fact that you only qualified for maternity allowance if you had paid 'enough' in National Insurance. Here, we can see the consequences of the politicization of maternal need: in this case, your status as a deserving mother – and by extension, your child's status as a deserving child – depended upon how much you had contributed to the national coffers.

In comparing domestic work to paid labour, some unions intervened in the ongoing disagreement about Wages for Housework.

On the one hand, a universal income was the only way – in the short to medium term, at least – to free women and children from financial dependence on a specific man; on the other, as one member said, 'the State's worse than a jealous husband.'[28] In *Women and Social Security*, Social Security claims expose the false logic of choice:

> No one can claim Supplementary Benefit if they are less than sixteen years old. Lots of girls get pregnant before reaching sixteen. Many are 'persuaded' to have abortions, or to place their kids for adoption by the fact that the State refuses to maintain them. In order to have the 'right to choose', one must have the right to an adequate income regardless of one's age.

Later on in the same publication, the welfare state itself – run 'by women for women' including social workers, teachers, nurses and claimants – is declared to be 'a con': 'State control over the working class. Fostering the work ethic. Supporting the notion of the nuclear family'. The system itself was 'built up around the idea of bonny babies, and healthy well-schooled children cared for by their neat and tidy mother who is a child rearer and home cleaner'. As soon as a person 'stops playing the "happy family" game', he or she becomes subject to state sanctions, such as the restriction on housing for single people, the rules prohibiting cohabitation for women, and the fact that there could be prison sentences attached to 'failing to maintain your wife and kids'.[29]

Above all, when it came to motherhood, the Claimants Union movement unequivocally rejected the idealization of 'women's work', either in the home or the workplace. In their focus on practical advice for claimants and the building of solidarity, they never lost sight of the fact that, for many, the arguments about the role of the state represented a clash between idealism and pragmatism: you might be between a rock and a hard place, but you still had to eat. In a letter titled 'Wages for Motherhood' sent by a reader called Lois Gulley to *Spare Rib* in 1978, responding to an ongoing debate in its letters pages about a piece Denise Riley had written about childcare, Gulley observes that, although not a total solution, 'wages for motherhood might alleviate some of the symptoms while the revolution goes on.'[30]

That revolution is still struggling to be born. Indeed, helped by the unholy midwife of the capitalist-feminist success story – the girl boss – both the practical and the ideological situation have worsened in many respects, especially in the alliances that are forming between the right and trans-exclusionary feminists, who are so keen to prioritize their myopic agenda that they see no problem endorsing calls for women to follow their duty to reproduce and aid the falling birth rate, or, as we have already seen, advocating the policing of womb transplants and the imposing of restrictions on gay adoption. A decade on from austerity, successive governments have implemented economic policy that further plunges the poorest households in the country – mostly single mothers – into debt, and draconian immigration policies which separate mothers from their children in detention facilities or deportation centres. If understanding motherhood as a political state has liberatory potential, its relationship to the state has to be twofold: immediate, practical assistance for mothers and children who need it, and a long-term focus on revolutionary reform. The politicization of motherhood, on the other hand, serves only to collaborate with and reinforce the violence of the state itself. The symptoms are proving fatal.

5.

Communal Experiments

Everything turns on the housing question.

Denise Riley, 'The Force of Circumstance'

To care for others, we ask specific questions: where am I safe? Where are my children safe? Where are we able to experience pleasure? Under which conditions are we able to merely live? Central to these questions, unifying all of them, in fact, is housing. The provision of adequate housing is another place where we can find the uneven seams that join the public with the private: in the UK, the selling off of council stock and the wild inflation of both house prices and the average monthly cost of private rent ensure that domestic stability is a privilege available to an increasingly slim proportion of the population, something which directly affects both the ability to mother and the ability to even make the decision to do so. It wasn't always this way. At the same moment that reproductive healthcare became available on the NHS, enfolded into the notion of the planned family, a movement was growing across the UK of people seeking new ways of living. Primarily, their solutions were communes, or 'intentional communities', and squats. Though communal, such living arrangements were not necessarily communist, and many actively defined themselves, in contrast, as founded on anarchist or anti-state political ideas, or a nascent green politics.[1] Still, collective ownership based on need, rather than private ownership for profit, was a fundamental ideological cornerstone of both squats and communes: they were resisting the aspects of life under capitalism that led to swathes of property lying empty while, as the 70s turned into the 80s, homelessness increased and council waiting lists grew at a staggering rate.

Collective childcare was an integral part of these experiments in housing. This was, in part, a response to immediate need: single women with children were particularly vulnerable to the vagaries of the housing crisis, as many private landlords didn't want children in their properties and mothers were more vulnerable to unemployment, since until the Sex Discrimination Act of 1975 it was not technically illegal for pregnancy to cause employee dismissal. It was also rooted in more complex negotiations over exactly *how* one is to raise a child in a manner that respects their autonomy, meets their needs and resists imposing prescriptive gender roles (one answer, perhaps, is that 'one' can't). In reordering this division of labour – in many such communities, domestic work was, at least in theory, divided between all residents – mothering was, in one sense, liberated. It was also destabilized, removed from its assumed positions: in many accounts of life in these communities, adults with no biological relationship to the children describe immense feelings of parental attachment, and decisions about children's welfare were not made unilaterally. This opens up a complex space for biological parents themselves: what to do with this new mode of relation? Is it freedom, or loss? And what happens to familial bonds when this kind of choice is introduced: do they slacken or grow stronger? (If you love someone, so the saying goes, set them free.)

Squatting

Squatting – the occupation of disused land or property – has a long history in Britain and Northern Ireland. After the First World War, amid a sharp rise in unemployment and rent strikes in the East End of London, municipal buildings were occupied by squatters who intended to set up neighbourhood relief; after the Second, rising homelessness and the lack of housing for veterans and their families instigated a wave of squatting across the country, often on disused army bases, aided by former soldiers, the Communist Party of Great Britain, and groups within the Labour Party itself. This was generally tolerated, even supported, by the public at large, but when squatters moved into luxury housing in central London, the national mood soured. Five CPGB members were charged with 'conspiracy to trespass', a new offence, and police blockaded the squats, cutting off food supplies. The Labour government framed their response as one concerned with fairness: the squatters had 'jumped the housing queue'.[2] Positivity towards squatters had relied upon the characterization of them as families in need, specifically veteran families in need. Now, a notion took hold that they were in fact depriving such families by circumventing two of Britain's most beloved institutions: private property and queueing. The distinction between deserving and undeserving, which still poisons discussions about social housing today, prevailed: families were privileged over single homeless people and those living in less identifiable groups. Yet even being part of a recognizable family unit guaranteed nothing, and between the end of the post-war squatting wave and the beginning of a new movement in 1968, the occupation of buildings continued to be a tactic employed out of necessity.

Necessity is not apolitical. Throughout the 60s, squatting was also used by communities in Northern Ireland as direct action resisting housing policy that discriminated against Catholics. In 1963, a group of women in Dungannon, the third largest town in County Tyrone, began a campaign to highlight the state of housing provision for working-class Catholics in the area. In a 1968 interview, Angela McCrystal, a factory worker and key figure in the campaign, described how her Protestant colleagues would marry and return from honeymoon to a house, while Catholic women in the factory were on waiting lists for ten years or more.[3] When McCrystal and two of her colleagues decided to do something, they were joined by 'about forty-six families' in setting up a Homeless Citizens League, and they picketed the council, wheeling their prams to the building to emphasize that this was a generational problem. (Motherhood as both an aesthetic and a political weapon.) When no response was forthcoming, they took matters into their own hands, squatting a group of houses that had been left empty by Protestant families who were moving to a new estate. Almost forty families took part, with some former tenants handing their keys to the squatters rather than to council officials; meanwhile, Patricia McCluskey and her husband Conn, a local GP, compiled evidence that detailed that discrimination on religious grounds was occurring.[4] Eventually, the council allowed the squatters to remain in the houses, and the building of a new estate was agreed on.

The McCluskeys went on to help found the Northern Ireland Civil Rights Association, a coalition of trade unionists, communists, liberals, socialists and republicans, who organized marches at the end of 1968 that are identified in many accounts as the turning point for civil unrest in the North: from the vantage point of 1979, the RTÉ journalist Tom Savage described this as the time when 'curdled acceptance' became 'smouldering resentment'.[5] Central to this transformation were events that occurred at a squat in Caledon, Dungannon, in 1967. Mary Theresa and Francis Goodfellow and their three young children had begun squatting in Caledon after all but one newly built council house went to Protestant families. After being given six months to vacate the property, the family were violently evicted by bailiffs and police, with Mary Theresa dragged from the house with a baby in her arms: this was undeniably a reproductive crisis. (The house that the Goodfellows were evicted from was given to a family who the council said had five children: they actually had just one.) The primary catalyst for the events that followed, however, was the allocation of the house next door to a nineteen-year-old unmarried Protestant woman, Emily Beatty, the secretary of a local Unionist politician. Beatty had no children, and as such became symbolic of the council's unscrupulousness: a symptomatic figure, in her childlessness, of the uneven distribution of resources along religious lines.

The nature of the housing itself was important, too: as it was a resource allocated by the state, rather than the luxury private property that turned the tide against the London squatters in 1946, everyone's claims were supposed to be equal, and judged on the basis of need. On 20 June, Austin Currie, a Nationalist MP at Stormont, and two others broke into and occupied the house that been allocated to Beatty, who had not yet moved in. Although they were removed within hours by the Royal Ulster Constabulary, the event marked the first time that the London-based national news had covered housing discrimination in the six counties.[6] The first civil rights march in the north followed, organized by groups including the Campaign for Social Justice and the Northern Ireland Civil Rights Association: 2,000 people marched from Coalisland to Dungannon, and the march was followed by a protest at the Guildhall in Derry, where housing discrimination was equally rife, due in part to the gerrymandering of constituencies that enabled the consolidation of Unionist power in a mostly Nationalist city. In March 1968, the Derry Housing Action Committee had formed, and they organized squats in the Guildhall in December 1968 and the January of the following year. These squatters, too, were homeless families. In images from the occupied council chamber, the austere wood panelling contrasts almost comically with the everyday domestic actions of its subjects: someone reaches across to pour milk into a cup of tea while a child looks on with interest; one child shields their face from the camera while another stares at it fully, a bottle of milk in their hand; a pram sits prominently at the front of the frame. The country's fundamental failure to take its duty to house its citizens seriously was powerfully embodied in the figures of these children, emblematic both of historic neglect and of the potential for a different path forward: unfixed, insecure and full of possibility.

Political Outposts

Reliable figures to do with the squatting movement that began at the end of the 1960s are, for obvious reasons, hard to come by, but historians have estimated that by 1975 there were 50,000 people squatting in the UK. By January 1977, there were an estimated 6,168 squats in

Northern Ireland Housing Executive property alone.[7] The unique situation of the north of Ireland meant that its squats were specifically politically contoured, but squatting was highly politicized in England, Scotland and Wales, too. Anti-squatting legislation was progressively strengthened throughout the 70s, and in 1977 the Criminal Law Act was introduced in England and Wales, which made it harder, although it did not criminalize it entirely: for its opponents, squatting was characterized as an act of theft, 'about the lowest form,' in the words of Brent Councillor Ron Dinsey, 'of stealing from society'.[8]

Between 1968 and 1980, the movement evolved, as the work of the historian Kesia Reeve details, from one which primarily involved homeless families – a family she interviewed who were squatting in 1968 included seven children and had been homeless for twelve years – to one with increasing numbers of single people, some of whom were looking for alternative communities. This became a bone of contention among squatters themselves, as divisions emerged between those who co-operated with local authorities in order to secure 'legitimate' housing and those who sought a different lifestyle altogether. In the national press, lines were drawn between the 'truly homeless' and a 'new army of parasites', with the former commanding sympathy and the latter deserving only reprobation.[9]

This division was a politically convenient one. The image of the homeless family, and particularly of a mother and children, softened the sharp edges of squatting, allowing housing provision to be depoliticized and understood through a philanthropic lens, which ignored the structural causes of the housing crisis: the myth of the deserving and the undeserving homeless was just as alive as that of the deserving and undeserving squatter. It also compounded existing discrimination against those who weren't part of family units: a man who was squatting in St Albans, Hertfordshire, at the end of his tether after endlessly playing 'bat and ball with the Council', wrote that 'Many times I have gone to the Council and asked them "What is homeless?"; they reply "A married couple with a child".'[10] One poster produced by squatters in the 70s read SINGLE PEOPLE NEED HOUSES TOO. By the mid-70s some councils, including the Greater London

Council, whose properties housed 5,000 squatters, offered permanent council tenancies in exchange for the vacation of squatted dwellings. This was heralded by some as a victory, but for others, this was community dispersal by another name. Another of Reeve's interviewees, talking about demolition of Elgin Avenue in west London, where around 200 occupants had squatted in one street, in 1975, observed that they 'did all get re-housed but where did they get re-housed? [. . .] on these huge GLC estates' and 'people got scattered.'[11]

For those for whom squatting was, as Tom Osbourn wrote in 1980, an 'outpost of a new culture' in which people began to 'change the nature of their relationships with one another' and build 'a classless society' – however optimistic a definition that may have proved in practice – it was crucial to resist individual rehousing.[12] The focus was on redefining the family itself: they rooted collective domestic life in trespass and subversion. The role of the mother changes, in these situations, from a socially approved marker of need – this normal family deserve normal circumstances in which they can raise their children – to a role in radical and productive flux. This was a threatening proposition, and collective childcare provision often met with a particularly heavy-handed response from the authorities. In 1985, a group of mothers started the Squatters Creche on Brailsford Road in south-east London: there was up to a three-year wait for local nurseries, many of which were being closed due to Margaret Thatcher's imposition of rate capping on local council budgets. When they tried to get a licence from the council to continue their successful programme, the council sent bailiffs and four vans full of police to evict the premises: witnesses accounts tell of children's toys being thrown out into the snow.[13]

Much press coverage suggested that squatters destroyed properties and neighbourhoods, turning them into unliveable slums: in fact, many were committed to learning and sharing the DIY skills to make abandoned houses inhabitable. Councils, on the other hand, resorted to destructive deterrence tactics, filling properties with concrete, ripping out bathrooms, and cutting off power supplies. It was the 'parasites' who were invested in creating and sustaining communities that state structures had neglected. A network of groups shared resources and information, allowing them to quickly mobilize and defend their peers against eviction, even assembling barricades against bailiffs. In doing so, squatters imagined new kinds of social responsibility. Often the buildings themselves were adapted to incorporate large communal spaces or connecting doors between terrace houses, and in some squats exchange systems were used instead of money.[14] Squatters set up food co-ops, health-care advisory drop-ins, and informal women's centres, and they were so successful that, by the mid-70s, official channels were unofficially referring people to the Advisory Service for Squatters; the squatted Brixton Women's Centre on Railton Road received between thirty and forty referrals in one week from Lambeth Social Services.[15] (A photograph of the Black feminist activist Olive Morris climbing onto the roof of 121 Railton Road in 1973, defying the police who had arrested her partner Elizabeth Obi earlier that day, became an iconic cover of the 1979 *Squatters Handbook*.) Squats, like benevolent mothers, begat other squats. There was an impetus to this self-reproduction, as density meant a better chance at permanence: it's harder to evict a whole terrace of houses than one flat.[16] Households were reconfigured to comprise mixed groups including single people, couples and children; the couple form was often subverted or at least complicated by sexually open relationships. Many squats considered themselves to be family groups. This was not an understanding shared by authorities, and the fight to be recognized as such was essential to their attempts to win the concessions necessary to keep communities together.

Family Ties

In *Squatting: The Real Story*, something that comes up with striking regularity is the failure of the traditional family structure. For some, like the London squatter who wrote in 1975 that 'I wanted to live communally in a large household with kids, and the only way to do that was squatting', it was a choice, but for many their circumstances were forced. In April 1977, one squatter wrote that

> I have been on Manchester Council's housing list for 12 months awaiting one bedroom accommodation. I live with my aunt and my 69-year-old grandmother who I have to share a bedroom with. My gran is bedridden with chronic bronchitis and emphysema. My aunt and I do not get on and due to this I have been in hospital twice with overdoses. My aunt has given me notice to quit but I have nowhere to go so I have thought of squatting.

Even for families, who were supposedly prioritized for housing, squatting might become a last resort. A mother in Bournemouth wrote in 1975 of the discrimination families without material wealth met from landlords:

> At the moment we live in a one room flatlet. We are my husband, myself and daughter (3 months old). We have been given notice to quit and can't just sit back and let it happen. I must do something. We have tried all sorts of rented accommodation, but with a child nobody wants to know. Even when we go down to the council, all they say is they can't do anything until we are evicted. Somehow I don't think I could face that.

In Oldham, one correspondent demonstrated that housing was contingent not on *being* a mother, but on the *kind of mother* you were:

> My wife is divorced and she has four children in voluntary care in Middlesbrough. Our situation is that we can't get a house unless we have the children and we can't have the children unless we have a house. We both work in or near the town and we cannot get satisfaction from any of the councils we have been in touch with. Therefore we have taken the law into our own hands to get my wife's children and ourselves together as a family.[17]

Here, the 'law' is actively working to keep the family apart. The withholding of the children until the house is secured and vice versa turns what should be a governmental duty of care into an ouroboros of refusal: in denying the mother a space in which she can care for her children, she is always already being punished for not having the means to create that space in the first place. These punitive mechanisms were famously documented in Jeremy Sandford and Ken Loach's 1966 Wednesday Play *Cathy Come Home*, which depicted the eponymous Cathy and her children being met by dead-ends at every turn, from the social services, the emergency homeless shelter and the council, before they are eventually separated. The film made a significant impact when it was aired, publicly exposing a 'hidden' problem: the homelessness charity Shelter launched their first appeal the next day, taking out advertisements that asked 'Did you see Cathy last night?', and the Minister of Health Julian Snow wrote an article for the *Labour Woman* announcing policy changes entitled 'How We are Helping Cathy to Come Home'. The actual circumstances for homeless mothers in labyrinthine custody proceedings, however, were slow to change: a decade later, the experience of Cathys across the country remained the same.[18]

Even when they did have somewhere to live, mothers were insufficiently protected within it. Today, women's refuges are generally accepted as a necessary service, although they remain severely underfunded. In the 70s, however, the marital home was almost exclusively understood to be a private place, with social services and law enforcement exercising few powers to intervene in violent or abusive situations. Legally, women were the property of their fathers or their husbands: it was not until 1975 that a woman could even open a bank account in her own name. Until the Domestic Violence and Matrimonial Proceedings Act of 1976, a woman could not seek a court order against an abusive husband that allowed her to access her home without him being present unless she first instigated divorce proceedings, which risked her losing custody of her children. The first refuge in the UK was a squat. Chiswick Women's Refuge, which became the national charity Refuge, was set up by

Erin Pizzey in 1971 in her own home, before spreading out across twenty squatted properties. Pizzey – who, having disavowed feminism altogether, is now a men's rights activist – recognized that there was 'no pigeonhole for a woman who is battered': not technically homeless, the social services could not offer her accommodation, while the police would rarely intervene. Women were understandably reluctant to press charges against their abuser who was also their husband, their financial support and the father of their children, especially given the lack of options for them to be safely accommodated elsewhere in the lead-up to the trial. (Even on the rare occasions court proceedings did occur, the consequences were frequently minor: in 1974, Pizzey recalled a case in which a man who had broken his wife's nose, cracked her ribs and cracked her spine was fined £5 and sent on his way.) Chiswick inspired squatted refuges across the country: premises were occupied in Grimsby, Stoke, Nottingham, Guildford, Birmingham, Manchester and Glasgow, rallying around the slogan 'How can she leave when she has nowhere to go?' In a 1976 *Spare Rib* article, a woman with two young children wrote of the Grimsby refuge that 'I have had nowhere to go in the past. I was advised to come here and haven't regretted it. I have been able to talk to all the members of the women's group and feel much clearer than I have for a long time.'[19]

Many women interviewed at refuges said that the abuse did not start until after they were married, often after their children were born. Violence was simply part of the condition of matrimony. Many spoke of 'putting up with it' for the sake of the children or as part of a marital duty: if a husband needed to release the stress of the working week, then wasn't he technically paying the wife for the privilege? In *Scream Quietly or the Neighbours Will Hear*, a 1974 documentary about the Chiswick refuge, one woman identifies her young son's response to violence – he began, aged two months, to tense up when he heard loud noises or raised voices in the street – as the catalyst for her flight. This is a woman who had previously received a beating so bad that it detached her retina, and another so violent that she went into premature labour in the street. The documentary shows eighteen women and forty-six children sleeping in crowded rooms on mattresses, cooking happily in the communal kitchen and having birthday parties, interspersed with first-hand testimonies of traumatic violence. Despite the overcrowding and lack of funding, the interviewees describe new relationships forming within the refuge: when someone new arrived, they often needed a few days or weeks to acclimatize and get over the shock, and during this time the other residents would rally round and cook their meals for them, give their children the bottle, play games with them, comfort them when they cried. Pizzey, towards the end of the film, voices her belief – and hope – that many of the women will seek communal living for themselves and their children once they leave the refuge.[20]

By the end of the decade, public opinion was shifting, and many refuges received some government or council funding; Women's Aid federations, meanwhile, were established across the UK. By the middle of the 80s, domestic abuse had also been made culturally visible in a far more prominent way than before, particularly via its inclusion in high-profile and sympathetic – if melodramatic – storylines in soap operas like *Coronation Street* (ITV), *EastEnders* (BBC) and *Brookside* (Channel 4).[21] Such stories frequently had wives and mothers at their heart: the ideal victim was one who could be understood to be innocent, put-upon, and traditionally feminine (maternal) but not provocative (promiscuous). The habits of blame that had formed were hard to banish, and it was not until 1994 that marital rape was criminalized, or rather, that marital rape legally existed at all: until that point, sex was considered to be included in the marital contract (love, honour and obey).

Resistant Communities

Squatting provided opportunities for women-only housing not just in the short-term solutions of refuges, but in the network of queer women's households that emerged during the 70s.[22] Many of these were concentrated in London: lesbian squats existed in Hackney,

Tower Hamlets, Camden, Islington, Westminster, Kensington and Chelsea, Lambeth and Southwark. The 'antithesis' of repressed suburban life, they provided an opportunity for women to seize control of their lives. In east London's Broadway Market alone, there were around fifty such squats by 1979, and most of their occupants identified as lesbians. The historian Christine Wall, herself a squatter and subsequently a member of a housing co-op in London Fields, recounts stories of local residents telling them when a house was going to be vacated because, as 'a recognizable group of new neighbours who repaired houses and, in many cases, put up blinds or net curtains', they were far preferable to empty properties. The inhabitants reclaimed traditionally masculine skills like bricklaying, plumbing, carpentry and repairing electrics, with many women going on to formally train in these fields or become active in the Women in Manual Trades campaign group.[23] In 'Learning to Learn', an article published in the *Squatter* in 1976, the wonderfully named writer Pat Moan describes such skill-sharing as something which both literally facilitated the growth of women's communities and began to repair the damage that patriarchy had done to interpersonal relationships: 'Differences become interesting instead of scary as men and women become friends. Ditto men and men and women and women.'[24] The realization that kinship with other women was possible was a liberating one: rather than instinctive competitors, supposed to leave school and set up an isolated family home of their own, they could live communally, collaborate, even raise children together.

In accounts of life in these squats, there are stories of group hockey and football games in parks and on commons and of Christmas Day trips out to paint over National Front graffiti. Former squatter Paddy Tanton remembers that, when she moved into a squat with two other women and a young child, 'I got very involved with that child's life and became a kind of third mum to her, and then, through that, got involved with other women who had children, and I remember often wheeling children round the streets and having days looking after kids.'[25] A third – not even a second – mum is a phrase that suggests a horizon not only beyond the heterosexual family but beyond the couple form: what freedoms are afforded to the category of 'mother' when it is allowed to be multiplied? What bondage is it freed from when it isn't understood only in relation to a male counterpart?

The law did not recognize this as a positive, or, as I discussed in Chapter 4, recognize lesbian motherhood as motherhood at all. In some custody cases, residence in a lesbian squat was given as primary evidence of maternal 'unfitness'. A *Spare Rib* report on the 1983 Lesbian Mothers' Custody Conference observed that, in court, 'over ninety per cent of lesbian mothers lose custody of their children.'[26] The extreme vulnerability of lesbian households, squatted or otherwise, only increased in 1988 when the Thatcher government brought in Section 28 legislation that specifically outlawed homosexuality as a 'pretend family relationship'.[27] As with squatters' battles to be rehomed together as families, these communities were held hostage to rigid definitions of what parenting could be, despite the successful care that they gave to both children and adults.

In some women-only communities, the anti-patriarchal stance was made nominally explicit. In the 'Wild communes' of the 1970s, which comprised ten loosely linked groups in Oxford, Hebden Bridge and Sheffield, mothers decided that they would 'subvert the blatantly phallocentric ritual of surnames'. Rather than passing on their own surnames, which, after all, had belonged to their fathers, to their children, they decided to come up with a new one: in the words of Sue Finch, 'How did I want her to be? I wanted her to be wild and free . . . so Wild just seemed like a good name.' Shelley Wild, who had four mothers, all of whom she called by their first names, told the *Guardian* in 2009 that 'I had four people interested in my wellbeing: reading bedtime stories, taking me swimming. It meant the adults who were looking after us were fresh and not tired.' She recalls no resentment towards the other children who had claims on her biological mother's attention – though it is interesting that the Wild children still knew who their biological parent was – and notes that, for her, 'Wild was simply to do with freedom, to be who we wanted to be.'[28]

Lesbian squat networks and Wild communes, necessarily political, were involved with local campaigning, most frequently with
Claimants Unions, Reclaim the Night marches and women's refuges. Much of this support coalesced around squatted women's
centres, in which multiple organizations and campaigns could come
together, support each other and learn. As we've seen, the Brixton
Women's Centre helped Lambeth women find housing. The Wom-
en's Centre in Camden, meanwhile, was a home for Wages Due
Lesbians, Women against Rape, Black Women for Wages for Housework and the English Collective of Prostitutes, among others. The
centre was also a focal point for resistance to the forced injection of
Depo-Provera in local hospitals, and succeeded in stopping it being
administered at a local level.[29] (It is now the Crossroads Centre in
Kentish Town, after a successful campaign for council premises
which included the occupation of the town hall.) Recognizing both
that there was a desperate need for a space in which women could
come together and that the likelihood of one being created through
legitimate means was slim, squatted organizations responded
immediately to the needs of the community, without interference
from the state.

South of the river, there was a network of squats and women's
centres around Brixton. These included the artist Pearl Alcock's
famous shebeen, an unlicensed bar that provided a meeting place
until the end of the decade, and gave rise to the Brixton Black Wom-
en's Group and the Brixton Women's Centre.[30] By the middle of the
70s, hundreds of council properties were being squatted in Brixton,
with community initiatives demonstrating and resisting the links
between police violence and racist education, labour and housing
policies. In the 1960s and 70s, as was revealed by the 1981 Rampton
report, Black children were often sent to ESN 'special' schools,
resulting in scandalous educational deprivation with long-term consequences. As the historian Kehinde Andrews has written about at
length, in the UK the 'liberation schools' run by the Black Panther
party inspired British supplementary schools organized by parents,
teachers, churches and community groups, where young people

were given the opportunity to learn outside of racist educational institutions and Black history was taught alongside maths and literacy skills. Supplementary schools were opened in squats, often alongside nurseries and crèches: Olive Morris herself, while a student in Manchester and a key figure in the Manchester Black Women's Co-operative, had campaigned to open a supplementary school and a bookshop. In the face of hostility and discrimination, these alternative spaces took on the responsibilities of child-rearing collectively: transmitting knowledge, making food and giving care were not individual projects but a collective endeavour, a matter of strength and survival.[31]

In east London, meanwhile, where there was a growing Bengali and Bangladeshi population, the Bengali Housing Action Group formed in 1976. In collaboration with the Anti-Racist Committee of Asians in East London, the Tower Hamlets Squatters Union and the Race Today collective (who published the eponymous political magazine from 1973 to 1988) the group squatted multiple properties across the area. These housing struggles, led by figures like the prominent Black Panther Mala Sen, connected to wider reproductive battles for Bengali and Bangladeshi women: the lack of housing fit for children was used by politicians to justify racist birth control policies like the Depo-Provera scandal. They were also linked with anti-fascist resistance. The construction of a Bangladeshi community that centred around Brick Lane was a crucial part of resisting the attacks of the National Front, who were very active in the area; in 1977, the BHAG had secured tenancy for 100 families in east London.[32]

As the decade moved to its close, the double blow of the Conservatives gaining control of the GLC in 1977 and Margaret Thatcher winning the 1979 election marked an end to this period of squatting in the capital. Communities perceived to be particularly threatening to the state were aggressively targeted. Railton Road, which had been a hub of the Brixton resistance to police oppression that took place in July 1981, was consistently and viciously assailed by law enforcement: in November 1982, 400 police evicted nine squats in the area. As council housing stock was sold off, 'homesteading' schemes, in which council-owned houses were sold on a 100 per cent deferred mortgage to first-time buyers, were offered to (mostly) middle-class professionals, and no more licences to squat were given out. Squatters in council properties were offered housing on estates that awaited refurbishment, mostly in single rooms. Those who wanted to retain some communal structure formed housing co-ops, which is what many of the women-only communities ended up doing, although some, like those living at Ivydene Road, Hackney, refused to leave the street they loved even as it was being demolished around them.[33] The lesbian squatting community, however, managed – in a variety of creative ways – to persist, remaining active in Brixton, Vauxhall, Peckham, Soho, Forest Gate and Hackney. Over the past few years, the Rebel Dykes History Project has been established, encompassing an archive – housed at the Bishopsgate Institute – an exhibition and a feature-length documentary. Many of these squatters met at the Greenham Common Women's Peace Camp, or through other political movements of that turbulent decade: the South London Women's Hospital occupation, support for the Miners' Strike, resistance to Section 28, ACT-UP, sex workers' rights, and the Poll Tax Riots; many of them, too, were deeply involved with the punk and fetish scenes.

Speaking at the British Film Institute in 2020, the artist and Rebel Dyke Atlanta Kernick – immortalized in an archival photo carrying a banner that reads: 'Brixton Dykes Demand Wages for Bashing Bailiffs' – noted that the conditions that allowed such squats to exist are almost entirely changed: leaving aside the criminalization of the act itself, there was no internet, no CCTV and a more generous social security system, meaning that both setting up a squat and living in it cheaply was an achievable goal.[34] The 'tremendous feeling of possibility' that lesbian squatters described in their interviews with Wall has dissipated in the intervening decades, replaced by, in Mark Fisher's famous phrase, the 'slow cancellation of the future'.[35] In 'Learning to Learn', the 1976 *Squatter* article, Moan captures the elation of futurity:

My daily life has been totally transformed. When you are no longer impaled on a 40-hour work week trying to pay the rent and indulging in expensive weekend, escapist diversion, what you are left with is time. Time to do things, time to make things, time for yourself, time for others. We have time to get down to the business of living.[36]

Austerity has privatized the imagination, and a forty-hour working week is no longer an upper limit. Anyone seeking to turn an empty building into a shelter for the night is at risk of arrest, let alone those who want to construct an alternative community. Mothering, under these circumstances, is pushed ever further away from more experimental structures of relation: if you're spending all your time and resources battling to stay afloat in the individualized way the state affects to support, your ability to imagine otherwise is sorely constrained.

Free Love and Nuclear Collapse

The prevailing mood of the 1970s, among socialist feminists in particular, was that progress could only be made by questioning the family itself: if, historically, it had functioned as the primary container and regulator of women's emotional lives, what possibilities might be found outside it? This held particularly true for mothers, both because mothering was the most labour-intensive aspect of traditional family life, and because of the emotional demands it placed on women: worry work, the labour of anxiety. Communes offered, for those who didn't want to squat, a way out of the bind of the marital home. The 'intentional communities' that began to proliferate in the 60s and 70s were not based in squatted premises, although they shared a foundational desire to reject privatized ownership, including the kind expressed in the family form.

The current network of communes in the UK, of which there are more than 400, is called 'Diggers and Dreamers', a tribute to their radical agrarian antecedents: the original Diggers were a group led by William Everard and Gerrard Winstanley between 1649 and 1650, who dug wasteland and cultivated common land. This history extends into the modern period, through Chartist land schemes, land-sharing Owenite communities in America and utopian experiments inspired by the horror of the First and Second World Wars.[37] In the latter part of the twentieth century, as the Cold War dragged on and the welfare state was stretched past its diminishing capacity, some communities anticipated the apocalypse and came together spiritually – Findhorn in Moray, Scotland, a notable example, is still going today – while others united around more practical considerations, like the rising cost of rent.

The practicalities of these domestic networks varied across the country, although they all relied on the availability of cheap housing, with groups buying up streets of adjacent houses, parts of large tower blocks, disused country houses, former mills and factories, and abandoned holiday and military camps. Unlike squatters, they needed a legal framework that allowed them to own one or multiple properties together and safeguard the rights of members. Although this often went against the anarchist tendencies of those who had come to the movement in search of an alternative lifestyle or as the logical next step from a squat, others believed this was a way to protect communities and make them accessible to those with little or no money: legality allowed them to shield themselves from, in the words of a member of People in Common in Lancashire, 'the arbitrariness of the state'.[38] Often, communities funded themselves via income pooling, which sought to upset the assumed balance between work and earnings, and in many instances benefits, including Family Allowance, were shared between all residents.

The Communes Network, which was set up in 1975 'to meet at least annually to discuss how we're doing – perhaps reorganize – and have a good time', sent out a monthly (at least in theory) bulletin and organized the Revolving Loan Fund, which groups could apply for with a specific project, 'no strings attached': the previous holders of the loan would approve your plan, and you would be in charge of passing it on to the next group once you had finished, with a little interest added if you could afford it. Communes organized work swaps, visits and celebrations with each other, and there was a Communes Network Directory where communities could find new members, and display their particular customs. Others emphasized their refusal of the title of commune altogether, like Crow Hall in Norfolk, a community established in 1965 that remained active until 2004, who declared 'We are not a commune', taking offence, it seemed, at the assumptions the term contained. 'Our lifestyle is literate, urbane and sophisticated,' they continue, and, 'We are not, nor do we pretend to be country folk', taking aim at the romanticized pastoral cliché: 'We live in the particular, not the abstract.'[39]

Whatever they preferred to call themselves, almost all alternative communities sought to reinvent heterosexual family structures. In 1977, Nell Dunn published *Living Like I Do*, an oral history in the same vein as *Talking to Women*, though unlike that book it has been almost entirely forgotten. Inspired by her own changing domestic situation as she split up with the father of her children, she visited communes across the country, interviewing their inhabitants. (One community she visited in Leeds subsequently wrote to her to clarify that they did not consider themselves part of the communes movement 'if such a thing exists' but rather a group trying to 'work out new forms of living and child-care relationships'; they pointed out, too, that she focused only on the adults' feelings, and did not treat the children as people.) Dunn's project was to challenge assumptions about family life: 'when the nuclear family collapses, society and the social worker are apt to think that's the end, the children and adults are lost. This isn't true.'[40] It's clear from her introduction that she doesn't see a meaningful distinction between the intentional community, set up with structure and subversion in mind, and the family that changes by chance, that collapses.

Free love, an easy concept to mock, was central to some British communities, particularly those formed in the 60s and early 70s.

The manifesto for the 1974 Windsor Free Festival – an anti-monarchist, anti-rent event held from 1972 until its brutal suppression by police in 1974 – advocated non-monogamous love as a way of resisting capitalist society: 'In the place of the rip-off employer/employee relationship we can have one of complete co-operation (we can all take part in the decision-making process at work as well as at home). But we have to learn this co-operation in the home and from an early age.' Loneliness and capitalism, in short, have a causational relationship. But free love is not in itself an antidote to feelings of isolation, and within communes that practised non-monogamy there were difficulties in squaring the ideal with the reality, with feelings of guilt and jealousy often proving difficult to avoid. The historian and commune veteran Chris Coates recalls, during a course called 'Alternatives' that ran at the Future Studies Centre in Leeds in the 80s, a woman from the Lifespan commune in rural Yorkshire answering the question 'Are you a free love commune?' with 'Do we have Free Love? No – it costs just as much as it does anywhere else.'[41]

In Dunn's book, there are several accounts of non-monogamous relationships that had emerged circumstantially, which are mostly unable to withstand the difficult feelings they engender. The more intentional relationships, although far from difficulty-free, had more success. A community in Leeds that spanned houses on Abbey Road, Penny Lane and Greystone Road, with shared living spaces and children moving from house to house according to a rota, centred on sexual freedom within their entire organizational structure:

> The reasons we decided to work through it all together lay in the wider, social, cultural, and political events going on at that time . . . In our household we were becoming aware of the politics of everyday life and realising that *all* aspects of the way people live, including things as prosaic as cooking or as private as sex, have political implications.[42]

Here Alex, a thirty-year-old man, is discussing the difficulties that arose between several members of the collective after their sexual relationships began: this scenario, in many respects a familiar tale of a love triangle, is clarified by a sense of its political ramifications and indeed the political characteristics of sex as a category, despite its 'privacy'.

Domestic labour was often regressively distributed in communes despite their stated intentions, and there are many stories of women ending up taking on the responsibility for cooking and cleaning.[43] It is difficult to construct a society that doesn't reproduce the hierarchies of the old one. (In Doris Lessing's 1985 novel *The Good Terrorist*, the protagonist, Alice, leaves her parents' house for a squat that she sometimes calls a commune, and becomes the mother figure who performs all the chores. At the end of the book, her own mother observes that 'it turned out you spent your life exactly as I did. Cooking and nannying for other people. An all-purpose female drudge.'[44]) Often, trying to redress this imbalance proved a steep learning curve. At People in Common, for example, Coates recalls that 'in response to women in the group calling for us to treat domestic work as seriously as we were taking our paid work' all communal home-based work was renamed Support, and the 'expectation was that everyone would do two days a week Support and three days paid work each week'.[45] In breaking down the divisions between men's work and women's work, other boundaries began to dissolve. In a special 'Women in Co ops' issue of *Undercurrents* magazine, published in July 1981, alongside articles suggesting living co-operatively should draw on the menstrual cycle and a call-out from 'Creches Against Sexism' is a report about the women-only weekends held at Lifespan in Yorkshire, in which one participant observes her desire to 'change my "sexist" attitude towards other women' and to 'talk about babies and laying bricks in the same breath'.[46]

A large part of this domestic labour was, of course, childcare. One of the longest features in the 'Women in Co-ops' issue is June Statham's investigation 'Childcare in Communities'. Concentrating on People in Common, Lifespan, Laurieston Hall in Dumfries and Galloway, Wheatstone in Shropshire and Redfield in Buckinghamshire, Statham interviewed mothers and non-mothers wishing to take on maternal labour who were 'trying to bring their children up in a less restrictive, non-sexist way'. After diagnosing the problem – the nuclear family – communities struggled to construct alternatives: in conversation with Statham many outline a trial-and-error process, with many women with children and pregnant people leaving after only a short time. At Laurieston, it wasn't until a long-term resident, Linda, decided she wanted to have a child that serious planning began: already 'one of us', there was more at stake, perhaps, in facilitating Linda's choice. One of the small cottages on the property was set up as a 'children's house', and a baby group was formed of people committed to supporting her through pregnancy and beyond. Before they could test these structures, however, another resident, Catriona gave birth to her son Finn. She told Statham that she particularly appreciated 'the sharing of worry':

> Because more than half the group has either had children or had a lot to do with them, they can answer my questions and fears and I trust the answers. They help without taking away my right to experience motherhood. They always encourage me to say what I feel and ask for what I would like. That has been especially true of the amount of time I spend with Finn. Originally we had expected to do an equal amount; one day a week each. When he was born I found I wanted to see him every day, so I did mornings. Then I began to feel I could let go a little bit more and appreciate being able to concentrate on other work in the commune for a day at a time. This coincided with other people wanting to do whole days themselves. If they had asked for more time before I wanted to give it I would still have tried to listen to that; as I believe they have rights too.[47]

These rights seem to stem from the burden of anxiety itself: those who alleviate Catriona's worries by caring for Finn inevitably generate their own, and in the process develop their own claim on him. Just as Catriona herself has a 'right to experience motherhood', the other members of the baby group have the right to develop their own specific relationships with the child – whether semi-, quasi-, or even wholly parental – and adjust their commitments accordingly.

Similarly, Lisa, a resident of the Abbey Road commune that Dunn spent time with, said that, in sharing the care for her one biological child with a group that included the mothers of three other children, 'I don't feel I've lost my role of "mother", because I'm mother to four instead.'[48] Motherhood, here, is not a finite resource: it multiplies with each use it is put to.

At People in Common, where Catriona spent some of her time (planning, in 1980 at least, to leave Finn at Laurieston when she did so), childcare experiments were a mixed success. Initially, according to a long-term resident, Barbara, the parents of the three children that were part of the group when the commune was established declared that 'kids are everyone's kids'. Yet in practice they were unwilling to share control or let go of their power. In the mid-70s, other children joined the community and Barbara herself gave birth, resulting in a chaotic period where eight children under eight were being cared for and educated. In 1978, they instigated a numbered system: '"ones" were equivalent to a parent, "twos" were fairly closely involved but had less power, and "threes" were like uncles or aunts. The children each had a number one who was not their biological parent, although there had been no decision that it had to happen that way.'[49] Although this system worked for a while, it eventually fell apart, not least because the older children in particular were used to being cared for primarily by their biological parent.

Even when the practical aspects of shared childcare worked, feelings of parental ownership were difficult to shake. Sally, who wanted to 'try and put into practice her feminism by living in an alternative to the nuclear family, with its oppression of women', told Statham that she was frustrated by parents' refusal to 'give up a bit of their power'. Another interviewee, who 'liked children but wasn't ready to have any of my own, and I wanted to be a kind of "third parent", taking a share of the responsibility and inconvenience as well as the pleasure', found that the 'basic difference' between parents and non-parents persisted: while mothers were happy to share tasks with other biological parents, they didn't feel comfortable asking for or accepting help from those who had no children of their 'own'.⁵⁰ The logic here is transactional – other mothers can be 'repaid in kind' – but it also speaks to a sublimated idea of an essential change that makes someone a mother, that equips them, somehow, for maternal work. Within this, perhaps, is fear: if you do let go of your power, how do you recalibrate your own relationship to your child? Acknowledging that care is work, and therefore can be learned, endangers the specialness of the category of mother. This special quality of biological relation also proved its power when a mother (it was almost always a mother who had primary custody) decided to remove a child from the community, sometimes after they had spent their whole life among its members. During one of Dunn's visits to Leeds, one commune member, Jan, was contemplating doing just that. Albert, another member, noted that 'I get freaked by Jan wanting to take Sam away. That's a big disadvantage, this insecurity because Jan is his biological mother, but it feels as if she can take my kid away.' It felt that way because it was that way: legally, the other members of the community had no rights over a child; their care was not recognized by the state.

Legal ownership intruded in other ways, too. A commune in Brighton set up in the former marital home of a woman called Sue, shared with three adult men and her three children, is described, with traces of bitterness, by one of the residents, Mike, as being 'in flux, according to Sue's relating to me or not [. . .] Primarily, the house exists as a home for Clare, Ben, Lucinda and their mother. This means that everyone else is to a degree dependent upon Sue for the present roof over our heads.' Although it seems clear to me from this and his other comments in the interview that Mike has trouble accepting a subservient role to a woman in control of property, it's also true that Sue – who in her own interview describes her 'alternative family' as her job – has taken on a conservative role that mimics the traditional position of the father, the head of the house; the children are caught up in the status negotiations of those who occupy the living space. (Sue's husband, who still owned the house, was unusually understanding; another interviewee, Frank, whose marital home became a commune after his wife became involved with the WLM, refers to his own 'tell-all' book about the 'most agonizing years of my life', which he attributed entirely to 'feminism'[51]).

No Father

A primary question of communal childcare, in these tellings, is who bears the ultimate responsibility for a child. Responsibility can, of course, tip over into possession and control. If the child has enough mothers, enough guardians, enough parental figures, then the question becomes: how can we all best help the child to feel like they have control over themselves? How do we keep them safe – don't touch that, it's hot; don't run out in front of that car; don't drink that, it's poisonous – without stamping them with a mark of ownership? (I'm reminded, again, of the Leeds community's response to Dunn, chastising her for not seeing that the children themselves deserved to be heard.)

In the Wild communes, for example, if the Wild surname refuted the stamp of paternal ownership, then questions emerge about giving them all the same surname: they become the children of a concept, both freer and less free in their own ways. There are lots of stories, in the sporadic articles and programmes that track down these former 'Wild Kids', of difficult teenage years, of being bullied, and of rebelling against the Wild principles, by, for example, becoming an investment banker or marrying a Tory. Their houses were often the site of local attacks, smeared with animal excrement and pelted with eggs, and most of them did not last into the 1980s, although many of the mothers and children moved on and into different intentional communities. The children, now adults, remember, too, a sense of being taken seriously, of being respected: Sam Sky Wild recalled in 2005 'being stimulated and getting challenging answers from adult company'. He goes on to describe children and adults, in this iteration of a communal life, as not a hierarchical structure but rather 'a series of satellites spinning around each other, with something common at the core'.[52]

Parenting hums with anxiety: how can you care for someone else well? One of Winnicott's most influential ideas about mothering is the notion of the 'good-enough mother': in 1971's *Playing and Reality*, he outlines the concept as a gradual progression from a mother with 'an almost complete adaptation to her infant's needs' – forgoing sleep, responding to every cry – to a mother who responds more partially, teaching her child, over time, to 'deal with her failure'.[53] The writer Emily Ogden offers a gentle correction to the notion that a mother who can reassure the infant that she can withstand their relentless demands on her is the liberatory concept it is often taken for. Ogden cites Adam Phillips, who asserts that if the mother 'insists upon being a real person, then the infant or young child has to invent a false self to deal with her'. A good-enough mother, then,

> is to hide that she is a real person! She is to do so *just enough*! Some number of lapses into personhood can be acceptable, but how many? How would one know? I imagine every caretaker does lapse. I imagine every caretaker does insist, from time to time, upon being a real person. I know I did, and do. I lapse. When I think about my failures, I feel the same dreadful wave of nausea I felt in third grade when I was responsible for another girl locking herself in her locker out of sadness. The abyss of myself as a harmful person opens up inside my heart.[54]

As Denise Riley writes in her critique of attachment theory in *War in the Nursery*, there is too much pressure placed on motherhood when a mother is the sole and only provider of emotional security to her child. If the aim of communal living is to alter such a punishing dimorphic structure – to become satellites, spinning around their common core – then perhaps there's a possibility within it not to prevent lapses made by caretakers, but to have ample cover for these natural lapses. If you're too tired to keep up the pretence that you aren't a real person, someone else can take over. But how to deal with the flipside of this? We have it culturally ingrained that sacrifice is central to parenthood: is part of the struggle of letting go of feelings of possessiveness, jealousy and ownership letting go of the centrality of sacrifice to maternal love? Or could we reclaim the selflessness allegedly inherent to maternity by making it the centre of a more expansive mothering that is directly political? By understanding this as rooted in collective responsibility, we might find a way to a form of child rearing that abolished the division between the public and the domestic once and for all.

These questions make me think of another piece by Riley. In 'The Force of Circumstance', published in *Red Rag* in 1975, she details the 'conservatizing' effect of being a single mother, 'effectively voiceless' within the women's movement, 'on all fronts at once: housing, geography, time, work, medicine, sexuality, love'. She continues:

> *Everything turns on the housing question* as the most visible uniter ('home') of structures of money and class. It's in respect of housing that my single motherness pushes me back hard into the most overtly conservative position. I'd hoped to live more or less communally with people I cared for and could work with (without pushing the commune ideology too far; mutual support/convenience not necessarily entailing good politics). But I never found/co-made such a group. Lacking one, I couldn't wait; and so I filled in such gaps as turned up in people's flats on a need-a-roof-over-my-and-child's-head basis (which many of us do). In the event we have moved seven or eight times in his lifetime; most of those moves I didn't want, but were forced on us as a result of overcrowding, emotional demands from people in a landlord position which couldn't be met, leases expiring, and so forth. The obvious solution to having a child alone is to live with people; but there are always a majority who can't or so far haven't had the massive good fortune of making it work, who cannot be consoled by the diminishing prospect of true communism. Though we know the utter brutal irrationality of living alone.[55]

Housing is determined by money and class for everyone, of course, but Riley's point is that having a child outside traditional family structures exacerbates the inequalities of both. Riley, who was

sceptical of traditional Marxist understandings of love and economics, but who nevertheless knew exactly how compromising the status
quo was for mothers and children alike, presents the 'commune ideology' as, in one sense, the opposite of conservatism, but the difficulty
of keeping such set-ups alive in practice turns the single mother to
hostile situations, crowded flats, demanding landlords. Simply *knowing* the utter brutal irrationality of living alone is not enough.

One of Riley's earliest publications was her 1977 poetry collection
Marxism for Infants. She attributes the title to George Orwell's *The
Road to Wigan Pier*, where it features as a disingenuous book written
by a bourgeois socialist, Comrade X, who hates the working class.
The academic Samuel Solomon has clarified this slightly unlikely
connection by pointing to a reading Riley gave at the 1977 Cambridge
Poetry Festival, in which she said something that has, for me, become
a personal mantra: she wanted to 'retrieve' that title and use it to say
that 'If Marxism does not have to do with infants and vice versa then
there's not much hope for either infants or for Marxism.'[56] In the
poems collected under this marvellous title, she offers a different
image of children and adults' lives; a different kind of entanglement
which is neither the disavowal of possession nor a defence of it:

You have a family?   It is impermissible,

There is only myself   complete and arched
like a rainbow or an old tree
with gracious arms descending
over the rest of me who is the young
children in my shelter who grow
up under my leaves and rain
In our own shade
we embrace each other gravely &
look out tenderly upon the world

seeking only contemporaries
and speech and light, no father.[57]

I find these lines almost unbearably moving. It's not just my own experience, the dubious contemporary concept of relatability, that colours them with such feeling, although I can't pretend that isn't part of it. 'No father' is both specific to Riley's circumstances (and my own, albeit from the perspective of a child) and conceptually tethered in something else, in the prospect of establishing relationships between men, women, adults and children that try to refuse hierarchies, seek 'only contemporaries'. It is very difficult to do, and it requires both a graveness and a tenderness, each contingent on the other.

6.

Spilt Milk

If the world hates you, you know that it has hated me before
it hated you. If you were of the world, the world would love
its own; but because you are not of the world, but I chose
you out of the world, because of this the world hates you.

John 15.18–19

In 1990, the Irish musician Sinéad O'Connor released her second
album, *I Do Not Want What I Haven't Got*, to considerable critical
acclaim. In her autobiography *Rememberings*, O'Connor describes
the album as a piece of work structured by maternal themes. The
song 'Three Babies' is about her three miscarriages, which she 'carries' with her, and 'The Emperor's New Clothes' documents the
breakdown of a relationship after the changes wrought by pregnancy and birth, as well as the vitriol directed at her for speaking
truthfully about her own politics in her music and in interviews.
Many tracks address her own mother Marie, who was abusive and
struggled with addiction, and who had died in a car accident in 1986.
According to O'Connor, 'Feels So Different', 'Stretched on Your
Grave' and the iconic cover of Prince's 'Nothing Compares 2 U' are
songs that she 'was always – and am always – singing to my mother'.[1]
The album takes its title from something Marie said when she
appeared to Sinéad in a dream: 'what I haven't got' is the forgiveness
of her other daughter, Éimear.

There is another kind of maternity at play in *I Do Not Want
What I Haven't Got*, one that stretched beyond personal experience.

The song that sits at the centre of the album, 'Black Boys on Mopeds', begins with the name Margaret Thatcher, referring to a televized speech in which she responds with shock to the massacre of pro-democracy protestors in Tiananmen Square in June 1989, despite the fact that similar 'orders' are 'given by her'. In the chorus, O'Connor elaborates on the false distinction made between the British state and the conduct of repressive regimes elsewhere: England, she sings, is not the rosy land of myth and legend, but rather a place where police officers murder indiscriminately the 'black boys on mopeds' of the song's title. It continues by connecting this observation to O'Connor's maternal desire to protect her own son, Jake, who was three years old at the time of the album's release: because she loves him, she's going to leave the country, in an attempt – always already doomed – to shield him from grief. In the third verse, O'Connor turns the maternal gaze outward, imagining a young mother at Smithfield market, begging for food in the early hours of the morning: the babies in her arms – three of them, like O'Connor's three miscarriages from earlier in the album – are cold, and when they learn to speak, their first introduction into language will be the word 'please'.

'Black Boys on Mopeds' is based, according to *Rememberings*, on a true story 'involving two young teenagers near where I lived in London. They had taken a cousin's moped without asking permission; the cops were called and gave chase; the boys got frightened, crashed and died.' O'Connor links this to the wider climate of racism in London at the time, one in which many young Black men were going suspiciously 'missing' while in police custody.[2] The story matches closely with that of Nicholas Bramble in 1989; it also chimes with many details of the death of Colin Roach, another 21-year-old Black man chased down by police while riding his own moped. Roach was found dead of a gunshot wound in the doorway of Stoke Newington police station on 12 January 1983. The official verdict on the cause of his death was suicide; the Hackney Black People's Association and other community civil rights organizations, who had been campaigning for several years for a public inquiry into police brutality in the area, disputed this verdict.

On the inner sleeve of *I Do Not Want What I Haven't Got* is a photograph of Roach's parents standing in the rain beside a poster of their son; the whole record could be interpreted as a dedication, either to them or to his memory. Roach's death, and the belief that it was a cover-up, became, for a time, a touchstone in the anti-racist movement: according to Benjamin Zephaniah, whose poem 'Who Killed Colin Roach?' was a feature of many of the demonstrations outside police stations, the case was 'a rallying point for the black community', though in the years to come it would be 'overshadowed' by the struggle against the National Front, the campaign against the SUS (stop and search) law, and the many other suspicious deaths in police custody.[3] The latter no doubt includes the riots in Brixton and on the Broadwater Farm estate in Tottenham that happened in the same fortnight in the September of 1985: in Brixton, Dorothy 'Cherry' Groce was shot by police who were looking for her son Michael, while in Tottenham Cynthia Jarrett, another mother accused of harbouring her son, died of a heart attack after police searched her house. Groce survived the shooting but was paralysed until her death in 2011; the Metropolitan Police did not issue an apology until three years later. (I want to emphasize, here, that when it comes to the racist misconduct of British police forces, I am barely scratching the surface.)

There is a long tradition of maternal imagery in protest song and poetry, from the bereaved mother grieving for their child to the radical mother leading the fight. (Often, the speaker doing the imagining is a white mother who reaches towards – in solidarity, but sometimes with an obscuring empathic greed – the suffering of Black mothers. Think of the variations, in recent years, on the slogan 'When George Floyd called out for his mother, he called forth all mothers'.) In 'Black Boys on Mopeds', O'Connor explicitly positions the multiple grieving mothers in the song against its very first image, their political opposite: Margaret Thatcher on TV. Nine months after the album was released, Thatcher was to leave office, deposed by her own party halfway through her third term. Throughout the eleven years of her premiership, which began with a landslide election win in May 1979, Thatcher's maternity, like her gender more generally, was a powerful tool both in her own self-fashioning and for her critics to wield.

O'Connor wasn't the first to use the Prime Minister's image in juxtaposition with a suffering child in a song. In 1982, Crass, an anarcho-punk band from Essex, released their anti-Falklands war song 'How Does It Feel (To be the Mother of 1000 Dead)?', which was the centre of a minor media flurry: Thatcher herself was asked on *Question Time* if she had heard it and the Conservative MP for Enfield North tried to prosecute the band under the Obscene Publications Act. In 1989, Elvis Costello released 'Tramp the Dirt Down', a song built around a refrain that imagines standing on her freshly dug grave as something to aim for, even live for. It opens with the description of a picture in a newspaper of the Prime Minister planting a kiss on an afflicted child – it's not clear whether the pain predates the kiss, whether the event is captured during a hospital visit or staged – an image, in Costello's hands, of a predatory avalanche of greed raining down on an innocent face: a grotesquely inverted Madonna and child.

Matron Knows Best

When it comes to the symbolic intertwining of maternity and Maggie Thatcher, it is difficult to know where to begin. The first female Prime Minister of the United Kingdom, her legacy continues to dominate the country like no other. Thatcherism, according to the sociologist Stuart Hall – an early adopter of the term – represented 'the decisive break with the post-war consensus, the profound reshaping of social life'. As an ideology, Hall believed, it forged new connections between 'the liberal discourses of the free market and economic man and the organic conservative themes of tradition, family and nation, respectability, patriarchalism and order'.[4] Harnessing a new economic agenda to profoundly regressive positions on gender and sexuality, compounded by the vicious paring down of the supportive state, it brought new pressures to bear on motherhood both practically and conceptually.

The image that Thatcher constructed of herself, an Iron Mother running the nation with a firm hand and its finances like a household budget, lent new force to the conservative maternal ideal.[5] It is not a coincidence that mainstream capitalist feminism today casts Thatcher ('politics aside!') as an example of a glass-ceiling-breaker, nor that she features in some of the plethora of anthologies released in the past ten years about 'gutsy', 'inspirational' and 'amazing' women in history: her particular mode of femininity was a reaction against the more radical possibilities that had been opened up in preceding decades. During her leadership and after it, 'women' and 'feminism' began to be used as interchangeable terms. (Following the 1979 election, Eileen Fairweather wrote in *Spare Rib* that the American press were shocked that feminists in the UK weren't celebrating: 'The recurrent question, from the land where even the mastectomies of presidents' wives are used to catch the feminist vote, was why hasn't the British women's movement put pressure on Thatcher to turn her into one of us?'[6])

Thatcher repeatedly emphasized her identity as a wife and mother while refuting and actively hampering the feminist gains that had allowed her to succeed in the first place. Throughout her political career, she treated herself as an exception: she could play the housewife while running the country, but all the housewives she implored to identify with her were to stay firmly in their place, at home. In 1975, at the Conservative Party women's conference, she honoured women's 'voluntary work' as the 'spirit of a real social contract', positioning womanly virtues as the opposite of paid labour, and advocating the privatization of the sectors that predominantly employed women.[7] In a Thames Television news interview in 1981, she stated that 'I don't think there has been a great deal of discrimination against women for years', and the following year she used an address in honour of the suffragist Margery Ashby to talk about the 'privilege' of the woman's role of wife and mother.[8] Although women have historically tended to vote Conservative, in 1979 there was a significant swing to Thatcher among male voters: as Beatrix Campbell wrote from the vantage point of 2015, 'it was not women who were being addressed by this woman, and it was not women who put this woman into Downing Street.'[9]

Her path there had not been guaranteed. Born Margaret Hilda Roberts in 1925 in Lincolnshire, she was the daughter of Beatrice, a housewife, and Alfred, who owned a tobacconist and a grocer and later became Mayor of Grantham (he was unseated by a Labour council victory). At the University of Oxford, where she read Chemistry, she was president of the Conservative Association; upon graduating, she worked as a research chemist for J. Lyons & Co., developing ice cream emulsifiers. In the general elections of 1950 and 51 she stood as a Conservative candidate in Dartford, and managed to lose well, reducing the Labour majority each time. It was then that she met Denis, a wealthy businessman who was assisting her campaign. They married in 1951, a union that gave birth first to 'Margaret Thatcher', and then, in 1953, twins Carol and Mark, and he funded her studies in law: she qualified as a barrister later in the same year their twins were born, and practised, briefly, in taxation and patent law. After a few false starts and a difficult – now much mythologized – election campaign, she was elected as the Member of Parliament for Finchley in 1959. During the premiership of Harold Macmillan, she was promoted very quickly, and was appointed to Ted Heath's shadow cabinet before the 1970 general election, after which she became Education Secretary before, finally, after the loss of the February 1974 election, becoming Leader of the Opposition in 1975. By 1979 Thatcherism had clarified itself as an ideology – 'the first time since the war,' according to Neil Kinnock, that the Conservatives were an 'ideological party' – that pitted a new everyman, the ordinary taxpayer, against the excesses of the bureaucratic state, the bullying trade unions, and the wicked, envious scroungers who sought eternal dependence. She declared her intention to revive 'a sober and constructive interest in the noble ideals of personal responsibility'. This, she said on multiple occasions, was something she learned from her father.[10]

This ordinary taxpayer lived, without fail, in an ordinary family. Thatcher was almost maniacally committed to a regressive view of family life and she weaponized her identity like a consummate professional: aware of the misogyny and classism leveraged against her – her Cabinet was referred to as a 'middle-class pressure group' – she turned these qualities into her calling cards, concocting a performance of womanhood that enshrined housewifely qualities as definitional virtues. She allowed cameras into Downing Street for the first time, insisted on doing (some of) the housework herself, and often cooked meals for her Cabinet if they were meeting late into the night (coronation chicken, apparently, was her signature dish). According to Shirley Williams, the Labour MP who became a founder of the Social Democratic Party in 1981 – assisting Thatcher with the 1983 'landslide' in the process – the ironing board in Parliament's 'ladies' room' was 'almost permanently occupied' by Thatcher during her premiership, who was often ironing Denis's shirts.[11]

This domestic vaudeville extended to her political communication, transforming the national stage into a living-room mirror. In one of her earliest political appearances, a 1949 meeting where she sought formal party approval for her candidacy, she shared a platform with her father and declared that 'the Government should do what any good housewife would do if money was short – look at their accounts and see what's wrong.'[12] Thirty years later, just after her election, she referred to a specifically gendered knowledge that brings to mind the apocryphal divisions between work and women's work: 'The women of this country have never had a Prime Minister who knew the things they know, never, never. And the things that we know are very different from what men know.'[13] This knowledge was domestic, emphasized by her repeated insistence that she, too, was a 'housewife' at heart: 'housewives know a lot about managing finance', she said on more than one occasion; 'every woman knows you can't make a soufflé rise twice.'[14] This housewife was always a mother, too. In 1981, a journalist for the Australian television programme *Sixty Minutes* asked her whether her famous toughness required being 'inhumane' on occasion. She responded in the language of mothering handbooks, conflating – appropriately, for an interview about the Commonwealth Games – the production of children with patriotic feeling: 'No, toughness is not being inhumane, any mother will tell you. If you're just over soft and sympathetic without being firm, without trying to bring your children up to responsibility you'll never do your children or your country any good.'[15]

In her particular country, where positions of influence were and continue to be dominated by former public schoolboys, Thatcher provided a canvas onto which others could project their maternal fantasies. Marina Warner, in *Monuments and Maidens* (1986), describes Thatcher's embodiment of a fantasy composite of 'women of discipline': 'Nanny, matron, governess: characters from the youth of the landed classes, of the Edwardian nursery and the prep school dorm'. Julian Barnes, who was educated at the City of London School for Boys, wrote that her second term in office promised 'the cold showers, the compulsory cod liver oil, the fingernail inspection, and the doling out of those vicious little pills that make you go when you don't want to go. No wonder the sick bay's overpopulated.'[16] The journalist Jon Snow declared in his 2013 documentary *Maggie and Me*, that

> My own one-to-one experiences with Maggie made me think about what life must be like in the cabinet. Because like the men who sat around that table, I'd been to a public school and the only woman any of us had ever known in authority was Matron. And now suddenly it was as if Matron was running the country.[17]

Such fantasies of matron had a certain erotic power that legitimized a latent desire to be dominated. It allowed Conservative politicians to adopt the passive postures of an institutional childhood: nasty medicine to be swallowed, but at least you don't have to make any decisions yourself. In his book *Thatcher and Sons*, which positions her as the symbolic mother of her successors John Major, Tony Blair and Gordon Brown, the journalist Simon Jenkins describes her fall in 1990 as a kind of matricide, before emphasizing – inadvertently, perhaps – her dual occupancy of the position of both mother and surrogate: 'The fall of Thatcher left the nation stunned. Nanny had been thrown out by the inmates of the nursery.'[18] (The chapter about Thatcher herself is called 'The Revolution in Embryo'.) Her class position is important, here. Nanny is the servant figure who is part of the family and exercises some power within it: both mummy and not-mummy, she is responsible for discipline that, untainted by the love we might assume to be the prerogative of a mother, wavers on the border of cruelty.

Thatcher's policies often directly resulted in deprivation, which was, for her supporters, excused by her gender – she must be in some way doing it for 'our own good' – and for her opponents a bitter irony. Perhaps the most famous example of this dates from her time as Ted Heath's Secretary of State for Education from 1970 to 1974, at the time traditionally understood to be a woman's role. Acting at the behest of the Treasury, Thatcher implemented budget cuts that included the removal of free school milk for primary school children between the ages of seven and eleven. Instantaneously, she became a figure of approbation in the press and from the opposition, despite the fact that the preceding Labour administration had abolished free milk in secondary school: the moniker 'Thatcher, Thatcher, Milk Snatcher' emerged almost overnight. During the hastily arranged media appearances that attempted to mitigate the PR disaster, it became clear that the public held her personally responsible. One woman in a daytime television audience, Mrs Booth, declared that she would 'never again' vote Conservative: 'this milk has finished me [. . .] hurting children is absolutely the end.'[19] The affair offered ample opportunity for misogyny: one headline read 'Mrs Thatcher Caned Over School Milk', while during the late-night Commons debate over the furore there were chants of 'ditch the bitch'. This is language – naughty nanny being caned in the nursery – in which the subtext is leaking all over the text.

Thatcher had also increased the price of school dinners, but it was the milk that stuck. The provision of free milk to children and pregnant women had begun in the 1940s, in the hope of staving off rationing-induced malnutrition; it became, as Carolyn Steedman's memories of it illustrate, a symbol of the welfare state as a whole. Milk is an appropriate symbol for Thatcherism, an unstable and profitable commodity, always at risk of oversupply, sitting at the intersection of the domestic and the global. The historian Emily Baughan has written about the slow disappearance of National Milk – a government-issued baby formula that was available either free or heavily subsidized between 1940 and 1976 – and its entanglement with both cost-cutting measures and the scandal that had erupted in 1974 about Nestlé's marketing of formula milk in the Global South. Nestlé's campaigns aimed to persuade women that the breast was not for feeding but was instead an aesthetic, sexualized object, and to substitute breast milk with an expensive product that was often diluted with fatally unclean water; in the UK, where reports of National Milk, improperly prepared, leading to infant death had been proliferating in the media, it was deemed appropriate that state resources be devoted to the encouragement of breastfeeding.[20] The provocative sexuality of the famous 'Got milk?' advertising campaign in the 90s, which featured American celebrities posing with milk moustaches, before its English and Scottish counterparts 'Make mine milk' and 'The white stuff', reinforced its uncomfortable erotic potential. Milk is, of course, intimately related to the maternal body, and it reminds us of our uncomfortable origins: our dependency on another, our permeability, and our need. (The 'Got milk?' campaign has been the subject of many parodies over the years, the most on the nose being the musician Fergie's 2016 video for her song 'M.I.L.F. $' – the chorus declares 'I got that milk money / I got that MILF money' – featuring Kim Kardashian, Chrissie Teigen and other famous and very rich mothers, and climaxing in Fergie pouring milk all over herself, wearing a t-shirt that asks – incomprehensibly – 'Got MILF?').

Thatcher was, of course, also an actual mother. The belief that she wasn't a wholly successful one, favouring her son and bullying her daughter, is now firmly embedded in the mythology that surrounds her personal life. In the first volume of her autobiography, *The Path to Power*, she briefly discusses the twins' surprise birth by C-section before – with characteristically unsettling briskness – detailing her experience of maternal ambivalence (not that she names it as such):

> Oddly enough, the very depth of relief and happiness at having brought Mark and Carol into the world made me uneasy. The pull of a mother towards her children is perhaps the strongest and most instinctive emotion we have. I was never one of those people who regarded being 'just' a mother or indeed 'just' a housewife as second best. Indeed, whenever I heard such implicit assumptions made both before and after I became Prime Minister it would make me very angry indeed. Of course, to be a mother and a housewife is a vocation of a very high kind. But I simply felt that it was not the whole of my vocation. I knew that I also wanted a career.

She continues, noting that a 'phrase that Irene Ward, MP for Tynemouth, and I often used was that "while the home must always be the centre of one's life, it should not be the boundary of one's ambitions."' Her genius was to effect a sleight of hand that used the conditions of the home to soften or feminize her occupation of the most high-profile job in the country. Thatcher expanded the metaphorical boundary of her home to encompass Downing Street.[21]

In the 2008 television film *The Long Walk to Finchley*, which dramatizes the same events as *The Path to Power*, Thatcher is pictured in the maternity ward telling Denis that this 'ready-made family' of a boy and a girl child coming all at once is 'perfect': now she can get on with her real work. In a 1985 interview with Miriam Stoppard, 'Woman to Woman', she phrased it differently, and more emotionally: she looked at the babies, newly born as they were, and thought, 'I'm not going to be overcome by this.'[22] This language is familiar: the engulfing, overwhelming need of the newborn is experienced as an oncoming tidal wave, threatening to obliterate everything that preceded it. Yet for Thatcher, giving birth didn't inspire any solidarity with other mothers. At the end of her three-week-long stay in hospital, she submitted her name for the Bar finals, a famous story that she takes evident relish in repeating in her memoir, offering it as proof that she was simply more willing to work hard than other women. In her pursuit of a 'career' – a rather understated term for her actual ambitions – she had to face repetitive questions about whether a wife and mother could balance her duties with those of an MP, which must have been both frustrating and demoralizing. In the same memoir, however, she asserts that these committees had 'every right' to ask her these questions, and she seems blissfully certain that the reason she could successfully perform this balancing act was her superior 'organization', something that chimes with her insistence throughout that she was simply more rational, more willing to face hard truths, than other people.[23]

The details she includes about her household, however, shed more light on how she accomplished these extraordinary organizational feats: she employed a nanny who also had the responsibilities of a housekeeper, and her children spent their educational lives at boarding school. (In a *Woman's Hour* interview, Thatcher dispatched her parenting advice: 'Try to set aside one afternoon a week for your little one, it makes such a difference to their sense of being loved.') This was the fundamental hypocrisy of her policymaking: for all her talk of housewifery, she herself was almost entirely free of the domestic obligations that she constantly reiterated were the rightful concern of all other women. In *The Path to Power*, immediately after stating that the home was not the boundary of her ambitions, she – with no apparent sense of irony – details her opposition to tax allowances for childcare for working parents:

I did not believe that working wives, who would presumably be bringing more money into the family anyway, should be in effect subsidized by the taxes paid by couples where the woman looked after the children at home and there was only one income. This was a straightforward matter of fairness. Of course, these general arguments were not ones which affected my own decisions as a young mother. I was especially fortunate in being able to rely on Denis's income to hire a nanny to look after the children in my absences.[24]

A straightforward matter of fairness, just like the straightforward matter of organization, when organization really just means 'money'.

Family Values

'Margaret Thatcher was my mother.' This is how the poet Lemn Sissay opens his celebrated 2012 TED talk 'A Child of the State', which recounts the abuse he experienced in foster homes and other institutions after being born in a mother and baby home near Wigan in 1967. Sissay, in declaring Thatcher to have been his *mother*, not a public-school-esque nanny or matron, illustrates that the stakes of her cruelty were much higher for those who weren't born with privilege. For those without the support of a family, she wasn't simply an unpleasant aspect of the general national circumstances, she *was* your circumstances. At the very end of his talk, Sissay circles back to its title: 'You can define how strong a democracy is by how its government treats its child. I don't mean children. I mean the child of the state.'[25]

If Thatcher was the mother of the state, she was by no means its advocate. In 1987, she gave an interview to *Woman's Own* which contains the most concise distillation of her approach to government, the statement often paraphrased as 'there is no such thing as society', in which she outlines exactly how little care the state should be responsible for. In popular memory, she was talking about adult slackers. In fact, even children aren't spared her disdain:

I think we have gone through a period when too many children and people have been given to understand 'I have a problem, it is the Government's job to cope with it!' or 'I have a problem, I will go and get a grant to cope with it!' 'I am homeless, the Government must house me!' and so they are casting their problems on society and who is society? There is no such thing! There are individual men and women and there are families and no government can do anything except through people and people look to themselves first.

She goes on to figure benefits as related to 'tragedies', both in their intended use – 'to reassure people that if they were sick or ill there was a safety net' – and in their misuse: the tragedy of the 1980s, a decade which saw more than three million people out of work, was apparently that 'there are some people who have been manipulating the system . . . when people come and say: "But what is the point of working? I can get as much on the dole!"' [26] The family is positioned here as a private unit of care and control, separate from and resistant to the interference of the state: it produces the individual men and women whom she exhorts to 'look to themselves first'.

Welfare dependency was an obsessive concern of Thatcher's, so embedded in her psyche that it preoccupied her even more after she left office. *The Path to Power*, which was published in 1995, is split into two parts. The first details her life up until she won the election, breezing matter-of-factly through childhood, adolescence, marriage and motherhood. The second part is devoted entirely to criticizing John Major, detailing the crisis that had befallen the family and her plans for solving it. (Reading this inspired in me both pity and genuine fear. It reads like the ranting of an exiled supervillain.) In a chapter called 'Virtue's Rewards', subtitled 'Politics to strengthen the family, curb welfare dependency, and reduce crime', she declares that it is 'welfare dependency' which weakens the 'traditional family'. Her reasoning is that benefits make it 'less worthwhile to work and less troublesome and more financially advantageous to have children outside marriage'. Thatcher's panic is threefold: first, that families are relying on benefits at all; second, that people are rejecting traditional models like marriage; and, third, that undesirable people are seeking to remodel the family structure in their own image. 'The family,' she writes, 'is clearly in some sort of crisis: the question is what. There are those who claim that the family is changing rather than weakening. At one extreme some of these people view *any* household unit, such as cohabiting homosexuals, as a "family" deserving the same degree of social recognition and respect as a married couple with children.'[27] (This is, after all, the government that introduced Section 28.)

Simultaneously terrified that the family was losing its appeal while she seeks to police its boundaries against those who wished to adopt the term, Thatcher accidentally confirms the central tenet of family abolition. 'A functioning free society cannot be value-free,' she writes, before laying out a frankly terrifying proposal for restoring family values by enshrining their institutional aspects through law, order and punishment.[28] Distinguishing between widows, who 'require financial help', and the 'exceptionally irresponsible' lifestyle of the 'never-marrieds', she advocates harsher punishment in schools and blames ethnic minority communities for a vast proportion of crime, vandalism, graffiti, drug trafficking and, seemingly, whatever else comes to her mind. This was nothing new: the 1981 report of the Home Affairs Committee on Racial Disadvantage, which influenced the policy of the decade that followed, stated that the 'West Indian family' was 'unstable' because of the failure of its matriarchal structures in a society governed by 'British values', which were defined as being those of the patriarchal nuclear family, ideally one which resided in their own, owned, house.[29]

After all this – which, I feel I have to remind you again, is in the second half of an autobiography that begins with recollections of childhood treats and schoolgirl high jinks – she zeroes in on her favourite topic: the single mother. In fact, she uses the term 'never-married mother', in the hope of pinpointing her target more accurately:

The never-married single parent would, however, receive the same benefits [as widows or ex-wives] under certain conditions: very broadly, if she remains living with her parents or, alternatively, in some sort of supervised accommodation provided by a voluntary or charitable body with other single parents under firm but friendly guidance. In such an environment, young mothers could be helped to become effective parents, young children could be cared for under proper conditions for part of the day if the mother went out to work, and undesirable outside influences could be kept at bay. Together with quicker and better procedures for adoption, this approach would safeguard the interests of the child, discourage reckless single parenthood and still meet society's obligations to women and their children who, for whatever reason, are in need and distress.

Essentially, Thatcher is advocating a vast, secular extension of the mother-and-baby homes of the twentieth century. It is not difficult to see beneath the surface of this language a desperately punitive instinct, a desire to restrict sexual freedom ('undesirable . . . influences') and to remove children from their parents at the whim of a conservative state. If the support offered to a mother is contingent on her submission to conditions that are tantamount to house arrest, it is not support, but punishment. (Thatcher deems such stringent treatment unnecessary for fathers, although she does discourse for a while on her belief that, without marriage, the only possible outlet for the expression of masculinity is either crime or irresponsible impregnation.) Children, here, are figured as a kind of inanimate bind, embodiments of the social contract and little else: lamenting that it would be logistically difficult to row back the liberalization of divorce law that occurred in the 1960s, she instead suggests that a 'clear distinction' should be made between a divorce where there are no children involved and one where there are dependants, where divorce would be actively and forcibly 'put off' to keep the home together, however unhappy or harmful it might be.[30]

Such a use of motherhood as a conservative ideological weapon was far from unique to the 1980s; its manifestation in this decade was simply a new spin on an old classic. In some respects, the Conservatives were the natural party to take on a maternal figure as their leader: Labour, the party of organized labour, had a complex relationship to gender equality, while conservative principles allowed for women's traditionally subordinate role to be celebrated and utilized to great effect. They had form when it came to pitting the respectable mother against the pernicious influences of the left: in the 20s and 30s they had used this tactic to oppose socialist Sunday schools, usurpers of the influence that rightly belonged to parents. Maternity, here, symbolized convention and law and order. What Thatcher opened up, however, was the heady possibility of a Prime Minister who united the national and the domestic, meaning the violence of her policy was dressed in the clothes of maternal betterment, cruelty performed as care.

Working Families

Beyond the woman herself, Thatcherite gender politics reconfigured the complex historical relationship between motherhood and work, and also the idea of 'women's work' in general. As more women were encouraged to re-enter the workforce under the sign of the first ever female Prime Minister they were not, in Beatrix Campbell's words, understood to have been 'proletarianized' but rather 'bourgeoisified': regardless of the actual work in question, it was aspirational to be a career woman, not a shop steward.[31] Women's magazines talked about 'having it all' and class consciousness got muddied: Julie Burchill, then one of the most well-known journalists working in Britain, declared in the *Face* in 1989 that 'I am a Thatcherite bitch I hear, which is middle-class liberal shorthand for a working-class girl who has made it.'[32] Melissa Benn, in her 1998 book *Madonna and Child*, writes that despite the 'murmuring' upon her election that Thatcherism would push women back into the home, in fact, 'at some point in the mid to late eighties, the burden of proof shifted from the working to the non-working mother.'³³ This is perhaps an overstatement. The Thatcherite position on the mother was that she both was and was not a worker, should and should not be one, and that she was simultaneously the foremost authority on economic necessities and entirely removed from the political sphere. She was, in short, an entirely ambivalent totem, central to the total politicization of the family on the one hand and its gushingly sentimental idealization as something beyond politics on the other.

The working mother of the Conservative imagination bore little resemblance to the working mother of reality, whose life was, more often than not, characterized by experiences of struggle and lack. In 1981, national unemployment figures stood at 2.7 million, highly concentrated among manufacturing jobs, and it remained over three million until the final years of the decade. (It's important to bear in mind, here, that there were many attempts by the government to manipulate the figures, and historians disagree over how much we can rely on the data. Many unemployed people were pushed to claim disability benefits instead of going on the dole. Two decades later, they were demonized by the Labour government for being 'workshy'.)

Ironically – and predictably – Thatcher's policies served to push people into the kinds of work she was so horrified by. Women who travelled to London from the north of the UK to sell sex, for example, were known as 'Thatcher's girls': their entry into work that Thatcher decried as symbolic of society's failures was, often, determined by the precise conditions of (un)employment that she had created. In 1982, the English Collective of Prostitutes, an activist group that had formed in 1975, occupied the Holy Church in London's King's Cross, the primary destination for those who were migrating to the capital in the hope of earning money from sex work.³⁴ Sex workers tend to be those who have been marginalized for many intersecting reasons: class, race, sexuality, gender presentation, addiction, homelessness and disability. Sex work also, crucially, allows those with caring responsibilities, particularly single mothers, to earn enough money to provide for their family and choose their working hours. The King's Cross occupation was led by mothers holding their infants, and those who had lost custody of their children; their list of demands emphasized the persecution they and their families received from the state:

1. An end to illegal arrests of prostitutes
2. An end to police threats, blackmail, harassment and racism
3. Hands off our children – we don't want our kids in care
4. An end to arrest of boyfriends, husbands, sons
5. Arrest rapists and pimps instead
6. Immediate protection, welfare, housing for women who want to get off the game

The occupation lasted for ten days, and during that time the only public figures who treated them as workers involved in industrial action were the Labour MP Tony Benn and his wife Caroline. Caroline brought cake to share, while her husband

> listened to our story and immediately made the parallel with a factory sit-in. He was the only visitor to compare us with other working-class people. When he had grasped our views and demands, he took out his pocket tape machine and dictated letters to the MPs for Camden and to the Home Secretary who is responsible for the Metropolitan Police. We corrected them: he rolled the tape back and re-dictated the corrected passages. That's when he got the applause.[35]

Selma James, a dominant figure in the Wages for Housework movement, was a spokesperson for the occupation, which she saw as fundamentally linked to Thatcher's policies: the action, she stated, was 'breaking ground not only on behalf of all prostitutes but on behalf of those women who are increasingly criminalised by the economic crisis'.[36] (This was something of a learning curve for Wages for Housework: in 1977, a group of sex workers in Birmingham had produced a leaflet, *Red Light*, emphasizing their frustration at the campaign's use of the term 'prostitute' when describing the labour of housewives and mothers.)

Joblessness, for many families, expressed itself as a lack of futurity: entire communities began to wither on the vine. In 1987, the feature-length documentary *Living on the Edge* was premiered on Central Television, accompanied by a limited cinema release. Conceived by its director, Michael Grigsby, and producer, John Furse, as a project exploring how the post-war dream of a better life for the working classes had been replaced by unabated free market capitalism, its central subjects included a farming family in Devon on the brink of bankruptcy, a mining community in the south of Wales discussing the aftermath of the 1984–5 miners' strike; Joanne, a young woman bringing up her baby on a housing estate in Birkenhead with the help of her mum Tess and sister Helen, and a group of young people forced to leave Glasgow and seek work in London. A primary theme of the film is isolation within families, as shared community responsibility for each other and each other's children is no longer the norm. In a pub in Birkenhead, a young man tells Joanne that 'the roots have all gone':

> I can remember when people used to take all the kids out on the block, have a party for the kids at the weekend, the neighbours would club together and make sure you had enough to manage but now they can't, they're struggling themselves. Sitting in that flat with the four walls around me it's like being in prison.

He continues: 'People like your [Joanne's] mum, people like my mum have never done a thing wrong in their life, have lived by rules and regulations that have been set down by society all their lives and where has it got them?' These maternal examples emphasize the invalidity of the social contract: 'And the likes of me and people that I know look at the likes of your mum and my mum and other people and think "Where's it got them?"'

Over repetitive and beautiful domestic footage – Tess silhouetted in the window, ironing; the slicing of a christening cake; a child helping wash the dishes; a cigarette moving back and forth from a lipsticked mouth – similar sentiments are repeated from Devon to Glasgow. Tess, hands immersed in the washing-up bowl, says that

'Years ago it used to be "I want my children to have what I never had", now it's "I want my children to have what I had."' Her children, passing the baby between them, agree:

> we do have dreams, obviously. You think to yourself, well, me mam might win the pools or something like that, you know, you always have your dreams but think about like our little Tessa, our Joanne's little girl: she won't have any dreams because we're getting that way now where we've got to face reality, and the more we face reality she's gonna grow up and say there's nothing better for us because we've got nothing to look forward to.

At least, Helen says, she and Joanne can remember some of the good life: they were born in the 60s. They might not feel like they have a future, but they have had a little bit of a past. In Wales, the wives of striking miners also discuss the failure of the promise that life would continue to get better generationally. Still entirely resistant to the idea of giving up, they figure this determination as a purely maternal quality: 'I think most people, and most women, are going to fight this for their children. If we give in, if we stop fighting, then our kids go down the river.'[37]

What Thatcher meant by 'there's no such thing as society' has preoccupied social scientists and historians alike in the long neoliberal dreariness of her wake. It was an ideology that eventually failed her, in the shape of the highly regressive Poll Tax, which led to her resignation as leader. In 1989, Thatcher's proposal to bring in a new Community Charge to replace the domestic rates system was met by enormous opposition: under the planned changes, everyone, regardless of the size of their home, their employment status or their wealth, would have to pay the same amount; for council tenants, who paid their rates through their rent, this was an entirely new tax. She decided to impose the new policy in Scotland first, which turned out to be a (deliciously) catastrophic mistake. Glasgow in particular was a hotbed of anti-poll tax activity and the headquarters of the Scottish Anti-Poll Tax Federation, with collective resistance against sheriff officers and bailiffs that drew on memories of the rent strikes of the early twentieth century, where women and children would ring bells and clatter pans to alert their neighbours that there was danger of eviction. Protesting the Poll Tax was a family affair: some of the most iconic images of the nationwide resistance feature children and their parents, wearing slogan t-shirts, holding placards and smiling: CAN'T PAY, WON'T PAY.

Thatcher could not understand that this mass opposition *was* society. In pitting the values of the (C)onservative 'family' against the state, she not only offered a rebuke to the communal caring practices that had been built in preceding decades, but also translated, in Stuart Hall's words, 'economic doctrine into the language of experience, moral imperative and common sense, thus providing a "philosophy" in the broader sense – an alternative *ethic* to that of the "caring society"'.[38] In positioning herself as the maternal guardian of common sense against the 'scroungers', Thatcher permitted a virulently small-minded nastiness to flourish under the guise of a concern with fairness. This violence was handed down like a nursery scolding: those who were struggling to survive the economic crises of the decade were 'moaning minnies' who needed to 'cheer up' and learn that 'change can't be painless'; that 'there isn't a pot of gold to draw on.'[39] Join the real world, she said to those who couldn't afford to heat their homes, who couldn't find work or enough to eat, to those who could imagine no future for themselves or their children at all. Sheila Rowbotham, remembering the decade, described this 'sneering contempt' as 'the only thing that hurt': 'If you had any thought or ideas of commitment to other people who weren't able to make it as individuals you were sneered at. I hated that.'

I first read Rowbotham's words in the aftermath of the 2019 election, in which I and many of my friends had spent long hours canvassing in December weather in the hope of electing an anti-austerity government, and they produced in me a feeling of recognition that was almost physically painful. Thatcher's most affective legacy is this sneering contempt, which lives in the way anyone with politics left of centre is spoken of in much of Britain today: if you suggest that there might be another way – a commitment to people who aren't able to make it as individuals – you're dismissed as childish, crazy, someone who simply doesn't understand how things work.

I feel that recognition, too, in the second verse of 'Black Boys on Mopeds', where O'Connor sings, defiant, that she won't be deterred by being called 'childish'. In the second half of the verse, she sings a refrain that will repeat later in the song: 'If they hated me they will hate you'. This is a quotation of a paraphrase of a Bible verse, John 15:18–19, where Jesus speaks to his disciples:

> If the world hates you, you know that it has hated me before it hated you. If you were of the world, the world would love its own; but because you are not of the world, but I chose you out of the world, because of this the world hates you.

On the album sleeve, this Bible verse is emblazoned underneath the image of Colin Roach's grieving parents.

7.

The Enemies Within

Since Ma died you're nothing but a useless twat.

Billy Elliot, *Billy Elliot*

Margaret Thatcher's political project relied on the division of the public into two distinct groups: citizens and enemies. The former were 'ordinary' self-supporting taxpayers; women, primarily defined by their relationship to the home and their roles as wives and mothers, were good citizens if they fulfilled their domestic duties supported by their own wages or their husbands, but never if they relied on money from the state. Enemies, meanwhile, were benefit claimants, unmarried mothers, the unemployed, communists, socialists, feminists, gay and lesbian people and, especially, strikers. Mothers who fitted into the latter category were doubly traitorous: to the country and to the appropriate domestic virtues of maternity itself. The period immediately before Thatcher came to power was characterized by an increase in industrial action, culminating, famously, in the 'Winter of Discontent': by the time she took office, the cartoonishly authoritarian elements of her own maternal performance positioned her as a bastion of common sense, the ultimate boss, admonishing the lazy workers. The history of industrial action in the 1970s and 80s is often remembered as a primarily masculine story, despite the concurrent increase both in women in the workforce and in women's trade union membership. This erases the maternal dimension of industrial action in the period: mothers were staking a claim on their identity as workers outside the home, but they were also identifying the punitive conditions in which their work took place.

By the beginning of the 1980s, women made up around 40 per cent of the total labour force, concentrated around the lowest-paid jobs in service work and manufacturing: the clothing and textile industry, for example, had a work force that was almost 80 per cent female. Women's working patterns were often dictated by their caring responsibilities, and the growing number of unionized women was a corrective to the fact that, historically, working unsocial hours had often resulted in alienation from other workers and from unionization as a whole.[1] One of the most significant examples of strike action by women workers was the 690-day-long strike that took place between 1976 and 1978 at Grunwick Film Processing Laboratories in Willesden, London. The conditions at Grunwick, where the majority of employees were Asian women, underscored multiple intersecting areas of discrimination: their pay was half the average for a female manual worker in London, and overtime was compulsory, with little notice given, meaning that childcare had to be frantically reorganized their childcare or their other caring responsibilities. The management, according to Amrit Wilson, Jayaben Desai and others who worked in the factory, exploited structural inequalities, turning away white applicants for the roles because they expected higher pay: 'Imagine how humiliating it was for us, particularly for older women, to be working and to overhear the employer saying to a younger, English girl, "You don't want to come and work here, love, we won't be able to pay the sort of wages that'll keep you here." '[2] Their fight for fairer pay and conditions was both a way to resist these discriminatory practices and, in a more diffuse sense, a way of laying claim to unionization itself, offering a corrective to the stereotypical image of the working-class subject in Britain.

The strike at Grunwick was ultimately unsuccessful – the Trade Unions Congress was controversially complicit in pressuring the strikers to end the action – but in relation to this latter objective, it achieved a huge amount. It built a community among those who were marginalized on multiple fronts, allowing for links to be identified anew between working conditions, living conditions, race and gender: one picketer told *Spare Rib* that the dispute had allowed her to combat the isolation she felt as the single mother of a four-year-old, as those she met at Grunwick were 'taking turns looking after him so I can join the picket. It is really breaking down the barriers between what is called personal and political.'[3] These barriers were particularly permeable in relation to NHS work: Wages for Housework, as Katrina Forrester has discussed at length, identified a crucial area of the 'public reproductive work' done by women as that which occurred in 'the home in the hospital'.[4] The end of the 1970s saw a mass walkout by NHS staff including nurses, auxiliaries and midwives as well as hospital maintenance and cleanliness workers, over cuts to pay and hospital closures, as well as demonstrations and partial strikes.

Indeed, pay and conditions were so bad for nurses and ancillary workers that recruitment was falling: wards were understaffed while many nurses sought work elsewhere. (In the early 80s, around 25 per cent of workers at the flagship London Marks & Spencer were registered nurses.[5]) Despite this unfolding crisis, and despite her declaration at the Conservative party conference in December 1982 that 'the NHS is safe with us', Thatcher remained committed to imposing cuts and market mechanisms in service of her ultimate – perhaps unattainable – goal: the replacement of the NHS with compulsory private health insurance.[6] The year 1982 saw the longest industrial dispute yet in the health service, with day-long work stoppages by nursing staff, porters and cleaners which steadily increased in duration. This was met with considerable public support, including a march of 120,000 people in London and smaller demonstrations across the UK, and expressions of solidarity from miners, dockers, newspaper and television workers and car manufacturers. Such action from NHS staff was a rare thing at that time: the nature of their employment meant that strike action was usually unpopular and difficult to organize. Indeed, the Royal College of Nurses had a blanket no-strike policy that lasted until 1995, which angered many of its members, and meant that only 2 per cent of the nursing workforce was officially on strike.[7] The characterization by Wages for Housework of hospital work as 'social housework' refers to the fact that the labour of tending to the living and dying has long been understood as somehow inherently feminine, and under-paid and undervalued accordingly. This, compounded by the RCN's policy, allowed Thatcher and opponents of their action to repeatedly characterize nurses as angelic women who were called to nurture: the few who did go on strike were bad apples 'hitting out deliber-ately at patients' or naive specimens who had been misled by 'extreme left wingers', as the Tory MP for Beaconsfield declared in the Com-mons. Thatcher repeatedly thanked the brave nurses who 'refused' to strike and would 'never dream of deserting their patients'. This language of vocation made nursing an obligatory feminized battle-field: to understand your labour as labour was to desert your cause.[8]

The most successful actions of the period used gendered stereo-types relating to maternal care and domestic life to their advantage. One of my favourite examples happened in the west of Scotland, an extremely hard-hit area for unemployment, where there was a long and rich tradition of women leading rent strikes, running socialist Sunday schools, and supporting the industrial battles of Red Clyde-side. At the beginning of the 80s, resistance unfolded at the Lee Jeans factory in Greenock, where the mostly female workforce sus-pected that the multinational Vanity Fair corporation was trying to close the factory: recent orders had been rushed through, and rumours abounded that operations were moving to Northern Ire-land. The factory had been opened by Lee in 1970 with significant financial support from government schemes trying to reduce unem-ployment in the area: when Vanity Fair took over in 1976, these grants were no longer operational. Their suspicions were proved right when the union shop steward Helen Monaghan was called into a meeting with management on 5 February 1981 which confirmed the factory's closure. The workers were prepared. Once Monaghan gave them the agreed signal, they began to occupy the factory, barri-cading the entrance to the shop floor with plastic canteen chairs. The sit-in lasted for seven months, and garnered significant support:

workers travelled the country addressing union branches and raising money; a march was organized from Greenock to Edinburgh to present a petition to the Secretary of State for Scotland; the Govan and Lower Clyde shipbuilders donated over £1,000 every single week. (The women's own union, the National Union of Tailor and Garment Workers, offered them little support.) The occupation was organized in shifts, with rotas for cooking and sleeping: Monaghan describes it as being like a 'big family'.[9] On the first night, realizing they weren't quite prepared to cook, two workers shimmied down the drainpipe and bought 240 fish suppers from a local chip shop.

Those participating in the struggle at Greenock were mothers, daughters and wives who all understood these roles to be fundamentally economic. Employees varied in age, from those who had just left school to those who had been garment workers for thirty years, but they all knew that if they lost these jobs others would not be forthcoming. The general perception of women's work was that it was done for 'pin money', supplementary to a male wage – this perceived disposability, according to the Scottish feminist magazine *MsPrint*, was why their jobs were targeted – but the reality in rapidly de-industrializing places like Greenock was that women were often the primary earners: they were fighting for their necessary work. (Some of the machinists ceremoniously set fire to their redundancy notices outside the factory.[10]) Although there were men participating in the occupation, it was understood to be fundamentally feminine in character: in statements of solidarity from other unions they were referred to as 'girls' and by the *Daily Record* as the 'petticoat rebels', despite the fact that they spent their days making denim jeans.[11] In a *Greenock Telegraph* article titled 'Now it's the great knit-in!', it was emphasized that 'the sit-in has given many of the teenage workers the chance to learn the basics of home craft.' It's true that domestic skill share was a large part of the occupation: younger workers were taught to cook large meals (and bash spuds) 'for their hungry "family" at the factory'.[12]

I love the story of the Greenock occupation, but to claim it as a straightforwardly feminist success story, in which the industrial space was domesticated and workplace bonds became familial, would risk simplifying its complexity. It would also be a political inversion of Thatcher's housewifely logic, but not a disavowal of its terms. On the thirtieth anniversary of the sit-in, the Scottish parliament debated a motion to formally recognize it. The SNP MSP Anne McLaughlin, who grew up in the area, gave an emotive speech about the part it played in the development of her own political consciousness, emphasizing the familiar theme of the frugally managed home:

> Those women were not political, and they certainly were not party political. What they were was determined. I believe that they had a distinctly female type of politics that makes me wonder how different the world would be if women were making more of the world's decisions – perhaps Greenock women, in particular. For instance, how many men would have thought to use Persil coupons? When Margaret Wallace and Catherine Robertson travelled across the UK to speak at rallies, they used two-for-one train vouchers from Persil packets, to save as much money as possible for the families at home.[13]

In part, McLaughlin is being faithful to the women's own representation of their action: feminism and militancy were both traditions that they rejected, and Monaghan in particular has been nuanced and forthcoming in interviews over the past forty years about her unease at attempts to retrospectively reframe it. And yet, what does it mean for an MSP to explicitly define the architects of a successful worker occupation as 'not political'? What is a 'distinctly female type of politics' in this context: small-scale? What precisely is it about 'Greenock women, in particular' that would, then, make them so good at political decision-making? The strike was a rare and remarkable success, but it didn't last: the factory closed for good in 1986.

Coal Not Dole

The defining industrial action of Thatcher's time in office was the 1984–5 miners' strike, one which has come to define, for many, the historical mood of the period as a whole. Although women's labour was central to pit villages, both in the household and outside it, women hadn't been permitted to work underground in mines since the passing of the 1842 Mines and Collieries Act. This meant that, unlike at Grunwick or Greenock, their involvement in the strike largely came from their positions as mothers of miners, wives of miners and inhabitants of the villages and towns themselves. (The Colliery Office Staff Association, which included canteen workers, cleaners and administrative staff, did go out on strike, and these workers were not offered large redundancy payments, but they made up a relatively small percentage of strikers overall.) Women in mining communities, then, were defending the livelihoods of their husbands and sons, but also fighting for a bigger cause: their way of life. For many of them, this manifested itself as an awakening both political and personal: rather than keeping them contained within their individual households, their maternal roles linked them together and afforded them the means of constructing a solidarity with other women and with the political landscape of the country as a whole.

The miners' strike was bigger than its immediate objectives from the very start. There are coalfields across the majority of Britain, in the Central Belt of Scotland, Northumberland, County Durham, Cumbria, North and South Wales, Yorkshire, Lancashire, the East Midlands, the West Midlands and Kent. (The last of Northern Ireland's coal mines had already closed in the 1960s.) The National Union of Mineworkers (NUM) was one of the strongest unions in the country, with a large membership, successful strikes within living memory and a reputation – false but powerful – for being responsible for the fall of Ted Heath's government in 1974; if Thatcher's government could defeat this union, others would surely fall in line. With the election of Arthur Scargill in 1982 to the leadership of the NUM and the appointment of Ian McGregor as his oppo-site number at the National Coal Board (NCB), who had a career of union busting in the US mining industry and mass redundancies at British Steel behind him, the stage was set for a generation-defining dispute. Scargill and the NUM were opposed to the closure of pits that the government termed 'uneconomic'. Pit closure meant extensive job losses – by 1992 the number of opera-tional mines would fall from 170 to fifty, reducing employment by almost 130,000 – and job losses meant destruction: mines were cen-tral to a way of life that extended beyond miners themselves.[14] A popular slogan throughout the strike was 'Close a Pit, Kill a Community'.

The family – the very thing that Thatcher's government pro-fessed to champion – was weaponized by the government from the start. Striking miners and their families were denied the full social security payments they were entitled to in the hope that this would force them back to work: their wives, it was assumed, would pres-sure their husbands back to work rather than see their children go hungry; maternal feeling was assumed to transcend class justice. This was a fatally, fantastically misguided assumption: what actually occurred was a groundswell of organization and support. Pit women refused to prioritize the welfare of individual families over that of everybody involved in the dispute. Local women's groups were set up across the country, and at the national conference held in Chesterfield, Derbyshire, in December 1984 'Women Against Pit Closures' was agreed on for their umbrella name. Their work began with one practical aim: feeding people. In the light of the punitive decisions being made by the state, miners and their families were going hungry. Sure enough, the community kitchens set up by the WAPC became what they were best known for, but they were also hugely present on the picket line, often facing significant police violence, and toured the country, raising funds and support.[15] (Many accounts note that women picketers humiliated the scabs more than the men did: perhaps this engages with the long misogynist history of the wife and mother as a nag and a scold, but it certainly takes that power out of the household and onto the streets.[16])

Although WAPC was a cause that was taken up by feminist activists across the country, and their support was often welcome – Betty Cook mentions in her memoir how appreciative she was of Sally Alexander, Jean McCrindle and Sheila Rowbotham in particular – the movement was at its core a working-class one.[17] Florence Anderson of Eppleton in County Durham told the journalist Jean Stead that they were determined for their efforts not to be taken over by middle-class feminists:

> We said it wasn't going to be like 1926, with people shuffling up to miners' soup kitchens demoralised and degraded. It was going to be miners' wives, miners' mothers, miners' sisters serving miners and their wives and families. We didn't want any sort of intellectuals coming down to play around in soup kitchens.[18]

The increased visibility of women's industrial action in the 70s and early 80s had shifted the realm of possibility. Cook recalls that

> I was determined that I wasn't going to stay at home like I had during the strikes in 1972 and 1974. I'd cried a lot then. I was cold and hungry all the time. I got sick and tired of seeing baked beans; beans and eggs, beans and chips, beans on toast. I told myself I wasn't going to cry this time and I wasn't going to go hungry. I was behind the strike from the start and I wasn't going to change my mind.[19]

What's more, they knew when they were being used. When the Department of Health and Social Security (DHSS) reduced the benefit families could claim, they stated that this was because strike pay was being distributed by the union, which wasn't true: the NUM was paying small allowances for picketers, but nothing more. In some parts of Kent, children of striking miners were refused free school meals.[20] If Thatcher, as she stated just after her election victory, really believed that there was a specific kind of women's knowledge – 'the things that we know are very different from what men know' – then she didn't consider that coal was just as central to these women's lives as it was to men's. As the journalist Jean Stead, who published one of the first accounts of WAPC, *Never the Same Again*, in 1987 puts it,

> women in the pit towns and villages had always known about the mining of coal. They knew where faces were being opened up, what the political reasons were for closing others, where seams were rich and where others were played out. They lived with coal mining, as their mothers had done. They knew more about it than many at NCB headquarters in London.[21]

Such knowledge included the fact that the NCB was winding down pits with thirty years of coal left in them; that their husbands and their sons were being given nothing to do and provided with no new machinery; that if the NUM got broken by Thatcher then the union movement as a whole would be fatally weakened. They knew that the strike, unlike those of 1972 and 74, was not about pay or conditions but about mining's very existence: the choice between coal and the dole.

In 1981, Vic Allen, a communist, activist and academic who had taught Arthur Scargill at an NUM day school in Leeds, published *The Militancy of British Miners*, research based in part on his own involvement with the union. In it, he writes that miners' wives 'functioned as vital elements in the organisation of mining': women 'have been adapted to meet the needs of mining as effectively as miners themselves'.[22] None of this is to romanticize the condition of life in pit villages – the 'adaptation' of bodies that Allen writes of was to a punishing, often shortened, life – or to retrospectively suggest that the emergence of WAPC was plain sailing. The nostalgic temptation is to paint the events of 84–5 as a new blooming of pre-existing female solidarity: this was not the case. By the 1980s, many miners' rows had been demolished in slum-clearance programmes, dispersing their former inhabitants, and women caring for husbands, fathers or sons who had been disabled in pit accidents were particularly isolated.[23] In the many collections of creative writing produced by local WAPC branches, the strike is frequently identified as a moment that allowed the writer to realize how little community, and how little pleasure, their lives had previously contained. Betty Cook, a founder of the Barnsley Miners' Wives Action Group and now a prolific writer, remembers her early days in a colliery village as being an experience of emotional hardening: 'A woman from down the row came with her baby. She said, "I don't know what to do, Betty." I told her that she would have to do what I had done, that was help yourself. I was becoming a right hard cow. Circumstances forced me.'[24]

In January 1985, Betty Heathfield, the well-known wife of an NUM official and a mother of four who was a key figure in Chesterfield WAPC, gave a speech in Newcastle in which she articulated what was at stake for all workers, not just miners: 'We are the only strong union, we are the only people who can put an end to this government's tyranny over all working-class people.' Heathfield, in an impassioned call to action, depicts those involved in the strike as the vanguard of a battle for society itself:

> They want your money, they want the destruction of your union, and they want the removal of your leaders. And if you let them get away with that, it'll be everybody else after, and you'll have stood the pace, and they'll still close your pits, and they'll still close your communities, and your kids will still be on the dole.

Although at the end of the speech, on a rallying note, she declares herself to be an optimist rather than a pessimist – 'I am not thinking about the past, I am thinking about the future!' – her specific invocation of the maternal perspective serves as a warning and as an acknowledgement of the damage that had already been wrought.

The threat of unemployment for their husbands was one thing, but WAPC members could not tolerate the idea of their children facing constant rejection. As Stead writes, 'There was nowhere for these young men to emigrate to anymore.'[25] This kinship went beyond immediate family: mothers who were active in the WAPC were not only acting in the interest of their own children but of children in general, and those without children were operating in an equally maternal space. (This is not necessarily a solely positive social phenomenon. Cath Cunningham from Fife told interviewer Vicky Seddon in 1987 that 'Mining women in particular have a protective attitude to their husbands; when you get married or go to stay with someone you take on the role of mother.'[26])

Not Just Tea and Sandwiches

'Video Number One' of the *Miners' Campaign Tapes*, an independent 1984 documentary project seeking to counter the official government narrative, subtitled 'Not Just Tea and Sandwiches', is a fourteen-minute-long film focusing on Chesterfield Women's Action Group. Positioned as it is on the border of Derbyshire and Nottinghamshire, where three quarters of miners were not on strike, Chesterfield was so heavily policed that a hard border between the counties was effectively enforced: women interviewed in the video discuss being stopped on their way to the shops and questioned by aggressive police officers, who often called women supporting the strike 'Scargill's slags'.[27] As well as cooking and picketing, this WAPC branch dispensed benefit advice. In one visceral scene, Janet Cunningham addresses the camera, visibly angry, and details the consequences of the DHSS penalization of strikers: she has seen, she says, a six-week-old baby who had gone without a bottle for two days, a family with children who had only eaten one biscuit, and a family with seven children getting a giro payment for ninety-one pence. 'They're getting thirty-four pound a week less than the base starvation level of supplementary benefit and they're expected to survive on it and they're not surviving on it.' At the end of the film, we see her again: 'I've got one thing to say to Mrs Thatcher, though I don't suppose she'll hear it. It's aren't you ashamed? Ashamed that you lead a country that can starve children? That can see children dying through wanting medicine that they can't get?'[28] Between 2018 and 2019, researchers from the Coalfield Women project created an archive of interviews in tandem with an exhibition at the National Coal Mining Museum for England in Wakefield, West Yorkshire (the project features women from Wales and Scotland, too). Their interviewees describe complex domestic mathematics, the relentless struggle to stay afloat on meagre benefits or one wage – Lorraine and Linda, two sisters from Kent, were living on £16 per week – and to keep their children in college or school, and then the long exhausting battle to pay back the debts that had accrued during the industrial action once it was over. Many families lost their homes.[29]

It was precisely these economic circumstances that meant WAPC kitchens in particular were so crucial to the longevity of the strike: anyone who came was fed. The exact combination of what they provided varied – sometimes it was a hot dinner, sometimes soup and a pudding – and food parcels were handed out and delivered, with nappies, soap, clothes and other necessities often included. This was all subject to donation, and women were instrumental in collecting these, both in their immediate community – in a 2014 interview with Channel 4, Angela Boulton recalls knocking on doors in the pouring rain with a three-week-old baby in her arms – and further afield, travelling nationally and internationally to raise awareness and support.[30] They organized raffles, coffee mornings, dances and auctions. Local shopkeepers offered free food to striking miners and their families, other unions organized collections, and donations arrived from abroad, particularly from France, East Germany and the Soviet Union: one detail that comes up frequently in the memories of WAPC women from all over the UK is the mystifying content of the Soviet food parcels in particular, with their bean soup and 'strange cabbagy things'. (The most generous assessment of these parcels comes from Cath Cunningham from Fife's tentative suggestion that 'It maybe widened our horizons instead of eating Norrie's pies all the time.' It was probably more interesting than the diet Liz Marshall recalls living on in Ayrshire: sausages and Spam.[31]) Sometimes food was even obtained through a more creatively redistributive approach. Anne Scargill remembers that, when her friend Sheila Capstick arrived on the day of the Barnsley march, 'She told us that she'd mugged the milkman. She'd realised that he hadn't given anything for the food collection so she took a tray of eggs, a crate of orange juice and a crate of milk off him.'[32]

Women's memories of donations emphasize how moving it was to be given things from people who also had very little – single mothers and pensioners come up repeatedly – as well as from unexpected places. My favourite story of surprising middle-class solidarity is Russell's account of May Hogarth, an elderly woman from Selkirk who invited strikers into her home for a meal with her family. 'She went on picket duty and they didn't know how to handle her because she was quite elderly then. She had great stamina, great guts, and it was an inspiration to a lot of us that somebody like that, who didn't have a background in mining, was happy to support us.' Elderly women, so often overlooked as if they are no longer truly part of society, were some of the strike's staunchest defenders. Another anecdote I treasure: the miner Andrew Stark remembers seeing an eighty-year-old woman go into a shop in Ballingry in Fife and buy a tin of soup. A Yuill and Dodds' lorry was parked outside (the firm was breaking the strike by moving coal after the train driver's union refused to do so). She walked out of the shop with her soup, and 'lamped it right through' the window.[33] The extensive campaigning by WAPC – as well as posters produced by the NUM that reminded the public not to 'forget about the miners' kids' – meant that those who felt uncomfortable with the picket violence they saw on TV could specify that their donations were to go straight to miners' families: in her punitive approach to wives and especially children, Thatcher had inadvertently created a sympathetic cause.

Still, the strike could pull communities apart as much as strengthen them, particularly in areas like Nottinghamshire and Kent where few miners were striking. One woman from Nottinghamshire told Stead that 'My mother blames Arthur Scargill for losing her only daughter. I mean, it couldn't have been a very close relationship if Arthur Scargill has broken me and my mother in two!' Even here, though, women described the WAPC as a worthy substitute for fractured relationships: 'My husband's family,' another Notting-hamshire woman told Stead, 'have completely cut us off and have said we all want sending to Russia . . . So that's it. We've lost a family. But we've gained a new family.'[34] Setting up kitchens and social spaces proved more difficult there than in areas where the majority of workers were on strike: at Clipstone colliery, women occupied a youth centre owned by the NCB and refused to leave until they were given premises that were appropriate for a kitchen. A Mrs Woodhead, in an interview with the BBC in 2019, remembers bor-rowing plastic cups from a local school to be used by the strikers' children. 'When she handed them back washed and cleaned, she says some of the wives of those who were still working threw them in the bin.'[35]

Even in areas where the majority of the community were on strike, the food preparation itself was a matter of complex commu-nal logistics. Any cooking that couldn't be done in whatever facilities the WAPC branch was using – often social or welfare clubs or church halls – would be done in members' houses and heated up later on; sometimes vast quantities of pots and pans were washed in showers. (There were also scuffles over who had proprietary rights to the menu. Anne Scargill remembers that, in Barnsley, 'Gladys was in charge of chips. Once she got going she insisted that only she was allowed to cook chips. I don't know why because they were only frozen ones.') The kitchens were also a place where intergen-erational learning and exchange could take place, just as with the Lee Jeans sit-in in Greenock three years prior. Scargill writes in her memoirs that 'We had some good lasses at that kitchen: old grand-mas came who could make a dinner out of a dishclout, sisters, daughters, our Joan was another, and two retired blokes used to wash up.' Cunningham recalls that in Cowdenbeath in Fife the committee included 'a couple of young, unemployed women and they played a tremendous role in the daily graft of providing for people': the task of sustenance was understood to be a crucial act of solidarity.[36]

Out of necessity, childcare became a collective responsibility, freeing their mothers' hands and time. Children were brought to the kitchens and played together, among a group of adults: many mothers in WAPC write of this a time when they felt they had moved beyond the isolation of caring for children all day alone. Joyce Coutts, secretary of the Lothian Women's Committee, which organized twenty-eight support groups in that region, told Jean Stead that this, in turn, had benefited the children. The 'wee ones' were 'spoilt' with treats like extra pennies, and the children thrived in a new communal setting. Coutts recalls it as being 'like a big play-school' where she watched babies develop over the course of the strike, starting to eat solids and talk: 'Their speech is perfect. It's good to watch them just walking up and getting their dinner, then coming back and sitting down and eating it.' They were at ease in the communal space, so 'If anyone at all needs a babysitter, there's no problem. The bairns know them all and will go with them.' Some mothers found, too, that doing something they previously would have baulked at – leaving their children at home while they travelled to raise funds – often changed their family relationships for the better. Pauline Radworth, from Blidford in Nottinghamshire, told Stead that, far from resenting their mother for leaving them, the children 'think more of you when you come back'.[37] Margo Thorburn in Fife made a direct link between the energetic organization of WAPC branches, including on picket lines, and the fact that 'we couldn't have done as much if our husbands hadn't been on strike, because they had to help out in the house.' Women were discovering that their partners were capable of doing housework, and many men were discovering how much they enjoyed childcare: with the normal routines of household labour disrupted, gender roles were losing some of their rigidity.[38]

Amid the public unrest of the strike, then, there was a fundamental transition occurring in the home. Betty Heathfield had declared that 'in our companionship with our men, our common struggle, we've wiped out the myth of the working-class wife.' Stead, considering this, asks:

What made up the myth of the working-class wife? That they had no interests outside their homes? That they did not make the political links between their own condition and what was happening in government? That they did not feel strong enough to change things through their own solidarity? That women were naturally right-wing and self-absorbed? If this were indeed so, it was an unfair myth. Working-class women had simply not had the time to do things before.[39]

Some marriages did not survive this change, but others changed for the better. (Anne Scargill, whose own marriage made it through the strike but ended in 2001, tells a story in her memoirs about a man approaching her and saying, 'Anne, I want my wife back. I don't want her I got now, I want the one I had before.'[40]) Many women remember finding the same new respect Radworth saw in her children in their husbands, or that their relationship had blossomed and expanded: to put it simply, they had something to talk about.

Mothers who took on more work to make up for the wages lost by their husbands during the strike, meanwhile, reported mixed feelings: loss, freedom and the awakening of ambition. Linda Chapman, who worked in Newcastle but lived eight miles away in Washington, told the Coalfield Women project that part of her was 'devastated' when she had to go full-time at work when her son was fourteen months old, but 'the other side of me was like, I'm enjoying this . . . I can see how I could progress my career.'[41] Many others actively sought work after the strike ended – out of both necessity and desire – or went back into education: Jackie Keating, who lived in Brampton in Yorkshire, went to adult literacy classes in Barnsley and wrote a book about her experiences of the strike, *Counting the Cost*; Norma Dolby from Arkwright in Derbyshire published her *Diary*, which recorded her growing commitment to the strike and her grief at the desolation of the community she loved; Cook began to study at Northern College, a progressive institution that allowed students to bring their children, who were found places at local nurseries and schools. Cook directly credits her creative inspiration to her work in the kitchens: 'There is nothing better than sharing food to bring folk together. I saw people who hadn't been acknowledging each other for years, sat talking. I was thinking about this one day and I was inspired to write my first ever poem.' It begins 'They tried to starve us out / You were there / We needed food and donations / You were there'.[42]

Changed Utterly

The 1984–5 strike has become highly mythologized in the years since it ended, particularly in a certain kind of British cultural product; the fact it was defeated, I think, plays a central role in the ease with which it is addressed from a position of nostalgic myopia. The most famous example of this is surely *Billy Elliot*. The 2000 film, adapted from a play by Lee Hall, became an unexpected box office success and, later, a legacy juggernaut: the stage musical, with music by Elton John, premiered in London in 2005 and ran in the West End for eleven years. Set in 1984, it follows Billy, an eleven-year-old boy living in Everington – a barely disguised Easington – in County Durham, who discovers a talent for ballet. His brother, Tony, and father, Jackie, are union stalwarts; his mother, Jenny, is dead. Gender is an extremely restrictive force in *Billy Elliot*, and much of the drama is produced by Billy's transgression of its rigid lines. Miners' solidarity is depicted as an extremely masculine affair, reminiscent of the images of picket line violence that dominated press coverage. Jackie and Tony are occupied with strike business and, occasionally, with hitting each other; Billy goes to dancing lessons in secret, makes eggs and toast, and cares for his Alzheimer's-ridden grandmother. In one symbolic scene, Jackie chops up his dead wife's piano, which Billy loves to play, for firewood.

The lineage Billy identifies himself within is a maternal one. His grandmother often remarks that she could have been a professional dancer: when they go together to visit his mother's grave, she is distracted by her own movements, performing a halting port-de-bras in the cemetery. The ghost of Billy's mother makes one appearance, wearing what looks like a nurse's uniform and lightly scolding him for drinking milk straight from the bottle. Conceptually, she haunts the entire film, in the absence of tenderness – Jackie's form of care being the axe, hers being the lullaby – and most notably in the scene where Billy's ballet teacher Mrs Wilkinson, a surrogate maternal figure played by Julie Walters, reads out a letter that she wrote to him before she died. When she observes that Billy's mother 'must have been a very special woman', Billy replies, breaking the viewer's heart, that 'she was just me mam.' This gesture towards the shared labours and triumphs of mothering – often the defining feature of such depictions of the working-class everywoman – lands curiously in a film that is otherwise completely devoid of actual mothers. The boxing studio is split in two so the ballet class can rehearse because their usual hall is being used as a miners' soup kitchen, presumably run by the WAPC, but this is something we never see. When the money is raised by the community to fund Billy's transport to London for his Royal Ballet audition, we see the boxing teacher, George, offering the twenty pence pieces he's collected from his students, and Jackie pawning Jenny's jewellery, but no active input from any women, despite the fundraising prowess they were, in real life, demonstrating across the country and beyond.

This has more to do with the noughties than the eighties. Clive James Nwonka has written that, opening as it did just three years after New Labour's landslide election victory, *Billy Elliot*'s success was 'a consequence of a craving for cultural products that chimed with the feel-good escapism of Blairism': a working-class hero was someone who had transcended his own circumstances, rather than improved them for his community.[43] (The musical is more political by far than the film, in which Thatcher is barely mentioned. On the day she died, its West End audience were given the chance to decide whether the song 'Merry Christmas Maggie Thatcher' – the general gist of which is that Christmas is worth celebrating because it's one day nearer to the day of her death – would be performed. They voted 'overwhelmingly' for its inclusion.[44]) Another film scholar, David Alderson, writes that the film 'presents the transition to neoliberalism as one from a repressive and repressed "masculine" past to a more tolerant, expressive, cosmopolitan, and "feminine" present': he reads Billy's triumphant performance as the swan in Matthew Bourne's *Swan Lake* at the film's climax as a success 'on the terms of an emergent system the miners were struggling against'. In response to readings of the film as a feminist or liberatory triumph over patriarchal gender norms and a 'dysfunctional family', Alderson asks what a 'functional family' could possibly have looked like during the year-long strike.[45] In a song from the musical called 'Expressing Yourself' the gender and sexual politics of the story are presented as a truism about choice and freedom (love is love), as Billy and his schoolfriend Michael duet, instructing the audience that if you want to be a dancer, all you have to do is dance, and if you want to be a miner, all you have to do is mine, with a repeated refrain declaring breezily that it's all equally fine. Hard to be a dancer, however, without the money for your train fare to the audition. Hard to be a miner if the mine's been shut down. Fine.

Continuing, in some senses at least, *Billy Elliot*'s legacy, exactly thirty years after the strike began the film *Pride* was released to general acclaim. (Following *Billy Elliot*, a stage musical is currently in development.) Written by Stephen Beresford and directed by Matthew Warchus, it tells the story of Lesbians and Gays Support the Miners (LGSM), an initially London-based organization who decided to raise funds for the strikers. Rejected by national miners' organizations, they decided to present the funds directly to the Dulais Valley in South Wales, driving Hackney Community Transport minibuses 200 miles to present their donation of over ten thousand pounds to the community in person. The film, which, like *Billy Elliot*, I find impossible to watch without crying despite my aesthetic misgivings, depicts two persecuted communities finding common ground and practical solidarity in their common enemies: the newspapers, Margaret Thatcher, her government and the police.[46] After a wildly successful 'Pits and Perverts' fundraiser – the name reclaiming an insult from the *Sun* – the group bought the Dulais community a minibus decorated with a pink triangle and the LGSM slogan; in 1985, the London

Pride march was led by miners and their families, and the TUC passed significant resolutions on gay and lesbian workplace rights.[47] *Pride* makes a fair amount of slapstick hay out of the differences between its two central communities, but according to those it fictionalizes, its representation of the solidarity between them is accurate. Mike Jackson, co-founder of LGSM, recalled in 2014 that

> It would be dishonest to say there was no dissent. Years later, we found out there had been a meeting following my letter explaining a bunch of queers wanted to support them. It had led to a very heated discussion. But the consensus was: we have been demonised by the press, maybe we should meet the gay people because they've also been demonized.[48]

Members of Lesbians Against Pit Closures, meanwhile, noted that rather than the 'mixed or hostile reaction' their baby pink banner often received at rallies and demonstrations, 'we were widely applauded and made to feel welcome marching alongside the fighting men and women of the mining communities.'[49]

Such support enabled a mutual broadening of horizons in ways that resonate with firsthand accounts of involvement in WAPC. Siân Jones, another key character in the film and a key figure in the kitchens, eventually became a director of Welsh Women's Aid and subsequently the first female Labour MP for Swansea East. She describes the period as one that reawakened her desires:

> I'd married at sixteen. At twenty, I had two children and was happy as a housewife and young mother. As long as my lace curtains were the cleanest, my children immaculately dressed, their hand-knitted clothes made with love, I was happy. Then along came the strike and all the things I'd thought about before getting married – such as getting A-levels – returned.[50]

For some, this (re)awakening of desire was sexual. The influx of lesbians and gay men into a previously very – outwardly at least – heterosexual community represented the arrival of new possibilities for personal desire. In an interview commemorating the thirty-fifth anniversary of Thatcher's egging outside the 1984 Welsh Tory Party conference in Porthcawl, Jayne Francis-Headon, whose mother Hefina features in *Pride*, said 'Because of the impact the lesbians and gays of London had on me, I'm now married to a woman and I'm part of the LGBT community.' A shy teenager at the time of the strike – 'I didn't used to go out much, I used to go everywhere with my mam' – it opened up, she says, 'a different world'.[51]

Although journalists at the time preferred to refer to the 'politicization' of these wives and mothers, 'awakened' is a word that occurs again and again in reflections from those actually involved in WAPC: whatever politicization was occurring, it stemmed from something within, rather than an externally imposed agenda. Their campaigning visits to Northern Ireland – fundraising miners were stationed in Belfast for the duration of the strike – demonstrated the hostility the British state was capable of both 'at home' and abroad. Newly alive to the violence of colonialism, the WAPC women were also inspired to join cause with the uranium miners in Namibia being exploited by British Nuclear Fuels Limited, with the Pacific Islanders whose homes had been used in nuclear weapons tests, with Chilean exiles from Pinochet's regime and with the coalition of organizations campaigning for food justice in the developing world.[52] In the Midlands, Asian communities had been extremely generous in their support of the strike, having faced their own share of police brutality, and the mining community then responded in kind: when the largely Asian workforce at the Kewal Brothers factory in Smethwick began industrial action in 1984, over a hundred WAPC and NUM members joined them on their picket line.[53] Jane Davies and Shirley James, WAPC members from a village in Caerphilly, went to the Fête de l'Humanité in France and were so inspired by the support the French Communist Party gave the miners that they became committed activists in the CPGB. (Previously Labour voters, they were disappointed with their local MP, Neil Kinnock, who was so much a fence sitter that, in their words, 'It's a wonder he didn't have splinters.') In Fife, Cath Cunningham, Suzanne Corrigan and Margo Thorburn reflected that the experience of the strike had widened their own empathetic perspective, and encouraged them to extend friendship and help to those who were experiencing poverty: 'You don't realize till you're on strike just what it is to be unemployed or on a pension.'[54] In a 2014 interview, Scargill and Cook compared both the experience of the community pulling together and its long lasting effects to that of the Second World War: 'It brought a community together in a way they hadn't been together since the war, and it was a war. And we were fighting it along with the men.'[55]

Despite this wartime service, ultimately the women who had been so central to the strike were forced to expand their perspective beyond the industrial action itself: even after everything they had done, the NUM in England and Wales refused to allow them to become associate members (Scotland did). But the dispute had demonstrated that they had qualities that they had not previously believed themselves to have, and that another way of living was possible: the personal was political, and the political was profoundly, physically, personal. Although most WAPC members did not – and many still would not – describe themselves as feminists, one of the strongest alliances that came from the strike was with Greenham Common Women's Peace Camp in Berkshire, which is one of the subjects of the next chapter of this book. Active for nineteen years, the camp originated as a protest against the nuclear cruise missiles placed at the RAF base at the Common, started by a Welsh group called 'Women for Life on Earth' who marched from Cardiff to Greenham in 1981, and became an alternative community for the women and children who lived – some of whom were even born – there. Many WAPC members had visited before the strike had begun: nuclear power was a natural bridge between the interests of miners and the interests of Greenham women, and they formed an organization, Links, that formalized this common ground.

There was initial dissent at Greenham about supporting the strike: although some of the first marchers had come from Welsh mining communities and were on board from the start, others were sceptical of the unecological nature of mining and the issue of joining forces with men (Greenham became women-only in 1982). By the middle of 1984, however, coaches were running from Greenham to pickets in Wales and Nottinghamshire, camp-dwellers spoke at the NUM Scottish Area gala in Edinburgh, and they had produced a badge that declared 'At Greenham or on the picket line'. WAPC members, in turn, frequented the camp, where there were a lot of useful skills to be shared: the Greenham women were experts in dealing with police violence and the threat of arrest, and they knew how to keep out the cold. (Both communities were also extensively targeted by undercover police officers, or spycops, from the London Metropolitan Police.[56]) Mining women found themselves useful at Greenham in surprising ways. Anne Scargill recalls,

> We used to take our own bacon, lard and frying pan to Greenham. A lot of the women had decided to be vegetarian so they turned their nose up at us at first. Then there would be this smell of bacon frying and we'd see women coming out of the woods like fugitives creeping about. 'Will you make me a bacon sandwich Anne, but don't tell the others please.' They were all at it. We ended up like the Salvation Army, frying bacon and handing it out.[57]

Not by Bread Alone

When I began researching the WAPC in earnest, I knew that involvement in it had offered a space for self-expression and creative flourishing that was – unlike that depicted in *Billy Elliot* – directly related to political action, rather than some kind of transcendence of it. In a neat coincidence, one particularly collective iteration of this occurred in Easington, although this time it was the real place that inspired the work, rather than the fictionalized Everington. In 1984, the writer Margaret Pine and the director Nobby Dimon were employed by Durham Theatre Company, an Arts Council-funded touring company based in Darlington, to work on 'a play about women in the 1984–5 miners' strike', which was to be workshopped and performed by people from the Easington district. (The initial idea came from the Artists' Agency in Sunderland, which placed professional artistic practitioners in community projects.) Called *Not by Bread Alone*, it explored, as its programme explained, the strike and its antecedents through a focus on one particular support kitchen. As research for the project, Pine moved to Easington, living with a retired miner and his wife, interviewed families, met with union officials, and picketed: most importantly, however, she worked in the kitchen. The production toured the country, a first for almost all involved: although there was a tradition of political touring theatre in the UK and of residential drama weekends funded by the NCB in coalfield communities, the programme states that 'Only two of the group had any previous experience of acting, let alone of mounting a touring production'; this was a step up.[58]

It is very difficult to find a copy of *Not by Bread Alone*. Once I knew of its existence, I became obsessed, not least because I was teaching at Durham University at the time, an affluent and frequently exclusionary institution that often sits at odds with its surroundings. While I was looking for it, I first found a film by the same title, directed by Ian Krause, which documents the twelve months that followed Pine's arrival in Easington. Interviews and rehearsals are interspersed with footage of the women smoking and talking, of Arthur Scargill thanking WAPC from a podium, of Pine working alongside women peeling potatoes and washing dishes, of the women's banner on pickets and marches. In an interview, Pine declares that the support group has become a political organization in its own right: 'It isn't just preparing a meal each day, they have seen the link between that activity and all the political aspects of the strike.' The women themselves talk frequently about their own political awakenings, characterizing the process as one of realization:

One of the lasses was saying 'Well, I don't know anything about politics.' And one of the things I did say was, 'Well, if they were making six teachers at your child's school redundant, meaning your child was going to be in a class of fifty, would you not go down to the school or to the local authority and complain?' and she said 'Yes, I would,' and I said 'Well that's politics. You're getting yourself involved in politics.'[59]

When I finally tracked down a copy of the script it was in the archives at Beamish, the 'Living Museum of the North', where you can visit, should you wish to, a 1900s pit village, a 1950s town, and participate in a traditional carriage-driving contest. Sitting in an uncomfortable chair next to a large pantomime-costume pig's head, several discarded Singer sewing machines and some threadbare bunting in red, white and blue, I soon saw that the play itself was centred around maternity, both conceptually and practically. Threaded throughout it is the motif of a pregnant Victorian pitwoman, running from police, who describe the foetus in her belly as 'Another little bastard for the workhouse!' before pursuing her offstage.[60] A little later, this 'nineteenth-century union woman' tells the audience about her own maternal lineage, writ as it is in coal:

My mother was born down a pit. My grandmother brought her up, found the light too much and disappeared, leaving the child. She took with her bread, water, and would you believe it, the poems of William Blake. She had to sell my mother's milk to make her way south. There were occasional reports of her labouring for radical groups – then – silence. Now she exists only in my mind and, if you choose, in yours.[61]

The image of her grandmother selling her breast milk to survive makes clear not only her desperate circumstances but the erosion of her maternal identity as she leaves her community and makes her way further south: with no possibility of return she has to leave that behind, too.

Not by Bread Alone combines a naturalistic representation of the day-to-day organization of the kitchens – the logistics of sharing kitchen utensils – and the interpersonal conflicts that reared their heads – marriages feeling the strain, resentment towards those who remain well-off enough to get their hair done – with more experimental interludes. As well as the Victorian pitwoman, we meet Beddoes, Whitaker and Carstairs, representatives of the Coal Board past, conducting an investigation into the lives of pitwomen and children: they meet a Mrs Wilson, whose daughter has 'born four but only one has lived':

[*She takes a small piece of wood and nails it down on the cradle, transferring it into a little coffin. She picks up the coffin, curtseys to the commissioners, and exits.*]

Although they never adopt such terminology, as the play progresses the contemporary characters find that the kitchen has become a space akin to that of feminist consciousness-raising groups. At the beginning, as they're introduced one by one, many credit their involvement in the WAPC simply with practical desires for their own families: Sandra Hughes, says, 'What would I want with revolution! I want my own house. Peter and me don't follow politics much. Just want our bairns to do well, especially our Philip.'[62] As the strike progresses, we see them begin to recognize every aspect of their life as political: they discuss their deepening strength of feeling, learn what to do if they get arrested, and learn that the police and the government are actively working against them. Rage becomes a defining feature: one member, Joan, says to the group after a particularly difficult confrontation that she's 'frightened, lasses. I'm beginning to hate.'[63] Later, she says, 'Sometimes I wonder if I'm in me anymore. I'm sorry.'[64] The most distressing conflict in the play happens within the group itself. Maureen, a character we've grown to know and like, reveals, distraught, that her husband, Clive, is going to scab. The committee – her other family – do not respond with empathy and there is a bitter argument. Eventually, though, they welcome her back, but soon the situation becomes a tragic one: after returning to work – socially alienated and wracked with guilt – Clive dies by suicide.

This death remains present throughout the rest of the play, even as it ends with new life – that reliable symbol of futurity and hope – when Ann, one of the committee's youngest members, gives birth. The pregnancy, which was announced as 'Another for the revolution', is knitted into the story of the strike itself: the audience hears the news of the birth from Sandra, who recounts that Ann was 'bouncing around as usual on the picket line Friday dinner time and had the baby Friday night. She makes you proud to be a woman.' The baby itself becomes collective property: the women march into the maternity ward, 'demanding to see "our baby" or else'. The multiply mothered infant is later brought onstage, as the group present her with some things to commemorate the strike, which has just ended. 'Out there,' Joan elaborates, 'they'll say this is a defeat', but really 'it's for history to say . . . that depends on who's telling the story.' They come forward one by one and ceremonially place the items they've chosen around the carrycot:

SHEILA: We've got letters of support from all over, Wales, London, the Continent.
LESLEY: And photos, pamphlets, everything we've collected during the strike.
JOAN: In particular, these smashing letters from Ethel, our anonymous pensioner.
EDNA: Here's a list of our menus and the numbers fed.
MAUREEN: And the accounts, showing how we raised the money.
TED: I offer the union rule book.
ANN: Ted! She'll need a degree in law to understand it!
SANDRA: I'd like her to have copies of my diaries.
MAISIE: A piece of coal and what the best dressed pickets are wearing.
[*She offers her cap covered in badges.*]
Mind, these are from all over the country.
ANN: Thanks Maisie.
MARY: Our poems and stories. All of us here – all our feelings.

MAUREEN: A copy of a personal letter.

ANN: Oh Maureen!

LIZ: And just in case we're all getting a bit sentimental, here's
    something practical – a breadknife for when the next strike
    comes!

ANN: Eee thanks lasses.

[*She cuddles the child.*]

How about all this then. My baby.

LIZ: What do you mean, your baby. She's *our* baby. [65]

Easington WAPC deposit history into the baby, knowing as they do
that this is a gesture of defiance: the strike has failed, and they know
how high the stakes were. The baby, her life stretching away into the
future, unknowable and unknown, is the living proof, in this
moment, of the communal existence they have shared and their
sentimental practicalities: the breadknife next to the collection of
poems. The personal letter given to the baby by Maureen is Clive's
suicide note: the baby cannot only know, her gesture says, of the
strike's metaphorical losses. Maureen's last gift, however, is a practical one: an offer of babysitting, if Lesley ever does get round to
doing that college course she's been talking about.

Ann's baby – or rather, I should say, Easington WAPC's baby –
would be almost forty now. The strike has not faded from cultural
memory and will perhaps always remain a favoured setting for a
certain kind of sentimental British film, but some of its legacies are
less celebrated than others. Although some kitchens closed immediately after the strike, others were transformed into community
spaces. In Easington, the WAPC evolved into the Easington Unemployment Committee, campaigning against local bank and hospital
closures. In Cortonwood in south Yorkshire, the site of the sponta-
neous walk-out where the strike began, the kitchen became the
Cortonwood Comeback Community Centre, a space which tries to
mitigate the brutality of council cuts, dispenses benefits advice and
provides a place for people to gather. These bright spots, although
brilliant, are not enough: in Maerdy, in the Rhondda Valley, a local

campaign to reopen the library cannot disguise the complete and total neglect of the place by the government, with its unemployment rate sitting at almost double the Welsh and British average.[66] Many of the sites where community kitchens once stood are now, as Dawn Foster wrote in 2014, central to local fights against austerity:

> A lot of the women around the country fighting government cuts now are working-class women who were involved in WAPC or remember their mother's involvement, and are again galvanized by cuts directly affecting them and their community. The strike remains in the collective memory of the areas most affected by austerity, and the sense of history repeating itself as the government continues to cut benefits to the poorest in society is often voiced in local anti-cuts meetings.

Like the women recorded in the documents of 84–5, like the Victorian pitwoman running across the stage, Foster figures this as a maternal lineage: 'it's noticeable in what's been passed down, from generation to generation. Women involved say their children and grandchildren are more politically active', having learned stories of resistance at their mother's knee.[67]

If women's work is the work of continuance, it is also the work of memorialization. As well as the writings that emerged from WAPC kitchens and pickets, and more recent works like Maxine Peake's play *Queens of the Coal Age*, there are also more personal elegiac labours. Over the past decade, many obituaries to members of WAPC groups have appeared in local newspapers, all of them detailing extraordinary ordinary lives lived with political commitment, compassion and joy, often encompassing further union work, anti-apartheid activism and anti-nuclear campaigning.[68] In their own way, they weave the history of this definitional, defeated struggle into the landscape of the country itself. At the end of Scargill and Cook's joint memoir, *Anne & Betty: United by the Struggle*, Scargill describes what she did after ending up the custodian of Dougie

Stables' ashes, a Barnsley man and WAPC ally who had been the secretary of the Swaithe Working Men's Club for forty years:

> At the time of his death they were building a memorial to the industrial heritage of Worsborough on the road to Sheffield, near the Red Lion pub. I wrote to the council and asked if I could bury Dougie's ashes under it. The council turned me down. The night before they laid the concrete, a good friend of mine helped me to dig a hole. I fetched the ashes and placed them into the hole with a message saying 'Douglas Stables. He did a lot of work and should be recognised.' Then we filled it back over. The next day the council workers came and put the concrete down and not long after that erected their monument. I always think of Dougie when I go past.[69]

In this quietly defiant act of remembrance, she adds a footnote to the official structures of commemoration. Rebelliously, she tends to history, tries to carry something of the past into the future.

8.

Mother Earth and Mother Courage

Men are not each exploited in the same way.

Roland Barthes, 'Seven Photo Models of "Mother Courage"'

Mother is a powerful metaphor. I mean this both in the sense that the word itself has a rich and varied history of this kind of use, and that very often its metaphorical employment has explicitly to do with power: mother country, motherland, mother earth. Within these metaphors is a kind of violence. It is a primary insight of psychoanalysis that hatred is as inherent to maternity as love – D. W. Winnicott, in 'Hate in the Counter-transference', lists eighteen reasons a mother 'hates' her baby 'from the word go' – but the metaphorical violence attributed to mothers exceeds this recognizable feeling: the counterpoint to the canonized image of the virtuous mother is the monstrous one (think of Euripides' Medea sacrificing her children, Shakespeare's Volumnia withholding nourishment from Coriolanus, the camp horror-show incarnation of Joan Crawford in *Mommie Dearest* . . .).[1] This canon is generally one of private violence: traumas inflicted on children by their mothers. In this chapter, however, I am going to pay attention to the way the image of the maternal is used to instigate, encourage and legitimize violence of a more public kind. In the 1980s, this question took on a particular force, with matron-nanny-mummy Margaret Thatcher at the country's helm, and waging war in – most visibly, anyway – Ireland and the South Atlantic, while other women were tying children's toys to the wire perimeter fence at Greenham Common.

When it comes to representations of war, the image of a mother that comes most immediately to mind is that of the grieving woman left behind, her sons taken from her for some larger purpose (usually, making money for other people by killing somebody else's sons). This obscures the fact that women, historically, have been essential components in the wider machinery of war both at the level of domestic propaganda – even the suffragettes handed out white feathers – and in active decision-making. Remember the band Crass, threatened with legal action for their anti-Falklands war song 'How Does It Feel (To Be the Mother of 1000 Dead)?', which not only attributes the losses of the conflict entirely to Thatcher but charges her with using their 'corpses as moral blackmail': 'You accuse us of disrespect for the dead,' they sing,

> But it was you who slaughtered out of national pride.
> Just how much did you care? What respect did you have
> As you sent those bodies to their communal grave?[2]

One of the most enduring cultural representations of a kind of maternity complicit in, rather than victimized by, warfare comes from the German dramatist Bertolt Brecht's 1939 *Mother Courage and Her Children*. The play is often heralded as one of the greatest of the twentieth century, although its first performance was felt by Brecht himself to be severely belated, failing as it did to premiere before the Second World War began in earnest. Set during the Thirty Years' War, which wrought destruction across the Holy Roman Empire in the seventeenth century, it stages the travails of the eponymous mother, Anna Fierling, and her children Eilif, Swiss Cheese and Kattrin, as they follow the increasingly bedraggled armies with their cart, eking out a living selling provisions to soldiers. By the end of the play, all three children are dead, and Courage pulls her cart on alone, singing the same song she did at the beginning:

> The new year's come. The watchmen shout.
> The thaw sets in. The dead remain.

Wherever life has not died out.

It staggers to its feet again.[3]

Brecht is perhaps most famous for his use of *Verfremdungseffekt*, often translated as defamiliarization or estrangement, which employed a variety of techniques to emphasize, rather than dispel, the artifice of theatrical performance: he wanted to dissolve the complacency of catharsis, to startle with direct address. Roland Barthes, in his essay 'Seven Photo Models of "Mother Courage"', writes that this distancing is in the service of one of the 'essential meanings' of Brechtian theatre, which is that 'men are not each exploited in the same way': it is not individual feelings, actions and circumstances that signify but rather the 'political relationship of situations' to each other.[4]

When it comes to the specifics of exploitation, for Barthes Mother Courage is 'doubly alienated: as the exploited and as the exploiter'. She exploits those to whom she sells her extortionate wares, but she is still 'no more than a plaything' in the war waged by her social superiors: 'she is culpable and she is wronged.'[5] The war devours her children, yet she continues to follow its armies. Swiss Cheese is captured and shot, and Courage tries to haggle for his release, barters for too long, and then has to disown his body ('Chuck him in the pit').[6] Eilif is executed for looting, the same act he was previously awarded military honours for (he was forcibly enlisted while Courage was busy making the sale of a belt buckle). Finally, Kattrin, who loves children but, in her mother's estimation, will never have them, being mute and facially scarred, sacrifices herself to save a settlement of families, drumming frantically to alert them to an oncoming danger until she is permanently silenced by a military bullet. There is a brutal cyclical logic at play here: as the Recruitment Sergeant reminds Courage, mockingly, in Act One, 'like the war to nourish you ? / have to feed it something too'. *Mother Courage* is very moving, full of the absolute cruel pathos of circumstance. I feel it the most acutely in the death of Kattrin: in her drumming, in her unfulfilled desires, in the way Courage cradles her as she lies on the ground, singing 'Eia popeia' ('Lullaby baby'). It's not true that there are no displays of maternal feeling in the play: Courage sings Kattrin to sleep, she protects her from unkind comments, and she tries to save Swiss Cheese's life when he is captured. What there isn't, however, is maternal sacrifice. Barthes again: 'To be sure, there is a profound motherliness in Mother Courage. But this motherliness can never be dissociated from the regular running of a business.'[7] He thinks that her cart 'is like one of her children'; I think it exceeds them, and demands more loyalty, precisely because of its ability to sustain without depending.

Brecht believed that audiences and critics alike misunderstood *Mother Courage* when it was eventually performed in Switzerland in 1941. He altered the text in an attempt to make Courage less sympathetic but still the audience had too much sympathy for her and did not take her active participation in the war seriously.[8] Such misinterpretation has continued: Courage is often praised for her vitality, her status as that perennially appealing thing, a 'strong woman'. In 1976, the German leftist-feminist newspaper *Courage* was founded by ten women from the West Berlin Women's Centre in Kreuzberg, named after a character they believed to be a 'self-directed woman . . . not a starry-eyed idealist but neither is she satisfied with the status quo'. In 1991, the women's rights organization MADRE went on a 'Mother Courage Peace Tour'.[9] Whenever a new production is staged – often starring a renowned actor in her middle years and described as 'the female Lear' – the coverage and the dramaturgy is related to its political circumstance. Fiona Shaw, talking about her role in a 2009 National Theatre production of Tony Kushner's translation, declared that 'The political situation in Iraq and Afghanistan absolutely informs the decision to stage the play now. Its speeches – about forcing liberty on other countries, for instance – are so pertinent, sometimes I just want to insert the name George Bush.'[10] (Where? None of the characters in the play work as Bush substitutes. And by this logic, wouldn't Courage work for an arms dealer?)

The 2009 production, which was directed by Deborah Warner,

opened with Shaw riding in a battle helmet atop her wagon, an image that reminded contemporary reviewers and reminds me now of the famous image of Margaret Thatcher riding a British tank in Fallingbostel, West Germany, during an official 1986 forces visit, albeit with a more steampunk aesthetic than Thatcher's headscarf and pearls. Peter Thomson, in his 1997 monograph on the play, writes that

> I received a postcard some years ago, one of those satirical photo-montage images in which the then Mrs Thatcher had taken Helene Weigel's place between the shafts of Mother Courage's wagon. It was the play's final tableau, and the card asked where Mrs Thatcher was dragging the wagon from, and where to. A production which cast Lady Thatcher as Mother Courage would provide a nice exercise in dialectics.[11]

But Thatcher, like Bush, is not Courage: she is offstage making decisions while other mothers struggle to survive, are corrupted by their circumstances, and receive no bodies to bury.[12] She was not following armies, but leading them: on the day of the 1983 General Election, the front page of the *Sun* featured a large mock-up of Thatcher as Britannia, replete with a trident, a Union Jack-emblazoned shield and a lion, headlined 'She is carrying the banner for ordinary people.'[13] Part of the persistent misreading of *Mother Courage* that so bothered Brecht himself is rooted in the desire to understand maternity as the opposite of violence, and the fantasy that warfare is a solely masculine pursuit. This ignores the sorry mess of history.

It was difficult to hold on to that notion in the 1980s, with a mother in Downing Street inflicting violence at every level of her policy. In an article published in 1988 called 'Margaret Thatcher and Ruth Ellis', Jacqueline Rose constructs a psychoanalytic analysis of the relationship between Thatcher and violence. (Ruth Ellis was the last woman to be hanged in the UK, in 1955; Thatcher was a keen advocate for bringing back the death penalty.) Contemplating her approaching third term in office, Rose observes that Thatcher is 'especially difficult for feminism because she is a woman, one who embodies some of the worst properties of what feminism has defined as a patriarchal society and state'.[14] Reading her housewifely performance and her embrace of the symbolically phallic 'Iron Lady' moniker as the lynchpins of a deliberately ambiguous positioning in relation to gender, Rose argues that Thatcher posed a challenge to a feminism that had previously gendered the violence of the state as male: in short, 'the fact that Thatcher is a woman is allowing her to get away with murder.'[15]

Her command of state violence was central to the image Thatcher projected of herself as someone unafraid to make difficult decisions: she allowed a vote on capital punishment in 1983 and was firmly in favour of corporal punishment in schools; in 1961 she voted, against her party, to reinstate birching. Stuart Hall credits her with placing an actively authoritarian 'social gospel' at the centre of government, depending upon a cycle of moral panics that push society sharply towards the right, to a 'law-and-order state', capable of acting swiftly and brutally against an enemy that 'is lurking *everywhere*'.[16] On the international stage, she was personally and politically aligned with Ronald Reagan during the Cold War, a staunch supporter and friend of the Chilean dictator Augusto Pinochet and obstructed international efforts to sanction apartheid South Africa (she was a friend of the Prime Minister P. W. Botha, and famously denounced Mandela and the African National Congress as 'terrorists'). Her stance on the conflict in Northern Ireland was profoundly aggressive: although she surprised many, and attracted the ire of unionists, by signing the 1985 Anglo-Irish agreement which granted the Irish government an advisory role in the governing of the six counties, her premiership's policy towards the north in general, as the next chapter will discuss, was to escalate the British presence and authorize collusion between the security services and loyalist paramilitary groups. Thatcher's foreign and domestic policy – as the convergence of the conflict in Northern Ireland could be said to represent – used any isolated instance of violence directed towards British people or institutions to legitimize an escalation of the violence that the state itself controlled and enacted. This found its most symbolic outlet in the Falklands War, which presented her with an opportunity like no other to demonstrate how far she would go in defence of 'British values'.

Iron Ladies Love Milk Tray

The Iron Lady was initially an unflattering sobriquet invented by a Soviet journalist. Thatcher repurposed it, as Marina Warner details in *Monuments and Maidens*, around the time of the Falklands War: 'I have the reputation as the Iron Lady. I am of great resolve. That resolve is matched by the British people.'[17] The Falkland Islands and their territorial dependency, South Georgia and the South Sandwich Islands, have been inhabited by said British people since the beginning of the nineteenth century. A living relic of colonialism, their residents are mostly descended from British settlers; so are the sheep. Since 1841, the islands have been embroiled in a protracted sovereignty dispute between Britain and Argentina, the islands' closest neighbour. In early April 1982, Argentina – then a military junta led by Leopoldo Galtieri – occupied the Falklands, invading South Georgia the next day. Three days later, the British government dispatched a naval task force to the territory. The conflict lasted for two and a half months, until Galtieri's forces surrendered: 649 Argentinian soldiers, 255 British soldiers and three Islanders died. A total of 777 British combatants were injured, with almost one hundred 'maimed for life', something belied by Thatcher's triumphal attitude towards the conflict.[18] Although war was never officially declared by either nation, this was a significant international event: Reagan, whose government had previously funded the Argentinian junta as a bulwark against communism ceased to co-operate with Galtieri, and the UN Security Council called for a withdrawal of Argentinian troops from the territory.

Conflict in the Falklands was very good for Thatcher. It allowed her to distract from domestic dissatisfaction with a re-enactment of Britain's 'finest hour': leadership in wartime and the aggressive defence of a waning empire. In defiance of advisers who cautioned against dispatching military personnel 8,000 miles away to defend a territory that was neither particularly politically important nor highly populated, Thatcher saw an opportunity. She described her motivation in grandiose terms in the second part of her autobiography, *The Downing Street Years*: 'what was the alternative? That a common or garden dictator should rule over the queen's subjects and prevail by fraud and violence? Not while I was Prime Minister.'[19] In interviews she presented the conflict as a national crusade, telling ITN that 'We must recover the Falkland Islands for Britain and for the people who live there who are of British stock.' (The journalist Max Hastings, interviewed in 2022 for a Channel Four documentary that revealed catastrophic military mismanagement, said that the conflict showed that, although Britain could no longer compete with international manufacturing of cars and household goods, it could still win in a 'jolly old colonial conflict'.[20]) Thatcher deliberately invited comparisons to Elizabeth I and Queen Victoria, whom she frequently quoted: ' "Failure?" Queen Victoria once said, "The possibility does not exist." That is the way we must look at it. We must go out calmly, quietly, to succeed.'[21] And succeed she did, on her own terms: amid accusations from the Labour Party of 'glorying in slaughter', 1983 saw the most decisive victory in a British election since 1945. A *TV Eye* poll a week before the election asked if the 'Falklands Factor' was helping Thatcher's election campaign: 44 per cent of respondents said it definitely was. She polled particularly well with women voters; a few days before polling day, the *News of the World* declared 'The Mums back Maggie.'[22]

Unlike the women's peace movement, which understood warfare as inherently masculine – a popular song at Greenham Common was 'Take the Toys from the Boys' – Thatcher positioned herself as an aggressive matriarch, a protective commander: not warmongering but simply doing what was necessary. The progenitor of 'our boys', her femininity generated and authorized violence, emphasizing even more the pageantry of her gender performance: as the conflict ran on, she invited guests back to Downing Street after the Trooping of the Colour, where she had prepared a meal for a dozen children and their families. In the 2013 documentary *Maggie and Me*, following footage of her in fatigues, flirting with troops, trying on ear protectors over a headscarf and firing an automatic weapon, Major General Julian Thompson recalls being asked to organize a military display in her honour. He decided that 'The first chap up over the side of the ship, dressed in his sort of ninja suit, was to give the prime minister a box of Milk Tray', in reference to the popular advert in which a suave James Bond character defeats many obstacles to deliver a box of chocolates to a woman's pillow. 'All because,' read the tagline, 'the lady loves Milk Tray.' Thatcher loved it, and why wouldn't she? Despite being the orchestrator of their comrades' loss of life and limb, she was canonized and fetishized by the military.

Representations of the Falklands War in popular culture delight in emphasizing Thatcher's femininity – her confusingly glamorous dowdiness – as both antithetical and foundational to her battle-ready spirit. In the terrible 2011 film *The Iron Lady*, directed by Phyllida Lloyd, there is an exceptionally twee set-piece in which Thatcher (Meryl Streep) declares to a sceptical US Ambassador that 'Many men have underestimated me before. This lot seem bound to do the same.' Dramatic music swells, until, abruptly, she holds up a teapot, her tone matter of fact: 'Now, shall I be mother?' In season four of the popular British television show *The Crown*, created by Peter Morgan, the timeline of the war is shifted, placing it immediately after the six-day-period in which her son Mark had gone missing in the Algerian desert during an attempt to complete the Paris–Dakar rally. Thatcher, played by Gillian Anderson, tells the bank of reporters' on-camera cameras that, although they are used to thinking of her as 'PM', above all else 'I am a mother.' Journalists and historians alike frequently speak of the that difficulty dispatching troops posed for Thatcher 'as a woman' and 'as a mother', and *The*

Crown likewise sets up an equivalence between Thatcher and other concerned mothers, and between Mark and other endangered sons: the fact that he was a child of immense privilege participating in a rally for fun is left out of the picture.[23] Rather than spend any time on these ordinary lives, however, *The Crown* prefers to centre the Queen's maternal problems. Taken aback by Thatcher's assertion that Mark is her favourite child, the hapless monarch spends the rest of the episode meeting her progeny one-on-one to ask them painfully stilted questions about their lives. We learn that Andrew is her favourite: arriving by helicopter for their meeting, we are encouraged to remember that he is about to distinguish himself – in his family's terms – by serving in the Falklands. It's difficult to forget, from the vantage point of 2023, the other violence inflicted by these two mummy's boys: Mark Thatcher was to go on to fund a coup in Equatorial Guinea, and Prince Andrew to step back from his duties after his association with the convicted sex trafficker Jeffrey Epstein became impossible for even the Royal Family to ignore.

It is not just sons who are involved in these strange wartime acts of maternal historicization. In 2007, Carol Thatcher – allegedly the least favourite child – travelled to the Falklands to make a documentary called, and I wish I was joking, *Mummy's War*, capitalizing on her success on the reality television show *I'm a Celebrity . . . Get Me Out of Here*. (This was not her first journey in her mother's footsteps. Once a journalist, in 1983 she published her *Diary of an Election*, a breathless account of the campaign trail, dogged by pesky CND demonstrators and 'irrelevant' questions about unemployment, in which she characterizes her mother as 'resolution in power heels' and a 'loner' who never sleeps, nor, it seems, has much time for her daughter. Daddy Denis is mostly golfing in Kent.[24]) In *Mummy's War*, which is full of ruminations on the 'unmistakeable British character' and 'British stock' of the islands, Carol reminisces about what she saw of her mother during the conflict (basically nothing, it turns out), and jollies around the island talking a fair amount of nostalgic nonsense. On her way home, she visits Buenos Aires – she is met by protestors with signs reading THATCHER GO

HOME – and meets a group of bereaved mothers whose sons died on the *General Belgrano*, the Argentinian boat controversially sunk by a British submarine outside the mutually agreed exclusion zone. They tell Carol in no uncertain terms that her mother killed their sons, that their most fervent hope is that God will punish her for it, and they speak of the pain of grieving without a body. Carol refuses to apologize: Mummy, she tells them, was right to do it.[25]

Very Sane and Very Angry

Critiques of the conflict grapple with the contrast between Thatcher's emphasis on her own maternal identity and the actual experiences of bereaved mothers and wives. The most successful of these embrace the Prime Minister's larger-than-life performance, focusing on her artificiality, her monstrousness. Raymond Briggs, best known for the beloved Christmas tale *The Snowman*, published a picture book in 1984 called *The Tin-Pot Foreign General and the Iron Old Woman*. 'Far away over the sea' from the 'sad little island' that the Tin-Pot Foreign General desires, 'there lived an old woman with lots of money and guns. Like the Tin-Pot Foreign General, she was not real, either. She was made of Iron.' Above these words is a garish illustration of the gigantic iron woman's naked body, baring her silver buttocks to the viewer in a pastiche of a seductive pose, surrounded by phallic stacks of coins and missiles. A few pages later, as she 'flies into a rage', we see her front-on, cannons firing from her breasts, breasts we next see being removed to reveal hordes of treasure as she says, grinning, 'It's so exciting to have a real crisis!'[26] The second half of the book dramatically deviates from its previous grotesque, colourful style: in place of the caricatures are monochromatic line drawings of the dead and the maimed: 'Some men,' Briggs tells us, 'were shot'; 'some men were drowned'; 'some men were burned alive'; 'some men were blown to bits'; 'some men were only half blown to bits and came home with parts of their bodies missing.' After this interlude, the coloured illustrations return, sharing space with these muted memorials: the victory parade is in blazing colour, bedecked in Union Jacks, while the injured – who were initially banned from participating in the real parade by the London Lord Mayor for fear they would sour the mood – watch on TV. The final image is of three people gathered around a headstone above the closing line, 'And the families of the dead tended the graves.'[27]

This is not the stereotypical image of a family bereaved by conflict. Rather than a young widowed mother and two children, there are two adults and one child in the image: the figure in the centre with its bent back and white hair appears elderly, while the crouching woman to the left is of indeterminate age. The average age of the soldiers dispatched to the Falklands was nineteen, and teenagers made up 50 per cent of those who died there. With nothing ahead of them at home except dole queues, young working-class men armed forces recruitment relied, as ever, on to swell its ranks. In Jean Carr's 1984 book *Another Story: Women and the Falklands War*, the widow Lynda Gallagher, newly pregnant with her third child at the time of the conflict, recounts how her husband Lawrence had joined the army at fifteen instead of going down the pit in the Yorkshire village he came from. The actual experience of bereaved wives and mothers across the country was swallowed up into a general sense of noble sacrifice: something regrettable but necessary, a loss in the service of the greater good. Many felt themselves to be isolated and forgotten, and the perceived pointlessness of the war which wasn't a war exacerbated their grief. Caroline Hailwood told Carr that she had thought that if her husband ever died in a conflict it would be 'The Big One, all or nothing'. Her husband, Christopher, had been planning to leave his job at the Ministry of Defence to spend more time with their baby son, Jim: 'He loved his work but after those twelve weeks at home with our new baby he did not think he could cope with being separated from Jim for months on end. We were very lucky to have that time together as a family, it was bliss.'[28] Both Caroline and Christopher were in their mid-twenties.

In a review of *Another Story* in the *London Review of Books*, Diana

Gould writes that, as well as those interviewed, 'another woman, also a wife and mother, looms large, the Prime Minister, Margaret Thatcher.' Thatcher had 'given the Falkland Islanders something denied to all other British citizens. This is the right to follow their way of life *in situ*, no matter what the cost in money or wasted young lives. This right has been denied to the miners, for example, who have seen whole communities destroyed.'[29] For Gould, this stages a battle between two kinds of motherhood: 'the maternal, caring, compassionate and, therefore, peace-orientated instincts of women' that prevent them from becoming leaders in the first place, and the 'ironized' version exhibited by Thatcher, in which compromise is recast as 'womanly weakness'.[30] Indeed, throughout Carr's book, women – many committed Conservative voters – express their astonishment that Thatcher was not listening to their appeals *as a mother*. Theresa Burt, whose teenage son Jason died, began campaigning for the return of his body. She wrote to Thatcher, detailing that she had seen her crying on television when Mark was lost in the desert: 'So surely she would understand why I wanted my son's body brought home. I got a formal acknowledgement saying the matter was being considered.'[31] (Until the Falklands, the general expectation was that the bodies of soldiers who died in combat would be buried where they fell.)

Those at home had to piece together information about their loved ones from rumours and press coverage, both of which were often inaccurate. The government and military provided inadequate support and communication to families: relatives of the twenty men who died on the *HMS Sheffield*, for example, heard of its sinking from a news bulletin. The families of the injured had to constantly chase information about the severity of injuries and the prognosis, without which they were unable to prepare for their return. Lynda Gallagher observed, 'It was only after nineteen SAS men had died in a helicopter crash that weekly information sessions for families were held at their Hereford base'; some wives were told mistakenly that their dead husbands had survived. Gallagher also spoke of the toll grief took on her pregnancy: she 'tried to keep from the doctor' the fact that she had lost a stone and a half and was smoking forty cigarettes a day. Jane Keoghane, who was also pregnant, describes the agonizing wait to discover whether or not her husband had died: she later found out that he had been taken off the military payroll the day after his ship was bombed, four days before she was told he was presumed dead. Her father-in-law, who was a member of the same regiment, the Welsh Guards, was informed an hour before her, as a military courtesy. A regimental representative was supposed to come and explain the financial arrangements – 'I was not the only widow expecting a baby' – but nobody ever did.[32] Pregnant wives received half the money those with children did, and there are many reports of benefits being delayed or cleared for the wrong amount, causing serious anxiety. The families of bachelors, meanwhile, lobbied for their lives to be properly valued: in the absence of other forms of memorial and acknowledgement, the lower financial settlement allotted to single men was insulting. The medically discharged received painfully little. A South Atlantic Fund was set up and badly distributed and administered; public charity was relied upon to compensate for the losses of a war orchestrated by the government.

Military communities are, generally speaking, socially conservative, based as they are around strict regulations and hierarchies. The heterosexual family is both of the utmost importance and continually subjugated to the homosocial 'family' of the military unit itself: 'The Commanding Officer is the father and his wife is mum.' Within the aggressively conventional theory of life in a barracks community, however, is the fundamental flexibility of the family unit in practice: they become, at regular intervals and for long stretches of time, single-parent (single-mother) families living communally. In 1982, Pirbright Barracks in Surrey, the home of the 1st Battalion of the Welsh Guards, was, in Carr's words, 'a community left almost devoid of men': 'A few of the soldiers' wives with children at local schools and jobs of their own moved in with neighbours to keep each other company and share the child-minding and household bills.' June Evans, who lived in Landrake in Cornwall, recalls that after her husband Andy died the community rallied round her at once: 'It must have looked a bit like a scene from a Greek tragedy, a room full of women who just came and sat with me for hours until my relatives arrived.'[33] Many of those left behind shared premonitions and bad dreams that felt like prophecies of deaths that later came. They could do this communal worry work with others who understood it and were also performing it, and distribute childcare and emotional support among whoever could handle the most at that particular moment. These ad-hoc communities, however, were blips. Once the war was over and the men came back, those who had lost their husbands had also lost their anchor to the military community: no matter how long they had spent there, no matter how close their friendships, they had to leave. Widows, like the mothers of servicemen who died very young, had no ongoing connection to the organization that had given them a home and had taken so much from them.

Memorialization, historically women's work, was a source of bitter discord in the months that followed Thatcher's victory parade. There was such confusion over who had been allocated tickets for the state memorial service that many bereaved mothers and widows did not attend at all. The Archbishop of Canterbury Lord Runcie, himself a recipient of the Military Cross in the Second World War, gave a controversial sermon at a thanksgiving service honouring the war in St Paul's Cathedral: making a point of remembering the fallen of both sides, he criticized 'those who stay at home, most violent in their attitudes and untouched in themselves'.[34] (Thatcher herself was initially not invited to the unveiling of the memorial to the Falklands dead in 1985.) Many of the bereaved received parcels unceremoniously in the post that contained posthumous medals, unassembled. As there was no identifying information on the envelopes, they were taken aback by being so suddenly and mundanely confronted with these supposedly meaningful objects. Petty Officer Frank Foulkes's posthumous medal arrived in the post in three pieces in a jiffy bag: 'When his widow, Dorothy, not knowing what it was, tugged the bag open, one of the pieces flew across the room and it took her a week to find it at the bottom of the fruit bowl.'[35] The Queen's (now King's) Regulations for the Armed Forces forbade its members to publicly criticize them, or to speak directly to the media, meaning it was often up to family members to act as proxies. It is hard to criticize an institution that was your home, which is also the sole guarantor of bestowing your loved one's death with meaning. For some, however, the critique becomes an unearthing, a cathartic release. It's easier, it seems, for bereaved mothers to do this than wives: they still occupy a protective role in relation to their children. Some, like Theresa Burt, emphasize repeatedly that their sons were just children: babies, really, with no idea of the gravity of life and death. Such grief doesn't disperse. Years after he died, she still kept her son's room as it was when he left, and on Saturdays she watched the football scores and put Chelsea match reports in his room along with his pocket money. 'I am very sane,' she told Carr, responding perhaps to imagined critiques of her inability to 'get over' the loss of Jason. 'I am very sane and very angry, and I do not want people to forget how, and why, my son died.'[36]

Bairns Not Bombs

To many of the bereaved mothers, the Falklands conflict itself seemed a shocking anachronism. Invasion and trench warfare was something they had assumed to be a thing of the past; their generation had believed that all future conflict would be nuclear. The very real threat of nuclear war was another site of deeply felt associations between violence and maternity: resistance to the production and storing of nuclear warheads, in the 1980s and beyond, drew heavily on children as the image of the future, and of mothers as their primary protectors. It is not incidental that, as I briefly discussed in the previous chapter, the maternal politics of WAPC found kinship at the Greenham Common Women's Peace Camp in Berkshire. Doreen Humber, a Nottinghamshire member of WAPC, who visited the protest camp and alternative community in 1984, made such connections explicit:

> Sometimes I look at my little lad; he's five, and I think, 'I wish I'd never had him.' That's how it makes me feel. Because I think if we lose what we have in this world, either by making nuclear bombs or putting people on the scrapheap, if we lose this fight, there is nothing to bring up kids for.[37]

WAPC used their identity as (mostly) wives and mothers to sustain industrial action, both through repurposing typically domestic actions like cooking and caring for children and by subverting them on the picket lines. Greenham women may have been more overtly concerned with gender politics, but they, too, repurposed and subverted: they made homes out of tents, cooked for each other, cared for children, lived on donations and the dole, sang together; they also faced extreme levels of police violence and repeatedly broke into a high-security military base. Beth Junor has written that 'the truest history of the Women's Peace Camp's work is to be found in the Criminal Records Office.'[38] (There was some freelance violence, too: there are accounts of locals throwing faeces and offal over tents, passing drivers throwing bottles and stones, and sleeping women being kicked and beaten in the middle of the night. It was so bad that Yoko Ono, or so the story goes, bought a small strip of land near the base that had a caravan on it that women could use as a safe haven.)

The Common first became a base for the US Air Force during the Second World War, something locals believed to be a temporary sacrifice of the green space known as 'the lung of Newbury'. The land was never returned to the people, and, after more was purchased by the Ministry of Defence, large areas of it were fenced off. In 1979, the decision was made by NATO to house ninety-six ground-launched USAF cruise missiles there and, despite the incredible violence contained within each nuclear warhead – sixteen times more capacity than the bomb that was dropped on Hiroshima – this was seen by many residents as a relief: exercises would take place nocturnally, in secret, and there would be no overhead aircraft noise.[39] The camp itself began in September 1981 when, at the culmination of a ten-day-long march from Cardiff organized by the Welsh group Women for Life on Earth, thirty-six women chained themselves to the fence: these women were swiftly removed, but, undeterred, they soon established another camp on the perimeter that would remain active for nineteen years, until the fences themselves were dismantled. Women and children were central to the action, and the camp formally became women-only in 1982; men were involved as supporters, but the group wanted to draw attention to the fact that women's work in the peace movement often got overlooked, and to capitalize on the symbolism of maternity: the creation and protection of life, rather than its destruction. Upon arrival they presented a letter to the base commandant which emphasized that they were acting as mothers:

> Some of us have brought our babies with us this entire distance. We fear for the future of these children. We fear for the future of all our children, and for the future of the living world which is the basis of all life . . . We want the arms race to be brought to a halt now – before it is too late to create a peaceful, stable world for our future generations.[40]

The first missiles arrived in 1983, and their arrival was marked by two large actions: a fourteen-mile-long human chain organized by the Campaign for Nuclear Disarmament linking the base to the nearby villages of Burghfield and Aldermaston, and a teddy bears' picnic organized by the Yellow Gate of the camp itself. In the latter, hundreds of women dressed in bear costumes entered the base, drawing on the imagery of the traditional children's rhyme: a humiliating framework for a military security breach. In July of the same year, during an Air Tattoo, seven women managed to gain access to the area where the planes were being kept and 'decorated' them with brightly coloured paint: apparently, it cost the MoD almost two and a half million pounds to restore them.

The identity of women as mothers, potential mothers, or 'universal' mothers – custodians of the earth and of human life – dominated the aesthetics and politics of Greenham. (Grand-maternal identities were included in this: some of the most iconic images from the camp include elderly women holding signs reading GRANNIES AGAINST THE BOMB.) This was an understanding of maternity that refused to countenance it as anything other than *conceptually* peaceful; the camp was defined by the principle of nonviolent resistance. Thatcher, by this logic, was betraying her maternal self, not utilizing it. (As her lack of response to Theresa Burt's letters shows, this avenue of persuasion was something of a dead end in practice.) Women keened and ululated – traditional mourning rituals – and dressed in black, performing pre-emptive grief for the children who would be lost to nuclear warfare; they fastened teddies, pictures of loved ones and children's toys to the perimeter's wire fence.[41]

The centrality of maternity at Greenham was literal as well as metaphorical. In Beeban Kidron's landmark 1984 documentary *Carry Greenham Home*, we see a group of women in a tent, bustling around heating up hot water bottles and rearranging blankets. Their purpose is to provide warmth and comfort to the woman inside the tent, Sarah Green, who is giving birth. (It's likely that some of the women assisting the birth were midwives, nurses or doctors, but self-administered DIY healthcare was understood at Greenham, as in other feminist movements, to be essential to the rejection of patriarchal systems.) Holding her newborn, the mother tells the camera that 'It's really important that women can have babies in the way that they want to': she wanted to give birth at Greenham because 'it's all about whether there's a future or not.' She seems to have found her answer: 'I think that there is a future now. I'm absolutely certain of it.' Green's son was the first child born at the camp: he was named Jay Greenham. In August 1983, the *Newbury Weekly News* ran a story titled 'SECOND PEACE WOMAN EXPECTS BABY AT CAMP' in which Green confirmed that another camp-dweller was expecting. She also emphasized that Jay was surrounded by caring adults, spent a lot of time outside – 'which I feel is an advantage' – and received care packages from those involved in the peace movement around the world.[42]

There were older children living at Greenham too, and their care and entertainment was shared – and argued over – like other domestic tasks, although there were fewer attempts to deconstruct parental ownership than in communes and squats: most Greenham mothers interviewed in the press at the time were keen to stress their own ongoing responsibility for their children, who were children of the camp only for as long as the camp made sense as a place to raise children. (Jay Greenham's surname, then, is a response to the absence of a father, rather than the absence of 'special' parental relationships entirely.) For some, the absence of their own children was as much of a motivating factor as their presence was for others. Mary Millington told the *Guardian* that she was 'free to go and live at the camp' when her daughter moved in with her father: it was, from Millington's perspective, 'the best way to live under Margaret Thatcher – to work for peace and live off the meagre dole money'; perhaps this would not have been possible had her daughter remained in her custody. For Fran De'Ath, the camp became a way of channelling otherwise frustrated maternal energies and anxieties: 'I was divorced and my children, who were five and twelve at the time, were living with their father. I felt like when the bomb dropped I wouldn't be able to even hold their hands, so I just wanted to do everything in my power to stop it.' The camp, here, becomes a way of protecting her children, of caring about them without caring *for* them: 'I thought if I was an artist or poet I would have a voice, but all I could do was sit in the mud.'[43]

Long-Blond-Haired-Pregnant-Mother Images

Greenham was not the first or the only iteration of a women's peace movement in the UK, and neither was it the only one to claim a maternal prerogative.[44] Yet it is Greenham that has been remembered as if it is entirely representative of political maternity and even, sometimes, of British feminism as a whole. (The title of a 2021 documentary about the camp, *Mothers of the Revolution*, is a case in point.) In fact, Greenham was a topic of fierce disagreement: an anti-Greenham conference was held in London in 1982, with criticism including that it diverted energy from the WLM, that it bent feminism to un-radical and un-feminist ends, and that it relied upon a stereotypical idea of femininity. Although there were groups, like Babies Against the Bomb, who argued for a kind of maternalism that transformed the love you had for your own children into something applicable to all children, the vision of motherhood that characterized the peace camp was uncomfortably essentialist.[45] The art historian Alexandra Kokoli has argued that the visual language of anti-nuclear activism constructed at the camp, with its baby bottles and blankets, directly contradicted the WLM's emphasis on maternal ambivalence and the burdens of social reproduction. Greenham's approach reinforced the idea that care and nurture were somehow essentially female, not socially constructed: maternity was natural, it was spiritual, and it was linked to the earth itself. In the first issue of *Trouble and Strife*, a radical feminist magazine that launched in 1983, Ruth Wallsgrove described these as 'long-blond-haired-pregnant-mother images'.[46]

The feelings Wallsgrove expressed towards the camp, however, were contradictory. On the one hand, there was frustration and sadness that so many women felt they could only care about the world once they'd had babies, on behalf of these babies rather than themselves; on the other, the unignorable fact that Greenham had reached so many 'ordinary' women – in some cases convincing them to radically alter their lives – whom, for whatever reason, the WLM had not been able to galvanize.[47] In Beatrix Campbell's *The Iron Ladies*, many of her Conservative-voting interviewees acknowledged that, although they didn't agree with their lifestyle choices, the Greenham women had raised awareness of the presence of the missiles. Some, like Barbara Stone in the Scottish Borders, even envied 'that they'd got out of their boring lives. I still have that, and a tremendous admiration – they'd been despised, the butt of everyone's jokes, but I admired their courage for standing up for what they believe.'[48] Although socialist feminists had their own concerns, many acknowledged the success of Greenham at making connections with groups like WAPC and forging international links: in 1986, a group of women from two of the eight Hackney Greenham groups wrote in *Feminist Review* that the longevity of the camp alone was a powerful means of counteracting political despair during the Thatcher years.[49] The philosopher Mary Midgley noted that, despite the fact that the mainstream media tried to write Greenham women off as 'a handful of lesbian maniacs from the North London suburbs', it is 'undeniably clear how various are their backgrounds and how large, over the whole time, have been their numbers. The strength of the feeling which has been able to unite this great range of diverse but mostly ordinary and representative women sticks out at once.'[50] Not all of these 'ordinary' women lived at Greenham: much of the food, wood and medicinal supplies that the camp relied upon was brought by those who did not live there full time.

Although nuclear disarmament was Greenham's unifying cause – with, relatedly, environmentalism, given the linked issues of ecological damage and nuclear waste – it would be a simplification to suggest that the camp was ever of unified mind. Kokoli compares the 'radical diversity of views and tactics' at Greenham to 'a wildly bricolaged tool kit'.[51] (There is a neat example of this from the moment of its inception: Ann Pettitt, an organizer of the march from Cardiff, describes in her memoir that, as the initial declaration of occupation was being read by Karmen Cutler, Reading Women for Peace arrived dressed in black and loudly keening, making it almost impossible to hear Cutler's words.)[52] Many Greenham women were drawing on their experience of organizing in trade unions, social housing campaigns and against gendered violence; as Fran De'Ath writes in *Greenham Women Everywhere*, many were simultaneously campaigning for free childcare, better public service pay, social housing and against public spending cuts, by making the argument that funding nuclear weapons diverted money from these essential services, disproportionately affecting women.[53]

The diversity of opinion at Greenham expressed itself in daily life as well as in its tactics. Personal accounts make it clear that there were a lot of delays and a lot of arguing, but this confirms Kokoli's point about bricolage: even if you could see the joins, they still managed to construct something. Laborious processes of agreement were not an impediment to life at Greenham but essential to it, and taking the long way to reach decisions was an active choice made by the Greenham women, who – like the WLM – sought to avoid masculine hierarchies. In a *Marxism Today* round-table discussion, Helen John – who had been at Greenham since its inception – described this as an ability to 'live the subject', and 'discuss something until we get it right'. (Caroline Blackwood, in her controversial 1984 account of life at Greenham, *On the Perimeter* – she took an anti-lesbian stance and extensively interviewed representatives of the organization Ratepayers Against the Greenham Encampments, or RAGE who, supported by local Conservative councillors, campaigned to have the women taken off the electoral register – noted that 'No one ever told anyone else to do anything. If no one felt like cooking, no one cooked . . .'[54])

Though hierarchies were avoided, the camp was divided into different gates, Yellow, Red, Orange, Green, Blue, Indigo, Violet and, later, Woad, Emerald and Jade, each with its own specific identity. The differences between the gates often dominate the accounts of those who were there. Cheryl Side, for example, remembers that Green, which had always been exclusively female, was 'the muesli gate'.[55] The Orange gate, close to Crookham Common, was safe for children and older women and was also known as 'music gate'; Turquoise was vegan. Sarah Hipperson notes that Yellow was the most dangerous: to live there was to accept continual police harassment. In Lucy Robinson's account, Yellow was also the gate where much of the conflict and critique over Greenham's broader politics was played out.[56] For many, this was the first time they had experienced either police violence or sustained media hostility, and certainly the first time they had felt their ability to mother was in question, and this forced some painful recognition of the privileges of class and race.[57] White middle-class mothers were not used to the idea that their status as 'good' mothers was dependent on certain expectations. Although some documents, like the one distributed at the Embrace the Base action in December 1983, made an attempt at class analysis – 'We will not verbally abuse those police officers, messengers and office workers who have few options in choosing their occupations, due to the economic realities of sex, race and class in this country' – assumptions about the 'power' of non-violence were a source of tension when members of the NUM came into contact with Greenham, and for Black and brown women in the movement itself, all of whom were much more likely to have violence forced upon them.[58]

In 1984, Amanda Hassan, an elected member of the CND National Committee, published 'A Black Woman in the Peace Movement' in *Spare Rib*:

> I was holding on to the fence [at Greenham] along with some other women (all white) and from nowhere a big burly policeman gave me a chop on my arms and sent me reeling into the mud. None of the other women who were also holding on to the fence got this treatment. When I commented on this, a woman said: 'Well, you're only picked on because you're short.' (I'm under five foot.)
> *Couldn't they see it was because I was Black?*[59]

This wilful blindness was something Beverley Bryan, Stella Dadzie and Suzanne Scafe used in *The Heart of the Race* to contextualize the 'white ideology' of the women's peace movement more broadly:

> It's as if they've just discovered imperialism, and they're only worried about it because it threatens their particular lifestyle. They say they don't like violence, but there are a lot of other forms of violence around they've never bothered about before now.

Greenham did, at least, open many of its participants' eyes to these 'other forms of violence'. The experience of the British justice system was for many a revelatory one, unveiling the mechanisms of the democracy they lived in for the first time. Bryan, Dadzie and Scafe note this too:

> I think a lot of white women are beginning to wake up. When they get kicked around by the police and check the media's version of events, they begin to see what Black people have to face every day of their lives. And when they get thirty days in Holloway for being assaulted, and find that nearly half of the women inside are Black, it forces them to confront the realities and to start making links. That's the point at which any allegiances will be made between Black and white women. Until then, it's all rhetoric.[60]

Central to this awakening was the realization that neither their non-violence nor their maternal status would protect them: it doesn't matter if your weapons are teddy bears and you're holding your baby if you're perceived as a threat to the state. In Wilmette Brown's 1983 *Black Women and the Peace Movement*, one of the most important texts that addressed this divide, there is also a cautious optimism (better later than never). Charitably, she writes that the willingness of white women at Greenham to address 'the issue of Black participation self-critically' was a testament to what the struggle had already taught them: 'For me that was already a victory: another victory of Greenham Common. But it's a hard row to hoe.'[61] Brown was a seasoned activist hailing from the US, where she had been involved in the civil rights movement, the peace movement and the Black Panther Party. In the UK, she co-founded Black Women for Wages for Housework in 1975 and was heavily involved in the squatted King's Cross Women's Centre. Brown became a principal character in divisions at Greenham in 1987 when, under her leadership, the Yellow Gate unofficially split from the rest of the camp supported by members of the King's Cross Women's Centre. This controversy generated much comment in the left-wing press: the 'King's Cross women' were accused by some of weaponizing racism and of 'Leninist' entryism, while the women themselves, in a reply to their critics published in the queer feminist magazine *Shocking Pink*, said the split was to do with 'non-alignment' – the refusal to align the movement with either power bloc in the Cold War – 'women's autonomy and Black autonomy', as well as anti-racism more generally.[62]

Black Women and the Peace Movement feels remarkably contemporary in its reading of the movement's failure to grapple with the overlapping legacies of colonialism and imperialism, and its critique of the demand for 'peace' itself. 'Black women's experience – surviving, resisting, demanding, organizing – at the bottom of the world hierarchy of work and wealth,' Brown argues, 'is a living critique of the many slogans so far put forward to connect peace with other issues and or to rally the peace movement to a "wider cause": slogans such as "jobs not bombs"; "bread not bombs"; "disarmament and development"; "people before profits"; "money for human needs".' She addresses, too, the fact that not everybody can demonstrate for peace: 'the Nationality Act and internal passport controls terrorize Black people and immigrants into not demonstrating for peace; while the Police Bill threatens to drive underground everybody's organizing, whether for peace or for any other issue.' Brown compellingly traces her example of Black 'welfare mothers' organizing in the US back to the feminism of Virginia Woolf, in whose work she finds an argument for wages for housework, 'a money wage for the unpaid worker', and the broader point that 'the military was able to thrive because women did not have the economic power to speak out against them' and, vice versa, that 'the military budget prevented women from winning that money' for work in the home. Although I don't agree that there is something inherent in the female or any gender that can always be relied upon to seek peace rather than conflict, Brown, via Woolf, argues that one 'contribution of Black and white women's leadership to the peace movement has been to show how private personal violence is of a piece with nuclear and military violence'.[63] The way motherhood was put to political use at Greenham, with its blind spots and stereotypes about gender and race, demonstrates that this private personal violence is the province of maternity, too.

The Mummy Returns

It is tempting to draw a clear line right down the middle of the 80s: Thatcher riding a tank on the one side, Grannies Against the Bomb on the other. It wasn't that simple. Ultimately, maternity and violence are each foundational to the other: the labour pains, the struggle for self-individuation, the production of sons for battle, the handing out of white feathers, the doling out of smacks, the feeding, the clothing, the bathing of wounds, the construction of an imagined future. There is no singular maternal position on the violence committed by the state. In *Greenham Common: Women at the Wire*, Lynne Jones describes her distress upon encountering a fellow protestor regaling an anti-nuclear demonstration with tales of her son's distinguished performance in the Falklands.[64] Rose, I think, was on the money in 1988:

> One of the things that Margaret Thatcher is doing, or that is being done through her, is to make this paradox the basis of a political identity so that subjects can take pleasure in violence as force and legitimacy while always locating 'real' violence somewhere else – illegitimate violence and illicitness increasingly made subject to the law.[65]

Riots were violent, but their causes were not. Non-violent resistance at Greenham was an assault on the state, but the sinking of the *Belgrano* was a matter of national self-defence. The IRA used force illegitimately; British troops in Northern Ireland were simply keeping the peace.[66] The enshrinement of extreme violence into the legitimate means of the state was not new, but in Thatcher it was bound up inextricably with her identity as a woman and a mother, with these traits becoming so cartoonishly relevant that she began to exceed the category entirely. In the 1993 *Spitting Image* annual *Margaret Thatcha: The Real Maggie Memoirs* she is represented as a face-hugger from the film *Alien*, bursting out of her own mother's chest. Denis, a few pages later, is pictured in a housecoat and curlers, heavily pregnant with the twins.

Her 'sons', as Simon Jenkins would have it, continue her legacy. David Cameron, interviewed on the *Today* programme before Thatcher's funeral in 2013, linked his admiration of her to both the Falklands conflict and her opposition to the 'eccentricity' of the Greenham camp, which was not far from where he grew up, although he was away at Eton and Oxford for most of its existence.[67] In May 2001, Thatcher came out of retirement to speak at the Tory party conference in Plymouth, deep in its New Labour wilderness years and led at the time by William Hague. She spoke for ten minutes and received a three-minute-long standing ovation. She began:

> It's wonderful to be here this evening, campaigning for a Conservative victory, in this enterprising port of Plymouth. I was told beforehand my arrival was unscheduled, but on the way here I passed a local cinema, and it turns out you were expecting me after all. The billboard read *The Mummy Returns*.

I'm loath to end this chapter on such a horrifying image. Let's finish where we started: with Brecht, in a manner of speaking. The 1980s were perhaps the last decade in which the tradition of socialist touring theatre thrived in the UK. One of the most influential of these companies was the Scottish troupe 7:84, founded in 1971 by John McGrath, Elizabeth MacLennan and David MacLennan; its name refers to a 1966 report that 7 per cent of the country owned 84 per cent of its wealth, and they were passionately committed to bringing shows to communities who were overlooked in terms of cultural programming and funding.[68]

Often described, slightly embarrassingly, as 'Britain's Brecht', McGrath combined Brechtian theatrical constructions with the vernacular of popular entertainment: he aimed above all to provide a 'good night out'. In 1986, his play *Blood Red Roses* was televised in three parts by Channel 4. It follows the political awakening of Bessie Gordon, a working-class woman from East Kilbride in the west of

Scotland. A 'domestic epic', in McGrath's words, it begins in 1986, with the funeral of Bessie's father in the highlands, proceeding to tell in flashback the story of the preceding thirty-four years. The central event of the series is the multinational takeover and subsequent closure of the factory, Scottish Accounting Machines, where Bessie, her friends and her husband, the Communist shop steward Alex McGuigan, work; she becomes a vocal trade unionist herself and is lauded and eventually ostracized for her trouble. Despite her powerful character and her bravery, Bessie, representative of her class and her gender, is burdened by care. Alex, initially drawn to her because of their shared politics, expects her to stay at home and look after their two children, and they eventually divorce: 'My politics,' he tells the camera in a confessional monologue, 'has always been to overthrow the capitalist state first and foremost. But unfortunately along with that seems to go this old-fashioned need for the wife to look after the weans til after the revolution.' When her beloved father suffers a stroke that leaves him entirely dependent upon her on the same day she discovers she is pregnant with a third – illegitimate – child, she tells the viewer, 'I had acquired the two weans in the one day.'

Motherhood, for Bessie, is a fundamentally political state because she herself is a fundamentally political creature. The birth of each of her daughters coincides with what McGrath believed to be the three largest defeats for the left in his lifetime: the Conservative election victory in 1959, Harold Wilson's victory in 1964, and Thatcher's 1983 landslide after the Falklands War. At the end of the final episode, discharged from the maternity ward too soon due to bed shortages, she watches Tony Benn lose his seat while her two elder daughters help her care for the baby: the election, they say, is 'torture', the Tories will 'crucify us'. Bessie is overcome as she holds them and cries 'my girls, my girls'. *Blood Red Roses* ends with a montage of Bessie and her girls watching footage of the Battle of Orgreave in horror, raising money for the NUM, and marching in the Glasgow May Day parade alongside other mothers and children (Bessie is marching with the Communist Party; one of her daughters is carrying a solidarity banner for Nicaragua). Here, maternity is a metaphor for the ongoing fight, the way generations of struggle build on each other. To invert *Mother Courage* – 'like the war to nourish you / got to feed it something too' – if you want to nourish your children you have to try to nourish the social world around them, too. This, in the end, was what Greenham was: my own sympathies might lie more with Bessie's version of action, but their bravery deserves to be remembered, not least for all that it has helped make possible in the decades since.

PART THREE

The Metaphor

9.

Mother Ireland

I don't know of a mother in a working-class situation in
Ireland for whom every day is not a fight . . .

Bernadette Devlin McAliskey, *Mother Ireland*

Motherhood and nationhood – where mother country meets
mother state – are knottily entangled: there is no single link between
the two, but rather, like the roots of a tree now grown so long together
their separation can't be discerned, a living, changing system of
relationships. The personification of Britain is relatively mild in its
association with maternity, with many in England preferring to
romanticize the masculine endeavours of St George, although the
female Britannia still 'rules the waves'. Ireland, on the other hand,
has long been a maternal entity. Known by many names – Cathleen
ní Houlihan, Shan Van Vocht, Dark Rosaleen – the image usually
falls into two categories: a helpless mother weeping for her subjugated sons, or a leader calling her children into battle. Under British
censorship, which prevented the discussion of nationalism, Mother
Ireland became metonymic of the country as a whole.

The tangled roots between the two states are most clearly expressed
in the conflict in Northern Ireland, or the north of Ireland: the six
counties of the island of Ireland's thirty-two which were officially
declared part of the UK in 1921, after a long occupation of Ireland
by the British which dates back to the twelfth century. This, as the
writer Patricia Malone observes, raises some difficult questions at

the level of language itself: 'How is one to name or speak of a state whose very existence is a state of un-being, an annexation of one part of an island made to quell the violent and unsettled history of that same island, a splitting off that represented a psychic sacrifice on a national scale: 6 counties given to an uncertain future, so that 26 might know peace?'[1]

Throughout the previous chapters of this book, I've tried to show that motherhood, as both institution and experience, is a fundamentally political concept that has both been weaponized by the state and used as a means to resist it to resist it. The profound instability of the British state expresses itself violently, cordoning off sections of its own inhabitants and designating them enemies within. This is not a logic that can be simply applied to the conflict in Northern Ireland: although the British government maintained that their position was neutral, a democratic upholding of 'law and order', their presence was experienced by nationalists as that of an invading colonial force. By their own logic, then, those who were engaged in civil or military resistance to British rule were not 'enemies within' but dissidents resisting their very enfolding *in* to the state in the first place. In this way, republican mothers faced a particular dilemma, with a conflict between the conventional representation of mothering as peaceful and domestic, the gendered expectations of their own communities, and the reality of mothering during this brutally domestic war. In this chapter, I am mostly going to be paying attention to this iteration of politicized motherhood as a specific resistance to the British state, although – inevitably – it is not always possible to draw clear distinctions between nationalism and republicanism, and there is much to say, too, about how maternal resistance expressed itself also in loyalist and even unionist communities, though most research suggests that there were more women active in combat in republican movements than loyalist.

It is almost a standing joke – though not a funny one – that a war that lasted for at least thirty years and claimed at least 3,500 lives is all but forgotten by many, especially by those who should bear the political responsibility of remembrance. The media coverage of the riots that tore through London in 1981 adopted a tone of shock that such 'civil disorder' could possibly happen in Britain, despite the fact it had been happening in the north of Ireland for over a decade; 1998's Good Friday Agreement is primarily remembered as a successful solution to a 'senseless' conflict. In recent years, Brexit's reawakening of the question of a hard border in Ireland and tragedies like the shooting of the journalist Lyra McKee in Derry in 2019 have raised the profile of the Troubles, yet in 2022 there was no shortage of journalists claiming that the Russian invasion of Ukraine was the first time they had seen 'war in Europe' in their lifetimes.

When they are publicly discussed, the Troubles are mostly presented as a masculine concern, despite the fact that it was a war with no official battlefield, waged in homes, schools, nurseries, workplaces, shops and pubs; within families and marital beds. The line between the public and private – always unstable – was entirely transgressed, something the cultural geographer Bryonie Reid has described as follows:

> Because of the intimate nature of the Troubles, houses have been on the frontline of violent struggle, used as boltholes and weapon stores by paramilitaries, the carriers of political symbols of assertion of resistance such as flags; as the objects of invasion and search by the army and police, often the site of their inhabitants' murders, and in many places vulnerable to destruction as a result of their inhabitants' politics or religion, private family homes in Northern Ireland have been made full participants in the public world in ways specific to the province's history and politics.[2]

This gendered violence occurred on all fronts, and doesn't fit a convenient narrative: military forces intruded into domestic space – especially in Catholic homes – and so did paramilitary forces. Many men heralded as heroes in their communities were domestic abusers. Eli Davies, in her work on the figure of 'Mother Ireland' in the north, has made a compelling argument for attending to accounts which do not conform to the stereotype of 'victim or peace-maker', and, crucially, position the domestic as a site of resistance in itself.[3]

Maternal involvement in the Troubles has tended to be grouped by historians into distinct categories: mothers involved in the armed struggle; mothers against the armed struggle; mothers advocating for and supporting their relatives; and mothers engaging with indirect forms of resistance. (Historically, Irish society on both sides of the border has a reputation for a religiously inflected, conservative approach to gender.[4]) Regardless of category, motherhood provided a role in the public sphere that had not been available to those still understood to be girls, and, for many, this allowed them to fully realize the political nature of their maternity for the first time.[5] In 'Living with the Army in Your Front Garden', a 1976 *Spare Rib* article, Mary McKay defended 'the way the mass of women have been involved as a community' – to a 'sceptical' audience of British feminists:

> For example, in Derry, we heard that when the army first came in 1971, they took a school as their base. It was the women who got up a march and picket to move them out of the school. It is very much as *mothers* that women are moved to action against the army. That shouldn't make us over here [in Britain] too sceptical. The Catholic Church and economic underdevelopment do make the family conservative and cohesive in N. Ireland, and this obviously does circumscribe the part played by women in current events. But because so much of the action has been in communities, where whole families are involved together, domestic life and family relationships have been opened to change.[6]

This scepticism stemmed, in part, from the resistance within much of the British feminist movement to engage with the political life in the north: the conflict between republican communities and the state was perceived as masculine, violent and divisive, and turned away from accordingly.

Mother Ireland, Get Off Our Backs

In 1988, Anne Crilly, a member of the Derry Film and Video Collective, made a documentary called *Mother Ireland*. The Collective was a political space. Active until 1989, it was formed under the 1982 Workshop Declaration, a movement that brought together the resources of multiple British and Irish funding institutions in the hope of democratizing filmmaking; their films were broadcast on the newly founded Channel 4. A collective who also organized community cultural education, the Derry Workshop documented aspects of life in Northern Ireland that were consistently misrepresented. They learned as they went: Crilly remembers that when they first got the equipment, 'we literally did not know how to use it, but we decided that instead of just doing a training exercise for the sake of it we would pick a project and do it no matter how it turned out.' (That first project was a film about the strip-searching of prisoners in Armagh: it was used by the official anti-strip-search campaign, and later screened in the European Parliament.[7]) Motherhood was key to much of the Workshop's output: its final project, 1990's *Hush-A-Bye Baby*, followed fictional fifteen-year-old Goretti Friel through an accidental pregnancy, drawing on anonymous interviews with teenagers and a youth drama workshop, 'No Sex Please, We're Irish', held in Derry.[8] (One of Goretti's friends is played by a young Sinéad O'Connor.)

Mother Ireland is made up of interviews with a group including the former MP Bernadette Devlin McAliskey, the writer Nell McCafferty, the General Secretary of Sinn Féin Rita O'Hare and the IRA volunteer Mairéad Farrell. For Crilly, by the late twentieth century the national maternal figure had come to embody a central contradiction of gender in the Irish republic and the still-occupied six counties: Mother Ireland was revered in nationalist culture, especially as the progenitor of warrior sons, but when it came to 'the reality of the women who fought for Mother Ireland', feminism and republicanism came into conflict.[9] The symbolic creaked under the weight of the real. For Crilly's interviewees, there was a divide along generational lines: for octogenarian members of Cumann na mBan, the 'women's council' of paramilitary volunteers founded in 1914, the image was central to their motivation, while Farrell – who, aged thirty, had spent ten years in Armagh jail – declares that 'Mother Ireland wouldn't make me want to go out and fight, in fact it would do the opposite.' (A popular phrase among republican prisoners in Armagh was 'Mother Ireland, get off our backs.') Other interviewees were uncertain. On the one hand, the image had become softened and commercialized, exploited by the tourist board – although, as Crilly notes, this was more a 'pure unspoiled maiden welcoming people in' than a mother – but on the other, it was a 'framework' for the development of a nationalist consciousness. Devlin McAliskey repoliticizes the image by returning it to a material maternal reality: 'I don't know of a mother in a working-class situation in Ireland for whom every day is not a fight. Being a mother is certainly not a passive romantic image . . .' Often, she notes, mothers involved in nationalist resistance were working double time: 'Women in Derry were still providing three square meals a day and men were still eating them.'

Mother Ireland was unusual in its positioning of feminism and nationalism as 'two sides of the same coin'. There was a longstanding reluctance in the Irish women's movement to even discuss the north, ostensibly to avoid division. Republican feminism was marginalized: it was often blamed singlehandedly for causing frictions, or for 'silencing' Protestant women, in the words of Monica McWilliams of the Northern Ireland Women's Coalition (NIWC). Within the republican movement, feminism wasn't necessarily understood as a topic of primary importance: Devlin McAliskey, in a statement Crilly called the 'most provocative' of the entire film, declares that the 'best young feminist women today' are from the republican movement, 'those who have come to an awareness of their oppression as women through a growing awareness of other layers of oppression'.[10] (In this way, there was more of a kinship with the civil rights struggle in the US than with the WLM: Devlin (as she was then) visited Angela Davis in prison in 1971, and gave the key to the city of New York that she had been awarded to the Black Panthers.)

The sociologist Teresa O'Keefe spent seven years interviewing women active in the republican movement during the Troubles, aiming to correct the skewed representation of feminist organizing in the period as only existing in cross-community movements. O'Keefe describes the 'check-your-label-at-the-door policy', which the feminist movement tried to instil in the service of neutrality, as 'lowest common denominator politics'. Often in the women's movement in the north, those attending meetings were 'not allowed to raise issues that were not shared by all women. It silenced those who wished to talk about experiences of oppression as, for example, gay women, working-class women, or Republican woman.' Claire Hackett, a republican feminist and queer activist, told O'Keefe that 'no concerted efforts' were made to address state violence against women, which was seen as a republican issue rather than a feminist one: 'They didn't deal with it because they would have had to take up a position themselves on the state and that was too scary.'[11] Gendered violence was certainly enacted by both sides: there are many stories of punishment beatings, head shavings, tarring and featherings administered by the IRA to women who had been seen to transgress, often through having a sexual relationship – real or rumoured – with an enemy. And, as O'Keefe's interviews make clear, for women in Catholic communities, sexual harassment, verbal assault and rape threats from state forces were 'just the usual': these would come from soldiers in passing foot patrols, driving armoured vehicles, or shouted from the vantage point of watchtowers, where women were 'easily scrutinized'. Women's bodies were another territory upon which the lines of dispute were mapped: unwanted pregnancy, in particular, was weaponized by both sides.

The most disturbing of these stories, perhaps, is about Catherine, a 27-year-old mother of three from west Belfast whose pregnant body was caught between Irish abortion law and British border enforcement. Six years into her husband's twelve-year-long prison sentence for alleged membership of the IRA and possession of a weapon, raising her children alone in a damp council flat, she had a brief affair, fell pregnant and had to travel to England for a termination. Terrified she would be arrested – Special Branch knew she was the wife of a prisoner – she befriended another northern Irish woman at the clinic. The woman was a Protestant, and Catherine was too scared to tell her that her husband was in Long Kesh, and so couldn't tell her to lie if they were stopped by police. When they were, the woman who as a feminist 'felt fully justified' in doing so, told the truth: they had been to an abortion clinic. Catherine was taken to Castlereagh holding centre and interrogated. The aim of the interrogation was clear. Calling her an 'IRA whore' and a baby murderer, they wanted to scare her into becoming an informer in exchange for them keeping the information about the terminated pregnancy from her husband. Catherine refused, and prison guards used her abortion to torment her husband throughout the rest of his sentence.[12]

McCafferty recounts the story of a pregnant woman who was arrested and then taken from Castlereagh to Dundonald Hospital under armed guard, where she suffered three forced internal examinations, the insertion of forceps and a catheter. No reason was ever given, and after three days she was released without charge.[13] Sexual harassment and strip-searching were used as forms of intimidation both of prisoners and those in detention awaiting court hearing, intended to degrade and humiliate. Searches were sometimes accompanied by threats of sexual violence, and the experience is often compared to rape by those who undergo it.[14] There are many accounts of pregnant people being strip-searched, often in a state of heightened distress, and Jennifer McCann recalls 'a woman from Derry who was strip-searched when she was going out to hospital to deliver her baby and another woman who had a miscarriage and she was also strip-searched'. Liza McWilliams was strip-searched in 1984 after she had been informed that her mother had died: 'It was really hard when we were strip-searched, especially when I came in after the funeral. I had my period and they did not care.'[15] In excluding state violence from the definition of what counted as a feminist issue, then, the relevance of feminism itself to the reality of life in the north was truncated.

A mother's ability to make choices about her own life cannot be disentangled from the national context in which these decisions take place. As Farrell puts it in *Mother Ireland*:

> I am oppressed as a woman, and I'm also oppressed as an Irish person. Everyone in this country is oppressed and yet we can only end our oppression as women if we end the oppression of our nation as a whole.

Despite the contribution of women to the cause, and despite 'the saturation of scholarship on the Troubles', O'Keefe notes that 'republican feminist politics are, for the most part, hidden from view.'[16] Although there are icons like Devlin McAliskey and Farrell, most of the heroes in murals, ballads and poems are men; the most prominent female figure, still, is the allegorical Mother.

Mother Ireland, despite being commissioned in 1987 and finished the following year, was not screened until 1991, in a one-off series of 'banned films'. Five days after it was finished, in 1988, Farrell was killed by the SAS in Gibraltar, becoming perhaps the most famous female IRA martyr. The controversy around the circumstances of her death – some witnesses stated that she had been shot with her hands in the air – delayed broadcast until after the official inquest had concluded and then, in October 1988, new British broadcasting restrictions came in that prevented members of Sinn Féin and Cumann na mBan from being broadcast at all. (This applied even to archival footage of republican Maud Gonne speaking at a rally five decades before.) When it was eventually broadcast, Crilly had to agree to extensive cuts: Farrell and O'Hare's voices were over-dubbed, footage of Emma Groves being shot with a plastic bullet was removed, and contemporary images of masked women were taken out. The experience of complying with these regulations ser-iously affected her, and she went into 'self-censorship mode'. In the years between its commission and its broadcast, she found it hard 'to get any other work in the media, because there was that sort of taint over you'.[17] This was a seditions motherhood, under suspicion for what it might be capable of creating.

Overburdened with Struggle

Dolours Price was another republican icon. The first woman admitted to the IRA – she and her sister Marion were known as the 'Crazy Prices', a riff on the well-known Belfast department store – Price was imprisoned in HMP Brixton in 1973 for her role in car bombings in London and embarked on a 208-day-long hunger strike. By 1984, she had been released from prison, and was reviewing a new book called *Only the Rivers Run Free* in the Belfast-based magazine *Fortnight*. The book was a sustained piece of reportage about the lives of women – mostly Catholic – in the six counties, put together by Roisin McDonough from Belfast, and two English writers, Eileen Fairweather and Melanie McFadyean, who were involved in feminist publishing (Fairweather was in the *Spare Rib* editorial collective, and had published the article 'Abortion: The Feelings behind the Slogans' that had sparked significant discussion in 1979).[18] Price's review begins in a tone of wry exhaustion with the distraction of feminism:

> I have grown weary of the constant trek of English feminists up the Falls Road, tape recorder on one shoulder, sleeping bag on the other and a foot that can be stuck in any door in the name of sisterly love and learning. I have resented their intrusion for many years and I have been made uncomfortable by their seeming longing for my background, my working-class status, my oppression, my politics. I have been weary of them and I have avoided them, not wanting to share myself, my situation, not thinking them worthy of the experience. I have thought they had no contribution to make save the introduction of meaningless struggles into a society already overburdened with struggle.

The review continues, however, with a startling admission: 'I have read [*Only the Rivers Run Free*] and I have been wrong.' At the root of this wrongness, as the book has allowed her to discover 'the real women of Belfast and Derry, I have seen them as I never would have been allowed, being one of them'.[19] Price pays particular attention to 'all of the stories of misery, endless pregnancies, guilt laden self-abortion told without self-pity with an attitude of acceptance that this is what is meant for us, women'. Discussing the story of Nora, an older woman who details her twenty-five pregnancies, her constant physical discomfort and fear of sex, Price is movingly candid, imagining her own existence as part of a long history of reproductive misery:

> I realised that in my arrogance I had thought I was from these people, knew them and their suffering. But I did not know their lives, these lives spoken about in quiet and embarrassed whispers to strangers. Probably I did not know because I could be any of the daughters, one of the ones to survive the poison and pills.

Price's self-proclaimed ignorance illuminates the fact that many republicans were loath to discuss women's suffering at the hands of the Church or their husbands for fear of perpetuating stereotypes about 'thick, brutal, priest-ridden Paddies'. (Later in the book, Cathy Harkin, co-ordinator for Northern Ireland Women's Aid, which ran five refuges in 'neutral' areas that housed Catholic and Protestant women together, emphasizes that domestic violence crossed sectarian and class boundaries. Refuges, in her words, provided a space away from the general 'Christian concept of the indissolubility of marriage'). There is a touching symmetry in Price's imagining that she herself could be one of Nora's daughters. When the interviewers ask Nora how she learned, finally, about sex and reproduction she says, 'proudly', it was through her daughter, Cathy: 'she was better educated than I was, and very daring with it. She sent away to England for all these books.'[20] Daughters have something to teach their mothers, too.

Only the Rivers Run Free is a remarkable historical document: in Price's words, it tells 'the truth of how women cope in Northern Ireland in their marriages, their religion, their poverty and in war. It is a tribute to their survival and a litany against the institutions which demand too much of them.'[21] One such institution was motherhood. The book opens in Turf Lodge in west Belfast on the anniversary of the introduction of internment without trial of those 'suspected' of IRA involvement: the streets are 'thick with soldiers' and young people, with fires and fights. (Between August 1971 and December 1975, almost 2,000 people were interned; only just over one hundred were loyalists.) The first voices we encounter are maternal: a woman 'beside herself with fury' that her two sons have been hit with plastic bullets; Mary, a 'weary single parent with three children' observes that 'these kids are old before their time. They've seen what they've seen, injustice and brutality every day of their lives. Then they see the politicians on the TV and all that teaches them is that when you're in the ghetto nobody cares.'

For many young women, motherhood arrived as the only possible answer to an unprepossessing question. Josie, interviewed in Belfast on her nineteenth birthday, elaborates: 'Here, there's no jobs, nothing to do, and nothing to think about. So the most interesting thing to do would be to get married and make a job of looking after my family. That's all there is really.'[22] We meet Deirdre, a sex worker struggling to bring up two children on paltry social security: after the introduction in 1971 of the Payment for Debt Act, which only applied in Northern Ireland and was an attempt to curb rent and rates strikes, the British government took late rent payments directly out of welfare payments. We meet Eileen, whose son Seamus was arrested and held for two hours by the RUC when he was five years old, and we hear from those whose children were killed by plastic bullets, many of whom fought lengthy appeals for civil damages in the face of lies about what their children had been doing: for 'rioting', read, 'walking down the road' or 'going to the shops'.

The maternal impulse to defend and protect, frequently attributed to something mammalian inside us, an inheritance that exceeds the limits of the human, weaves together violence and care, and demonstrates that they are not, in fact, oppositional. What use is it to tend to your babies when the hostile state – or its opponents – might shoot them as they make their way down the street? Valerie Morgan, writing in 1996, noted that it was only relatively recently that historians of conflict began to question the received notion that women are less active than their male counterparts in times of war; Eilish Rooney, five years earlier, observed that for women on both sides of the divide, the only socially acceptable role was that of peacemaker, 'applauded for being uninterested in politics; for prioritizing the "personal" over the conflict ridden "political" '.[23] There is still very little acknowledgement of the fact that there were women who took an active role in the struggle, and that many of them were not just women who were mothers but, crucially, were engaging *as* mothers. In *The Price of My Soul*, Devlin McAliskey recalls that at the battle of the Bogside in Derry in 1969 the petrol bombs thrown at the RUC were 'made, literally, by pregnant women and children. Kids of seven and eight who couldn't fight made the petrol bombs, and made them pretty well.'[24] (Women's hands had a well-practised speed from working on factory assembly lines.)

Even those who didn't directly volunteer with paramilitary groups were on the frontlines: there was no clear boundary between the home and the war zone, making something of a mockery of the idea of 'voluntary' participation. After the British introduced internment without trial for anyone suspected of IRA involvement in 1971, so many men were either imprisoned or on the run that the majority of residents on Catholic estates were women: their domestic work became the work of enduring and resisting house raids, interrogations and army blockades; they led the street resistance to the army, 'hen patrols' warning of approaching soldiers and moving en masse to break curfews. This experience provoked its own political awakening. Christina Loughran's interviews with republican prisoners and their families in 1980 revealed a significant consistency of motivation: 'Mothers of prisoners have commented that harassment, house searches, spot checks and being bussed to school to avoid sectarian attacks are reasons for their daughters' involvement.'[25]

Women's right to join the IRA dates to the beginning of the Troubles. Cumann na mBan was an auxiliary organization, fundraising and providing combat-adjacent support like first aid and hiding weapons. In the late 60s – around the time pregnant women on the Bogside were making petrol bombs – many of its younger members began to express dissatisfaction with this subsidiary role. The IRA responded by allowing Cumann na mBan members to be seconded into the organization, before finally acquiescing and allowing women to become full members.[26] Cumann na mBan itself had a puritanical reputation. (Its motto is 'Strength in our arms, truth on our lips and purity in our hearts'.) Divorced women, those living with men out of wedlock and those with illegitimate children were not accepted; there were instances of women who got pregnant being forced to stand down while the fathers, were they IRA volunteers, faced no consequences.

Cathleen, a young woman from the Falls Road interviewed in *Only the Rivers Run Free*, linked this explicitly to our familiar stereotype: 'It all boils down to this romantic "Mother Ireland" image. They like to depict Irish women as very staunch and behind their men. But the only relationship you're allowed to have with a man is a married one.'[27] The IRA remained a forcefully masculine and often chauvinistic organization. In O'Keefe's interviews, many report that being a woman in combat was its own struggle: 'A lot of the women that were involved had to fight for their position . . . because we were just supposed to be making the tea or whatever.' They were not represented in its organizational structure, having only 'second-class status': 'Men make all the important decisions. Generally speaking, the Army Council is men and maybe a token woman.'[28] The IRA, did, however, have a maternity leave policy. One member, an explosives expert and new mother, was in 1984 'relieved of all [her] duties' until she chose to report back, with no pressure or time limit. She stayed in touch with her superiors in case of an emergency, but 'at the moment I just want to spend some time with my daughter. They understand that.'[29]

Having a baby often heightened political commitment: many

women with children who were involved in paramilitary activity saw the fight as one that would procure their children's freedom. One woman interviewed by Fairweather, McDonough and McFadyean emphasized that women had just as much of a practical vested interest in resisting the British occupation of Ireland as men: 'The point is that women aren't just involved the way they are because their men are inside. They're involved because *they* see their own interests as women in getting the Brits out of our country.'[30] In some families, engagement in armed struggle was passed down like a family crest: Price recalled that 'Our family motto wasn't "For God and Ireland", Ireland came before God.' In an interview with Evelyn Brady, Madge McConville, who was interned in Armagh in 1942 and 1975, remembers, when she was let down by contacts who were supposed to hide weapons she had in her possession, 'My ma said she would fix us up. She wrapped the stuff up in an old plastic Mac and buried it under a wee tree she had in her garden.'[31]

In loyalist communities, too, paramilitary involvement was understood generationally. There was a prevalent belief that Catholics, with their typically larger families, were attempting to eliminate or replace them, and there was a feeling of betrayal by the state: in a 1982 sermon, Ian Paisley declared that one could 'wring out the skirts of Maggie Thatcher' and find them 'soaked in the blood of Protestants she had betrayed'.[32] The historian Sandra M. McEvoy spent a decade interviewing loyalist paramilitary women. One interviewee, Karen, describes the stakes as being entirely familial in nature:

> I would say that I am a very warm, loving mother of three and grand-mother of four. When I was needed I was there. I am not a cruel person. I mean, if we've got Republican people that's willing to kill our people for their cause, I mean, you just can't sit back and let it happen.[33]

For some housewives, paramilitary activity was a way of participating actively in something beyond domestic isolation. McEvoy found that her interviewees emphasized the importance of their paramilitary service, rather than more traditional or romanticized notions of motherhood: maternity and combatant life coalesced. Maternal protection, here, is expressed through direct participation in violence. Yet, when McEvoy posed the question 'What would your feelings have been if your daughter wanted to be a member of the group?', very few responded positively, one 'noting that she would pass on her own knowledge of how "not to get caught"'. Another responds that she would have actively encouraged her because "I believed in what I was doing". Although most interviewees believe their own mothers were not supportive of the danger they put themselves in, one, Lynn, reminisces about intergenerational collaboration: they 'regularly worked in tandem to conceal weapons and ammunition in their homes by shifting these materials across the street to one another's houses in a well-orchestrated routine to avoid detection'. Her mother, knowing there was ammunition hidden in her daughter's house, took the head off a toy belonging to her granddaughter, hid it inside, 'sewed the head back on and set it back'.[34] Like Madge McConville's mum burying weapons in the garden, such mother-daughter teamwork occurred on both sides of the divide.

'My Son is Dying on the Blanket'

Whether loyalist or republican, maternal suffering was not easily borne, even by those who believed in the reasons behind their children's sacrifices. In Catholic communities, families realigned themselves around their (often multiple) incarcerated members. Thirty-three women were interned at Armagh jail between 1973 and 1976, while the majority of male prisoners were housed in Nissen huts at Long Kesh Detention Centre, formerly an RAF base; conditions at both were horrifying.[35] In 1972, William Whitelaw, Ted Heath's Secretary of State for Northern Ireland, had introduced Special Category Status: so named to reassure Parliament that it wasn't political status, it meant prisoners did not wear uniforms or undertake prison work, and were allowed to socialize, receive food parcels and have extra visiting hours. This special status was ended in March 1976 by the new Secretary of State, Merlyn Rees, and most men convicted of 'scheduled terrorist offences' were held in the eight H-shaped blocks at the newly named 'escape-proof' HMP Maze. When the first prisoner, Kieran Nugent, arrived, he refused to put on the uniform and instead wrapped himself in a blanket. By the end of 1976, forty more 'blanket-men' had joined him in the Maze, with those at Armagh and Crumlin Road jail in Belfast participating, too.[36] The prisoners were treated appallingly: as well as regular beatings, their letters were stopped and ofter confiscated, and visiting rights were denied, even for dying family members. Sometimes the guards would keep them in suspense for hours, refusing to tell them if their loved one was dead or living. Those on the blanket escalated their protest and refused to slop out: cell walls were smeared with faeces, their quarters shared with maggots. Finally, in 1980, the hunger strike began, which ended – famously – in 1981 after the deaths of ten strikers, including the newly elected MP for Fermanagh and South Tyrone, Bobby Sands.

In many families, internment was already a generational blight. In the 40s, the British government had launched a similar campaign in which hundreds of young men were imprisoned for suspected affiliation with the IRA. (In Bobby Devlin's Long Kesh memoir *An Interlude with Seagulls*, he recalls that internee 'was one of the first words I could say as a child', because his eldest brother, Paddy, was in Crumlin jail.[37]) In 1984, Fairweather, McDonough and McFadyean observe that, in Belfast, someone has written 'My son is dying on the blanket' 'in large, even capital letters the length of a side wall of a house.' They elaborate:

> those 'outside the wire' are also prisoners in this war: the mothers, wives and children who form part of the 60,000 people currently affected by the imprisonment of a near relative; those who remain behind, to wait, to campaign, to worry. Waiting is something to which Irish women have become accustomed. During the past decade of the Troubles, one in ten adult Catholic males have at some time been imprisoned.[38]

Incarceration is a thief of youth. Ronan Bennett, a former Long Kesh internee, recalled in 2008 that, although there was 'a scattering of ancient men in their 30s and 40s; veterans of previous campaigns', on the whole 'the men in Long Kesh and Crumlin Road and the women in Armagh jail were terribly, terribly young'.[39] Teresa, a mother interviewed by Fairweather in 1980 about her son Patrick, who had been on the blanket for three years, said 'at 21 he looks like an old, old man.' Patrick had previously been interned for nine months at the age of sixteen, before being sentenced to fourteen years for alleged membership of the IRA and possession of a rifle on the strength of a verbal confession after a three-day-long interrogation.

Youth offered no protection against the state, and mothers were engaged perpetually in the difficult maintenance labour of supporting an imprisoned child in full knowledge of the horrendous conditions in which they were living. Fairweather, using a false name, accompanies Teresa on a visit. First, they make up packages to try to smuggle contraband inside their vaginas: 'half an ounce of tobacco, a few cigarette papers and broken-off match heads, the inner tube of a tiny biro, four migraine tablets, a letter from a friend and a few pages from the writings of James Connolly. Both are written out, in tiny writing, onto toilet paper.' After reading, Patrick ate the paper (he had read nearly half of *Labour in Irish History* this way). The bus to Long Kesh was full of women – some old, some very young, many carrying babies and toddlers – and two men who, according to Fairweather, seem out of place; visiting prisoners is women's work, 'emotional housework'. At the prison, the visiting bodies are subject to an aggressive inquisition: pregnant people have to pull their tights down; those who are menstruating are told to remove their sanitary towels and nappies are removed from baby's bottoms. For Teresa, the violation of her own body is not the point: she is thinking of Patrick, of the repeated infractions on his physical boundaries. 'How do you console someone,' Fairweather wonders, 'whose naked son is undergoing an anal search?'

In theory, Teresa supports Patrick's protest: she believes the prisoners should have political status. In practice, she is desperate for him to give up. Terrified for his life, she describes shaking hands with him as 'shaking hands with a bone':

> I don't want to go back and see him anymore because I can't bear the sight of him. The prisoners are going through it on the inside, but the mothers are also going through it on the outside – they are on our minds morning, noon and night. You waken in the morning and your son's face is in front of you, your sons face is in front of you when you're going to sleep at night.

One thought has occupied her mind, she says: that she should 'do something to herself [. . .] "last night I wanted to kill myself. I thought it was the one thing that might bring it all to light." ' This is a fantasy – her death would have been just another statistic, guilty by association – but a fundamentally maternal one: she wants to exchange her own life for that of her child. Later in *Only the Rivers Run Free*, Fairweather describes a hen party on the Turf Lodge estate, where, towards the end, two men arrive: Blanket boys; she is told that they're always welcome, 'even at a party just meant for women'. A woman called Mairead, whose own son is in Long Kesh, observes that 'the mothers eat, sleep and die H-Block every day, every hour, every minute. Even while I'm talking here I'm wishing my heart and soul that my son was here.'[40]

A central part of eating, sleeping and dying H-Bock was the Relatives Action Committee, set up in 1976 (later the National H-Block/ Armagh Committee), which gained particular momentum during the 80–81 hunger strikes, with Father Piaras Ó Duill as its chairman and Bernadette Devlin McAliskey as its primary spokesperson. As well as campaigning, the group allowed those involved in the agonizing business of waiting to find purpose and community. This formalized something that had been true even prior to the RAC's formation. Deirdre Lennon, interned in 1974, recalled that 'I always thought of my mum who had to struggle like many other mums. But then she made many friends with the other mums who were going through the same thing.' Many former prisoners reminisce about the gargantuan efforts put in by their families: Maggie McClenaghan, who had seven incarcerated family members, remembers that, for years, her relatives 'did the rounds of the Crum, the Kesh, the Maidstone, Magilligan and the H Blocks. That was one hell of a struggle for parents to go through, never missing out on visits or parcels.'[41]

Prisoners' mothers were generally the most active demographic in the RAC: they tended to have more time to give than wives, with no young family of their own to bring up. The rules of the Belfast Committee dictated that it 'should concern itself with all matters concerning the arrest, interrogation, trial and sentencing of prisoners and their rights and conditions pending a general amnesty', recognizing that these all relate to the British policy of criminalization, and demand 'a total amnesty for all Irish political prisoners', the withdrawal of all British troops and restoration of the Irish republic. They also sought to mobilize national and international opinion in favour of the campaign, holding demonstrations and pickets attended by tens of thousands, garnering significant support from the socialist and communist movements in Britain especially. Many at the time spoke of the RAC as being unique in that it was a mass organization started and led pretty much exclusively by women. Some believed this to represent a shift in the dynamics of families in the north as a whole, with one member stating that:

> probably the only good thing to come out of this heart-breaking war is the great change in the role of the women. With things so bad we had to be active, and with that we've found a whole new identity for ourselves. No longer was the woman just a piece of property: your man's missus, your children's mother. As we've come more and more to the forefront we've discovered our own strength, and power.[42]

Rose McAllister, a female prisoner interviewed in *The Armagh Women*, recalls that it was 'amazing' to:

see women on the streets, in control of the streets, those public places; women with their families of children, women out at two or three in the morning. I remember once, near dawn, saying to this woman who had six kids, 'You'll be wrecked sorting those kids out when you get home', and she said 'They can sort themselves out!' There was a time when that remark would have been sacrilegious. Society used to class you as a good mother if you stayed at home and never set a foot out the door.[43]

Another former Armagh internee compared this shift in gender roles to that which took place during the Second World War, only more lasting, because, even after the men returned, women 'didn't go back into the home because men expected them to': 'Nothing's ever been the same since.'[44] Anne Scargill and Betty Cook, remember, made a similar comparison about the aftermath of the WAPC's involvement in the miners' strike. These struggles, however disparate, demonstrated that the transgression of the division between domestic and public life allowed mothers in particular to feel connected both to the wider struggles and to each other, recasting their maternal identities as sources of collective power.

In Armagh

Women were not just the campaigning mothers of prisoners: they were also prisoners themselves, primarily in Armagh jail, where conditions were horrific. *Troops Out*, the journal of the eponymous movement, reported that:

The wing the women are held in is the largest block in the prison, with three stories, and on the Governor's orders, only one orderly is detailed to clean it. So it is filthy. The women themselves have been on 21-hour lock up, so they have only three hours to clean themselves, their clothes, and their cells. There are two baths for the 33, the washroom has no hot water and regularly floods, there are no mops and one brush, Wing dirt gets walked into cells, landing bins are not emptied. The place is maggot-infested. The warders have cut down even more on toilet visits – twice a day only, and women are allowed only two sanitary towels daily, regardless of need. They have had to relieve themselves in the cells.[45]

According to Nell McCafferty, sanitary towels were precious: the women used them as masks against the putrid smell, and wore them even when they weren't menstruating, to prevent against infection.[46] In February 1980, hostilities escalated within Armagh when forty male prison warders were brought in, officially to search the cells. A violent clash ensued, in which the officers – many in full riot gear – beat the women viciously before locking them in their cells for twenty-four hours, with no access to bathrooms. When they were released, the toilets remained locked, and the women were repeatedly prevented from 'slopping out', leaving chamber pots overflowing in their cells and beginning to stink. In response, thirty-three of them embarked on a no-wash protest, smearing the contents of their chamber pots onto the cell walls. Pauline McLaughlin, a nineteen-year-old from Derry, became so unwell that she began to vomit after every meal, and became a poster girl – in the grimmest and most literal sense – both nationally and internationally for the horrific conditions in the jail: in October 1980, the British Socialist Feminist Conference pledged to campaign for her release, endorsing the political status cause for the first time.

Coverage of the no-wash protest was significantly gendered: menstrual blood, somehow more horrific or perhaps more private than faeces, became symbolic of Armagh's horrors. 'The menstrual blood on the walls of Armagh prison,' wrote McCafferty in the *Irish Times* in 1980 'smells to high heaven. Shall we (feminists) turn our noses up?' The answer, according to many who responded, was 'yes'. The divided women's movement in the north repeated old debates about the legitimacy of the nationalist struggle, its perceived masculinity and its use of violence. The no-wash protesters responded to their critics:

It is our belief that not only is our plight a feminist issue, but a very fundamental social and human issue. It is a feminist issue in so far as we are women, even though we are treated like criminals. It is a feminist issue when the network of this jail is completely geared to male domination. The Governor, the Assistant Governor and the doctor are all males. We are subject to physical and mental abuse from male screws who patrol our wing daily, continually peeping into our cells . . . If this is not a feminist issue, then we feel that the word feminist needs to be redefined to suit these people who feel that 'feminist' applies to a certain section of women rather than encompassing women everywhere regardless of politically held views.[47]

When the hunger strike began, its gendered dimensions were difficult to ignore. The republican leadership was initially reluctant to allow women to participate: they worried that Armagh would divert attention from Long Kesh, that they might be seen as men forcing vulnerable women to participate, and that the comparative biological weakness of women would make their strike less likely to succeed. Eventually, in November, Mairéad Farrell, Mairéad Nugent and Mary Doyle, all in their early twenties, were allowed to participate. Their statement was steadfast: 'We are prepared to fast to the death, if necessary, but our love for justice and our country will live forever.' The women dropped weight significantly faster than the men, and quickly became terrifyingly thin: fellow prisoners remember Farrell's face being 'just teeth' and nothing more, her skin stretched skull-like over her face.[48] Authorities maintained that there was no cause for concern, and prison staff tormented the strikers. Doyle recalled:

The cell was never without food. They took away breakfast and replaced it with lunch, took away lunch and replaced it with supper, etc. Jail food is notoriously rotten and cold: fat with a bit of meat through it. But all of a sudden the plates were overflowing with steaming hot chips that smelt so appetising. A screw would say, 'Those chips have been counted, so we'll know if you're eating.'

The physical vulnerability of the women was also an asset: although some did believe that they had been forced into participating, the image of a woman's body undergoing such hardship was a powerful symbol for the hostility of the invasive colonial state. Mother Ireland's canonical suffering was both aesthetically and historically linked to the 1845–52 famine. The strikers' families rallied round them, and Nugent's mother Margaret was particularly active in the support campaign, touring Britain and giving interviews to the left-wing press, clear in her belief in her daughter's heroism, and in her consent. She told the *Morning Star* that:

> It is not up to us. I just cannot imagine what they will look like after 40 days of hunger strike – but it is a choice I know they are determined to follow through . . . I know my daughter is determined to win or die.

Emphasizing the personal consequences of forty days of hunger on her daughter at the same time as declaring them subordinate to the larger cause, Nugent's maternal concern was expressed through support, not approbation. She told the *Socialist Worker* that she had not attempted to change her daughter's mind because the strike was the 'last hope' that the prisoners had; her role as a mother was not to protect her daughter from harm but to honour and even facilitate the bravery of her child.[49]

Throughout 1981, a debate raged on the pages of *Spare Rib*, sparked by an article by Róisín Boyd arguing that British feminists should support the hunger strikes. In November, a letter was published from the mothers of some of the strikers in Long Kesh, as well as Margaret Nugent. It read:

> The women's struggle is the same as the men's in the H blocks: they are the same freedom fighters for a united Ireland.
>
> As feminists and progressive women you can't remain silent, while the people of Ireland give their lives in a struggle, as long as the British remain on our soil . . .

There will be no freedom for women in Ireland, while British soldiers remain in our country, while our daughters and sons are attempted to be criminalized in British jails and our women and children are killed and maimed by plastic bullets.[50]

Maternal voices were again afforded a particular power: they endorsed the sacrifices made by their children, and implored other women, in solidarity, to do the same. Motherhood could not, in such circumstances, be understood as the opposite of conflict, or apolitical: in fact, these mothers were putting their political beliefs before their filial bonds. (After the strike ended, and despite their heroism, the three female hunger strikers were often forgotten or belittled: agency diminished, they were seen simply as 'the girls in Armagh'.)[51]

Armagh itself could be understood as a site of feminist consciousness-raising in the tradition of the WLM: imprisonment could provide an experience in political education, reading and discussing other struggles for social justice.[52] It was also a predominantly working-class space, as McCafferty observes:

The prisoners' previous occupations read like a roll call of working-class female life in Northern Ireland – cashier, hairdresser, shop assistant, stitcher, cutter, stitcher, clerk, student, housewife, shop assistant, stitcher, shop assistant, shop assistant, librarian, dental nurse, clerk, stitcher, stitcher, short-hand typist, tobacco worker, computer operator, stitcher, housewife, barmaid, florist, clerk, stitcher, tobacco worker, receptionist, shop assistant.[53]

Jail made the women feel more keenly the link between their class and their gender, and offered them opportunities to learn together. Maternal structures developed within the prison walls: Rosaleen Walsh remembers that everyone looked on Mary McGuigan, who 'never seemed to run out of teabags' and was in Armagh at the same time as her daughter and her daughter-in-law, 'as a surrogate mother; she was the essence of kindness'.[54] Though there were no formal classes like those that took place in Long Kesh, shared reading and discussion through cell walls was common, much of this centring around historical struggles. A former prisoner interviewed by O'Keefe said 'throughout jail my whole outlook was broadened', becoming a truly 'feminist outlook' for the first time.[55]

This was true of action outside the walls, too. One woman who helped organize Armagh pickets with the republican socialist feminist group Women Against Imperialism told O'Keefe that it was a 'learning process', particularly because many of the 'women who came over to help were lesbians and it was free and open'. Their conversations made her feel 'so ignorant', and she read *Our Bodies, Ourselves*, the iconic feminist book about women's health and sexuality, to educate herself: 'Once you broke out of your shell you wanted to know everything.' WAI expanded their feminist work within the wider republican community. Founder member Una Ní Mhearain told O'Keefe that the group believed that 'imperialism had distorted all the landscapes within Ireland, all the personal landscapes and political landscapes.'[56] As well as campaigning to end the IRA practice of tarring and feathering, they gave talks in pubs and clubs about domestic violence, an extremely controversial topic. After the organization disbanded in 1981, Ní Mhearain and others founded the Falls Women's Centre in west Belfast, hoping to provide a place for women to organize and support each other, not only with domestic violence and other highly taboo issues like abortion and rape, but with further education: there were computer classes, literary classes and 'confidence-building' classes, and there was an crèche on-site, ensuring that mothers could participate.[57] Volunteers from the centre escorted women to court and legal appointments and to see banks and debt collectors; they also liaised with Women's Aid to remove women and children from abusive situations.[58] (The Falls Road, like other Catholic areas, was not a community protected by the police, who were unlikely to intervene in domestic situations anyway.)

The 'personal landscapes and political landscapes' that imperialism distorted converged most clearly when prisoners were pregnant.

Despite what regulations stated, pregnancy ensured no special treatment. In 2016, the former Armagh prisoner Brenda Murphy recalled giving birth in Craigavon Hospital while handcuffed to a bed: she was not allowed to keep her daughter with her, instead forced to 'sign her out like a piece of property'.[59] Rose, a Sinn Féin member who was arrested in 1971 for wearing a combat jacket and carrying a hurley stick ('paramilitary uniform') to a protest, discovered her pregnancy while working in the prison laundry: 'There was no medical attention for women like me. You just got your prison food. That was it. It was served in a dixie, a tin can like a dog dish.'[60] In 1977, she was arrested again and sentenced to two years, once again pregnant: her request to remain with her baby was denied. Jacqueline Burke, who was imprisoned in Maghaberry in 1987, told Brady that throughout her pregnancy she had to attend weekly remand court hearings 'in a paddy wagon', despite her extreme morning sickness. When her son, Padraig, was born, the prison doctor did not believe her when she said she was in labour, and the only help she received was from her fellow prisoners: those who had experienced labour themselves comforted her and advocated for her need to be taken to hospital. She arrived in the labour ward ten minutes before he was born, surrounded by strangers and armed police:

When I had Padraig the two screws who were with me were crying. They probably knew what I had been through and were thinking of what it would be like if their own daughter had been treated the way I was treated. Nobody was really kind to me in the hospital.[61]

Bernadette Boyle from Derry was arrested in 1976 when she was three months pregnant; allowed only one visit per month, when McCafferty interviewed her in 1981 her daughter had just turned four and had spent a total of eighteen hours with her mother in her entire life. The stress of separation was particularly acute if your child was taken ill. Evelyn Gilroy (Armagh, 1974) had a daughter, Denise, who was taken to Lissue Hospital with 'inward convulsions'. Between her arrest and her release, she did not see her daughter once: social services declared the jail a hygiene risk, and prison authorities would not let Gilroy leave the premises. When they were eventually reunited, 'Denise would not come to me as she did not recognize me. She would only respond to my mummy when she put glasses on. Apparently she had bonded with a nurse in Lissue who wore glasses.'[62]

I hope it is not necessary for me to state that people should not be forced to give birth in shackles or denied contact with their baby: even if we accept that they have done wrong, and even if we accept that prison is an answer to this (I don't), this neither incriminates the infant nor justifies the denial of the mother's human rights. It is not a surprise that the British state's attitude to 'criminal' mothers harks back to the Victorian era: separation is one answer to the notion that a guilty mother might harm their child by passing on transgressions in their touch, in their milk, in their blood. Motherhood is a useful weapon for the state to use against prisoners: Rose remembers that, in subsequent interrogations, she was told 'I wasn't a good mother, that I was just IRA scum and no decent woman would be associated with me.' It wasn't only the state that looked on her unkindly. She felt that life was harder for women who had been in jail, who weren't heralded as heroes like their male counbterparts were, particularly if they had children: 'By going to jail you're destroying their idea of what a woman should be like and what a mother should be like.'[63] (In a 2012 interview, Rose Dugdale, an English aristocrat who – infamously – became an IRA volunteer and gave birth in Limerick prison, recalled the joy of waking up to her baby's face each morning, but that her son's life was 'harder' because of her.[64]) For those who were already mothers when they were charged, life was very hard. Margaret Gatt, also arrested at the hurley-stick protest, told Brady that, of the twelve women also arrested at the hurley stick protest, two were pregnant and the rest had thirty-six children between them. These traumatized children were left in the care of relatives, often elderly parents, because of fears that otherwise 'the children would be taken into care and that was the nightmare for us all.'[65]

In a republican context, what does it mean to decree what a 'mother should be like'? If one thing she shouldn't be is incarcerated, is freedom then a quality essential to motherhood? Where does that leave Mother Ireland? By this definition, life under the British occupation is certainly not what mothering *should* be like, either.

Mothers for Peace

The conceptual alignment of motherhood with suffering and sacrifice positions mothers either as the direct victims of violence or adjacent to it: dealing with its results, rather than participating. (Think again of Greenham's maternal metaphors, pitting Mother Earth against the 'boys' and their toys.) Indeed, the famous case of Jean McConville, who was 'disappeared' by the IRA in the early 70s after being accused of passing information to British forces, has retained such a hold on the public imagination not just because the former Sinn Féin leader Gerry Adams has been implicated in her murder but because of the fact that she was a single mother of ten, the youngest of whom was six at the time. Reporters covering Northern Ireland during the Troubles tended to privilege a certain kind of innocence: the death of children in IRA attacks was given coverage that the killing of children by the British Army was not (I am not, as I hope is obvious, suggesting that the attention given to the former was not justified, but rather observing its unequal application).

On 10 August 1976 in Andersonstown, west Belfast, Anne Maguire and her three children Joanne, Andrew and John, were run over by Danny Lennon and John Chillingworth, two IRA volunteers who lost control of their car after being shot by a British patrol. Joanne, who was eight years old, and six-week-old Andrew, whom Anne was wheeling in a pram, died at the scene. Two-year-old John died in hospital the following day. Anne herself was critically injured, but survived: three years later, the night before the inquest into the deaths, she died by suicide. The event was the catalyst for the formation of the Peace People by Anne's sister Mairead Corrigan (now, having married Anne's widower, Mairead Corrigan Maguire) and Betty Williams, a resident who claimed to have seen Lennon and Chillingworth firing at the Army first. (There were no weapons in the car except for a dismantled gun in the back. Anne herself believed that two of her children were shot dead before the car hit them.)[66] Initially called the 'Women's Peace Movement', it became a runaway success: Williams immediately began gathering signatures for a petition and organized a march of over 200 women in Belfast. A second cross-community march, which ended at the Maguire children's graves, was attended by 10,000 women: within a month, there were 35,000 people of all genders in the 'Community of Peace People'.

At the end of August, Betty Williams wrote an open letter addressed to 'wonderful courageous Northern Irish People', published in *Peace by Peace*:

> God in Heaven what wonderful people you are. At the rallies I try my best to hug as many as I can get near, but there are so many thousands of us it is difficult. While you are reading this, my arms are around you nice and tight, and my heart is ready to burst with pride . . . We can truly say we are like Gandhi's movement through India, or Martin Luther King's in America. Maybe I'm being bigheaded, but I think we are braver . . .[67]

Williams's global focus paid off: in 1977 she shared the Nobel Peace Prize with Corrigan – the youngest ever laureate – for their efforts. In reality, the movement of 'wonderful people' and love that she describes had rapidly soured in the face of real political questions, losing the support of republican women in particular: although they positioned themselves as defenders of children, they refused to support the hunger strikers in Long Kesh or condemn the killing of the thirteen-year-old schoolboy Brian Stewart by the British Army in October 1976; and there was consternation when they announced that they were going to keep the Nobel money rather than donate it. Some were more sympathetic, however, as Daniel Finn notes, observing that, although IRA supporters attacked them as 'stooges of the British', the protests also attracted many working-class Catholics, those who had protested against internment and marched for civil rights in previous decades who sympathized with the peace campaign's general aims.[68]

Perhaps the most jarring aspect of the Peace People's very public rise and fall was the juxtaposition between its fanfare and hyperbole (braver than Martin Luther King!) and the life of Anne Maguire. Taking the loss of her children as its inspiration, and her children's graves as a literal destination, it used her suffering as a symbol, removed from the actual circumstances of the final three years of her life, which were deeply, fatally private. Corrigan, writing after Anne's suicide, said that

> Anne never saw her children buried. In her own mind she refused to accept their deaths. She would often talk about seeing them playing in the garden. Their deaths and the brain bruising she suffered resulted in psychotic depression. Anne became a troubled soul, knowing no peace of mind. She seemed to lock herself in a private world with her dead babies.[69]

The Nobel prize offered her no consolation. In March 1993, another maternal loss inspired the formation of another peace campaign group. The day before Mother's Day, two IRA bombs exploded on a busy shopping street in Warrington, Cheshire. The blasts happened within a minute of each other, and many ran from the first blast directly into the second. Fifty-six people were injured, and two children died: three-year-old Johnathan Ball at the scene, and Tim Parry, who was twelve years old, whose life support machine was switched off five days later. Parry's health was the centre of extensive media, and caught the attention of Susan McHugh, a housewife and mother living in Dublin. McHugh and her spontaneously formed group Peace '93 organized a rally attended by 400 people on the day of the bombing, and one five days later that attracted 20,000 people; a condolence book was left outside the General Post Office. In 2018, the

BBC aired a dramatization of McHugh's relationship with Tim's mother Wendy, played by Vicky McClure and Anna Maxwell Martin respectively. Called *Mother's Day*, it centres on the way in which Parry, numb and agonized by excruciating grief, tentatively forges a bond with McHugh over the efforts she goes to 'for peace': they can relate to each other, as their relationship unfolds over tentative cups of tea in homely kitchens, as mothers.

Peace '93 attracted similar criticism to the Peace People two decades earlier: their focus was almost entirely on the violence perpetrated by the IRA, reinforcing the general lack of media attention that was paid to other deaths. Of course, the deaths of two children hundreds of miles away from the Irish border were likely to be treated very differently from, say, the shooting of four Catholic men in Castlerock and a seventeen-year-old Catholic civilian in Belfast by the loyalist Ulster Defence Association: they were symbolic, in their youth and their Englishness, of innocence. A crucial scene in *Mother's Day* sees McHugh in conversation with a group of bereaved republican mothers in Belfast who had protested the second rally in Dublin over its selectiveness. 'My wee girl,' says one of them, 'was innocent. She was murdered too. But because she was murdered by the security forces rather than the IRA, that means she isn't seen as innocent, and neither am I. Has she not the same value? Do you know her name?' McHugh cannot answer her. She continues: 'When I lost her, no one in Dublin picked up the phone. No one sent flowers.' McHugh is shocked when told that 134 children had been killed by British state or loyalist forces since the Troubles began: 'I didn't know,' she repeats. 'I didn't know.'

The Warrington bombing is often cited as the inspiration for the 1994 song 'Zombie', the biggest commercial hit of the Irish band the Cranberries. In this song, history is flattened: it begins with the description of a child being 'taken' and the grief of its mother, linking the tanks and bombs and guns of today with an unbroken chain of events that Dolores O'Riordan, in her astonishing, cracking, girlish voice, dates back to 1916, the year of the Easter Rising. The video to 'Zombie', initially banned by the BBC, featured monochromatic footage shot in Belfast of children playing, interspersed with shots of British soldiers and O'Riordan painted gold, standing in front of a crucifix surrounded by silver-painted children with bows and arrows: part pietà, part crucifixion scene, part vengeful mother goddess. At the 1998 Nobel Peace Prize ceremony, which was awarded to the Northern Irish politicians John Hume and David Trimble for their role in the Good Friday Agreement, the band performed the song live. In an interview with *Vox* magazine four years earlier, O'Riordan denied that the band were 'taking sides': 'I don't care whether it's Protestant or Catholic, I care about the fact that innocent people are being harmed. That's what provoked me to write the song . . . It doesn't name terrorist groups or organizations. It doesn't take sides. It's a very human song.'[70] What does human mean, here? Is suffering only suffering – only worthy of outrage and sympathy – if it is understood to be politically 'neutral'? The grief of a mother for her child certainly isn't, despite attempts to define it as such: it is more palatable for mourning to be understood as something that exists outside the sphere of the political, not least because it absolves us of our complicity in the conditions which led to it.

Maternal grief is powerfully symbolic but it is never only that. In accounts of mothers who lost children during the Troubles, the complexity is often lost, sacrificed in favour of a message, a symbolic point about guilt and innocence. Many of the British soldiers dispatched to the north were very young, and many were men from working-class communities with few other options (remember the Claimants Unions, compiling factsheets about the ways the state tried to use the unemployed as a military recruiting ground). Many of them had no idea of the history of the conflict they were about to perpetuate, and neither did their families. In 2000, Rita Restorick published *Death of a Soldier: A Mother's Search for Peace in Northern Ireland*, an account of the death of her son Stephen, the last soldier to be killed in the conflict, in which she admits that she didn't even know the names of the six counties before her son was killed in one of them. I do not want to diminish Restorick's loss by saying that the fact that hers was understood to be tragically bad luck – to die so close to the end of your tour – and the loss of Catholic sons and daughters at the hands of soldiers was not. This is emblematic of an absence in the wider culture, an inability to allow the political into maternal mourning. The army, here, is understood to be apolitical, simply doing a job, 'keeping the peace', unlike the deaths of those who sought to disturb it. But each is as political as the other.

One mother who was all of these things at once – an activist, feminist, author of violence and victim of it – was Bernadette Devlin, already familiar to this chapter. Called 'the baby of Parliament' when she took her seat in 1969 at the age of twenty-one, she was criticized for her 'wild' behaviour and her mini-skirted, long-haired appearance as much as for her behaviour in the Commons (slapping the then Conservative Home Secretary when he claimed that the Army had fired 'in self-defence' on Bloody Sunday, for example).[71] Particularly scandalous was the birth of her daughter, Roisin, out of wedlock in 1972. Although Devlin married the father, Michael McAliskey, and went on to have two more children – Deirdre and Fintan – an unmarried, pregnant Catholic was something for her critics to make hay with. In 1981, her family life again became a target, more seriously this time: the Ulster Freedom Fighters shot her and her husband in their house, while their three young children were present. Their injuries were severe enough that they had to be taken to intensive care. (British soldiers were watching the building at the time and did not prevent the loyalists' violent entry.) Addressing the psychic repercussions of this profoundly traumatic event in 2008, she stated that she believed that 'My kids would have survived the loss of their mother better than the loss of their physical security, which was home.'[72]

Devlin McAliskey, in interviews and in writing, constructs her own heritage as a matriarchal one: 'I come from a long line of strong women. My mother and grandmother were both widows. The level of poverty that I grew up in brings a degree of strength and creativity to women, because they have to manage.'[73] (After her mother died, the nineteen-year-old Bernadette combined her undergraduate studies with raising her younger siblings.) In 2016, she told *Jacobin* that somebody had recently contacted her to tell her that her maternal grandmother was in Cumann na mBan, which was a surprise: 'She never spoke about it – such must have been her disappointment with the revolution's outcome.'[74] Maternal inheritance can be a complicated blessing, or even a curse. In 1997, it seemed that the latter was true for her daughter: Roisin, seven months pregnant, was being held without a specific charge in HMP Holloway under anti-terrorist legislation while the government decided how to respond to an extradition request from Germany, where she had been named as a suspect in a mortar attack on a British Army barracks in Osnabruck.[75] Devlin McAliskey's solicitor reported that her mental and physical health was seriously deteriorating, with the PTSD that stemmed from the 1981 attack exacerbated by her week-long interrogation in Castlereagh. Once she was moved to Holloway, she was strip-searched seventy-five times in four months and was prevented from leaving her cell, where an electric light was on twenty-four hours a day; she was eventually transferred to a mother-and-baby prison unit 'after fears for the safety of her unborn child grew'.[76]

The case became a rallying point for intersecting causes. Although the imprisonment of those fighting extradition from the UK was fairly routine, there was no precedent for the detention of a pregnant IRA suspect in Britain, and the treatment of pregnant prisoners in general had been gaining attention as unjust: Women in Prison, co-founded in 1983 by the criminologist Pat Carlen and former Holloway prisoner Chris Tchaikovsky, had been building up a strong profile campaigning for the rights of pregnant prisoners. They were vocal in their opposition, with Tchaikovsky declaring that, in not granting bail, the government was 'willing to risk her and the baby and, God forbid, a conflagration in Northern Ireland – she is a symbol after all, Bernadette Devlin's daughter – to keep her in jail'.[77] A year previous, Channel 4 had broadcast secretly filmed footage of a Holloway prisoner shackled to warders only an hour after giving birth, with witnesses saying she had been restrained while she was having contractions. Prisons Minister Anne Widdecombe defended the practice, responding that, actually, the prisoner had only been shackled until full labour was established: the Prison Service, she said, 'has a duty of care to the mother, but this must be balanced against the needs of the service'.[78]

Signs waved at protests internationally usually bore an image of her next to her mother, their faces close, looking strikingly alike, underneath the slogan RELEASE ROISIN MCALISKEY! Her supporters were clear that the family connection was a governing factor in how Roisin was both treated and perceived by the state. In the *Independent* in March 1998, Ros Wynne-Jones wrote that 'the Devlin legacy' 'made' Roisin guilty: she was born in the month internment began; woken as a child to 'the sight of a masked gunman standing in the doorway'; her daughter Loinnir's father was Sean McCotter, a former republican prisoner and, most damningly, there was the often reprinted picture of Roisin, Bernadette and Gerry Adams carrying the coffin of the former head of the Irish National Liberation Army, Dominic 'Mad Dog' McGlinchey, at his funeral in 1994.[79] It was left to Bernadette and her lawyer Gareth Peirce to defend Roisin against this symbolic solidification, and against her history. She was being punished for her mother's crimes, or at least her associations. In 1998, Roisin and Loinnir were finally released. As her mother put it to a reporter, in a characteristically dry nod to her family's well-documented past, 'I can think of more traumatic things than finding out that my daughter is a terrorist.' To turn the mother into a symbol of conflict and aggression has its drawbacks; so does its transformation into a symbol of peace.

10.

No Father

If there are not many reliable men,
you can in effect marry the state instead.

David Willetts

I had a New Labour childhood. Although John Major's Conservative government was still in power when I was born in April 1993, exactly a fortnight after the Child Support Agency officially began operations, by the time I started school in September 1997, Tony Blair had won a landslide election victory. By the turn of the millennium, my brother – literally a New Labour baby, having entered the world a month after their government entered Parliament – and I had become part of a particularly zeitgeisty moral concern: we were children being raised by a lone parent, a Single Mum. This came with a particular glamour attached to it: earnest conversations with teachers about The Divorce, a few visits to a family therapist whom I have a distinct memory of believing myself to be running rings around, the sense that a grand adult significance, bigger than just the three of us, had been bestowed upon the changing circumstances of our lives.

It can be exhausting to be the offspring of a political concept: 1993 was the year in which the Tories froze one-parent benefit, a policy backed up by a 'pathologization' of single mothers that the government both encouraged and exploited, shoring up the symbolic power of the archetypal feckless single mum.[1] To me, however, my new life was made legible by the culture I and crucially, my peers were consuming: we were a Jacqueline Wilson generation, and her books and others like them widened our idea of what a family could be to include foster care, children's homes, temporary accommodation and psychiatric wards. I became quite obsessed, for a while, with a television film called *The Greatest Store in the World*, in which a very beautiful single mother, played by Dervla Kirwan, and her two daughters secretly move into and then subsequently save a department store after the van they've been living in explodes. A little later, there were American images – single *moms* – infused with the mystique of their origin: the *Princess Diaries* books, with scatter-brained, sexy artist Helen Thermopolis, and *Gilmore Girls*, a TV show which made a father seem like a superfluous, uncool accessory.

As a teenager, I somewhat unpredictably decided to become a dedicated reader of *Q*, a music magazine perhaps best described, in that period at least, as the journalistic embodiment of the protagonist of Nick Hornby's *High Fidelity* (I certainly absorbed more passive misogyny from those pages than from women's magazines). In it, I came across an interview with the musician Loudon Wainwright III, and became fascinated by the Wainwright–McGarrigle musical dynasty and their public playing out of divorce and all its attendant bitter feelings: the crumbling of Loudon's marriage to the folk icon Kate McGarrigle, the LPs in which his famous children, Rufus and Martha, process their archetypal shitty dad. In the interview, Wainwright describes listening to Martha's song 'Bloody Mother Fucking Asshole': 'At first I thought it was just about some guy who broke her heart,' he said, 'but then I listened closer to the lyrics and I realized it was to be taken literally.'

> And you have no idea
> No idea how it feels to be on your own
> In your own home with the fucking phone
> And the mother of gloom
> In your bedroom standing over your head
> With her hand in your head

In an interview in 2005, Martha Wainwright tells a particularly chilling story about her father's song 'I'd Rather be Lonely': 'I always felt terribly sorry for the poor woman I thought it was about because of the line: "Every time I see you cry / you're just a clone of every woman I've known." Then one time I was on tour with Loudon and he said to the crowd: "I wrote this song about my daughter." I had no idea. We lived together for one year in New York when I was 14 and it was a disaster, and "I'd Rather be Lonely" was about that year. He really crossed the line there.' You don't say.[2]

It was delicious to find myself so glamorously rendered: my angst was righteous and, crucially, identifiable. I performed a kind of therapeutic, oversized identification with my mother, taking pride in the fact that my difficult relationship with my father was not just because I was virtuously taking her side, but because I was in some way exactly like her: a repetition of the same dynamics, arguments and mistakes. I wonder if my mother found the same solace in cultural representation. Did she borrow the *Erin Brockovich* VHS from the library and see herself consolingly reflected? Probably not. Denise Riley's 1975 assertion that single mothers 'fit in around the cracks in everyone's theorizing like so much Polyfilla' remained, three decades on, depressingly relevant.[3]

Lone parenthood, which is the preferred term of most sociologists and historians – I am being neither neutral nor scholarly in my specific interest in the single mum – is, of course, not a new phenomenon. The historian Pat Thane, a leading expert on the subject, has repeatedly demonstrated that it is both 'an experience as old as marriage itself', and 'one with which few societies have been at ease'; in the UK, the nuclear family was only ever the norm for a brief period between 1945 and 1970.[4] Between 1961 and 1994 the number of families headed by a single mother increased fourfold, from 5 to 20 per cent of the country as a whole, something which has been attributed to the increasing separation of marriage and parenthood: in the 1970s, this was mostly due to divorce; while from the mid-80s onwards, more children were being born outside wedlock altogether.⁵ This reality was reflected in legislation: with the passing of the 1987 Family Law Reform Act, the term 'illegitimate' was removed from official legal vocabulary, giving all children 'broadly equal legal rights'. Yet attitudes towards the lone mother were still shaped by her traditional characterization as, as Thane and Tanya Evans have it, either a sinner, a scrounger or a saint.⁶ Single mothers were wronged, and deserve sympathy; they sinned, and deserve punishment; or they are seeking an easy ride, and deserve nothing.

The single mother is a convenient canvas onto which the anxieties of a period can be projected: during wartime, for example, the rise of illegitimacy was attributed to a loosening of sexual morals; for Thatcher, it was the demise of British family values. By the late 90s, the conversation had certainly shifted, and the material circumstances of single mothers were centred in some feminist campaigning. There was a sense that a single mother could be a good thing, was even, perhaps, a symbol of the new *girl power* thing, and in the process of becoming this more positive cultural touchstone, the single mother has taken on a kind of visible invisibility, solidifying into a figure of bad-luck-resilient-deservingness, so that the specific contours of each individual mother's life can be difficult to discern. The single mother suffers just as much from the lazy celebration of her as a 'radical' figure as she does from her castigation. It also creates a curious circumstantial time lag: when we talk about the family as a concept, even – perhaps especially – when we critique it, the particular qualities of a single-mother-family are not fully considered.

In *Landscape for a Good Woman*, Carolyn Steedman asks what happens to theories of patriarchy in households in which 'a man was not master, nor even there very much'. The mother, here, is not the patriarch's opposite but his replacement: Steedman quotes E. Ann Kaplan's theory that single mothers are 'forced to invent new symbolic roles'. Rather than a dynamic in which the mother is 'object to the father's law', in households governed by a lone mother it is her 'desire' which 'sets things in motion'.⁷ Writing three decades later, amid an ever-climbing rate of single-parent households on both sides of the Atlantic, Maggie Nelson offers a corrective to the idea that single or lesbian mothers offer some innate riposte to the patriarchy, a 'rejection', in Julia Kristeva's terms, of 'the symbolic'. Given, Nelson writes, how many families are helmed by them, 'you'd think the symbolic order would be showing a few more dents by now.'[8]

One thing which complicates the figure of the single mum is her especially heightened relationship to the state: anxieties about her cannot easily be separated from the question of material support. Thane writes that, since the sixteenth century, there has been significant confusion and disagreement over how lone mothers and their children should be supported: is the responsibility with the father, or is it with the state? If it's the former, how can money be extracted, and what if he doesn't exist? If it's the latter, how does this interact with the mother's role as a worker? Should she be forced to work outside the home for the sake of it – for appearances? 'Few social problems,' she observes, 'have changed so little over such a long time without effective resolution.' It's essential, however, to remember that not all single mothers are impoverished, or indeed even actually single, and private feelings are always more complicated than those recorded officially in public discourse.[9]

In the newly minted welfare state of the 1950s, 'unmarried mothers' could rely on social security: no longer required to register for work to qualify for income support if they had a child under sixteen at home, they could claim benefit even if they were living with their parents. Such benefits, however, were disqualified if they were living with a man, a policy which was the target of the Claimants Unions campaigns against welfare officer 'sex snoopers'. Single mothers were supported by the state on the condition that they devoted their entire self – their sexuality suppressed – to caring for their offspring. (We can see, too, how marriage was the only acceptable signifier of adult womanhood: in living with your parents rather than a man, you remained infantilized, an errant daughter.) In 'The Force of Circumstance', while detailing the *conservatizing* effect' of being a single mother, Riley also notes that:

It's not possible to live as a single mother and not confront, in a particularly immediate form, the real structured omnipresence of the bourgeois family and its economic correlatives. We are constituted by it automatically as deviants, economically as well as sexually. That is, ideology is not *merely* propaganda; if it were, the task of destroying it would be comparatively straightforward. I can detect myself being engineered into a series of conservatized positions which result directly from my position *as* a single mother under this phase of capitalism, and the process is not particularly mysterious, just saddening. We need a way of fully understanding our whole social and economic marginality.

Her warning is that the paradox of single motherhood is that being (generally) more financially vulnerable, more in need of an accessible anti-capitalist way of life, you are less able to resist the pressures of capitalism itself: you have fewer choices. The relative invisibility of single mothers in the wider politics of the left meant that the difficult choices of the socially and economically marginalized – such as, for example, deciding to continue renting privately to ensure your children remained housed rather than taking the risk of joining an experimental communal housing project – risked being understood as 'purely "irrational" private failures', rather than forming the basis for robust support of single mothers in order that they might not have to make such compromises.[10] The process that Riley is describing is recognizable in the stories some women tell about their lives in which they, having dealt with significant obstacles and overcome immense difficulties, are reluctant to help others with the same (think of the hardening that Betty Cook describes in her memoirs; think of Julie Burchill describing herself as a 'Thatcherite bitch').

Steedman's mother, meanwhile, was a lifelong Conservative, but her class position and her 'illegitimate' children made her an 'exile' from conventional society. Her decision to have children is figured by her daughter as a consequence of a bargain she struck: a decision which 'must have been made in the knowledge of herself as both bargain and bargainer', something she could 'exchange for a possible future'. This was a bargain with Steedman's father, who 'legalized us, by paying for us, supporting us, staying around', but also one 'struck between working-class women and the state, the traffic being a baby and the bargain itself freedom, autonomy, state benefits and a council house: the means of subsistence'.[11]

This is strikingly similar to the calculations single mothers were accused of making at the end of the century: producing a child to extract support from the surrogate paternal state. When it comes to the means of subsistence in the 1990s, I know that from a very young age I understood my entire life as one enabled by the Labour government. We lived in a very Conservative area, but my mum was a vocal Labour voter, a stridence I imitated long before I turned eighteen. The betrayal of the Iraq war hit us both hard – Tony B. Liar! – but there were no other options. New Labour, which to us meant Working Families Tax Credit, Family Benefit, Child Support and the Educational Maintenance Allowance, had ensured our survival. When I went to university, where I met the children of capital and – worse – the children of *cultural* capital, I embarked upon a strange performance of class, both self-aggrandizing and self-abnegating in turn. I emphasized the difficulties we had experienced that I understood to be virtuous – our single-mother-ness – without admitting to the aspects of our background I found difficult to deal with, difficult to understand. In 2011, the atmosphere was thick with the vocabulary of benefit fraud, but I was at an elite institution, I had a southern English accent, and I could use the benefits we had received as a trump card in arguments: I knew that I could confess to them and people would be *surprised*.

The Single-Parent State

Something had shifted in the 1990s in the realm of the single mum: as the social mores that had made illegitimacy and divorce shameful began to recede, the division between good and bad mothering was not erased but moved, transposed onto the old binary between the deserving and the undeserving poor. Celebrities, politicians even, would boast about having a 'single mum'; the richest and, at that time, most beloved woman in the country, J. K. Rowling, was one: the good kind, that is. A good single mother was one who had become such through no fault of her own – preferably via divorce – and, although she might claim some benefits, was either in work or had been before having children. A bad one was the opposite: someone reliant on benefits, who had had children outside marriage and even outside the couple or with multiple partners. These, regardless of their actual age, coalesced most intensely in the specific figure of the *teen mum*, which will be the focus of the next chapter.

By 1990, the dog days of Thatcher's premiership, one third of children were born to unmarried parents, with two million living in single-parent households, which earned on average just thirty-seven per cent of their two-parent equivalents. Correspondingly, the invective launched at them by politicians and much of the press reached a fever pitch. Thatcher's government had been committed to depicting single mothers as reliant on and motivated entirely by 'state handouts', accompanied by a classed and racialized caricature of the 'feckless father'.[12] The Conservative MP Rhodes Boyson declared at the Party conference in 1986 that single parents were 'evil', having made 'their case so well they have expanded their subsidies from the public purse from some £15 million in 1960 to £1 billion in 1983', constructing a baffling image of a single-mum cabal, sending out press releases and using ingenious guerrilla tactics like 'getting pregnant' and 'needing support'.[13] This continued, and even accelerated, under John Major: indeed, Melissa Benn suggested in 1999, the real crusade against single mothers at the level of policy as well as rhetoric began after Thatcher had left office.[14]

In 1993, John Redwood, then Secretary of State for Wales, caused a minor press sensation when, after touring the St Mellons housing estate in Cardiff, he described 'fatherless' families as 'one of the biggest social problems of our day'. In the same year, the murder of the toddler James Bulger by two ten-year-old boys was reported by many journalists as a direct result of their 'broken homes'; newspaper headlines declared that 'Single Parents Cripple Lives'. At that year's Conservative Party conference, where Major launched the much-ridiculed 'Back to Basics' campaign to restore 'traditional family values', the Secretary of State for the Department of Social Security, Peter Lilley, declared that his goal was to 'close down the something-for-nothing society', distinguishing between good single parents (widows, some divorcees) and bad ('benefits-driven', never married, young). The latter had risen, he believed, because it had become 'politically incorrect' to laud the virtues of the 'traditional family'.[15] Previously, he had delighted conference attendees with a refashioning of the Lord High Executioner's song from the Gilbert and Sullivan opera *The Mikado*:

> I've got a little list / Of benefit offenders who I'll soon be rooting out / And who never would be missed / They never would be missed. / There's those who make up bogus claims / In half a dozen names / And councillors who draw the dole / To run left-wing campaigns / They never would be missed / They never would be missed. / There's young ladies who get pregnant just to jump the housing queue / And dads who won't support the kids / of ladies they have . . . kissed / And I haven't even mentioned all those sponging socialists / I've got them on my list / And there's none of them be missed / There's none of them be missed.

It was in this frankly bizarre political climate – this was, to reiterate, a member of Cabinet singing about executing benefit claimants – that the Child Support Agency was established to implement the 1991 Child Support Act and ensure payments were made by the parent not residing with their children to the one who was: in practice, these were generally understood to be payments made by the father to the mother. The CSA ignored the advice of campaign groups and focused on penalizing fathers for not financially supporting their children; the amount paid by the father was then to be removed from the benefits the mother received. Although this was an ideological departure, legally categorizing the absent father for the first time as the 'sinner', in practice, it compounded discrimination against mothers. In Thane's words,

> For the first time, also, mothers were required to name the father of the child and were penalized by 20 per cent loss of benefit if they failed to do so 'without good cause'. Definition of 'good cause' was at official discretion and penalized some at least of the one in six divorced and one in ten single and separated mothers who gave violence as the reason for leaving the father and, reasonably, feared further violence if they named him.[16]

Poverty among lone-parent families was not reduced, and neither was the government's much-castigated 'benefits bill': single mums remained in the spotlight, a national problem.

Support for single mothers was, as many Tory MPs took pleasure in pointing out, the fastest growing part of the social security budget. Financial prudence and social hygiene have always been Conservative bedfellows, and they came together in the construction of an avaricious figure: a hustler, a grifter, the British equivalent of the American 'welfare queen' stereotype identified by Dorothy Roberts in 1991 as the latest prototype of 'bad mothering'.[17] Establishment media happily confirmed this notion: the BBC's *Panorama* broadcast several programmes that focused on the tantalizing spectacle of their 'cost to the state', including 1993's *Babies on Benefit*, which was filmed partially on the St Mellons estate. (One mother featured, from Wandsworth in south London, emphasized the economic realities of reproduction in the United Kingdom for those who weren't part of the middle and upper classes: 'If you're going to wait until you've got enough money to have a child, you're never going to have a child.') In 1994, Michael Portillo, then Secretary of State for Employment, personified state benefit as a corrupting influence in the style of a sexual predator or a brothel madam: 'Teenage girls,' he warned in *The Times*, could be 'lured into a life of poverty-stricken dependency by over-generous benefit'.[18]

Such comments declared their own paranoid motivations: the terrifying agency of a lone mother inspired a fear of replacement and usurpation. The Tory MP David Willetts wrote in the *Mail* in 1993 that 'The welfare state has taken over the traditional roles of the husband: it provides housing and a steady income. If there are not many reliable men, you can in effect marry the state instead.' In the same year and the same paper, the columnist Keith Waterhouse wrote that 'in the Single Parent State' lone mothers could 'rake in' over £100 per week and 'jump the housing queue': 'the majority of unmarried mums seem to regard the father as being as dispensable as the umbilical cord.' The political organization of lone parents was equally alarming: the Unmarried Mothers' Union was described as 'the single parents' militant wing where having a baby is not so much a happy event as a political statement'. Rife with classist references – 'You cradle the little mite to your boiler suit and carry a placard demanding crèche facilities at the bingo hall' – Waterhouse's article was reminding the reader that political identity was not something that working-class mothers were supposed to have.[19] The single mum, dispensing with fatherhood like medical waste, embodied the castration anxieties of those in control.

There were attempts to rehabilitate lone motherhood during these years. In 1994, to coincide with the United Nations 'Year of the Family', Virago published a collection of writings by single parents edited by Gil McNeil, in partnership with the charity Gingerbread; it is called, catastrophically embarrassingly, *Soul Providers*. Its contributors are mostly women, including the Labour MP and actor Glenda Jackson and the prominent feminist writer Lynne Segal, and it includes a variety of experience – stories from a refuge, parenting a child with Down's syndrome, the dual discrimination experienced by young Black single mothers, and a truly hair-raising account of international kidnap – with one consistent thread linking them all together: the lack of affordable childcare. Many of the stories emphasize the alternative system of relationships that exist in their families: Monica Tracey, in Liverpool, describes her elder daughters, Christine and Fiona, caring for the new baby, Rosheen, as a collaborative, equal arrangement: 'My new family had three parents.' Imani, in south London, identifies motherhood as the inspiration for her work in an Afro-Caribbean community centre, running writing classes and oral history classes (with a free crèche). Gender roles are pleasingly flexible: Greg Marsh recalls that after his partner left, their son started calling him 'mummy' and, in another chapter, Keith Hawkins refers to his son as his 'life partner'. Anna Keigh, in 'Not a Pretend Family', details the practical difficulties of lesbian mothering under Section 28, and the circular ironies of reproduction: speaking of an abortion she had ten years before her insemination, she notes 'I didn't take the decision to have an abortion lightly but I'm sure it was the right thing to do. The same people who would have wanted to prevent me from having Vicky would have tried to force me to have that child.'[20] Yet the book frequently reinforces conservative distinctions. In the preface, Claire Rayner invokes the Victorian notion of a mother fallen on hard times, declaring that many single parents would 'tolerate' this patronizing figure 'in exchange for the current stereotype of the single parent as at best feckless, and at worst an eager abuser of welfare "handouts", breeder of delinquent children and all round author of her own misfortunes'. She continues: 'in a wide experience of single parents, I have never *ever* met someone who had a baby to get on the housing list.'[21] So what if they did?

Old Problems

The 1997 general election was not, as many have observed, the radical break with the status quo it promised.[22] Families had changed, and this had to be reflected by the policies of a party that was branding itself as New: public opinion was significantly more tolerant than the mainstream representation made out.[23] Central, however, to Tony Blair's bid to win over the electorate was a commitment to the traditional family unit, as well as a promise from the Chancellor of the Exchequer, Gordon Brown, to follow the Conservatives' proposed budget, in the hope of banishing Labour's reputation for profligacy. In his first conference speech, Blair had declared that Marx was dead; he fashioned himself as a representative of 'middle England' and rewrote Clause 4 of the Labour Party's constitution, which, adopted in 1918, declared its purpose to be 'to secure for the workers by hand or by brain the full fruits of their industry' and 'the common ownership of the means of production, distribution and exchange', effectively ending the party's commitment to nationalization. In this 'radical centrism', a focus on the individual was encouraged. Despite – I cringe as I write it – 'Cool Britannia' – Blair was in many ways in political continuity with Thatcher, whom he called 'a radical, not a Tory', and who was the first former leader he invited to Downing Street.[24] Thatcher herself, in January 1997, told the Conservative Carlton Club that 'Tony Blair is a man who won't let Britain down.' (In Tony Benn's diary from 1995, he wrote, calling it presciently early, that Blair was 'the most popular Tory leader in Britain at the moment'.[25])

Blair, like Thatcher, put the family at the centre of the state: he professed that a 'strong society' needed 'strong families', linking this explicitly to Labour's stated aim to be 'tough on crime and tough on the causes of crime'; the prison population increased rapidly under his leadership.[26] (Fulfilling his role as national paterfamilias, he told the Police Federation that 'If we dare not speak the language of punishment then we deny the real world.'[27]) In 1999, the Family and Parenting Institute, which would come under attack a decade later when its incoming head Katherine Rake publicly declared that the 'days of the typical family are numbered', was established to 'actively support' families and children. Launched by the Home Secretary Jack Straw in a drive to deal with young offenders, it ran a helpline for parents whose children were deemed at risk of committing crimes. Straw wrote that families were 'the foundation' of society, and 'central to this Government's vision of a modern and decent country'.[28] The family was an arm, in other words, of the law-and-order state.

This necessarily perpetuated the stereotype of single motherhood as a drain on society, a contravention of the social contract.[29] Almost the first thing Blair's government proposed was to cut benefits for single mothers in order to reduce spending on social security. This was hugely controversial: forty-seven MPs voted against the government, over one hundred abstained and one minister and two Private Parliamentary Secretaries resigned their posts.[30] There was a public outcry, too, influenced by the Save Lone Parent Benefit Campaign, led by the Labour Women's Action Committee with support from major unions, the Single Parent Action Network and One Plus, the largest single-parent-focused organization in Scotland, and a protest was organized outside the Houses of Parliament, where Labour rebels were joined by mothers and children. The 'savings' worked out at around £195 million, relatively little in the context of the £100 billion total spent on welfare and – as many critics were quick to point out – the £800 million cost of the proposed Millennium Dome. This furore, coming so soon after an historic Labour victory, indicated that single mothers were not considered worthy of support or protection by this new version of the country's left-wing parliamentary party: their defence was a fringe issue, relegated to the 'hard left'.

The face of these cuts was Harriet Harman, MP for Camberwell and Peckham, Secretary of State for Social Security and the first ever Minister for Women. In her autobiography *A Woman's Work*, in a section called 'Transformation: Changing Politics to Match Women's Changing Lives' that is itself part of a chapter called 'Pressing Forward for Women' – the book is nothing if not committed to its theme – Harman mostly engages with the cuts as the cause of her own embarrassment and subsequent sacking from the front bench in 1998. She does briefly note her regret at not refusing to propose them, as well as explaining that they were a trade-off, made to protect benefit spending on the retired and the disabled.[31] Single mothers were acceptable collateral damage: it was easy to paint them as undeserving. The government's focus was on incentivizing single mothers to enter the workforce, and the 'New Deal for Lone Parents', implemented in 1998 and co-developed by Harman and Yvette Cooper, included childcare for working mothers, the right to flexible working hours, support in looking for work from Job Centre

Lone Parent Advisers, tax credits to top up their income if working part time, and changes to the system that ensured the continuity of benefits if employment ceased. It also withdrew benefits from those who had school-age children and did not find paid employment. As Thane observes, although the percentage of single mothers in employment did increase, it's unclear whether this was due to such policies or to the general reduction in unemployment, although they were certainly successful in implying that paid work should be the default, regardless of the needs or desires of the child and the mother themselves.[32]

In her autobiography, Harman defends the 'New Deal', positioning it and by extension herself in the reasonable centre: criticized by the right, who believed a woman's place was in the home – she doesn't engage with the fact that reducing benefits for single mothers also gave them exactly what they wanted – and castigated by 'the traditional left'. There were successes: as well as the (limited) childcare provision and flexible working policies, many mothers were keen to get back into work, and some even became Lone Parent Advisers themselves. Those who wished to could now seek advice from the Job Centre, which, classed as 'not available for work' until their youngest child turned sixteen, they previously had not been able to do until a time when many had been out of the workforce for so long that they had become 'unemployable'. Yet Harman continues to draw on the old framework of deserving and undeserving: 'The Tories denigrated lone parents as feckless women who'd had babies in order to get a council house, but most were lone parents because of divorce, rather than having started out as "unmarried mothers".' She also laments the 'rift' between married women and unmarried women, with 'many married mothers' resenting the fact that they were not 'entitled to benefits, enabling them to stay at home', as if it were some kind of luxury and as if the cure for resentment was to reduce entitlement, rather than extend it to everyone.[33]

New Labour's impact on single parents and their children has been heatedly relitigated in recent years, particularly after the 2015 election of Jeremy Corbyn to the party leadership and the subsequent, short-lived move away from the neoliberal consensus. Certainly, New Labour policies had a material impact on child poverty: there were 600,000 fewer children living in households with less than half the median income by the end of their time in government than in 1997. Between 1999 and 2003 child benefit for first children increased by 25.3 per cent, and for subsequent children by 3.1 per cent, and a more generous working families tax credit was introduced. Yet, in 2004, child benefit was withdrawn totally for migrants with no 'right to reside' as part of broader anti-immigration policies.[34] Childcare policies, meanwhile, relied, as Thane and Evans note, on an 'oversimplified' understanding of the problem: more childcare was available, but it wasn't affordable, and provision for older children and children with disabilities after school and in the holidays was still far from adequate. The amount of childcare provided by family members, meanwhile, was increasing, most often performed by grandmothers and 'often at some cost to themselves'.[35]

Although the state of childcare in the present day makes it difficult to resist idealizing New Labour's provisions, by the end of Blair's time in office, the childcare sector itself was in significant trouble, with unrest across the UK among its workers. This included in 2004, the largest all-out strike in Scotland since the miners' strike, when 5,000 nursery nurses struck over a pay dispute that had been raging for two and a half years. Demand for childcare had increased, due in no small part to the free hours now on offer, but the pay and conditions of childcare workers – often mothers themselves – were stagnant. In interviews conducted by the sociologists Gerry Mooney and Tricia McCafferty, the striking workers articulated the gap between Labour's professed priorities and the reality:

> Lots of people think that all we do all day is change nappies, sing nursery rhymes and paint pictures of cows or hills or the like. They don't see the physical and emotional demands that go with the job, or the extra unpaid work we often do, often with kids from very

poor and disadvantaged backgrounds. And what they don't see either is that we are providing an education service, and an important service that helps to shape a child's future. (Susan, 24, nursery nurse, Glasgow, with 4 years' experience)

What is often hidden from public view is the educational and social work aspects of nursery nursing. These were always there – but more so now. Being a nursery nurse is rewarding in some ways, less so now as a result of recent changes perhaps, but also emotionally and physically draining. (Mary, 52, pre-school worker, Glasgow, of 26 years)[36]

In the places where the public and the private met, like nurseries, the new status quo was the same as the old one: normative families were prioritized, while care work was overlooked, underestimated and underfunded.

Lady Macbeth and the Queen of Hearts

In the 2006 film *The Queen*, written by Peter Morgan, who would later go on to create *The Crown*, Cherie Blair (Helen McCrory) muses on why her husband, played by Michael Sheen, can't see the resentment towards the 'unfeeling' royal family in the aftermath of the death of Princess Diana as an opportunity to modernize the monarchy. 'It's not a mother thing, is it?' she asks, continuing: 'Well, were she alive now, your mother would have been exactly the same age [as the Queen]. I mean, you were always saying how stoical she was. Old-fashioned, uncomplaining, lived through the war.' Diana's instincts – to hug and kiss her children, for example – were frequently compared with the emotional and often literal distance favoured by her mother-in-law: in many respects, particularly after her divorce from Prince Charles, Diana's maternal mode was read as emblematic of an entire generation, a revolt against the wartime stiff upper lip represented by Elizabeth II.[37] Diana's death in a Paris tunnel in 1997, combined with the events of her last years – her charity work, her status as wronged wife and her celebrity – afforded her a Madonna-like memorialization: she became, and remains, the figure of a particularly feminized virtue. In the roster of single mums, Diana is a saint: Sara Maitland, writing in 1998, recalls several friends and acquaintances comparing the flower-strewn scenes of mourning outside Buckingham Palace to Lourdes. On the Mall, as the crowds of mourners gathered, Ross McKibbin attempted mass-observation: 'A very large proportion of the bouquets and messages – probably a majority – came from children, often collectively; from playgroups, kindergartens, primary schools.'[38] One of the most abiding images is of the card placed on her coffin, which said 'Mummy'. (Roger Scruton declared that the 'most important fact about the Princess was also the most obvious. She was a woman'; he blamed women, in general, for the 'feminization' of society, which had led to the breakdown of the traditional family.)

The historian Helen McCarthy writes in her history of working motherhood *Double Lives* that, asked in 1997 to 'name the prominent women they most admired', a group of female sixth-form students awarded Cherie Blair first place, with Princess Diana, Margaret Thatcher, Nicole Kidman and Nicola Horlick (an investment banker with six children, written about frequently at the time as a 'superwoman') following behind. One of the students, who was seventeen, said of Blair that: 'She is successful, having her own career and looking after her children. She must be under pressure but the image she portrays is one of a happy, ordered and stable family life. These days girls want to have it all, and women like her prove it's possible.'[39] The 90s was a decade in which motherhood had the gleam of celebrity, bookended by Demi Moore's naked, pregnant *Vanity Fair* cover shoot in 1991 and Cherie Blair's surprise pregnancy announcement in 1999, the first baby to be born to a serving Prime Minister since the nineteenth century. The domestic life of the Blairs was a popular subject for tabloids and celebrity magazines alike. Tony got mostly favourable coverage – he was voted 'Britain's top family man' by the readers of *M* magazine in 1998 – but Cherie became the object of a consuming media hunger, something best illustrated by the paparazzi photograph of her opening the door to a delivery of flowers the day after the 97 election victory, dishevelled, hungover and wearing a nightdress: she was a woman who promised to disclose too much. In an interview with the *Guardian* about the photograph almost two decades later, she remained 'very upset' that 'the press said I was wearing some sort of nylon thing; it was a high-quality, cotton nightie from Next and I bought it especially for the campaign . . . It was a lot better than you might expect from a mother of three.'[40]

Tony Blair's 'family man' image was part of a highly considered media strategy, another way to performatively disrupt the establishment: he was young, knew how to navigate the media and was not averse to celebrity, and, when his family commandeered Number Eleven Downing Street because Number Ten wasn't big enough, his virility was gratifyingly visible. At times, such a policy could backfire; when it did, this was blamed on Cherie. In 2000, there was a media frenzy when their former nanny, Ros Mark, announced her intention to publish a book about her time working for the Blairs, with the proceeds going to Refuge. They immediately responded by taking out a gagging order and threatening further legal action should the book ever see the light of day. Mark's mother, Margaret, interviewed on the *Today* programme, attributed this to Cherie, who was herself a lawyer. Defending her 'absolutely terrified' daughter, she said that the distressing confusion could have been avoided if Mrs Blair had not 'played the lawyer's card with such a heavy hand.'[41]

By the turn of the millennium, with many highly publicized 'gaffes' behind her, Cherie was a magnet for negative publicity and accused by Tory frontbenchers of being 'the power behind the throne', a cross between Hillary Clinton and Lady Macbeth.[42] Despite the newly glossy aesthetic of aspirational maternity, the media were far less generous than sixth-form schoolgirls when it came to famous women's maternal qualities. Both Diana and Cherie were perfect targets for the tabloid press, not only because of their celebrity and their affiliation with the highest offices of state in the UK, but because of their proximity to the old titillating stereotype: one became the most high-profile single mum in the country, the other was the daughter of one.

At first, Cherie was the perfect foil for her husband. Her career as a barrister – 'high-flying' and 'ambitious' – was a direct contrast to her more traditional predecessor Norma Major, and allowed her to perform a very modern kind of motherhood. Blair was the first Labour Prime Minister to have a wife in office since Harold Wilson, whose wife Mary had been born in 1916: there was a significant amount of pressure on Cherie to be both representational and inspirational. Matters were complicated by the fact that she herself had wanted to become an MP: rumours circulated in Whitehall and the media that the couple had made a pact that whichever of them got elected to Parliament first, the other would stop seeking a political career and practise law instead. There was a consensus in some circles that it was in fact Cherie who was the real political thinker, that her husband's beliefs were less firmly held, and that he was less interested in politics altogether. (There is a painful television interview from 1994, just after Blair had become the Leader of the Opposition, with the two of them looking very young, standing on the front steps of their house, as Cherie tries very hard to deny this, building up an image of her husband as the true politician. All that she manages to do is elicit a 'funny' confession from him that when she had been seeking election in Thanet in 1983, he had handled being an 'MP's wife' with bad grace; it was 'ghastly' to be expected to help with mundane tasks like washing up while his wife talked strategy.)

Euan Blair, the couple's first son, was born the year that Tony got elected to Parliament: he got the political career and the family, and Cherie became a prominent voice highlighting gender inequality in the legal professions. In 1995, she spoke on *Channel 4 News* about the way women practising law 'have problems when they come to be mothers', remembering having to juggle appointments with antenatal clinics – barristers are technically freelancers. Cherie, writing in 2013, constructed a narrative that in this campaigning she was honouring her own background:

> As my pregnancy became more visible, I noticed a perceptible change in the attitude towards me of my colleagues, who were all men. I was by nature a stubborn 'Scouser' and was determined to prove I could have both a career and a family life. My mother, who gave up her career as an actress to look after my sister and me, was abandoned by her husband and, with no maintenance forthcoming, took a job in a fish and chip shop to support us. This experience, as well as my professional ambition, instilled in me a strong feeling that maintaining a career and a family life was both desirable and necessary.[43]

Cherie Booth, as she was born and remained professionally, had a famously working-class childhood. Her parents, Gale Smith and Tony Booth, were actors: her father became a star of *Coronation Street* and *Till Death Do Us Part*, and was a classic bohemian hell-raiser, having (at least) eight children by five different women, and leading a merry dance for the tabloids until his final years. Booth left Smith when Cherie and her sister Lyndsey were in primary school, and Smith brought them up, with support from their grandmother, in a small flat in Sefton, just north of Liverpool. Cherie often spoke, as she does in the interview above, of her own success as something that was transmitted maternally, through the labours of her mother, her grandmother's passion for Rose Heilbron, the Liverpudlian lawyer and later high court judge who had been the first woman to win a scholarship to Gray's Inn, and the encouragement of her teenage boyfriend's mum, who thought she could make it as a lawyer.

Paternal inheritance was a more sensitive topic, even if we put to one side the difficult feelings that might arise from such a flamboyantly absent father. On the one hand, Booth was a traditional, socialist Labour man through and through, useful in establishing her own and later Tony's left-wing credentials: he campaigned for

Blair's election in Sedgefield on the arm of the *Coronation Street* icon Pat Phoenix. On the other, his antics brought with them a sizeable threat of embarrassment. Ultimately, though, it wasn't his alcoholism or his womanizing that put a spanner in the works of this uneasy alliance between Labour's present and its past: Booth became a staunch critic of Blair's government, famously over the decision to invade Iraq but also over the 1995–8 Liverpool Dockers' strike, which Blair refused to support. Cherie, in marrying Tony and embracing the right-leaning left-wing politics he both enacted and symbolized, renounced any convincing claim of politically advancing the position of the working class she came from, despite her frequent invocation of her origins. Throughout her time as Prime Minister's wife she garnered a reputation for extreme greed – gendered, certainly, in its lip-smacking coverage, but difficult to deny – and of flagrant financial corruption. Journalists would often attribute these impulses to her impoverished childhood, as Cherie herself would in her 2008 autobiography *Speaking for Myself*, perhaps hoping to portray a sympathetic compulsion, a fear of destitution; this performance, increasingly desperate as years pass and her extraordinary wealth builds, served only to telegraph her lack of self-awareness, playing into the hands of those who wish to categorize those from a working-class background as gauche, grasping and embarrassing.[44] It also indicated her absolute lack of solidarity, her total disavowal of the world she came from.

Speaking for Myself, published long after the Blairs' fall from grace, also included details about the conception of Leo, which happened at Balmoral because Cherie – embarrassed – had left her 'contraceptive equipment' at home. There was a lot of exaggerated media disgust about the way Blair described the physical aspects of motherhood – on the birth of Euan, she wrote of a 'third-degree tear . . . blood all over the place' – which, to my mind, simply reinforces the taboo around childbirth. I am inclined to agree with her assertion that there is a feminist aspect to including such details in an autobiography: 'I feel very strongly about contraception even though I know people say that, as a good Catholic girl, I shouldn't.

But I disagree because I think one of the keys to women's progression in the 20th century is being able to control their fertility.' This is one of the things that is so frustrating about Cherie Blair: sometimes, she's right, and you glimpse – fleetingly – the different path her life might have taken.[45]

Princess Diana and Cherie Blair, as those sixth-formers intuited, were prominent, perhaps definitional, figures of the decade who both incorporated the image of the single mum, the state of single-mum-ness, into their stories: the former as one, the latter as a daughter-made-good. Crucially, despite their wildly different circumstances, Diana and Gale Smith were both divorced, 'victims' of extramarital affairs, and, although Smith lived in poverty, her daughter translated it into a story about 'work ethic' – that famous fish and chip shop – and so they were both the good kind of single mother: they were not reliant on the state. (Diana actually was, but it was and remains true that the general consensus in this country is that the royal family 'work' for their money.) For Diana, her perfect beginning set in motion a reversal of fortune, a fairy tale backwards: she attained the status of single mum as a culmination of a story so powerful it started, in the words of Hilary Mantel, to tell her.[46] Cherie's plot was the inverse: she used her own single-mum-ed beginnings to craft a narrative of success, of bootstraps pulled and glass ceilings smashed and, in the process, she hardened, attaining success, status and acceptance through the very institutions that bore some responsibility for the mechanisms of her earlier exclusion. Yoking her life to Tony Blair – public-school-educated, charming, an Oxford man, everything she wasn't – she sheltered the child Cherie within the vast, adult carapace of financial and professional success and personal convention. Of Diana and Cherie, one was, eventually, beloved; one was, pretty much consistently, ridiculed. (Both women, however, have more in common than that which divides them: wealth.) For those without such advantages – that is, being very, very rich – New Labour promised much and delivered little. Growing up, it is not original to say, is a difficult process, one in which previously treasured beliefs reveal their limits.

One of the hardest aspects of transitioning from adolescence into adulthood, and the expanded political consciousness that came with it, was for me the realization that my view of the New Labour government had been a rose-tinted one. I had mistaken being merely permitted to exist for encouragement; I had mistaken the neoliberal state for a socialist one. Things could have been worse, it's true, and they certainly got worse rapidly, but they also could and should have been better. The attacks on mothers, particularly single mothers and teenage mothers, that were to come in the years that followed were building on foundations that New Labour themselves had built.[47]

If you had been paying attention to Blair's position on the family, the signs were there from the start. In 1996, Peter Flannery's *Our Friends in the North* was broadcast on BBC Two. Although its existence was initially jeopardized by Flannery telling the channel's commissioner Alan Yentob that it was a show 'about housing policy, Alan', it's now heralded as a classic, a piece of work that 'exemplified the idea that "the personal is political" '.[48] Beginning in 1964, it charts the lives of Nicky, Tosker, Geordie and Mary, four friends from Newcastle, over thirty-one years of turmoil. By the final episode, set in 1995, Mary (Gina McKee) has become a Labour MP. Her story begins with a young pregnancy and a depressing marriage, before evolving into a representation of a single mum equipped with the political will and intelligence to mount serious attempts to improve her own life and the lives of others. Living in a shoddily built social housing estate so riddled with mould that it's making her children unwell, she becomes a housing campaigner and then deputy leader of the council. Mary is a mother of her time and her place: a supporter of the miners' strike, we see her speak at a WAPC benefit and we see her give her son Anthony – a police officer – the space to realize that he can and should testify against his violent colleagues in court in the defence of two miners being prosecuted on trumped-up charges. For much of the series, she is a political and moral constant: we trust her, we like her, and we believe in her noble motivations.

In the first year of Blair's leadership of the party, however, Mary's story comes to an uneasy conclusion. Anthony, at a meeting with social services about a local boy who is frequently in trouble with the police, rages against the unfeelingness with which his mother, in her role as the local MP, is pushing the party line on council cuts and antisocial behaviour: 'Mother,' he spits, 'if you and your New Labour party sound any more like the Tories, they'll sue you for plagiarism.' Later, he tells her that he is leaving his marriage, and his two young children. He blames this on her, laying his own domestic failures at her door: 'I didn't have a mother, I had a martyr, so I married one the same.' Anthony's frustration, however he articulates it, seems to be not so much with the martyrdom of his mother, but rather with her falling short of her own standards: he watches her become complicit in the state's failures to protect working-class children like those she used to advocate for and – crucially – raise; domestic and political disappointment landing on top of one another. The Labour government, such a long time coming, came, when it did, like a heartbreak.

Teen Mom UK

She's the real future, she tells the world that we
broke the rules and got away with it, for better and
for worse, we're part of the shape of things to come.

Lorna Sage, *Bad Blood*

Yes I am!

Kat Slater, *EastEnders*

As the outwardly progressive 1990s marched into the new millennium, the definition of acceptable mothering was expanded to include *good* single mums – those who had become single inadvertently, despite doing everything 'right'. Left on the other side of this boundary of appropriateness was a mother whose 'badness' was historically familiar but somehow newly powerful, differently rendered: the Teen Mum. Regardless of their actual circumstances, these mothers were understood to be women who had had children without the supportive frameworks of marriage or wealth and who were consequently reliant on the state. The teen mum, always understood to be conceptually if not literally single, coalesced in the late 1990s into a figure that would cast an outsize shadow on culture and policy in the new millennium.

When I was a teenager, the film *Crossroads* (2002) loomed exceptionally large in my imagination. A vehicle for Britney Spears, written by Shonda Rhimes, it follows three estranged childhood friends on a road trip across America after they graduate from high school. As in many classic feminized coming-of-age stories, reproduction looms large: the two most prominent strands of the plot revolve around underage pregnancy and maternal abandonment. The purpose of the trip is for Kit (Zoe Saldana) to see her fiancé, for Mimi (Taryn Manning) to audition with a record company in LA, and for Lucy (Britney) to find the mother who left when she was a baby. This long-lost mother, played by Kim Cattrall – or rather, having no character to speak of in this film to distinguish her from her famous role in *Sex and the City*, icon of sexual permissiveness Samantha Jones – rejects Lucy once again. Meanwhile, Mimi, the most overtly classed of the trio, living as she does in a trailer park, is five months pregnant after being raped by Kit's fiancé. At the climax of the film, she falls down the stairs and loses her baby. *Crossroads* was a staple of sleepovers populated by girls who were all completely obsessed with the horror of teenage pregnancy, which our government-mandated sexual health classes had revealed to us as an ever-present threat, even if you had literally never had sex before and weren't planning to for a long while. Mimi's miscarriage presented to us the perfect solution to the problem of abortion, which we had been taught to view as a sad, tragic necessity for some girls, whom it would inevitably scar for life. She was going to give the baby up for adoption anyway! Now she doesn't have to bother with any of that! (Mimi also has to give up her place at the talent audition for Lucy. This, we felt, with the tidily punitive minds of adolescent girls, was only right: this was Lucy's reward for her good sexual hygiene and compensation for her bad mom.)

The teenage woman's body is sexualized, industrialized and exploited on a significant scale: it is used both as a powerful symbol of innocence and corruption, emblematic of social good and social ruin, and a joke, easy to mock, revealing of a fundamental unseriousness. Cultural representations of teenage sexuality are various, and can be nuanced, erotic, inappropriate, tragic, funny: this is not the place to embark upon a roll call from Nabokov to *Euphoria*, but we're all aware of the literature. Cultural representations of teenage pregnancy, on the other hand, tend to follow a specific set of aesthetic and moral guidelines. Unlike stories of sexuality more generally – the first blossoming of desire, the first heartbreak, growing up, letting go – they are almost always distinctly and narrowly classed. The pregnant teenage body is, almost always, read as a working-class one: even if the pregnancy happens, tragically, to a nice middle- or even upper-class girl, the drama is created by the loss of the glistening future – university! Marriage! A different, better pregnancy, at a different, better time! – that had generously been lain down ahead of her. Regardless of its specific circumstances – and young motherhood, like any other kind, is a far more varied experience than it is frequently understood to be – teenage pregnancy has mostly been represented as the first in a series of doors closing, the glum certainty of being, in some way, a burden: a life over before it had really had a chance to get going. This has been useful, unsurprisingly, for policymakers.

Strategies of Reduction

In 2018, it was widely reported that the teen pregnancy rate in the UK had fallen significantly, the ninth successive annual fall in rates, spawning headlines like 'Are teenagers swapping social media for sex?' and '(Less) Risky Business'. Two decades previously, the country had one of the highest teenage pregnancy rates in western Europe. According to Alison Hadley, the director of the Teenage Pregnancy Knowledge Exchange, the decline in in England is the result of a strategy launched by the Labour government in 1999, which aimed to reduce the conception rates of under-eighteens by 50 per cent in ten years and, unusually, was funded and sustained for the entirety of that time.[1] It utilized the expertise of practitioners who had been talking to young people about their sexual health for decades, and ringfenced funds to provide advice in schools, mount public campaigns, and license the over-the-counter provision of the morning-after pill at chemists from 2001 onwards, although it was not licensed for under-sixteens until 2015.

The strategy covered England alone, but teenage pregnancy rates were dropping in Scotland, Wales and Northern Ireland too, with devolved governments setting up similar reduction plans in the years following the millennium.[2] The general reasons behind such statistics are the same: an increase in sex education, an increase in those choosing to terminate pregnancy, and rising numbers of young women remaining in education. Despite these successes and the general downward trend in teen pregnancy that was already clearly observable, in the run-up to the 2010 election the Conservatives ran an aggressive campaign against Labour that used incorrect statistics: in a twenty-page document called 'Labour's Two Nations', they claimed that 54 per cent of under-18s in the most deprived areas of the country were falling pregnant. The real figure was 5.4 per cent.[3] (This campaign, part of David Cameron's programme of 'compassionate conservatism', was fed by the reports on 'Broken Britain' provided by a think tank funded by Iain Duncan Smith, the former party leader and then Secretary of State for Work and Pensions.) Regardless of the facts, perception was in the Conservatives' favour, as they well knew: polling consistently showed that voters believed that twenty-five times more under-sixteens were falling pregnant than was actually true, a misconception shared by young people themselves, who believed that 40 per cent of their own generation conceived before they could legally drink.[4]

Demonization works, and works so well that teenagers discounted their own experience: 40 per cent of each classroom being in various stages of pregnancy would certainly have been noticeable. But the representation of teen mums as being a different kind of person entirely, an embodied morality tale, perhaps meant that such maths *felt* real, on a symbolic level, despite the lack of evidence. (During my own teenage years, the category of the teen mum never really felt like it applied to the girls we knew who actually got pregnant, but to the wild rumours that circulated about girls from other schools, girls in someone's cousin's class, girls who gave birth in toilet stalls between Maths and PE, girls who had triplets before their year-nine SATS.)

Whether they are figured as individual failures or failures of the state, it is generally assumed that teen pregnancies are a tragedy of unsuccessful prevention. In a 2013 article that declared falling teen pregnancies the 'success story of our time', Polly Toynbee wrote:

> A modest investment of £25m has led to the probable non-birth of 60,000 babies to very young mothers, children whose lives on every measure would have been harder than average. Local clinics, nurses and well-trained teaching in sex, relationships, anti-bullying and resisting peer pressure had an immediate effect. Results were markedly different between places that cut pregnancies dramatically – Lambeth, Hackney and Hull – and similar areas that didn't, attributable to where there was good sex education, with good contraception services, and where too little was done.[5]

Of course, the things that Toynbee lists here are all social goods: it's hard to dispute the value of accessible sex and relationship education and free contraception. But I can't agree with her ethical mathematics: these 60,000 'probable non-births', she seems to be saying, would all have resulted in lives not worth living: harder than others, less valued and less valuable. Statistically, she is correct that the children of teenage parents are, on average, born into more difficult circumstances than their peers, and the number of underage pregnancies correlates with indices of multiple deprivation. But to be born to a teenage mother is not a reason for your life to be considered invalid. Within a reproductive justice framework, this is dangerously close to a eugenic perspective: not all teenage pregnancies are unwanted, and to assume they are is to undermine the very people you believe yourself to be protecting. We can advocate better provision of abortion, contraception and sex education without making these assumptions, and without categorizing the births as somehow hopeless by default: to do so denies the agency of the child as well as its mother.

Those who are otherwise committed feminists have long exhibited a particular blindness when it comes to class and teen motherhood.

Here's Anne Enright – a writer I admire – writing in 2003's *Making Babies*, her collection of essays about motherhood:

> All women with buggies look as though they are on welfare. Pushing a buggy makes you look like you're on the way to the methadone clinic. You look as though you had this baby in a working class, selfish sort of way – you had this baby even though you couldn't afford a car. A man pushing a buggy looks as though he is someone the global economy has left behind.

She continues with another joke about 'junkie mothers', before observing that

> women with buggies, as we know, became recklessly pregnant at an early age, so that they can drag their trashy kids around town, while using them to bark the shins of respectable shoppers. Women with buggies do not love their children, they are too busy slapping them at bus-stops, after getting them overexcited with E-numbered sweets.

Enright here is ostensibly making a joke about class, later identifying that her target is the very wealthy, those whose belief is that 'If you want to shop, then you should leave the child with the hired help.'[6] The joke hinges, though, on a slapstick mistaken identity: Enright being mistaken for what she isn't, a teenage mother. This is rooted in two classist assumptions, that take for granted that her readers share her perspective. These are that a) childcare is so expensive that *even* nice middle-class mothers like her – even writers! – are unable to pay for it all the time, and b) before she had a child, *even* a nice middle-class mother like her thought that buggies were entirely the preserve of the working classes. Although Enright is accurately critiquing the flawed planning and navigation of urban space that makes people with pushchairs (and many disabled people, too – if you can't get a pram through a space, then you won't be able to fit a wheelchair either) feel like nuisances and obstructions, with less of a right to access the street, this worthwhile point gets derailed by her compulsion to make repetitive jokes about teenage mothers and their many flaws. (I'd like to stress, lest I be accused of joylessness, that it's not that I don't believe that there are good jokes to be made about methadone clinics; it's just that this isn't one.)

Enright is writing from the Republic of Ireland, where there was also a dramatic reduction in teenage pregnancies over the same two decades: between 1998 and 2018, they fell by 73 per cent, something attributed by sexual health professionals to an increase in education, the availability of contraception, and the successful nationwide Teen Parents Support Programme.[7] Despite our difference in national context, Enright's attitude is intimately familiar to me. This characterization of teenage mothers was so fully saturated into my own understandings of pregnancy at a formative age that when I read *Making Babies*, seventeen years after its publication, I recognized the image immediately, as well as its attendant feelings of superiority, disgust and shame. I can understand why, in 2003, the joke seemed funny. We have been taught that teenage mothers, with a few honourable exceptions if their child grows up to be a success story, are bad mothers, sustained by the umbilical cord of the state: it's still common to hear people speak of underage conception as if it's directly motivated and rewarded by the immediate provision of a well-appointed council flat, which is, quite frankly, a ludicrous statement to make in the housing-crisis-riven landscape of 2023. The teenage mother is a scapegoat for structural problems: middle-class mothers like Enright who find that motherhood has altered their lives and made them newly proximal to these pariahs try to differentiate themselves from these undesirable reproductive spectacles in whatever way they can. These are real feelings of isolation and exclusion, and they could, seen from another angle, be cause for solidarity: maternity could provide the common ground from which a more liberatory politics of support could be constructed.

Celluloid Conceptions

My generation, teenagers in the early to mid-2000s, the test subjects of governmental strategizing over our uteruses, didn't really need the imported lessons of *Crossroads:* we were exposed again and again to televised representations of teenage motherhood. In 2003, the same year that Enright was pushing her buggy to the fake methadone clinic, the BBC sketch show *Little Britain* premiered. Written and performed by David Walliams and Matt Lucas, it became phenomenally successful, with its popular catchphrases dominating the playground. Amid the plethora of incredibly offensive characters – including Walliams playing a 'transvestite' and both men blacking up – were many which attempted to satirize benefit culture. This in effect functioned as two privately educated white men shoring up the dominant societal perspective: the sketches were Conservative Party broadcasts in fairground costumes. The writer Rhian E. Jones, in her 2013 book *Clampdown*, reads one of the show's most enduring characters, Vicky Pollard, as a grotesque continuation of the stereotypes set out in Peter Lilley's benefit-offenders-executioner's-song at the 1992 Conservative party conference ('I've got a little list . . . ').[8]

Pollard is played by Lucas in drag, wearing a pink tracksuit, long hair scraped back, pushing an exaggeratedly large stroller: the pantomimic incarnation of the teen mum who got pregnant on purpose to claim benefits. (Pollard's character was so loved by the nation that her mother was played in a Christmas special by the 'national treasure' Dawn French, and she was featured in a special Comic Relief sketch alongside Kate Moss. One of the stated aims of Comic Relief is to raise money to help children in poverty in the UK. This is certainly one way of approaching the issue.) In an interview, Lucas said that Pollard was intended as a parody of 'chavs' he had encountered while a student at the prestigious University of Bristol: her voice is a heightened version of the already heightened West Country accents frequently used in British culture – think of the archetypal rendering of the Shakespearean fool – to represent stupidity.[9] Pollard describes herself repeatedly as having had 'six children by seven different men' and, in one episode, describes herself as being jealous of a nine-year-old acquaintance who has only had three children and yet has already been given a council house. When these six children appear, they are dressed exactly like her, the belief that benefit dependency is transmitted generationally made manifest and broadcast into living rooms nationwide. Rather than producing future members of the workforce, Pollard simply multiplies her demands on the state, and never pays anything back. This is the most horrifying thing about the catastrophized teen mum: how much they cost. (In the BBC copy describing *Panorama*'s 1993 'Babies on Benefit' episode, the programme is described as investigating 'the cost to the state of young single motherhood'.) In 2022, *Little Britain* was removed from the BBC's streaming service, iPlayer, before being added with edits to 'better reflect the cultural landscape', removing all the sketches in which blackface was used. The Vicky Pollard storylines remained intact: a cultural low point, preserved for posterity.

There were other fictional representations of teenage pregnancy that were less relentlessly pernicious. In the 90s, the mature end of children's literature had evolved into a new genre: young adult fiction. This is often attributed, frequently by the writer himself, to the publication of Melvyn Burgess's controversial *Junk* in 1996, a novel which featured two teenage heroin addicts falling pregnant, with one pregnancy providing a redemption story: Gemma, after seeing her friend Lily continue to inject heroin while she's breastfeeding, leaves their squat, gets clean, gives birth, and returns to her home town to raise her daughter, Oona. Before Burgess, however, there were many writers whose work helped to establish the genre: Anne Fine, Judy Blume, Malorie Blackman, Berlie Doherty and Jacqueline Wilson, to name a few, all of whom touched upon teenage pregnancy – and pregnancy scares – in their work. (The fact that most of these writers are women perhaps explains why it's so easy for Burgess to forget them.) Particularly in Blackman's and Wilson's work, non-traditional family dynamics were frequently represented without idealization or demonization, letting a little light in for those young readers who did not have the kind of family or home which most visual media designated as 'normal'. By the mid-2000s, there were many texts in which readers could find stories that mirrored situations they might be experiencing in their own lives, and even a taboo subject like pregnancy might be accessible in the school library, or broadcast on children's TV: *Dear Nobody* by Doherty was shown on the BBC in 1998, and both *Grange Hill* and *Byker Grove* included stories of teenage pregnancy in their long-running narratives.[10]

Grange Hill, a show set in a fictional borough in north London, which ran from 1978 to 2008, and the Newcastle-upon-Tyne-set *Byker Grove* (1989–2006) were both BBC shows which functioned like juvenile soap operas, modelled, in their longform structure and their continuous setting, on the great British television tradition that had evolved from the kitchen sink dramas of the late 1950s. In a *New York Times* article called – hilariously – 'On British Soaps, the Poor and the Jobless', published shortly after Blair won the 1997 election, an American writer describes in a puzzled tone, as if observing specimens in a zoo, the difference between the aspirational milieux of American soaps, in which 'the fashionably dressed and the beautifully coiffed lead lives of highly improbable suspense in homes of well-heeled elegance', and their British counterparts: focusing almost entirely on working-class communities, these have characters who 'work in gas stations, fish-and-chips shops and corner grocery stores (and are actually shown working) or who have no jobs and live on the dole'.[11] In British soaps, emotional extremity is represented melodramatically, yes, but also embedded within the unexceptional contours of daily life: traumatic experiences occur and are dealt with in pubs, corner shops, market squares and launderettes.

Unconventional maternity stories have long been a fixture of soaps, with the scandalous pregnancy and the dramatic birth key features of the genre, and have provided some of their most famous storylines: *EastEnders'* 1985 'Who's the daddy?' plot centred around the pregnant schoolgirl Michelle Fowler; at the turn of the millennium Sonia Jackson had a 'surprise baby' on matriarch Dot Cotton's sofa. Also in 2000, *Coronation Street*'s Sarah Platt discovered that she had become pregnant at the age of twelve. Sometimes, such pregnancies reproduce themselves generationally: in *Emmerdale*, Charity Dingle had her daughter Debbie when she was a teenager; Debbie herself gave birth in a shed at the age of fifteen in 2005. In *Pobol y Cwm*, the Welsh-language soap that has been running since 1974, a child was born to 'wild teenager' Sheryl Hughes in the local pub, the drama of birth leaping out from the boundaries of privacy and into the living rooms of 70,000 people. Many of the longest-running examples of the genre are invested in matriarchal societies, with *EastEnders* the most prominent example: Jacqueline Rose and Sam Frears, writing in 2022, describe women as 'the moral barometers of life in Walford'. The endurance the women show both generates and necessitates a continuity of maternal trauma: Walford women survive 'sufferings that pass from generation to generation'.[12]

I don't watch *EastEnders* any more; I've become one of many people for whom the show, despite its revered ongoing-ness, exists in a very specific personal era. Perhaps this is a central trick to the longevity and emotional purchase of soaps in general: I hear familiar names, Mitchells and Slaters and Beales, if I walk into a room where an episode is on, or read some discussion of it online, and it feels like hearing the name of a cousin you used to play with in the paddling pool on family holidays, whom you now know only from their annual Facebook posts celebrating their wedding anniversary. For me, a fan in the early 2000s, the Slaters were what *EastEnders* was about. In a show which functioned like a many-headed matriarchy – Peggy at the helm of the Queen Vic, Dot looking anxious in the launderette, Pat Butcher resplendent, having a fag on the beige carpeted stairs – this family of complicated sisters felt like its beating heart: I loved to watch them fight, laugh and adjudicate each other's personal dramas. The most iconic storyline from that period hinged on the revelation that the Slater house was a more tightly knotted nest of maternal relationships than was previously assumed. Honestly, it still sends a chill down my spine to think of it: Zoe Slater (Michelle Ryan) arguing with her sister Kat (Jessie Wallace) on the cobbles of Albert Square, shouting 'You ain't my mother!'; Kat, face a perfect mask of pure tragedy, a moment of total anagnorisis, turning round and screaming back: 'YES I AM'. We acted that one out in the playground for months.

Less famous is the conversation that followed this scene. It is a remarkable piece of television, understatedly theatrical in its blocking, a duologue between Kat and Zoe which mostly takes place on either side of a bedroom door. We learn that Kat was sexually assaulted by her uncle Harry at the age of thirteen; we learn that she couldn't have an abortion, that she was terrified to tell her parents, who thought she was a good girl. Maternal ambivalence, horror and blame are unspooled for the viewer, with Zoe asking her mother, with breathtaking cruelty, 'Were you raped or weren't you?' Later, she screams through the door of her existential crisis: 'I shouldn't even be here. I'm only here because it was too late for you to have an abortion.' Kat replies: 'If I could have cut you out myself I would have done'; this wasn't Zoe as she knows her now, she explains, her beloved sister, but 'a thing' colonizing her insides. Their relationship eventually resolves itself into something tentatively positive that defies categorization, and then in 2004, Zoe leaves Walford. Kat, however, cannot escape the familiar fate of fictional sexually transgressive young women. She gets punished with an unbearable litany of reproductive misery: sexual abuse, forced adoption, several miscarriages, post-partum depression, the apparent loss of a child to Sudden Infant Death syndrome, which is later revealed to have been infant abduction, the trials of IVF, and a DWP investigation into the accusation that she was working while claiming maternity benefit. She was also one of the best-loved characters on the soap, and was afforded second, third, fourth, fifth chances: pain and struggle dogged her, but never swallowed her. She never got what she really wanted, though: a nuclear family.

In Real Life

Perhaps the most influential cultural product of the new millennium – itself influenced by the quotidian melodrama of the soap opera – has been reality television. Although the concept can be dated back to the 1974 series *The Family*, which offered a fly-on-the-wall view of a family living in Reading, the premiere of *Big Brother* in 2000 was the moment the generic floodgates opened. A popular subgenre focuses exclusively on teenage pregnancy, from MTV-style reality shows to semi-serious documentaries: as well as *Teen Mom UK* – a direct descendant of the successful American version *Teen Mom* – there was *Sixteen and Pregnant, Underage and Pregnant, Teen Mum Academy, Britain's Youngest Mums and Dads*, and various editions of the Channel 4 documentary series *Cutting Edge* including 'Pramface Babies' and 'Kimberley: Young Mum Ten Years On'. The latter was broadcast in 2009 and was a follow-up to 'Fifteen: This is Me': both programmes were made by the film-maker Daisy Asquith.

In the first, which aired in 2000, we meet Kimberley, a teenager from Camberwell in south London, and follow her as she dates and then has her heart broken by a nineteen-year-old pirate-radio DJ called Pete. Kimberley has a pregnancy scare while she's with Pete, but it ends up being just that – a scare – although in talking about it she reveals that her own mum fell pregnant as a teenager and is consequentially and vocally terrified of the same happening to her daughter. In 'Young Mum Ten Years On', we learn that Kimberley actually did get pregnant less than a year after 'Fifteen' was filmed, and eventually lost custody of her son because of the physically abusive nature of the relationship she was in at the time. In 'Young Mum', we follow her as she struggles to prove to the various state institutions that are monitoring her that she can look after her second child, Harvey, on her own. Her weekly income, which is derived from benefits, is £110.

The relationship between Asquith and Kimberley is evidently a very trusting one – Asquith is now the godmother to Kimberley's fifth child – and it is particularly moving, ten years on, to see a relationship delicately unfolding between Kimberley and her new partner, who is also a single parent. Towards the end of the programme, we learn that Kimberley is pregnant again: she decides to keep the baby, despite some initial reluctance from her partner, and gives birth to a daughter. In an interview with Asquith filmed in 2018, Kimberley speaks of being hurt by some of the hostile responses to the programme, many of which accused her of 'living off the state' and 'having a baby with whatever man she could'. Contemporary reviewers could barely contain their moralizing snark: in the *Independent*, Alice Azania-Jarvis wrote that in response to the pregnancy, 'a little exasperation set in. Of course, it's her right to have children, but it's clearly the last thing she actually wants.' (How, we might wonder, does Azania-Jarvis know?) She finishes her piece by insinuating that, in deciding to keep the baby, Kimberley is perpetuating a 'vicious cycle': 'there may be another documentary in 10 years' time.'[13] In *The Times*, Tim Teeman complained that the film was simply too sympathetic towards Kimberley, which he evidently experienced as a personal affront:

> It was clear where Asquith's sympathies lay – squarely, and understandably, with Kim. So what did that make the viewer at home, feeling uneasy about Kim's ability not to be a good mother or good parent, but to mother or parent at all? Intolerant? Unempathetic? A snob?

Teeman wanted Asquith to face the following 'tolerant' questions that occurred to him:

> Why was she shoving junk food down her son's mouth? What were the violent rows that supposedly took place between herself and her new partner? Did she think she was able to be an effective parent? What was she doing about marshalling her temper? Was she doing anything about trying to find work, an education, anything to raise herself out of the benefits dependency that she was enmeshed in?

Had she considered birth control? Why was she smoking during (a new) pregnancy?

He finishes the review by invoking the tragic death of Baby P, which had occurred two years previously, and was widely attributed to social services being too hesitant to act when children's safety was concerned. 'Sometimes,' he writes, 'people shouldn't be parents. Sometimes children should be put into care for their own good.'[14]

Repeat pregnancy fascinates and appals critics, something evident in their responses to programmes that document the lives of teen mothers. In *Teen Mom UK*, which began its life on air in 2016, seven years after its American inspiration, news of second pregnancies for members of the cast is often met with mixed reactions on screen, and sparks fierce commentary online: in Season Five, when Shannon Wise, a nineteen-year-old from Buckinghamshire, announced her second pregnancy, a result of forgetting to take the morning-after pill, she was accused by the public as well as by her then partner of 'trapping' him in fatherhood. Young women's access to contraceptive knowledge – another legacy of the New Labour reduction programme – is often weaponized against teen mums' first pregnancies, too. In 2016, as part of the press circuit promoting the show's launch, three of its subjects – seventeen-year-old Chloe Patton from Nottinghamshire, seventeen-year-old Amber Butler from Bolton and nineteen-year-old Mia Boardman from Southampton – were guests on the popular ITV chat show *This Morning*. They were sympathetically, if patronizingly, questioned by Holly Willoughby and interrogated by her co-host Phillip Schofield, who repeatedly, irritably, asked them 'How did you let this happen?', at one point suggesting that the fact they had all seen their US counterparts on *Teen Mom* should have had more contraceptive power.

Teen Mom UK can prove difficult to watch. The young mothers on the show are often seen to be struggling financially as well as emotionally with their rapidly changing lives. The dynamics are complex and varied: some of them have partners who have multiple children, and their relationships with their own parents is altered by the joys and difficulties of young mothering in an extended family unit. At times, the structure of the show feels, like all reality television, exploitative, although it gives the mothers themselves more of a voice than other shows in the genre; they provide their own voiceovers to the footage, in which they often retrospectively narrativize the on-screen events. (Their children, of course, have not consented for their early years to be so extensively documented in public in this way.) On the whole, the show's portrayal of teenage motherhood is more nuanced than its cartoonish graphics and curated playlists of dramatic YouTube clips suggest. Crucially, we see that the women in the show value their motherhood very highly: these are wanted pregnancies, if not planned ones.

This is a difficult issue to navigate. In a 2009 episode of *Underage and Pregnant* – which is narrated by Natalie Cassidy, whose voice is most famous for being that of teen mum Sonia Jackson from *EastEnders* – we meet fifteen-year-old Zena, who lives in Great Yarmouth with her mum and dad, and has intentionally conceived a child with her seventeen-year-old boyfriend Chris. Throughout the episode, Zena and her parents reiterate the fact that she has been adamant that she wants to have a baby since the age of eight. She vividly describes this desire as her only ambition: she wants to devote her life to raising a family, and we learn that when her older sister, Emma, fell pregnant the previous year at the age of sixteen, she struggled with fierce resentment and jealousy. Zena, who is physically tiny, a smoker since the age of eight, sounds like a woman far older than her years, especially when she speaks about the process of 'trying' for a baby for eighteen months and its pressures and disappointments, and when she describes her birth plan to the camera: she is very well prepared. When she takes a pregnancy test that returns a positive result, she declares that her dream 'has finally come true'.

When we listen to what the teen mums in such shows are actually saying, rather than projecting a particular set of values onto them, we realize that they are asking questions about the purpose and meaning of their lives, and these questions are in part material ones: they are as much questions about class and race as they are about gender. This is not a new phenomenon: remember Josie in *Only the Rivers Run Free*, interviewed in Belfast on her nineteenth birthday, saying that, with 'no jobs, nothing to do, and nothing to think about' the most interesting thing available to her 'would be to get married and make a job of looking after my family. That's all there is really.'[15] In 1989, the American writer Toni Morrison responded to a question about teenage mothers 'losing' their potential: 'They can be teachers. They can be brain surgeons. We have to help them become brain surgeons. That's my job. I want to take them all in my arms and say, "Your baby is beautiful and so are you and, honey, you can do it. And when you want to be a brain surgeon, call me – I will take care of your baby."' Later in the same interview, she elaborates further: 'I don't think anybody cares about unwed mothers unless they're black – or poor. The question is not morality, the question is money.'[16] For Angela Davis, writing in 1993, this was obvious:

> Is it really so hard to grasp why so many young women would choose motherhood? Isn't this path toward adulthood still thrust upon them by the old but persisting ideological constructions of femaleness? Doesn't motherhood still equal adult womanhood in the popular imagination?[17]

Culturally, we require teenagers to grow up fast, and Black women in particular are often hypersexualized from an early age. It might seem shocking, it might be concerning, to hear a teenager describe having a baby as her only ambition, but can we really pretend that this isn't a response to what she has been told about her own place in the world, her body's essential value, from the very start? In 2008, as the Labour teenage pregnancy prevention strategy reached its end, the artist Tracey Emin created *Baby Things*, a site-specific artwork featured in the Folkestone triennial, composed of bronze simulacra of baby clothes, deposited at various places around the town. Folkestone, like Emin's hometown of Margate, has historically had a very high teenage pregnancy rate. *Baby Things* was written of in its press coverage as a kind of elegy, a 'forlorn reminder' of these young mothers and the other lives they could have led. When Emin herself discussed the work, however, she positioned it as a far more ambivalent piece, centring the agency of teenagers themselves, and acknowledging the attraction of motherhood as an escape from your own childhood: 'There are some girls out there,' she said, 'who just don't want to be girls; they want to grow up . . . they want to get away from their childhood as quickly as possible.'[18]

Emin is an artist famous for her candid discussion of events in her personal life. She has been particularly open about her experiences of abortion, including one termination, just after she had finished college, which inspired a strongly prohibitive episode of guilt that stopped her painting for a time, something she now describes as a kind of 'deranged punishment' she inflicted on herself.[19] Her discussion of this was taken up gleefully by the Society for the Protection of Unborn Children, who seize any opportunity they can get to discuss the 'impact' of abortion on women's mental health. Emin's own relationship to reproduction, which remains a guiding force in her work, is not a coherent philosophical or political position, but rather an expression of ambivalence, pain and the complexity which characterizes the conditions of any unplanned – I don't want to say 'unwanted' – pregnancy. The co-option of such complexity by the SPUC reveals their reductive understanding of 'mental health', as well as the useless binary created by the cultural battle over teen pregnancies, a distinction implicit in the ongoing reproductive injustices of our time.

If pregnancy can be a means of escaping childhood, perhaps the appropriate question to ask is what we mean by the term 'underage'. Generally, rather than a reference to the age of consent, which has only been consistent across the UK since 2008, when it was lowered from seventeen in Northern Ireland – it was lowered from eighteen for homosexual acts in England, Scotland and Wales in 2000 – an underage pregnancy is understood by the World Health Organization as one which occurs in someone under the age of twenty. (The WHO is primarily concerned, in its literature on the subject, with the rate of underage conception in 'developing countries', and with the health issues than can ensue from early childbearing.[20]) There are things which, in an ideal world, would make teenage pregnancy less likely to happen, but these are the same things that would make it an easier experience for everyone involved. It is sad, of course it is, to think of some of the circumstances which might encourage a young person to have a child while they're still technically a child themselves – why they might want to escape their youth and become responsible for somebody else's. But by the same token, within these situations – which are by no means the situation that *every* teenage pregnancy emerges from – isn't there exactly as much to respect, to support, to celebrate? No pregnancy produces a future that is already plotted, guaranteed.

At the very end of Lorna Sage's *Bad Blood*, a memoir of teenage pregnancy, she discusses a photograph. Reproduced in the book, it shows Sage and her then husband, Vic, on their graduation day from Durham University, and it appeared on the front page of the *Daily Mail* in 1964: they were the 'first married couple of ordinary student age to graduate in the same subject at the same time, both with firsts'. Their daughter, Sharon, is between them in the photograph, now four years old:

> Sharon is the one looking beyond the ending, nobody seems to know yet that it's the 1960s, except perhaps for her. She's the real future, she tells the world that we broke the rules and got away with it, for better and for worse, we're part of the shape of things to come.[21]

Sage, who went on to become a literature professor, succeeded on the terms of a society that, when she became pregnant in 1959 at the age of sixteen, sought to define her by her perceived indiscretion and nothing more. Yet she and Vic were also supported by mechanisms that allowed them to exceed the limits that had been imposed on them: they both received full scholarships which covered their living costs while they studied, and Sharon was looked after by Sage's parents during term time, something she herself later recalled as a successful experiment in intergenerational living: 'When I was little, I had a great time, and it didn't matter who was delivering it.'[22] They broke the rules and got away with it, but, as Sage knows better than anyone, it wasn't an escape they could have pulled off without financial and educational support. Today, would they – could they – have been so fortunate? The landscape of higher education alone is almost unrecognizable, paying researchers poverty wages as, in the humanities at least, the possibility of securing even a fixed-term contract shrinks by the minute. It's important to note, too, that the unusual aspects that characterized Sage's approach to motherhood – leaving to spend a summer in Italy when Sharon was thirteen, for example, and regularly hosting parties late into the night – are the kind that, transposed from a university campus in the 1970s to a different time and place, would be met with opprobrium and the involvement of social services.

Lessons

Catastrophizing teen pregnancy is actually a response to the social deprivation that occurs when the kind of environment which would allow teens to parent, if they want to, is not created.[23] Studies conducted in 2003 and 2006, for the Institute for Social and Economic Research and the Joseph Rowntree Foundation respectively, found that the pervading belief that teenage pregnancy was a uniformly negative experience ignored the fact that the primary shaping condition of these negative experiences is poverty. In fact, as Suzanne Carter and Lester Coleman, the authors of the 2006 report, observe, 'Young mothers often see parenthood as providing a chance to create a loving family – often compensating for their own bad experiences of childhood.' Many interviewed said that 'their life would have been worse if they had not become a parent, pointing to family insecurity, a growing sense of worthlessness and lack of direction.'[24]

In this way, the opportunity to become a mother is rich with transformative possibility, and the 'lack' of the traditional familial structures that teenage mothers are castigated for – regardless of the fact that, as we have seen, these structures are no longer the norm – affords new possibilities for kinship that don't repeat the traumas of the past.

In 2011, the *Guardian* journalist Amelia Hill visited Moat House in Stockport, Cheshire, a school dedicated to helping young women who were pregnant or already mothers to continue their education. The school, which has its own crèche, teaches the core GCSE curriculum as well as sex and relationship education and parenting classes, with dedicated advisory services to assist its students with the next step, whether that might be further education or into the workplace. It aims to fill the gap that many teenage mothers found in their education: after falling pregnant they were functionally if not formally excluded from school, with their places of learning making it practically impossible for them to continue learning. The students that Hill interviews make it clear that their pregnancy had provided them with a new kind of opportunity. Annie, who was effectively illiterate when she arrived at the school, had plans to go on to study animal care at college: 'I've learned I can read if I try – and I want to try now, I want to be a good role model for Tara. Without her, I wouldn't have done anything with my life but now I've got plans and ambitions.' Being pregnant, Annie says, 'calmed me down a lot. I had a lot of anger, but I've grown up.' Natalie, who was seventeen at the time of her interview, observes the difference between her experience at Moat House and society in general. Although being a teenage mother is hard,

> the most difficult thing is the way I'm judged and treated by people who assume bad things about me, just because of my age. They don't know how much I love my baby. They don't know I'm a good mother. They don't know any of that, but they assume all sorts of things about me. And that makes changing the future for me and my child so much harder.

Moat House, which relied on Stockport local authority funding, was in 2011 expecting 'cuts of no more than 7 per cent' the following year; they were getting off relatively lightly.[25] Still, throughout Hill's article it's clear that the coalition government's austerity agenda cast a concerning shadow over its future. With austerity came the belief that opportunities like those offered by Moat House were simply too expensive to be paid for by the state: they were weighed and measured on an unfeeling scale and found wanting.

12.

Austerity Parenting

What are we going to do with a world that places targets on children's backs before they can even understand they are in danger?

Lola Olufemi, *Experiments in Imagining Otherwise*

I experienced the 2010 election, in which I was less than a year away from being able to vote, as a complete and total devastation. The prospect of a Conservative government represented not only the destruction of a political belief system I had fully subscribed to, but the real and imminent destruction of many of the practical aspects of my way of life in general. The programme of vicious budget cuts instigated by the 2010 coalition government of Conservatives and Liberal Democrats, with David Cameron as Prime Minister, George Osborne as Chancellor of the Exchequer and Nick Clegg as Deputy Prime Minister, slashed everything: social care, libraries, road maintenance, housing assistance, the judicial system and the police. (I do not consider the compromises made by the Liberal Democrats, such as the introduction of the five-pence plastic bag charge in exchange for punitive welfare reform, worth considering as any kind of ameliorative or dilutional force.)

Austerity was figured as a 'necessary' response to the economic downturn that had been ongoing since the 2008 global financial crash: Osborne spoke of the country as a domestic household which had been 'living beyond its means', conjuring ghosts of Thatcher's housewives and purse strings; Cameron said that the reduction in government spending would reduce the need for the state and instead lead to the 'Big Society', a concept in which spending cuts were figured as an opportunity for communities to take the initiative and look after themselves, never mind their vanishing resources.[1] In his victory speech upon being elected to the leadership of the Conservative Party in 2005, Cameron had declared that 'There is such a thing as society; it's just not the same thing as the state.'

This book has, in many ways, been about austerity throughout. In the first few chapters, I foregrounded our route back to the 1970s in the maternal crises of the present: we've seen how the state's provision of housing, childcare, healthcare and other services has been at best insufficient and at worst actively punitive, and how hard mothers campaigned and protested for better. Derica Shields, in *A Heavy Nonpresence*, an oral history of anti-blackness in the post-austerity welfare state, emphasizes that this is not simply a consequence of austerity, but rather a distinction between deserving and undeserving citizens embedded in the very framework of the welfare state itself, something far harder to fully reckon with.[2] The post-2011 programme compounded pre-existing problems and unravelled much of the progress that had been made. Its impact has been monumental, definitional.

In 2011, the Organization for Economic Co-operation and Development reported that not only was austerity reversing the progress that had been made on child poverty reduction in the UK, but in combination with the rising cost of childcare it meant that many parents could not actually afford to be in work.[3] Almost a decade later, the Child Poverty Action Group reported that 3.9 million children were living in poverty in the UK, equivalent to eight children in a class of thirty, and 75 per cent of these children lived in a household where at least one person was in work. Half of children living in single-parent households are in poverty, and of those, children who aren't white are significantly more likely to be living in poverty than their peers. In 2019, the United Nations declared it to have caused 'social calamity', forcing millions into poverty.[4] Despite the alleged protection by the NHS, researchers who studied the impact of the combined cuts to healthcare, public health and social care between just 2010 and 2015 concluded that they had led to 57,550 more deaths than average.[5]

In the almost thirty billion pounds' worth of cuts to welfare payments, housing subsidies and social services implemented since 2010 we can see the culmination of the persistent demonization of single parents and benefits claimants: regardless of the fact that employment was often irrelevant to whether people earned enough to survive, the government were able to repurpose old notions of value and virtue. Cameron and Clegg used Thatcher and Blair's playbook on family breakdown: incentives to marry were frequently discussed, the flipside of the sanctions doled out to those whose familial circumstances were not deemed appropriate or intelligible by the mechanisms of the state. Cameron's 'compassionate conservatism', for single mothers – teenage and otherwise – translated as an immediate child benefit freeze when the coalition government came to power in 2010, and the lowering of the age of the youngest child at which families would cease receiving income support from seven to five. In 2011, the Welfare Reform Bill replaced existing benefit systems, including Working Families Tax Credit, with the catch-all Universal Credit, which – and I say this as a former claimant – is fundamentally unfit for purpose.

In the service of this lionization of the family as an individual unit, responsible only for itself, Cameron fashioned himself as a young family man in Tony Blair's image. Between 2002 and 2010, he and his wife Samantha had four children, and his decision to take paternity leave from his role as Leader of the Opposition in 2006 was highly publicized: Cameron, who asked people to call him Dave so often that the media christened him 'Call-me-Dave', was cast as a new, modern kind of Conservative man, photographed playing with his children and talking about his 'dad dancing'. The nation's 'dad', he described himself on multiple occasions as 'a marriage man'. His role in the legalization of same-sex marriage can be seen, in this context, both as liberal pink-washing by a government still hostile to much of the LGBTQ+ community and part of the drive to expand the parameters of marriage as a norm, with its regulating management of sexuality and domesticity, to all citizens. The Camerons' eldest son, Ivan, was born with the very rare combination of Ohtahara syndrome, a severe form of epilepsy, and cerebral palsy, and he required round-the-clock care until his death in 2009. This experience – extremely painful and difficult as it must have been – did little to affect Cameron's policymaking. In 2011, the charity Kids, which had helped care for Ivan and of which Cameron was a patron, had its funding cut by £250,000. In bringing this up, I don't mean to make any comment about Cameron's paternal grief, but rather to emphasize, again, the limits of applying a virtue or knowledge to parenting that 'transcends' the political: whatever his own experiences, he did not, in his role as Prime Minister, believe that disabled children and their families deserved to be supported by the state.

Just over a year after the 2010 election, 'Broken Britain' was made manifest in the rioting that began in Tottenham, north London, on the 6 August and spread across the city and much of the rest of England.[6] The catalyst was the fatal shooting of Mark Duggan, a 29-year-old Black man, by the Metropolitan Police, and the subsequent Independent Police Complaints Commission investigation into his death, during which a spokesperson gave out false information to journalists. Journalists and politicians alike avoided structural explanations for the civil unrest, however, locating the blame squarely within the family, or rather, its 'failure', instead. The 'instant communities' of technology and trouble – the stampeding cavalry of BlackBerry Messenger – took root because of absent fathers and bad mothers, because of welfare dependence and no role models. David Cameron, David Lammy, Melanie Phillips, Peter Hitchens: all were explicit in their lament that these riots were a direct consequence of 'lone parenthood', meaning single motherhood, meaning social corruption and 'casual sex'. (Cameron blamed 'a lack of proper parenting, a lack of proper upbringing, a lack of proper ethics, a lack of proper morals', suggesting that the latter could only be transmitted by 'proper' parents. So much for the Big Society.[7])

In *London's Burning*, the exquisitely bad docudrama that aired on Channel 4 in December 2011, a policeman recites a text that was circulated on Facebook, in chain emails and on Mumsnet, the 'looter's prayer':

> Our father who art in jail
> Mother knows not his name
> Our Chavdom come
> Give us this day our welfare bread.[8]

The coverage of the riots was doubly gendered: as well as the repeated insertion of the figure of the single mother on benefits into the story, images of women wreaking havoc became titillating media staples as prosecutions wore on, though government data suggested 'only 10 per cent of those who took part were female.' Less than a year before, the British establishment had been up in arms about the prominence of young women in the student protests against the trebling of tuition fees. The *Mail* ran a piece filled with images of young women and 'truanting schoolgirls' disturbing the peace, headlined 'RAGE OF THE GIRL RIOTERS: Britain's students take to the streets again – and this time women are leading the charge'.[9] (One woman, Louise Malone, was quoted as saying she had taken the wheel of a police van simply because she felt like it.) The rioting women included mothers, as one bystander interviewed in the *Guardian* observed:

> I saw a woman and she came out of her house with her daughter and she was like: 'Oh, where's Debenhams?' And I was like: 'Why?' and she was like: 'Oh, we're going to go looting.' I was like: 'You're with your daughter and you're going looting?'[10]

The figure of the irresponsible mother became a key focus in the aftermath, with her violence doubly disgracing her and her maternal role, despite the efforts of some mothers to reject such a framing. Adrienne Ives, the mother of the Olympic Ambassador Chelsea, who received a two-year prison sentence for allegedly throwing bricks at a police car, had called the police on her own daughter after seeing her on television. This case got a lot of attention: scapegoats were wanted, and any association with the Olympics was useful ammunition for the media. It is easy to see how, in such a political climate, you might feel forced to prove your own worth, your law-abiding parental status, by calling publicly for the incarceration of your child. (Chelsea's father, Roger, later gave an interview in which he called on prison authorities to make his daughter serve the full sentence, 'so she learns the severity of her crimes'.[11])

In the wake of the riots, Keir Starmer, then the Director of Public Prosecutions, introduced 24-hour rolling courts. Over 2,000 people were convicted, with prison sentences totalling more than 1,800 years: in this mania for symbolic justice, sentences were far longer than for those who had committed similar offences the previous year. Half of those accused were under twenty, a quarter were technically children, and 50 per cent of those arrested were Black or mixed race; in the UK, where the prison system is already heavily racialized, this compounded the injustice that had underwritten the riots in the first place. The reoffending rate for those incarcerated for participating – held in overcrowded prisons with no counselling or assistance, serving time for stealing a pint of milk – is substantially higher than the reoffending rate in general.[12] Nicolas Robinson, a 23-year-old with no prior convictions, was sentenced to six months for stealing water from Lidl in Brixton. Ursula Nevin, in Manchester, was jailed for a week, separated from her two children aged one and five, for accepting a pair of shorts that were stolen by a friend, despite the fact that she wasn't present at the looting: in his sentencing, the district judge made explicit reference to her motherhood, admonishing her that she was 'supposed to be a role model for her children'.[13] Whenever scapegoats are sought, the bad mother is always close at hand.

In the austere law-and-order state, poverty is criminalized, and the guilt is transmitted generationally. In London, the Conservative-run Wandsworth council threatened to begin eviction proceedings against tenants who were involved in the riots, beginning with a mother whose son had appeared in court charged with disturbance in Clapham Junction: though she had not been present, the council believed she was violating the terms of her tenancy agreement. Cameron, whose personal wealth was valued at £10 million in 2009 by the *Sunday Times* Rich List, supported the council's decision, dismissing suggestions that the loss of a council tenancy would only aggravate the primary cause of criminal behaviour, poverty and conflating the mother with the son in the process: 'Obviously that will mean they will have to be housed somewhere else and they will have to find housing in the private sector and that will be tougher for them. But they should have thought about that before they started burgling.'[14]

Punishing Mothers

The prison population in the UK grew by 15 per cent between 1970 and 1992; from 1993 to 2012, it almost doubled, increasing from 44,500 to 86,600 incarcerated people, a level at which it has since stabilized. During austerity, the overall spending on prisons was reduced by 22 per cent, engendering serious consequences for the health and wellbeing of those incarcerated: as well as the severely limited availability of legal aid, such measures reduced the viability of voluntary services that work with the prison population.[15] In 2021, the EU Committee for the Prevention of Torture noted that many UK prisons do not meet the minimum requirement for the conditions of detention due to extensive budgetary cuts. In 2019, the Prison Reform Trust published a report that found such a disparity in incarceration rates that women in the north of England and the south of Wales are four times more likely than those in more affluent southern counties to be imprisoned, something the Trust's Jenny Earle describes as a 'postcode lottery'. Again, we can see that Margaret Thatcher was the mother of the present. Tracey McMahon, the head of the SHE Project in Lancashire which houses female ex-prisoners, linked this to the ongoing legacies of de-industrialization and the closing down of mining, steel, manufacturing, fishing and the car industry: these, she declares, are 'third generation problems'.[16]

According to Women in Prison, who were so vocal in the fight for the release of Roisin McAliskey at the turn of the millennium, 8,000 women a year enter prison on average, mostly receiving short sentences for non-violent crimes.[17] Almost two thirds have experienced domestic abuse, and over half have experienced emotional, physical or sexual abuse during childhood. Nearly half of these women leave prison with nowhere to stay: a short sentence is still long enough to lose your home.[18] Crucially, approximately 60 per cent of women in prison have children under the age of eighteen, and 95 per cent of children have to leave their homes when their mother is incarcerated, often putting them into temporary or permanent care (many women in prison have experience of the care system in their own childhoods). On average, an estimated 600 of the women sentenced each year are pregnant.

The incarceration of pregnant people criminalizes an infant before it is born, and makes a mockery of any concept of equal maternity care: when it comes to carceral maternity provision, austerity's reduction in basic standards has hit particularly hard. Of the prisoners who give birth during their sentences, one in ten give birth in prison rather than in a hospital, something which increases the likelihood of stillbirth fivefold, as well as significantly raising the probability of a premature birth, or the necessity for the child to be transferred to a neonatal unit. In 2022, the conditions faced by pregnant people in prison received significant media coverage after several harrowing stories came to light: that of an eighteen-year-old in HMP Bronzefield in Surrey, who gave birth alone in her cell and was found lying beside her dead baby the next morning, and that of Louise Powell, who gave birth to a stillborn baby in a toilet at HMP Styal in Cheshire. Powell was given no medical help or pain relief, and three emergency calls went unanswered. She described the extreme trauma she experienced in a BBC *Newsnight* interview: 'I felt like I was dying.'

In a feature in *Cosmopolitan* magazine that covered pregnancy in prison, 'Anna' described her own experience of pregnancy in jail: she was forced to endure an internal hospital examination while handcuffed to an officer, received minimal healthcare, and endured a very painful labour. Prison officers ignored her requests to contact her mother and the baby's father, and they both almost missed the birth.[19] Other women interviewed anonymously in the piece describe the isolation and fear they experienced in Mother and Baby Units inside prisons: there's nothing to distract you, nobody to help you, and no assurance that staff will even respond to the emergency buzzer. If your sentence is longer than eighteen months, you live in the shadow of the knowledge that your baby will be taken from you as soon as it reaches that age.

The austere state has an insatiable appetite for punishment: the government is at present planning to build new prisons capable of holding 10,000 more prisoners. Its hunger extends to asylum seekers and refugees: as the government increasingly agitates for harsher immigration policies, mothers and children are separated from each other for significant stretches of time in detention centres like Yarl's Wood in Bedfordshire and the newly opened Hassockfield in County Durham. (Hassockfield is a site of historic trauma: it was formerly Medomsley Detention Centre, where young men were systematically abused throughout the 60s, 70s and 80s.) In 2010, women held in detention in Yarl's Wood embarked upon a six-week-long hunger strike, which led to the 'ringleaders' being transferred to HMP Holloway in London: in the eyes of the state, there is no distinction between the 'holding' of those whose immigration claims are being processed and criminals.

In 2017, a report compiled by Gemma Lousley and Sarah Cope found that the government was actively endangering 'adults at risk' – a category which includes pregnant people – by detaining them indefinitely. Outside of detention centres, housing provision for asylum seekers is not fit for purpose either, and certainly not fit to raise children in. In Glasgow, which was until 2022 the only asylum dispersal area in Scotland, housing was outsourced by the government to the private company Mears Group Ltd. One of Mears's residences was the Mother and Baby Unit for asylum seekers who are pregnant or who have recently given birth in the city. The MBU was deemed 'cramped and unsafe' by the Children and Young People's Commissioner Scotland: the building is infested with mice and damp and each room measures just five metres by three, with radiators and gas cookers dangerously close to the cot, no natural light, and an uncomfortable single bed.[20] The safety of the mothers and children housed there is second to financial gain: Mears Group turned over a profit of £25 million in 2021. In 2023, in Rochdale, Greater Manchester, reports came out in the media that a social housing landlord had failed to treat the severe mould in asylum seeker housing – saying these conditions were acceptable for this 'kind' of inhabitant – that led to the death of two-year-old Awaab Ishak. A significant part of the narrative of austerity in the UK has relied upon the scapegoating of refugees and asylum seekers as the reason why poverty is so prevalent, why life is so unbearable for many in one of the most affluent countries in the world. Maternity, far from a reason for protection or empathy, is cause for greater suspicion.

In 2019, the story of Shamima Begum showed us that being 'from here' is no protection either. A few years earlier, at the age of fifteen, Begum along with two schoolmates had left her home in Bethnal Green to join ISIL in Syria. Sajid Javid, then the Home Secretary, announced that Begum would be stripped of her British passport, rendering her technically stateless. At the time this decision was made, Begum had just given birth to a son, Jarrah, who later died; she had carried and lost two other children since leaving the UK. In the House of Commons and in the media, motherhood was central to the debate over her request for repatriation. Diane Abbott, the Shadow Home Secretary, insisted that Begum should have been allowed to return, both to care for her baby in a safe place and to face the legal repercussions of her actions; Javid, in telling language, declared that 'The death of any British child, *even those children born to a foreign terrorist fighter*, of course is a tragedy – but the only person responsible for the death of that child is the foreign terrorist fighter.'[21] Begum, here, is not a mother in relation to her child but a 'foreign terrorist fighter': despite fulfilling all the 'necessary' biological qualities of even the most conservative definition of maternity, she was not considered to truly *be* a mother.

Without denying the violence of Begum's alleged actions after leaving the country, it is clear that her subsequent treatment was shaped by systemic Islamophobia: despite being legally a child when she was radicalized online, and despite her own newborn child's right to shelter and care, she was never afforded the protection of the state. (In 2022, it was alleged that the person who trafficked Begum was in fact a Canadian state spy.[22]) In contrast, the resurgent far right in the UK have in recent years become invested in projecting an image of themselves as heroes helping 'protect' white women and girls against the spectre of 'Muslim grooming gangs', with the former leader of the English Defence League Tommy Robinson a prominent figure in the perpetuation of this unsubstantiated crusade.[23]

Prisons and detention centres alike are interwoven legacies of trauma and abuse, both the kind which violates the law, as was the case with Medomsley, and those which result from its enforcement. This can prove fertile ground for resistance. In May 2017, the feminist anti-austerity group Sisters Uncut occupied the former Holloway Women's Prison Visitors Centre: the prison had been closed in 2016 and its residents transferred to HMP Downview and Bronzefield, both already overcrowded. The purpose of occupation was, in the words of Angela Davis during an address she gave during a visit, both to draw attention to the repurposing of the land in the present – it was bought by Peabody, a housing developer – and to respond to the 'the carceral feminism of the past'.[24] Holding a week-long community festival, the group 'transformed a space of state violence' into one where workshops, activities and meals were shared, leading by example: their overarching demand was that the land continued to be used for such 'public good', including genuinely affordable housing and the provision of services 'to all women and non-binary people affected by state violence, especially supporting survivors of colour, LGBTQ+ and disabled survivors'.[25]

Sisters Uncut's actions often include the occupation of premises in protest at the failure to rehouse mothers and children, fleeing domestic violence – something familiar from the origins of the refuge movement, as well as the squatting movement more generally. But they resist the use of the term 'occupy' itself, which had slipped into easy parlance in part because of the transatlantic Occupy movement that began in 2011, and use instead the term 'reclaim':

> Through our direct action of an empty council home, we have reclaimed what rightly belongs to the people and should be used to serve people in need, to provide homes for survivors fleeing violence. How can she leave if she has nowhere to go? The space is not one dominated by outsiders but owned and run by the community and in solidarity with non-hierarchical women and non-binary people who share in the struggle for justice against sexist austerity.[26]

'How can she leave if she has nowhere to go?' is a phrase which can be applied equally to those leaving prison with no secure housing, and to those incarcerated in detention centres threatened with deportation to a place where their life would be in danger, where they have never lived, or simply where they do not wish to be. 'Sexist austerity' blames mothers that exist outside the norm while materially making every aspect of mothering harder, more relentless and more isolated: it turns 'the people' into individuals and the raising of children into a solitary test of virtue.

Easterhouse Modernizers and E15 Mums

The reactionary logic of austerity is that 'we' don't have enough money to support people who aren't 'us': the state needs to look after its own. But it doesn't do that either, shifting the responsibility to communities themselves. When community organizing actually happens, however, it is perceived as a threat, and obstructed accordingly. In this contradiction lies one of the chief ironies of the centrality of Iain Duncan Smith's 'Broken Britain' narrative to Cameron's later 'compassionate conservatism'. Duncan Smith claimed that his belief in the necessity of aiding the working poor – a belief which apparently underpinned his resignation from Cameron's cabinet in 2016 – was inspired by a visit to Easterhouse in 2002. Easterhouse, which lies six miles to the east of Glasgow's city centre, was, like East Kilbride, one of the new towns built in the 1950s as part of the programme to move inhabitants of the city out from their 'sub-standard' living conditions, something which can also be read as a move to divorce working-class people from their wider social networks. Recalling his 2002 visit from the vantage point of 2010, Duncan Smith described its 'damp, rundown, grey concrete housing blocks scattered across acres of needle and litter-strewn, job-free wasteland'.

Yet Easterhouse provides an example of successful community organizing of exactly the kind that these newly compassionate Conservatives purported to believe in. For a decade, culminating in 1992 with the completion of the first ever tenant-led solar housing energy conservation project, the Easthall Residents Association campaigned for their damp-ridden council housing to be made safe and environmentally sustainable through remodelling and refurbishment using solar power techniques.[27] The association was led by the residents, with many of them mothers whose campaigning was primarily motivated by their children's health. Cathy McCormack, a writer and activist who became a figurehead of the project, described her experience in 1985 as a generational one:

> Although I had always lived in a freezing cold damp house and spent a lot of my childhood in hospital and even remember my own mum referring to our flats as pneumonia houses, in my ignorance I had never made the connection between our living conditions, ill health and the social environmental climate. I only started to make the links when the dampness started to affect my mental health . . . I found myself having to choose between feeding my hungry children or hungry fuel meters . . .[28]

The changes fought for by the Easthall Residents worked: energy bills were dramatically reduced and chronic health conditions alleviated. But in the first months of their existence, it became clear that the Labour council were reluctant to spend the money that would take the improvements to other council housing stock.[29] Joey Simons writes that 'the crucial lesson' to take from the victories in Easterhouse and from the contested history of Glasgow's urban redevelopment more generally is 'not that the vision of council housing that the city's working class fought for throughout the twentieth century is doomed to failure, but that without fighting, we'll get nothing at all'.[30] This is a lesson applicable to the rest of the UK, too; so is the fact that, in a society which weaponizes the rhetoric of social collapse to demonize mothers, any attempt to rectify the situation will be met with suspicion at best and obstruction at worst.

In using Easterhouse as a symbol for the ravages of poverty, Duncan Smith was ignoring its more complex history of activism, and refusing to learn the lessons of past successes, however limited they may have been. In 2010, he discussed his plans to address social deprivation with the journalist Amelia Gentleman, who notes that, although he had won praise from some charities and even some left-leaning politicians for his commitment to the subject, 'somewhere along the way, the thread of his argument takes an uncomfortable turn, and somehow seems to mix up being poor and being broken.' Poverty in Easterhouse, Duncan Smith declared from 400 miles away, is indelibly linked to 'bad parenting', to the fact that there is a 'a growing underclass of people increasingly incapable of rearing their own children'. This, as well as erasing efforts like those of the mothers of the Easthall Residents group, returns us to a familiar argument, eugenic in its character: poor people have too many children, and the blame for the deprivation they experience lies solely within their reproductive lives.[31]

After the Easthall housing project was completed, McCormack became a prominent figure on the Scottish left, working with STV and later the United Nations to raise awareness of the links between poverty, poor housing and ill health. A point she frequently made was that there was a war being waged against the global working class, a war 'without bullets', waged 'with briefcases instead of guns'. McCormack links 'sick housing' with 'sick babies' and with the 'sick planet': social justice, in Easterhouse, was global, environmental, and understood that there were identifiable perpetrators that were not the parents themselves.[32] This kind of violence continues, as the tragic death of Awaab Ishak in Rochdale illustrates, as well as many other deaths, each an unforgivable act of public neglect. In 2013, the death of nine-year-old Ella Kissi-Debrah was the first death to have air pollution officially recorded as its cause after the extensive campaigning of her mother, Rosamund: Kissi-Debrah's asthma was exacerbated by spikes in air pollution, which, in Lewisham in south London, where she lived, were frequent and, ultimately, fatal.[33]

It's not only in the quality of the housing provided for mothers and children to live in that the brutality of poverty is made manifest, but in the existence of such provision at all. In 2013, a group of twenty-nine single mothers, along with their neighbours, was served with eviction notices from the Focus E15 hostel in Newham, an area of east London where eleven billion pounds had recently been spent on the Olympics. The hostel provided one-bedroom apartments for women who had been made homeless to live in with their children, or while pregnant; it also provided training, education and support to help the women find work. Many of the residents in the below-market-rate rooms were teenagers, studying or engaged in part-time work in the area, with at least one mother applying for university courses in London. When state funding was slashed, it was announced that the hostel would cease to be an 'appropriate environment' for young mothers and children, meaning that Newham Council gained the responsibility for rehousing them. The mothers were told that they should expect to be placed outside the borough and even the city, maybe in Manchester or Birmingham, hundreds of miles away from their children's schools, their families, their friends, their support networks and each other. In the past, they would have been placed in temporary housing until local accommodation was found;

in 2013, five years into austerity, if they refused to take the homes they were offered, they would be deemed intentionally homeless, and evicted from their accommodation with nowhere else provided for them to go.

Like the mothers of Easthall, the residents chose resistance over acceptance: they banded together and launched the Focus E15 campaign, joining with their neighbours and some left-wing organizations. In September 2014, during London's Open House weekend, members of the group broke into two empty flats in the nearby Carpenters Estate, which had lain empty for years. Dawn Foster, writing about the campaign in 2016, noted that, 'walking around', it was 'remarkable how many windows were boarded up, so close to the 2012 Olympic site, which had promised regeneration and wealth for a poor area. Members of the Tenant Management Organization responsible for the site told me Newham Council had refused to allow them to rent properties that became empty if families moved out, slowly turning the red-brick estate into a ghost town.'[34] It's remarkable, too, to note the proximity between the eviction of these young mothers from their homes in the East End, and the national mania for *Call the Midwife*: when it came to the contemporary reality of mothering in the area, there was significantly less sympathy to be found.

In the occupied flats, the mums declared their own Open House, and prepared to open their newly precarious homes to the public, decorating them with toys, soft furnishings, banners and posters. A social centre was opened up for the community, a family friendly space which ran events: a felt-tipped rota held in the campaign's archives at the Bishopsgate Institute lists a 'Debt workshop: bring your bills, get advice'; 'Kids Kitchen! Parent-toddler cooking'; a basic plumbing and electrics workshop and community theatre performances. There was a guest book signed by visitors, and many cards, donations and tokens from across the country, from trade unions, single mothers and community groups. In the archives, I was particularly moved by a card saying, 'Dear E15 Mums, Here is £50.00 collected from our Ealing Trades Union Council public meeting last night. You are an inspiration to us all!! Absolutely brilliant', and by a postcard with a view of the Nevis mountain range from Loch Eil, reading, 'Dear E15 Mum's. Wishing you all the best at this difficult time. Please stay strong, the support is rising, and we are thinking of you here in Scotland. Don't let them bring you all down! Good luck Ann (mother of 3, and one of the 45%).' Banners were draped outside the occupied flats with a variety of slogans:

- EVERY MOTHER IS A WORKING MOTHER
- These HOMES Need People: These People Need Homes
- HOUSING IS OUR RIGHT
- GLOBAL WOMEN'S STRIKE
- SECURE TENANCIES NOW!
- WE ARE NOT ALONE
- People in East London say keep us in Newham
- Repopulate the council estate

My favourite poster looks a bit like Francisco Goya's famous painting of Saturn devouring his son but it's a mother holding her baby, both howling in horror at the word 'RENT'.

Much of the media, especially the London newspaper the *Evening Standard*, patronizingly declared the occupation to be a result of the 'hijacking' of the mums' campaign by seasoned left wingers. Andrew Baikie, the mayoral adviser for housing, stated his disappointment at seeing 'empty homes in the Carpenters Estate being occupied by agitators and hangers-on'.[35] The suggestion here is both that the young mothers themselves couldn't have come up with such an effective political strategy and that the campaign was not relevant to others who lived on the estate: that it was a highly specific set of circumstances, unfortunate perhaps, but not really *political*. In fact, the E15 mums knew very well that their campaign stretched beyond their own problem, however pressing that problem itself might be. Jasmin Stone, who was twenty at the time, told the *Standard* that 'Since we started our campaign last September we have met hundreds, if not thousands, of people who are really suffering with housing problems of all ages. We need to stand together and fight for decent housing for everybody.' Theirs was an issue that affected the whole community, and was applicable, too, to others around the country. One leaflet distributed by the campaign and its supporters said that 'When we met Newham's Labour mayor, Sir Robin Wales, he told us: "If you can't afford to live in Newham, you can't afford to live in Newham." We grew up in Newham. We find this attitude disgusting. No one on low wages or benefits, or even an average income, can afford to live here.' Transcripts of interviews conducted by Emer Morris held in the Bishopsgate Institute show that the remaining residents on the estate, who were also facing eviction, supported the mums. Mary Finch, a resident for forty-three years and facing eviction, described her reluctance to leave: 'I've been quite happy here. And this is where I want to stay.' When Morris asked what her feelings were about the occupation, she said:

> Fine. It's livened the place up again. I've got no objections. They're lovely. No problems . . . I've enjoyed a couple of nights over there. If I'd have been in a better mood I would have given you a couple of songs on the old karaoke! But no, it's been quite good, quite lively, like it used to be.[36]

The Focus E15 mums' fight to access suitable housing for themselves and their children became a symbol, both for the continuation of community – 'like it used to be' – and, in their single motherness, for a network beyond the traditional family. In December 2014, the graffiti artist Stik painted the tallest street artwork in the UK; called *Big Mother*, it stands at 125 feet tall. Describing its motivations, Stik, who began painting while homeless in Hackney, said: 'Affordable housing in Britain is under threat, this piece is to remind the world that all people need homes.' The mural, he continued 'is a symbol of solidarity with the pockets of resistance across the country', including the 'Focus E15 single mothers community'.[37] It was painted on Charles Hocking House, on the East Acton Estate, visible from both the Piccadilly line and flight paths over the capital. Charles Hocking

House was built in 1967 for low-income families; it was demolished in 2016, the artwork along with it. The destruction of communities is often adjacent to events like the Olympics – in Glasgow, there were plans announced to demolish the Red Road flats, a 1960s social housing project, live on television as part of the Commonwealth Games opening ceremony, with footage broadcast to screens in Celtic Park – something which emphasizes the gulf between displays of national pageantry and the lived reality of the country's inhabitants. The call to 'repopulate the council estate' is a call to reject not only austerity but its characterization of estates themselves as being broken, somehow, the site of generational trauma rather than the bare minimum a country should provide for its inhabitants: an affordable place to live. The accumulative effect of deprivation is real, but the community built up over decades is equally so: when families and networks of neighbours are able to stay in one place, the connected dwellings of estates can become, as the E15 occupation showed, a place where neighbours can work together, where life can be lived – and children raised – more collectively.

Disintegration

Any consideration of motherhood in the contemporary British state has to confront the fact that there may not be such a thing for much longer. As the ravages of austerity deepen, hysteria builds around immigration, more prisons are built to be filled and laws are passed to restrict the rights to free speech and free assembly of its citizens, it's possible to discern signs of its impending fracture. The grip tightens over the harness when the horse shows signs of bolting. Scottish independence has long been a contentious and definitional issue, and the prospect of a reunited Ireland is coming into clearer focus after the landmark victory of Sinn Féin in regional elections in 2022 and their stated intent of holding a unification referendum before the decade is out. In 2021, it was reported that the support for Welsh independence, which historically rested around 10 per cent of the population, has increased to one in three Welsh citizens. (This does not necessarily mean, of course, that the states that would replace the UK would necessarily be good, or even any better.[38])

The conservative version of the mother figure has historically played a significant role in the justification of the existence of the UK. This was most obviously embodied by Queen Elizabeth II, whose seventy-year-long reign ended in September 2022, with her cranky septuagenarian son ascending the throne with less charisma, less public goodwill and the legacy of his younger brother's alleged paedophilia to contend with. As the matriarchal monarch recedes, perhaps we will see a new prominence afforded to a more multi-faceted understanding of maternity, concerned with the urgent material problems of the contemporary moment.

In the 2014 Scottish Independence referendum, although only 43.4 per cent of female-identified voters voted Yes, compared to 53.2 per cent of their male-identified counterparts, within the broad Yes campaign there were multiple organizations making an explicitly feminist case for independence that recognized the concerns of the domestic as urgently and inherently political. Key among them was the umbrella group Women for Independence and the maternity-focused organization Mums for Change. In their 2018 study of the campaign for the women's vote in the referendum, the academics Craig McAngus and Kirstein Rummery concluded that, unlike Women Together, which shared the 'elite, top-down approach' of its parent organization Better Together, Women for Independence and its affiliated organizations were directly engaged in their communities and explicitly advocated independent statehood as part of the wider feminist movement in Scotland as a whole. Some of the most successful events that Women for Independence ran were held at community centres or outside shopping precincts at times that accommodated the school run, or featured beloved female celebrities talking informally about their lives, families and politics in their home towns.[39]

Throughout the official Independence campaign, the SNP emphasized the many brutal legacies of austerity. Nicola Sturgeon spoke repeatedly about benefit sanctions and Alex Salmond about the Bedroom Tax, something Gordon Brown's eleventh-hour intervention into the flagging Better Together campaign responded to cannily by highlighting Labour's role in the post-1945 consensus and the creation of the British welfare state. The left coalition of the Radical Independence Campaign – who prioritized enfranchising working-class communities through voter registration drives – campaigned under the slogan 'Britain is for the rich; Scotland can be ours'. Ultimately, of the thirty-two council areas in Scotland, the four that returned a majority for independence were the four most deprived areas in the country.[40] Without turning a blind eye to the regressive elements of a nationalist quest for separation, the integrated grassroots feminist campaigning for independence was something that used the elusive quest for 'the women's vote' to lay out its vision for new ways of living. Focusing on strengthening the community ties loosened by cuts and the ongoing violence of poverty, advocating for this kind of care-centred resistance invests the figure of the mother with a fresh political vitality.

In an interview with *Jacobin* in 2016, Bernadette Devlin McAliskey described the experience of 'seeing things come full circle' in the north of Ireland: 'I have lived to see food banks in Dungannon, where I work. When we were young and angry enough to be marching here against poverty in the 1960s, there was nobody living on food banks. The social housing waiting list in this town is now greater than it was when the Dungannon Housing Action movement started.' Emphasizing the difference between loyalism and unionism – and comparing middle-class Unionists to 'Falkland Islanders' – she writes that, despite their commitment to the continued existence of the UK,

the sense in the loyalist community is that they actually lost. They lost to everybody despite unwavering loyalty to the regime, even to those who challenged it by force. The anger in loyalist communities is fuelled by them still not having the price of a loaf and seeing Martin McGuinness up running the country.[41]

In acknowledging that loyalists are discriminated against for being working class or unemployed, there is the potential for a coming together in response to shared oppressions of class, rather than sectarian divides.

In August 2022, the Irish-language rappers Kneecap unveiled a mural in west Belfast of a PSNI Land Rover in flames, with the slogan 'Níl fáilte roimh an RUC' ('The Royal Ulster Constabulary aren't welcome'). Uproar ensued, with many politicians criticizing the mural for 'grooming' young people into 'sectarian hatred'. In an interview with the *Guardian*, Kneecap member Mo Chara pointed out that it was telling that the burning police car was interpreted as being sectarian at all: 'We took the design from a PSNI colouring book sent out to schools because they had such poor support from young people in the community.' Móglaí Bap, another member, tells a story about attending a Twelfth of July street party in the loyalist area of Sandy Row, and hearing 'like 14 young loyalists' singing their song CEARTA in Irish. He ended up drinking Buckfast with them: 'It's working-class people that get our craic.'[42] In 2020, Kneecap released a collaboration with the rapper DYRT, called 'Mam', which they described as 'a tune about something real, our Mothers'. The lyrics, a mixture of Irish and English, are structured around a refrain:

> Thank fuck mams don't do a runner /
> 'Cause some dads spend years buying butter'.
> I just took another line with my brother
> So I want to tell my mam that I love her

At one point in the song, DYRT addresses his absent father without blame, attributing his disappearing act to 'Peter Pan syndrome' and inherited trauma. He sympathizes with the difficulty for a mum who had to play the father, when their sons are 'Trapped in their self-centred thoughts about all that they lack / because they're missing a bond with their dad'. Later, we have lines about dinners of pasta pesto and spuds and salami, and the repeated line 'Seo ceann do na mná, a bhíonn ag obair gach lá' (''Cause there's nothing harder than single mas'). The song is defiant and never sentimental, alive both to harm and to joy. It celebrates, without naivety, one miraculous maternal act: not even fighting, but simply staying. Against a collection of near insurmountable odds, persisting.

Coda

Three Babies

One

The first birth I was ever present for, apart, I suppose, from my own, took place at the Queen Elizabeth University Hospital in Glasgow, on a beautiful Monday in June. It was an experience beyond language, and certainly the closest I had ever come to the sublime. I was there in my capacity as a voluntary birth companion, working for an organization, Amma, which provides pre- and post-natal support to pregnant people who would otherwise be giving birth alone. I was there, in other words, in a capacity which sits right on the boundary between the public and the private, a role which, in its very essence, reveals the absolute inseparability of the personal and the political.

The previous Saturday, we had spent a long night together on the induction ward. It was very quiet and, approaching the summer solstice, the sky outside the window never seemed to darken until, all of a sudden, I saw it had become an inky blue by stealth while I was looking the other way. In the hush and gloom of the empty ward, we listened to the sound of the foetal heartbeat monitor. One beat, pulsing, underwater and curiously crunchy: analogue, no matter how sophisticated the technology was. (All NHS machinery, however new it is, looks so implacably dated: the diagrams, the Vac and Sac font, the sterile blue plastic that seeps its colour sheepishly out into the atmosphere.) On Monday morning, the ward was far busier. There were ringing phones, the squeak of rubber soles on hospital flooring, chatter in the hallways. And there were three different foetal heartbeat monitors, all running at the same time, syncopating off each other. Squish, slosh, pulse.

Later in the day, labour not having 'progressed' along the timeline the midwives were hoping for, I took a break. I walked through the labyrinthine new hospital buildings to the price-gouged M&S and ate a four-pound-fifty sandwich on the grass, watching the various uniforms walk by. I followed the sandwich with a terrible coffee from the hospital café, and I was struck by how familiar it all felt. I spent a lot of time in East Surrey Hospital, where I was born, as a child and young teenager: when she couldn't find or afford childcare, my mum would often take my brother and me into work with her. Hospital spaces, so aesthetically singular in their attempt to convey absolutely nothing, remind me of her. I missed her: I wanted to thank her for having me.

By the evening, I wasn't thinking about myself at all. How to describe it? To be the hand someone squeezes and pinches during their contractions; to be the arms entrusted with a baby just, exactly, completely newly born, handed to you in the operating theatre before they can be fastened to their mother's chest. For a moment, I believed in the future. I could see it.

Two

Stories about motherhood are stories about giving and taking. (Lauren Berlant describes the 'female complaint' in their book of the same name thus: 'Everyone knows what the female complaint is: women live for love, and love is the gift that keeps on taking.')[1] In this book, I have struggled to maintain a commitment to utopian thinking: it's hard to strike a balance between a belief in what liberated mothering could be and an accurate representation of how it has been. This is true, particularly, of motherhood's relationship to gender: the fact that it is not by default a gendered state is coloured and contoured by the fact that it has been understood as a definitionally feminine one. When I try to unpick my own prospective relationship to reproduction, I feel myself chafing against, in the words of Denise Riley, the 'exhaustingly decisive' experience of my own gender. I'm now of an age where every other sponsored advertisement that targets me is about fertility: choice is knocking insistently at the door.

In *A Woman's Story*, Annie Ernaux writes about her mother's death, which happened eight days, she notes, before Simone de Beauvoir's: 'She preferred giving to everybody, rather than taking from them. Isn't writing also a way of giving?' Later, she writes that 'I believe I am writing about my mother because it is my turn to bring her into the world'.[2] My mother was always open about having miscarried many times before she had me, her first child. I appreciated this: yes, it sometimes felt like a haunting. But it made me feel so lucky to be alive. (In 'Three Babies', a song from her maternal album *I Do Not Want What I Haven't Got*, Sinéad O'Connor addresses her three miscarried foetuses, telling them that the images of their faces and the smell of their bodies will remain with her. In *Rememberings*, she says that song is also about the four children she does have: the not-babies are there with the babies that are, intertwined, for ever).[3]

My mother: now there is a woman who has given to everybody. In theory, I'd like to give her a baby – a grandchild. She wants one, for sure. To be honest, I'm not sure how well writing stands up as a replacement. But maybe the lines of possession don't need to be so clearly drawn. After all, in her mothering of me and my brother, hasn't she enfolded the lives of the not-babies, the ones that could have arrived before I did, but didn't? And hasn't her mothering of me, in turn, been repurposed in my own relationships with the babies in my life, those of my friends, those whose births I attend, those I try to think about in my politics, in my unsteady but committed hold on imagining a political future that differs from the present? In the 1980s, the Sisterhood of Black Single Mothers called families 'motherful' instead of 'fatherless'. Can the world also be understood to be babyful? Would that help us understand ourselves as interconnected subjects, not rugged individuals? Can we turn the psychic echo of the baby crying in the nursery into a sound that knits us together?

Three

In the middle of writing this book, I took a pregnancy test that produced a positive result. The next pregnancy test I took was negative, as was the next, and the one after that. How to explain it? A mistake, a faulty cheap test left in a drawer for too long, a fluke. A 'chemical pregnancy': as tests get more sensitive to hormone production in urine streams, they pick up the very early stages of pregnancy too early, pregnancies which usually end without being understood to be pregnancies at all. Whatever it was, it manifested itself at that moment as an experience of profound alienation: I did not want to have a baby. If you google a positive-negative-negative-negative pregnancy test, you find a chorus of posts on various forums documenting an utter desperation to conceive, the single lines on the second and third and sometimes fourth and fifth and sixth tests coming like body blows, a tragedy in stages. All I can say is that that is not how it was for me.

Often, the decision not to have children is represented in literature and culture as one that leaves a significant psychic mark. The question is not whether it is right or wrong to decide against reproduction, but rather whether to do so creates from some displaced energy, some absent matter, the ingredients for a haunting. I think, historically, it has done. The question is so circumscribed by the harm done by legal, religious and social institutions that even when 'choice' is utilized, encouraged or identified, it is never fully enacted. It can't be: the foundational tenets of reproductive justice – the right to reproduce, the right not to, the right to do either in *safety* – are still so far from being fully realized for everyone.

In *Happening*, when Ernaux writes of pregnancy as something that allows the spirits of previous generations to move through her, I wonder where they would otherwise have gone. What would have been their conduit? Does it have to be through the uterus? Is my only hope of passing on what I learned from my mother (for example: look after your knees) a route that involves a nine-month gestation? I didn't learn what I learned from her through the umbilical cord, or some other process, while I was in utero. I learned it the way I've learned everything else in my life: repetition, proximity, commitment and desire. I learned not at my mother's knee, but from it.

Despite the tantalizing promise of futurity contained within the figure of the child, none of us can predict the future. I certainly have no desire to be as foolish as to commit myself to print in a prediction for the way my own life will proceed. What I do know is that the faulty display of a pregnancy test that July produced in me a new relationship to choice, even though I did not have to enact my decision after I had made it. And what I know, too, is that the choice I made in July, however many other times I have previously made it – prevention, easier than a cure, counts here too – and however many other times I will make it in the future, has no bearing on my ability, capacity, desire to do the work of mothering in my own time and in my own way. These are difficult times. We have to construct conduits for each other.

Acknowledgments

Appropriately for the acknowledgements to a book about interdependence, I count myself very lucky to be so indebted to so many people. This does, however, make it hard to know where to begin.

Thank you, first, to every single person at Allen Lane who has worked on this book. *Mother State* was a long time in the making, and one of its beginnings was in a conversation with my brilliant agent Emma Paterson, to whom I am extremely grateful for that and for everything else. The introduction to the book began its life as an essay in the *New Statesman*, commissioned by Lola Seaton. I presented an early version of Chapter Five as part of 'Clear Away the Rubble / Glan an Spallaí ar Shiúl' at Project Arts Centre in Dublin in 2022, and a version of Chapter Seven at Arika in Glasgow, also in 2022: thank you to Sara Greavu at Project and the whole Arika team, and to the audience members who asked such generative questions. Parts of Chapter Twelve emerged in an essay I wrote to accompany Joey Simons' 2021 exhibition, 'The fearful part of it was the absence' at Collective Gallery in Edinburgh, and I'm grateful to Joey for the conversations about housing struggles we've had over the last few years. I was able to finish the first draft of this book with the help of a generous grant from the Francis W Reckitt Arts Trust and the Society of Authors. I'd also like to thank Željka Marošević and Francesca Wade for supporting my early writing during their editorial tenure at the much-missed *White Review*: the current indefinite hiatus of this magazine is a shameful indictment of the current state of arts funding in the UK.

Much of the thinking and reading that underpins *Mother State* developed during my postgraduate research, from 2014 – 19. I am happily indebted to my MPhil supervisor, Robert Macfarlane, my doctoral supervisor, Jan-Melissa Schramm, my doctoral advisor, Ruth Abbott, and my PhD examiners, Corinna Russell and Adelene Buckland. Emmanuel College, Cambridge, and the Arts and Humanities Research Council provided me with the grants that enabled my studies. During the time I was writing this book I was mostly engaged in fixed-term or hourly-paid teaching positions at universities across the UK. I'd like to thank those who persist in trying to advocate for better working and learning conditions in higher education despite the many disappointments of the last few years, and my students, who I learn such a lot from.

This book, like me, is a creature formed in a public library. I'd like to thank staff at Dorking Library and at libraries across Glasgow, especially Langside and the Mitchell, and to those who campaigned for public libraries to reopen on the Southside after lockdown and those trying to resist Glasgow City Council's harmful cuts to public services. I'm also grateful to staff at the Bishopsgate Institute, the British Library, Cambridge University Library, the Feminist Library, Glasgow Women's Library, and the Regional Resource Centre at Beamish Museum. Thanks, too, to Nobby Dimon of Durham Theatre Company who answered my questions about *Not by Bread Alone*, and to Emer Mary Morris for giving me permission to quote from her Focus E15 interview transcripts. Thanks to Kneecap and Penny Rimbaud for generously granting me permission to quote from their lyrics, and to Eli Davies for helping with my licensing queries.

Training with Amma Birth Companions, the charity that supports parents in Glasgow who might otherwise give birth alone, was a truly transformative experience. Thank you to everyone who works and volunteers at Amma, to those who contributed to the training programme, to those I trained alongside, and, of course, to the mothers who allowed me to accompany them through labour and the children whose first moments of life I was privileged to witness.

The daily work of writing can be both an isolated and an isolating experience, and those who alleviate this are very precious. This is not a book of poetry, but I am always grateful to the community of poets who I've read alongside and shared work with over the years, many of whom are keeping the fires of experimental publishing burning in hostile conditions. Thank you to my friends in Glasgow, London, Cambridge and elsewhere. I won't list you here, but I *love* you. Particular thanks are due, however, to Caitlín Doherty, Holly Isard, Daisy Lafarge, Conrad Steel, Chris Vardy and Emilia Weber, who read drafts of chapters of this book and vastly improved them. Quentin Beroud, Trish McKeown, Leyla McLennan, Anna Pearce, Liene Rozīte, Jo Shaw, and Joel White talked me through many knotty problems. Hannah Proctor read several versions of the stickiest part, and I look forward to many more exchanges of our mutual bad objects over the coming years. Thank you to Lilí Ní Dhomhnaill for Irish translations and for constant support since we met on a picket line in 2018, and to Rory Williamson for reading so many drafts, for intermittently housing me, and for the last twelve years of friendship. Thank you to my family, including my dad Clifford, my stepdad Nick, my stepmum Louise, and my step and half siblings. Thank you, too, to Grace, Stephen, and Stephanie Law. And to Christopher Law: thank you for living with me throughout this book's long gestation with such generosity, intellectual comradeship, and love.

This book is dedicated to my mother Jane, and to my brother and best friend Tom, whose story some of this is too.

Notes

NOTE: References followed by an asterisk are listed in the Bibliography with a web link.

Preface

1 Carolyn Steedman, 'Middle-Class Hair', *London Review of Books*, 39:20 (19 October 2017).
2 Carolyn Steedman, *Landscape for a Good Woman* (London: Virago, 1986), p. 122.
3 Jacqueline Rose, *Mothers: An Essay on Love and Cruelty* (London: Faber and Faber, 2018). See, in particular, Julia Kristeva, *Powers of Horror: An Essay on Abjection* (New York, NY: Columbia University Press, 1982).
4 Simone de Beauvoir, *A Very Easy Death*, trans. Patrick O'Brien (London: André Deutsch Ltd and George Weidenfeld and Nicolson Ltd, 1965), pp. 19–20.
5 Steedman, *Landscape*, p. 2.

Introduction

1 Angela McRobbie has diagnosed this as the neoliberal 'intensification' of mothering. See 'Feminism, the Family, and the new "Mediated" Maternalism', *New Formations*, 80/81 (2014).
2 Imogen Tyler, in 'Introduction: Birth', *Feminist Review*, 93:1 (November 2009), 1–7, quotes the British government report *Fairness and Freedom: The Final Report of the Equalities Review* as saying 'Our new research reveals clearly that there is one factor that above all leads to women's inequality in the labour market – becoming mothers.' In *The*

Phenomenal Woman: Feminist Metaphysics and the Patterns of Identity (Cambridge: Polity Press, 1998), Christine Battersby writes that all women – regardless of their fertility – are assigned 'a subject-position linked to a body that has perceived potentialities for birth' (p. 16).

3 Joseph Rowntree Foundation, 'UK Poverty 2022', 18 January 2022*.

4 Lola Olufemi, *Feminism, Interrupted* (London: Pluto Press, 2019), p. 25.

5 Liz Heron (ed.), *Truth, Dare or Promise: Girls Growing up in the 50s* (London: Virago, 1985), p. 6, and Beverley Bryan, Stella Dadzie and Suzanne Scafe, *The Heart of the Race: Black Women's Lives in Britain* (London: Verso, 1985), p. 198.

6 Jacqueline Rose, *Mothers: An Essay on Love and Cruelty* (London: Faber and Faber, 2018).

7 See Denise Riley, *'Am I That Name?': Feminism and the Category of 'Women' in History* (London: Macmillan, 1988). See also Lola Olufemi on womanhood as a 'strategic coalition', borrowed from Gayatri Chakravorty Spivak and Chandra Talpade Mohanty, in an interview with Josie Sparrow, 'A commitment to care . . . and to disobedience', *New Socialist*, 15 April 2020*.

8 Alona Ferber, 'Judith Butler on the culture wars, JK Rowling and living in "anti-intellectual times"', *New Statesman*, 22 September 2020*.

9 See Angela Y. Davis, *Women, Race & Class* (New York, NY: Random House, 1981); Hortense J. Spillers, 'Mama's Baby, Papa's Maybe: An American Grammar Book', *Diacritics*, 17:2 (Summer 1987), 64–81.

10 Hannah Summers, 'Black women in the UK four times more likely to die in pregnancy or childbirth', *Guardian*, 15 January 2021*.

11 Kate Briggs, *The Long Form* (London: Fitzcarraldo, 2023), p. 168.

12 Virginia Woolf, 'Professions for Women', *Collected Essays*, ed. Andrew McNeillie and Stuart N. Clarke, 6 vols (London: The Hogarth Press, 1986–2011), vol. 5: 1929–1932.

13 Nancy K. Miller, 'Mothers, Daughters, and Autobiography: Maternal Legacies and Cultural Criticism', *Mothers in Law: Feminist Theory and the Legal Regulation of Motherhood*, ed. Martha Albertson Fineman and Isabel Karpin (New York, NY: Columbia University Press, 1995), p. 17.

14 The cultural historian Mary Poovey argues that idealization and repression were two sides of the same coin – these maternal angels were

characterized 'not only as dependent but as needing the control that was the other face of protection' – and rooted in the popular belief that biological difference associated women with emotion rather than reason: the female body was the device of its own suppression. Mary Poovey, *Uneven Developments: The Ideological Work of Gender in Mid-Victorian England* (Chicago, IL: University of Chicago Press, 1988), p. 11. See also Valerie Fildes, *Wet Nursing: A History from Antiquity to the Present* (Oxford: Wiley Blackwell, 1988); Margaret Hewitt, *Wives and Mothers in Victorian Industry* (London: Rockcliff, 1958); Ruth Perry, 'Colonizing the Breast: Sexuality and Maternity in Eighteenth-Century England', *Journal of the History of Sexuality*, 2:2 (October 1991), 204–34 (p. 206).

15 See Angela McRobbie, 'Inside the socialist nursery: welfare maternity and the writing of Denise Riley', *Feminist Review*, 23:1 (2020), 287–96.

16 Denise Riley, *War in the Nursery* (London: Virago, 1983), p. 119.

17 Riley, *War in the Nursery*, p. 196.

18 Katrina Forrester, ' "In and against the state": revolutionary feminism during deindustrialization', lecture delivered on 9 June 2023, University of Cambridge. See also Christine Delphy, *Close to Home: A Material Analysis of Women's Oppression*, trans. Diana Leonard (London: Verso, 2016).

19 Anushka Asthana, 'Take care of your elderly mothers and fathers, says Tory minister', *Guardian*, 31 January 2017*.

20 Tithi Bhattacharya, 'Introduction: Mapping Social Reproduction Theory', *Social Reproduction Theory: Remapping Class, Recentring Oppression*, ed. Tithi Bhattacharya (London: Pluto Press, 2017), p. 19.

21 Lisa Baraitser, *Enduring Time* (London: Bloomsbury, 2017); Stella Sandford, 'What is Maternal Labour?', *Studies in the Maternal*, 3:2 (2011), 1–11.

22 Holly Pester, 'Songs of Rest: An Intervention in the Complex Genre of the Lullaby', *The Restless Compendium: Interdisciplinary Investigations of Rest and Its Opposites*, ed. Felicity Callard, Kimberley Staines and James Wilkes (London: Palgrave Macmillan, 2016), p. 113.

23 See Sophie Lewis, *Full Surrogacy Now* (London: Verso, 2019); M. E. O'Brien, *Family Abolition: Capitalism and the Communizing of Care* (London: Pluto Press, 2023); and Jenny Turner, 'Dark Emotions', *London Review of Books*, 42:18 (24 September 2020).

24 Sheila Rowbotham, *Beyond the Fragments: Feminism and the Making of Socialism* (Newcastle upon Tyne: Newcastle Socialist Centre, 1979).

25 Shulamith Firestone and Anne Koedt used it as the title for an article by Carol Hanisch about therapy and politics published in *Notes from the Second Year: Women's Liberation* (New York, NY: Radical Feminism, 1970).

26 Although internationalism and 'third world women' were on the agenda for the 1971 Ruskin conference, there was no initial consideration, as Gail Lewis, Gerlin Bean and others have noted, of how race might feature in their own movement. See Margaretta Jolly (ed.), *Sisterhood and After: An Oral History of the UK Women's Liberation Movement, 1968–present* (Oxford: Oxford University Press, 2019); Kimberley Springer, 'Third wave black feminism?', *Signs*, 27:4 (Summer 2002), 1059–82.

27 A. Sivanandan, *Communities of Resistance: Writings on Black Struggles for Socialism* (London: Verso, 1990), p. 57

28 Akwugo Emejulu and Leah Bassel, 'Minority Women, Austerity and Activism', *Race & Class*, 57:2 (October 2015), 86–95.

29 Frances Ryan, *Crippled: Austerity and the Demonization of Disabled People* (London: Verso, 2018).

30 Riley, *War in the Nursery*, p. 196.

31 Jacqueline Rose, *Mothers: An Essay on Love and Cruelty* (London: Faber and Faber, 2018), p. 82

32 See Angela McRobbie, 'Feminism, the Family and the New "Mediated" Maternalism', *New Formations*, 80 and 81 (Winter 2013), 119–37 (p. 119).

33 See Candice Brathwaite, *I am Not Your Baby Mother* (London: Quercus, 2020), and Sara Petersen, 'Victorian Era-Inspired Momfluencers are Taking Over Instagram', *InStyle*, 25 March 2021.

34 Brian Walden, Margaret Thatcher, TV Interview for London Weekend Television, *Weekend World* ('Victorian Values'), 16 January 1983.

35 Jacqueline Rose, *Women in Dark Times* (London: Bloomsbury, 2014), p. x.

36 Jean McCrindle and Sheila Rowbotham (eds), *Dutiful Daughters: Women Talk about Their Lives* (London: Pelican Books, 1979).

37 Margaretta Jolly, *Sisterhood and After: An Oral History of the UK Women's Liberation Movement, 1968–present* (Oxford: Oxford University Press, 2019), p. 5.

38 Lauren Berlant, 'For Example', *supervalent thought*, 16 May 2012*; Hazel Carby, *Imperial Intimacies: A Tale of Two Islands* (London: Verso, 2019); Saidiya Hartman, 'A conversation between Hazel Carby and Saidiya Hartman', *Paris Review*, 21 January 2020*.

39 Lorna Sage, *Bad Blood* (London: Fourth Estate, 2000), p. 236.

40 de Beauvoir, *A Very Easy Death*, p. 69.

41 Virginia Woolf, *A Room of One's Own* (London: The Hogarth Press, 1929), p. 114.

42 Tillie Olsen, *Silences* (London: Virago Modern Classics, 1994), pp. 19, 33; Maggie Doherty, *The Equivalents: A Story of Art, Female Friendship, and Liberation in the 1960s* (New York, NY: Penguin Random House USA, 2020), p. 48.

43 Roland Barthes, *Camera Lucida*, trans. Richard Howard (New York, NY: Hill and Wang, 1981), p. 65

44 Sigmund Freud and Josef Breuer, *The Standard Edition of the Complete Psychological Works of Sigmund Freud, Volume II (1893–1895): Studies on Hysteria*, ed. and trans. James Strachey (London: Vintage, 2001), p. 7.

45 Freud and Breuer, *Studies on Hysteria*, p. 305.

46 Shulamith Firestone, *The Dialectic of Sex* (New York, NY: William Morrow and Company, 1970), p. 30. This isn't a problem that has been solved. Gail Lewis, writing in 2023, phrased it thus: 'First, if each generation has its own thoughts, how can a temporal frame that is always "now", and also one that simply repeats, be avoided? The now/repeat dilemma poses profound issues of vision and strategy. Struggles for social transformation in pursuit of justice and freedom always raise the challenge of how to draw from history whilst avoiding being constrained by it (a dilemma embodied in intergenerational dynamics).' 'Whose movement is it anyway? Intergenerationality and the problem of political alliance', *Radical Philosophy*, 2:14 (April 2023), 64–74.

47 Sally Alexander, *Becoming a Woman* (London: Virago, 1994), pp. 109, 99.

48 Denise Riley, *The Words of Selves: Identification, Solidarity, Irony* (Stanford, NY: Stanford University Press, 2000), p. 22.

1. *Suffering*

1 See Lynsey Hanley, *Estates* (London: Granta, 2007), and E. P. Thompson, 'The Peculiarities of the English', *Socialist Register 1965*, 311–62. In 1936, an antisemitic march through the area by the British Union of Fascists, led by Oswald Mosley, was defeated by east Londoners in the Battle of Cable Street. This antifascism intersected with feminism: Sylvia Pankhurst, disillusioned with the mainstream suffrage movement's failure to engage with working-class women, founded the East London Federation of Suffragettes in 1914. A friend of Rosa Luxemburg, Pankhurst devoted her life to antifascist and anticolonial struggles, refusing to see women's rights as a single issue and refusing to capitulate to the middle- and upper-class demands of the Women's Social and Political Union, run by her mother and sisters: she refused to renounce her association with the Labour Party, and was ostracized by her family for her opposition to the First World War and her support for communism.

2 James Burton notes that in the storylines that do deal explicitly with racism, the blame is often laid on the shoulders of working-class women, with the middle-class characters rising above it. 'Reframing the 1950s: race and representation in recent British television', *Adjusting the Contrast: British Television and Constructs of Race*, ed. Sarita Malik and Darrell M. Newton (Manchester: Manchester University Press, 2017), pp. 71–89.

3 Caitlin Moran, 'Call the Radical Feminist', *Sunday Times*, 26 January 2013.

4 Hilary Garratt, 'Call the Midwife sends out a poignant message', *NHS England blog*, 27 February 2017.

5 Toby Helm and Michael Savage, 'More nurses, better care – Tories' 10-year pledge on maternity services', *Guardian*, 29 December 2018*.

6 See Denis Campbell, 'Concerns over birthing options as NHS shuts midwife-led centre', *Guardian*, 11 February 2019*; Harriet Sherwood, 'Left in the lurch: mothers-to-be devastated as maternity scheme ends', *Guardian*, 2 February 2019*; Maya Oppenheim, 'Maternity services at risk as midwives plan to quit over pandemic stress', *Independent*, 31 March 2021*.

7 Lisa Baraitser and Imogen Tyler, 'Private View, Public Birth: Making Feminist Sense of the New Visual Culture of Childbirth', *Studies in the Maternal*, 5:2 (July 2013), 1–27 (p. 1)*. Mary Poovey, in an essay about the use of anaesthetic in childbirth in the nineteenth century, reminds us that representation, as 'the arena for negotiating values, meanings, and identities' stages 'the workings through of the dominant ideology'. Mary Poovey, ' "Scenes of an Indelicate Character": The Medical "Treatment" of Victorian Women', *The Making of the Modern Body: Sexuality and Society in the Nineteenth Century*, ed. Catherine Gallagher and Thomas Laqueur (Berkeley, CA: University of California Press, 1987), pp. 137–68 (pp. 138–9).

8 Louise Fitzgerald, 'Taking a pregnant pause: Interrogating the feminist potential of Call the Midwife', *Upstairs and Downstairs: British Costume Drama Television from the Forsyte Saga to Downton Abbey*, ed. James Leggott and Julie Anne Taddeo (Lanham: Rowman and Littlefield, 2015), pp. 249–63 (p. 253).

9 Adrienne Rich, *Of Woman Born: Motherhood as Experience and Institution*, 2nd edn (London: Virago, 1977), p. 128.

10 Rich, *Of Woman Born*, p. 13.

11 Ciara Breathnach, 'Handywomen and Birthing in Rural Ireland, 1851–1955', *Gender & History*, 28:1 (April 2016), 34–56. See also Tania McIntosh, *A Social History of Maternity and Childbirth: Key Themes in Maternity Care* (Abingdon: Routledge, 2012). See also The Midwife's Tale Oral History Collection, at the Royal College of Obstetricians and Gynaecologists, London.

12 Silvia Federici, *Caliban and the Witch: Women, the Body and Primitive Accumulation* (New York, NY: Autonomedia, 2004). Federici's methodology in this book has been questioned: see Yann Kindo and Christophe Darmangeat, 'Caliban and the Witch: A Critical Analysis', *Intransigence*, 5 (2019).

13 See Adrian Wilson, *The Making of Man-Midwifer: Childbirth in England 1660–1770* (Cambridge, MA: Harvard University Press, 1995), and Irvine Loudon, *Death in Childbirth: An International Study of Maternal Care and Maternal Mortality 1800–1950* (Oxford: Clarendon Press, 1992).

14 Rich, *Of Woman Born*, p. 128.

15 See Poovey, ' "Scenes of an Indelicate Character" ', pp. 139–41.

16 Riley, *War in the Nursery*, p. 151.

17 Sarah Campion, *National Baby* (London: Ernest Benn, 1950).

18 See Angela Davis, *Modern Motherhood: Women and Family in England 1945–2012* (Manchester: Manchester University Press, 2014).

19 See Marjorie Tew, *Safer Childbirth? A Critical History of Maternity Care* (London: Chapman & Hall, 1995).

20 Annabel Sowemimo, 'Learning the African history of caesarean sections will help us better challenge stigma', *gal-dem*, 27 August 2020*.

21 Emily Martin, *The Woman in the Body: A Cultural Analysis of Reproduction* (Boston, MA: Beacon Press, 2001 edn), pp. 45, 57.

22 Susanna Rustin, 'All British women have the right to a caesarean – they're not "too posh to push" ', *Guardian*, 29 March 2016*.

23 See Elizabeth Mahase, 'Doctors question NICE recommendation to induce labour at 39 weeks in ethnic minority women', *BMJ*, 6 July 2021*; Denis Campbell and Pamela Duncan, 'Is "incessant increase" in caesarean births putting first-time mothers' health at risk?', *Guardian*, 31 January 2016*; Nadeem Badshah, 'Shropshire maternity scandal: 300 babies died or left brain-damaged, says report', *Guardian*, 26 March 2022*.

24 Jolly, *Sisterhood and After*, p. 79.

25 Jolly, *Sisterhood and After*, p. 228.

26 See Samantha May Shapiro, 'Mommy Wars: the prequel', *The New York Times* magazine, 27 May 2012*; and Brathwaite, *I am Not Your Baby Mother*, p. 107.

27 See Lorel Mayberry and Jacqueline Daniel ' "Birthgasm": A Literary Review of Orgasm as an Alternative Mode of Pain Relief in Childbirth', *Journal of Holistic Nursing*, 34:4 (December 2016), 331–42; Thierry Postel, 'Childbirth climax: The revealing of obstetrical orgasm', *Sexologies*, 22:4, 89–92.

28 Audre Lorde, *Zami: A New Spelling of My Name* (Watertown, MA: Persephone Press, 1982); 'Uses of the Erotic', *The Selected Works of Audre Lorde*, ed. Roxane Gay (New York, NY: 2020); Bethany Jacobs, 'Mothering herself: manifesto of the erotic mother in Audre Lorde's *Zami: A New Spelling of My Name*', *MELUS*, 40:4 (Winter 2015), pp. 113–14.

29 Maggie Nelson, *The Argonauts* (London: Melville House, 2016), p. 55.

30 See *Thinking through the Skin*, ed. Sara Ahmed and Jackie Stacey (Abingdon: Routledge, 2001).

31 Réka Kinga Papp, 'Decriminalizing childbirth', *Eurozine*, 28 June 2017*.

32 Scott Roxborough, 'Toronto: Hungarian Filmmakers on the Personal Trauma behind "Pieces of a Woman" ', *Hollywood Reporter*, 16 September 2020*.

33 Nicole Veach, 'Our trauma, by baby death couple', *Observer*, 16 May 1999*; Susie Steiner, 'Natural birth: "I felt brilliant. I was in utter ecstasy" ', *Guardian*, 1 June 2013*.

34 Sarah Davies, 'Albany midwives exonerated – ARM demands apology', *Midwifery*, 7 March 2017*; Lucy Atkins, 'A happy birthday every day', *Guardian*, 24 July 2007*; Jude Davis, 'Albany Midwifery Practice', *AIMs Journal*, 26:3 (September 2014); Clare Finney, 'A group of midwives like no other', *East London Lines*, 25 January 2010*.

35 Roxborough, 'Personal Trauma behind "Pieces of a Woman" '.

36 Sheila Heti, *Motherhood* (London: Harvill Secker, 2018), pp. 198, 144, 162.

37 Jolly, *Sisterhood and After*, p. 228.

38 Maggie Nelson, *The Argonauts* (London: Melville House, 2016), pp. 167, 163.

39 Rose, *Mothers*, p. 192.

40 Sandeep Parmar, 'An Uncommon Language', *Poetry* (April 2019).

41 See Sabina Spielrein, *The Essential Writings of Sabina Spielrein: Pioneer of Psychoanalysis*, ed. Ruth I. Cape and Raymond Burt (Abingdon: Taylor & Francis, 2018).

42 Nelson, *The Argonauts*, p. 155.

43 Rachel Cusk, *A Life's Work* (London: Picador, 2021), pp. 48, 104.

44 Alice Notley, 'A Baby is Born Out of a White Owl's Forehead – 1972', *Mysteries of Small Houses* (New York, NY: Penguin, 1998), p. 38.

45 Barbara Claire Freeman, *The Feminine Sublime: Gender and Excess in Women's Fiction* (Berkeley, CA: University of California Press, 1995), p. 3.

46 Sheila Lintott, 'The Sublimity of Gestating and Giving Birth', *Philosophical Inquiries into Pregnancy, Childbirth, and Mothering*, ed. Sheila Lintott and Maureen Sander-Staudt (Abingdon: Routledge, 2012), pp. 237–50 (pp. 238–9).

47 Zadie Smith, 'Joy', *New York Review of Books* (10 January 2013).

48 Maggie Nelson, *The Art of Cruelty: A Reckoning* (New York, NY: W. W. Norton, 2011), p. 23.

49 See Elin Diamond, 'Realism and Hysteria: Toward a Feminist Mimesis', *Discourse*, 13:1 (Fall–Winter 1990–91), pp. 59–92 (pp. 60–66); see Sigmund Freud and Josef Breuer, *Studies on Hysteria*, trans. Nicola Luckhurst (London: Penguin Classics, 2004).

50 Peter Wollen, 'Alphabet of Cinema', *Paris Hollywood: Writings on Film* (London: Verso, 2002), pp. 2–3.

2. Choosing

1 'Cowboys and Nomads', *I Love Dick*, dir. Andrea Arnold, written by Sarah Gubbins and Heidi Schreck, Amazon Prime Video, 2017.

2 Linda Nochlin, 'Why Have There Been No Great Women Artists?', *Art News*, January 1971.

3 Rebecca Solnit, *The Mother of All Questions* (London: Granta, 2017), pp. 1–3.

4 Rich, *Of Woman Born*, 2nd edn, p. 158.

5 Tobi Thomas and Jessica Elgot, 'Women from poorer backgrounds three times more likely to have abortions', *Guardian*, 23 March 2021*; Department of Health and Social Care, 'Abortion Statistics, England and Wales: 2019', 11 June 2020*.

6 See Clare Parker, 'From Immorality to Public Health: Thalidomide and the Debate for Legal Abortion in Australia', *Social History of Medicine*, 25:4 (2012), 863–80; British Medical Association, 'The law and ethics of abortion', September 2020*.

7 See Rachel Moss, 'Two Women in UK are Facing Criminal Charges for Abortion. Here's Why', *Huffington Post*, 18 July 2022*; Sally Sheldon, Jane O'Neill, Clare Parker and Gayle Davis, '"Too Much, Too Indigestible, Too Fast?" The Decades of Struggle for Abortion Law Reform in Northern Ireland', *Modern Law Review*, 83:4, pp. 761–96 (pp. 763–5); Susan McKay, 'Northern Ireland's women won abortion rights but its politicians won't accept that', *Guardian*, 20 March 2021*.

8 Joanna Biggs, 'Diary: Abortion in Northern Ireland', 39:16 (17 August 2017).

9 Erica Millar, *Happy Abortions: Our Bodies in the Era of Choice* (London: Zed Books, 2017), p. 1.

10 Victoria Browne, *Pregnancy without Birth: A Feminist Philosophy of Miscarriage* (London: Bloomsbury, 2022). See also Browne, 'The politics of miscarriage', *Radical Philosophy*, 2:3 (December 2018), 62–72.

11 Annie Ernaux, *Happening*, trans. Tanya Leslie (London: Fitzcarraldo, 2019), p. 39.

12 See Stephen Brooke, ' "A New World for Women"? Abortion Law Reform in Britain during the 1930s', *American Historical Review*, 106:2 (April 2001), 431–59.

13 Juno Mac and Molly Smith, *Revolting Prostitutes: The Fight for Sex Workers' Rights* (London: Verso, 2018), p. 15.

14 Mac and Smith, *Revolting Prostitutes*, p. 23. See also Jacqueline Rose, *Sexuality in the Field of Vision* (London: Verso, 1986); Judith R. Walkowitz, *Prostitution and Victorian Society – Women, Class, and the State* (Cambridge: Cambridge University Press, 1980).

15 Caroline M. de Costa, 'The king versus Aleck Bourne: the case that established the lawfulness of terminating pregnancy to preserve women's health', *Medical Journal of Australia*, 191:4 (2009), 230–31. See also John Keown, *Abortion, Doctors and the Law: Some Aspects of the Legal Regulation of Abortion in England from 1803 to 1982* (Cambridge: Cambridge University Press, 1998); Barbara L. Brookes, *Abortion in England 1900–1967* (London: Routledge, 1988).

16 Stephen Brooke, *Sexual Politics: Sexuality, Family Planning, and the British Left from the 1880s to the Present Day* (Oxford: Oxford University Press, 2011), p. 160.

17 Diane Munday, Colin Francome and Wendy Savage, 'Twenty-one years of legal abortion', *BMJ*, 298:6682 (May 1989), 1231–4.

18 Nell Dunn, *Talking to Women* (London: Silver Press, 2018), pp. 179, 130, 205.

19 Jolly, *Sisterhood and After*, p. 69.

20 Brooke, *Sexual Politics*, p. 185.

21 See Brooke, *Sexual Politics*, p. 207. Wendy Bourton, 'Abortion Rights Cardiff', Casgliad Y Werin Cymru / People's Collection Wales <https://www.casgliadywerin.cymru/items/1151991>.

22 See Brooke, *Sexual Politics,* p. 207. Wendy Bourton, 'Abortion Rights Cardiff'.

23 Kristin Hay, ' "More than a defence against bills": feminism and national identity in the Scottish abortion campaign, c. 1975–1990', *Women's History Review,* 30:4 (July 2020), 594–612 (pp. 600, 596); see also Lucy Grieve, 'The Scottish Government is failing women when it comes to abortion', *Scotsman,* 5 June 2022*.

24 See Sally Sheldon, Jane O'Neill, Clare Parker and Gayle Davis, ' "Too Much, Too Indigestible, Too Fast"?', pp. 768, 765; see also Monica McWilliams, 'Struggling for Peace and Justice: Reflections on Women's Activism in Northern Ireland', *Journal of Women's History,* 6:4 and 7:1 (Winter–Spring 1995).

25 Ruth Elliott, 'How Far Have We Come? Women's Organization in the Unions in the United Kingdom', *Feminist Review,* 16:1 (July 1984), 64–73 (p. 66).

26 Peta Steel, 'Terry Marsland: Union leader who devoted her career to fighting for women's rights', *Independent,* 25 June 2011*.

27 Jolly, *Sisterhood and After,* p. 102.

28 Hay, ' "More than a defence against bills" ', p. 9.

29 Laura Beers, 'Amy Coney Barrett, Enoch Powell and IVF politics', *History Workshop,* 30 October 2020*.

30 Brooke, *Sexual Politics,* p. 221.

31 Jolly, *Sisterhood and After,* p. 111.

32 Brooke, *Sexual Politics,* p. 201.

33 Jolly, *Sisterhood and After,* p. 111.

34 Ana Kinsella, 'Anything Else Would Not be Good Enough', *n+1,* 15 June 2018*.

35 Sally Rooney, 'An Irish Problem', *London Review of Books,* 40:10 (May 2018).

36 Lucy Ward and Riazat Butt, 'Too many abortions: Lord Steel', *Guardian,* 24 October 2007*; Jamie Doward and Denis Campbell, 'British women treat abortion as the easy option, claims angry Archbishop', *Guardian,* 21 October 2007*.

37 Berlant, 'America, "Fat," the Fetus', *boundary 2,* 21:3 (Autumn 1994), 145–95 (pp. 149–50).

38 Brooke, *Sexual Politics,* p. 214.

39 Jolly, *Sisterhood and After*, p. 104.

40 Jolly, *Sisterhood and After*, pp. 105, 107; Gail Lewis, 'Birthing Racial Difference: Conversations with My Mother and Others', *Studies in the Maternal*, 1:1 (2009), 1–21.

41 Jolly, *Sisterhood and After*, p. 108.

42 Barbara Katz Rothman, *The Tentative Pregnancy: How Amniocentesis Changes the Experience of Motherhood* (New York, NY: W. W. Norton & Company, 1986), p. 9.

43 See Marion Dain, 'Society for the Protection of the Unwanted Child', *Red Rag*, 7 (August 1974), 12–13; P. Shiels, 'Letter', *Red Rag*, 8 (February 1975), p. 23.

44 'The Black Woman', reprinted in *The Body Politic: Women's Liberation in Britain*, ed. Michelene Wandor (London: Stage 1, 1972), p. 89.

45 Jolly, *Sisterhood and After*, p. 206.

46 Juliet Mitchell, *Woman's Estate* (London: Verso, 2015), p. 38.

47 Drucilla Cornell, *The Imaginary Domain: Abortion, Pornography and Sexual Harassment* (London: Routledge, 1995), p. 35.

48 Ernaux, *Happening*, p. 42.

49 Ernaux, *Happening*, pp. 42, 53, 74, 69, 74.

50 Sophie Lewis, 'Free Anthrogenesis: Antiwork Abortion', *Salvage*, 12 (1 June 2022).

3. Family Planning

1 Emma Heaney, 'Is a Cervix Cis? My Year in the Stirrups', *Asterix Journal*, 18 February 2021*.

2 See Judith Butler, *Gender Trouble* (New York, NY: Routledge, 1999), p. 115. See Berlant, 'America, "Fat," the Fetus', p. 152.

3 Victoria Gillick, *Dear Mrs Gillick* (Basingstoke: Marshalls, 1985), p. 22; Beatrix Campbell, *The Iron Ladies: Why Do Women Vote Tory?* (London: Virago, 1987), pp. 182–6.

4 Deborah A. Cohen, 'Private Lives in Public Spaces: Marie Stopes, the Mothers' Clinics and the Practice of Contraception', *History Workshop Journal*, 35:1 (Spring 1993), 95–116.

5 Kate Fisher, 'Family Planning and Sex in Britain 1900–1960', *British Library*, 23 October 2020*; Cohen, 'Private Lives in Public Spaces', p. 105.

6 See Steffan Kühl, *For the Betterment of the Race: The Rise and Fall of the International Movement for Eugenics and Racial Hygiene*, trans. Lawrence Schofer (New York, NY: Palgrave Macmillan, 2013).

7 Margaret Sanger, 'The Eugenic Value of Birth Control Propaganda', *Birth Control Review* (October 1921).

8 Letter from Sanger to Dr Clarence Gamble, held in the Sophia Smith Collection, Smith College, North Hampton, Massachusetts, cited in Linda Gordon, *Woman's Body, Woman's Right: A Social History of Birth Control in America* (New York, NY: Grossman Publishers, 1976), p. 332.

9 Advances in modern medicine led to a longer life expectancy, unmatched by the lack of economic growth deemed necessary to support it, making these 'territories' far harder to control. See Beverley Bryan, Stella Dadzie and Suzanne Scafe, *The Heart of the Race: Black Women's Lives in Britany* (London: Verso, 1985), p. 182.

10 Angela Y. Davis, *Women, Race & Class*, p. 215.

11 See Laura Briggs, 'Discourses of "Forced Sterilization" in Puerto Rico', *Differences*, 10:2 (1998), 30–66; Iris Ofelia Lopez, 'Agency and Constraint: Sterilization and Reproductive Freedom among Puerto Rican Women in New York City', *Urban Anthropology and Studies of Cultural Systems*, 22:3/4 (Fall 1993), 299–323; Committee for Abortion Rights and against Sterilization Abuse, *Women under Attack: Abortion, Sterilization Abuse and Reproductive Freedom* (New York, NY: Committee for Abortion Rights and against Sterilization Abuse, 1979). This is not an isolated incident of clinical trials being performed on populations who were deemed in some sense reproductively inferior, non-citizen citizens: the 2021 report into the Irish Mother and Baby homes revealed that vaccines and clinical non-commercial formula milk were tested on incarcerated children and their mothers until 1973, facilitated by the Wellcome Foundation and Glaxo Laboratories. Mass sterilization programmes, meanwhile, continue globally: in India, for example, the Gates Foundation and UK governmental aid are implicated in funding an ongoing programme of forced operations. See Ciarán O'Kelly, Ciara Hackett, Samantha Hopkins and Clare Patton, 'Businesses, Remedy and Vaccine Trials', *Cambridge Core*, 14 April 2021.

12 Vanessa Heggie, '54 years of the Pill (on the NHS), and how Birmingham women got it first', *Guardian*, 4 December 2015*.

13 See Valerie Amos and Pratibha Parmar, 'Challenging Imperial Feminism', *Feminist Review*, 17 (Autumn 1984), 3–19.

14 Bryan, Dadzie and Scafe, *The Heart of the Race*, pp. 179, 180.

15 See 'Women and the National Front', *Red Rag*, 14 (1978), 28–31.

16 See Bayan Abusneineh, '(Re)producing the Israeli (European) body: Zionism, Anti-Black Racism and the Depo-Provera Affair', *Feminist Review*, 128:1 (21 Jul 2021), 96–113.

17 'Rowena Arshad discusses contraception and controlling poor women's bodies', *British Library**.

18 Jill Nicholls, 'Going Back to the Beginning', *Spare Rib*, 47 (June 1976), p. 27.

19 See 'I prayed, "Just let my baby see her first birthday"', *You* magazine, 13 December 2020*.

20 See Cari Romm, 'Before There were Home Pregnancy Tests', *Atlantic*, 17 June 2015*; Ben Frampton, 'Escapee pregnancy test frogs colonised Wales for 50 years', *BBC News*, 29 June 2019*.

21 Jesse Olszynko-Gryn, 'The feminist appropriation of pregnancy testing in 1970s Britain', *Women's History Review*, 28:6 (2019), 869–94 (pp. 880, 873).

22 Michèle Roberts, *Paper Houses: A Memoir of the 70s and Beyond* (London: Virago, 2007), pp. 136–7.

23 Olszynko-Gryn, 'The feminist appropriation of pregnancy testing', p. 883.

24 Kate Brian, 'The amazing story of IVF: 35 years and five million babies later', *Guardian*, 12 July 2013*.

25 Sarah Franklin, *Biological Relatives: IVF, Stem Cells, and the Future of Kinship* (Durham, NC: Duke University Press, 2013), pp. 38, 57.

26 See Katharine Dow, '"The men who made the breakthrough": How the British press represented Patrick Steptoe and Robert Edwards in 1978', *Reproductive BioMedicine and Society Online*, 4 (2017), 59–67 (p. 63); Robert Edwards and Patrick Steptoe, *A Matter of Life: The Story of a Medical Breakthrough* (London: Hutchinson, 1980).

27 Ciara Nugent, 'What It was Like to Grow Up as the World's First "Test-Tube Baby"', *Time*, 25 July 2018*.

28 Rebecca Jennings, 'Lesbian Motherhood and the Artificial Insemination by Donor Scandal of 1978', *Twentieth Century British History*, 28:4 (2017), 570–94 (p. 570).

29 See Hera Cook, *The Long Sexual Revolution: English Women, Sex, and Contraception 1800–1975* (Oxford: Oxford University Press, 2004), p. 286.

30 Jennings, 'Lesbian Motherhood and the Artificial Insemination by Donor Scandal', p. 572.

31 See Gillian E. Hanscombe and Jackie Forster, *Rocking the Cradle: Lesbian Mothers: A Challenge in Family Living* (London: Sheba, 1982); Marilyn Archer, 'Gay Wives and Mothers', *Spare Rib*, 31 (January 1975); 'Lesbian Mothers Unite', *Spare Rib*, 47 (June 1976); Susan Hemmings, 'In the Best Interests of the Children', *Spare Rib*, 74 (September 1978).

32 Ray Malone, 'Gay Sweatshop Theatre Company', *Unfinished Histories* (November 2013)*.

33 Cited in Jennings, 'Lesbian Motherhood and the Artificial Insemination Scandal', pp. 588–9.

34 Jennings, 'Lesbian Motherhood and the Artificial Insemination by Donor Scandal', pp. 588, 582.

35 See Susan Hemmings, 'Horrific Practices: How Lesbians were Presented in the Newspapers of 1978', *Homosexuality: Power and Politics*, ed. Gay Left Collective (London: Verso, 2018).

36 Jennings, 'Lesbian Motherhood and the Artificial Insemination by Donor Scandal', pp. 582, 583, 585, 593.

37 Raekha Prasad, 'I didn't have to have a man', *Guardian*, 4 June 2011*.

38 See Margarete Sandelowski, 'Fault lines: Infertility and Imperilled Sisterhood', *Feminist Studies*, 16:1, 33–51.

39 Shulamith Firestone, *The Dialectic of Sex*, p. 190.

40 Sophie Lewis, *Full Surrogacy Now* (London: Verso, 2019), p. 1.

41 See Sophie Lewis, 'Defending Intimacy against What? Limits of Antisurrogacy Feminisms', *Signs*, 43:1 (Autumn 2017), 97–125.

42 See Franklin, *Biological Relatives*, pp. 187, 204, 201, 193.

43 Historical and sociological studies of surrogacy before Lewis's have also illustrated that becoming a parent through surrogacy productively problematizes narratives of biological reproduction and creating new forms of relation including, in Helena Ragoné's words 'conception in

the heart'. See Ragoné, *Surrogate Motherhood: Conception in the Heart* (London: Taylor & Francis, 1994).

44 Franklin, *Biological Relatives*, p. 213. See also Charis Thompson, *Making Parents: The Ontological Choreography of Reproductive Technologies* (Berkeley, CA: MIT Press, 2005).

45 Lisa Jardine, 'A Point of View: IVF and the marketing of hope', *BBC News*, 25 October 2013*.

46 See Victoria Browne, *Pregnancy without Birth: A Feminist Philosophy of Miscarriage* (London: Bloomsbury, 2022).

47 See Lucy van de Wiel, *Freezing Fertility: Oocyte Cryopreservation and the Gender Politics of Aging* (New York, NY: NYU Press, 2020).

48 Zoe Williams, 'Where's all that grief going?', *Guardian*, 27 September 2013*.

49 Franklin, *Biological Relatives*, pp. 218–19.

50 Lauren Berlant, *Cruel Optimism* (Durham, NC: Duke University Press, 2011), p. 1.

4. Making Claims

1 Shaul Bar-Haim, *The Maternalists: Psychoanalysis, Motherhood, and the British Welfare State* (Philadelphia, PA: University of Pennsylvania Press, 2021), p. 3.

2 See Adriana Cavarero, *Inclinations: A Critique of Rectitude* (Stanford, CA: Stanford University Press, 2016).

3 The Care Collective, 'COVID-19 pandemic: A Crisis of Care', *Verso* blog, 26 March 2020*.

4 See Demise Riley, *War in the Nursery: Theories of the Child and Mother* (London, Virago, 1983), p. 151.

5 See Bar-Haim, *The Maternalists*.

6 Both of these narratives are founded in falsehood: in their 2012 study of single motherhood in Britain the historians Pat Thane and Tanya Evans concluded that the former was 'very rarely to be found', while most migrants are prevented from claiming state benefit in the UK due to their status as having No Recourse to Public Funds; the very small and difficult-to-access state funds that are available through

Section 17 for people with NRPF are only available to those with children. See Pat Thane and Tanya Evans, *Sinners? Scroungers? Saints?: Unmarried Motherhood in Twentieth-Century England* (Oxford: Oxford University Press, 2012), p. 29.

7 See Lynne Segal, 'Subject to Suspicion: Feminism and Anti-statism in Britain', *Social Text*, 18:1 (Spring 2000), 143–151.

8 See Juliet Mitchell, *The Longest Revolution: Essays on Feminism, Literature and Psychoanalysis* (London: Virago, 1984), pp. 41–2.

9 Mitchell, *Woman's Estate*, p. 150.

10 Mitchell, *The Longest Revolution*, p. 48.

11 Elizabeth Wilson, *Women and the Welfare State* (Abingdon: Routledge, 1974) p. 7.

12 Wilson, *Women and the Welfare State*, pp. 7–8.

13 See Amia Srinivasan, 'Who Lost the Sex Wars?', *New Yorker*, 6 September 2021.

14 Sheila Rowbotham, Lynne Segal and Hilary Wainwright, *Beyond the Fragments: Feminism and the Making of Socialism* (London: Islington Community Press, 1979), p. 4.

15 Socialist Feminist Social Policy Group, 'Rest in Pieces', *Red Rag*, 9 (August 1980), p. 34.

16 Mary Giles and Jane Hutt, 'Life on Social Security', *Spare Rib*, 85 (August 1979).

17 Nell Dunn, *Living Like I Do* (London: Futura Publications, 1977), p. 186.

18 See Donna McLean, *Small Town Girl: Love, Lies and the Undercover Police* (London: Hodder Studio, 2022); Veronica Clark and Helen Steel, *Deep Deception: The story of the spycop network, by the women who uncovered the shocking truth* (London: Penguin, 2022).

19 Leaflet in Denise Riley's donated items, Bishopsgate Institute, London.

20 National Federation of Claimants Unions, *The Fight to Live* (Birmingham: 1977), pp. 1, 56.

21 National Federation of Claimants Unions, *Women and Social Security* (London: 1977).

22 Marsha Rowe, 'What happened at Heywood', *Spare Rib*, 31 (1975).

23 *The Fight to Live*, pp. 1, 37. See also the National Federation of Claimants Unions, *Claimants Union Guidebook* (Birmingham, 1978), inside cover.

24 *The Fight to Live*, p. 44.
25 See Toru Yamamori, 'A Feminist Way to Unconditional Basic Income: Claimants Unions and Women's Liberation Movements in 1970s Britain', *Basic Income Studies*, 9:1–2 (2014), 1–24*.
26 *Women and Social Security*, p. 27.
27 *Claimants Union Guidebook*, p. 21.
28 Sheila Rowbotham, *The Past is Before Us: Feminism in Action since the 1960s* (London: Penguin, 1990), p. 24.
29 *Women and Social Security*, pp. 3, 29.
30 Lois Gulley, 'Letters', *Spare Rib*, 68 (March 1978), p. 5.

5. Communal Experiments

1 See Sally Howard, 'Is the boom in communal living really the good life?', *Guardian*, 17 January 2021*.
2 See Sam Burgum, 'The 1946 Squatters', *Squatting London*, 18 July 2017*; see Howard Webber, 'A Domestic Rebellion: The Squatters' Movement of 1946', *Ex Historia* (2012), pp. 134ff.
3 ' "I Have No Confidence in Dungannon Urban Council Whatsoever" ', 1968, RTÉ*.
4 See Myrtle Hill, Lynda Walker and Margaret Ward, 'A Century of Women – 1970s', *A Century of Women**.
5 See the Campaign for Social Justice Northern Ireland, *Northern Ireland: Why Justice Cannot Be Done* (1964)*; see also *RTÉ Eye Witness*, 1979: 'Background to the Caledon Protest, 1968'*.
6 See 'Austin Currie in Housing Protest', 1968, RTÉ*.
7 Miriam Turley, 'Squatting Belfast', *Vacuum*, 11*. See *Squatting: The Real Story*, ed. Nick Wates and Christian Wolmer (London: Bay Leaf Books, 1980); Sinead McEneaney, 'Home Sweet Home? Housing Activism and Political Commemoration in Sixties Ireland', *History Workshop Journal*, 87 (Spring 2019), 5–26 (p. 5).
8 *Squatting: The Real Story*, p. 1.
9 See Kesia Reeve, 'Squatting in Britain 1945–1955: housing, politics and direct action', *Housing Studies*, 33:1 (October 2017), 141–3; 'Squatting

since 1945: the enduring relevance of material need', *Housing and Social Policy: Contemporary Themes and Critical Perspectives*, ed. Peter Somerville and Nigel Springings (London: Routledge, 2005), pp. 197–217; 'The UK Squatters Movement 1968–1980', *Jaarboek voor Socialistische Discussie en Analyse*, ed. Leendert van Hoogenhuijze (Amsterdam, NL: Kritiek, 2009), pp. 137–59. See also Alexander Vasudevan, *The Autonomous City: A History of Urban Squatting* (London: Verso, 2017).

10 *Squatting: The Real Story*, p. 9.

11 Reeve, 'The UK Squatters Movement 1968–1980', p. 153.

12 *Squatting: The Real Story*, p. 186.

13 See *Crowbar: Squatting News*, 44 (6 August 1985); see also 'This is the real Brixton Challenge', *Past Tense*, 18 April 2021*.

14 Reeve, 'The UK Squatters Movement 1968–1980', p. 149.

15 *Squatting: The Real Story*, p. 48.

16 See Christine Wall, 'Sisterhood and Squatting in the 1970s: Feminism, Housing and Urban Change in Hackney', *History Workshop Journal*, 83:1 (Spring 2017), 79–97.

17 *Squatting: The Real Story*, pp. 4, 11.

18 Shelter, 'Shelter', *The Times*, 12 January 1967; Julian Snow, 'How We are Helping Cathy to Come Home', *Labour Woman*, 56:3 (1967).

19 'Women take the space they need', *Spare Rib*, 46 (May 1976).

20 Michael Whyte, dir., *Scream Quietly or the Neighbours Will Hear*, 1974 (London Screen Archives)

21 See Elaine Aston and Ian Clarke, 'Feminist theory and the matriarchal soap: *EastEnders*', *Critical Survey*, 6:2 (1994), 211–17.

22 Rowan Milligan has recently argued that women's squatting is an inherently radical act. See 'The politics of the crowbar: Squatting in London, 1968–1977', *Anarchist Studies*, 24:2 (2016), 8–32.

23 Wall, 'Sisterhood and Squatting in the 1970s', pp. 86, 49.

24 Pat Moan, 'Learning to Learn', *Squatter* (London, 1976), p. 182.

25 Wall, 'Sisterhood and Squatting in the 1970s', p. 90.

26 Lynne Harne, 'Lesbian Mothers' Custody Conference', *Spare Rib*, 129 (1983), 22–3 (p. 22).

27 See Lynne Harne, *Valued Families: Lesbian Mothers' Legal Handbook* (London: The Women's Press, 1977).

28 See Sally Williams, 'My four mums', *Guardian*, 4 July 2009*; and Gerry Kennedy, 'Wild side of life', *Guardian*, 27 April 2005*.

29 Rob Logan, 'Crossroads Women's Centre', 2014 <http://crossroads-women.net/watch-our-film>.

30 See Oluwatayo Adewole, 'Remembering Pearl Alcock, the Black bisexual shebeen queen of Brixton', *gal-dem*, 2 February 2021*. This was not without its tensions: 'Around 1974–1975, white middle-class squatters took the political initiative away from the coloured working-class squatters and had set themselves up as leaders, creating isolation among the black and the white. This group had the knowledge, skills and access to information and facilities. I learned a bit in this period, useful skills in painful situations' – from an anonymous piece of writing titled 'Lonely among the Feminists', *Spare Rib*, 132 (1983).

31 See Kehinde Andrews, *Resisting Racism: Race, Inequality and the Black Supplementary School Movement* (London: Institute of Education Press, 2013) and 'The Black Supplementary School Movement is as Essential as It's Ever Been', *Black Ballad*, 13 December 2020*.

32 Anon, '"Redevelopment", Housing & Squatting – Bengali Housing Action Group', *maydayrooms**.

33 Wall, 'Sisterhood and Squatting in the 1970s', pp. 92–3.

34 Kate Lloyd, 'Meet the lesbian punks who've been written out of London's history', *Time Out*, 25 April 2017*.

35 Wall, 'Sisterhood and Squatting in the 1970s', p. 84.

36 Moan, 'Learning to Learn', p. 182.

37 Chris Coates, 'The Basis of Communal Living', *Utopia Britannica*, 20 March 2013*.

38 Coates, 'We fought the law and the law changed', *Utopia Britannica*, 28 February 2021*.

39 See Coates, 'A wonderful anarchic-jumble-sale-of-a-disorganisation', 13 June 2020*.

40 Dunn, *Living Like I Do*, pp. 67, 9.

41 Chris Coates, 'The Price of Free Love', *Utopia Britannica*, 16 May 2020*. Hippy free love was particularly prevalent in North American communes and, as Chelsea Cain's *Wild Child: Girlhoods in the Counterculture* (Cypress, CA: Seal Press, 1999) documents, in the absence of boundaries, the

exploitation of young women and children could pass under the radar more freely.

42 Dunn, *Living Like I Do*, p. 38.

43 See Dinah Jeffries, 'My children grew up in a commune', *Guardian*, 14 June 2014*, and Annie Brown, 'From illiterate hippy kid to boss of major Scottish arts festival, Gwilym Gibbons talks of his amazing journey', *Daily Record*, 29 March 2011*.

44 Doris Lessing, *The Good Terrorist* (London: Cape, 1985), p. 329. See Sarah Bernstein, 'After the good life: squatting and the politics of the commons in *The Good Terrorist*', *Studia Neophilologica*, 92:2 (May 2020), 209–21.

45 Chris Coates, 'Your Children are Not Your Children', *Utopia Britannica*, 30 May 2020*.

46 *Undercurrents*, 'Women in Co-ops', 46 (June–July 1981), p. 27.

47 June Statham, 'Childcare in Communities', *Undercurrents*, 46 (June–July 1981), 9–18 (pp. 14–18).

48 Dunn, *Living Like I Do*, p. 47.

49 Coates, 'Your Children are Not Your Children'.

50 Statham, 'Childcare in Communities', p. 16.

51 Dunn, *Living Like I Do*, pp. 46, 81, 175.

52 Kennedy, 'Wild side of life'.

53 D. W. Winnicott, *Playing and Reality* (London: Routledge, 2005), p. 14.

54 Emily Ogden, *On Not Knowing: How to Love and Other Essays* (London: Peninsula Press, 2022), p. 33.

55 Denise Riley, 'The Force of Circumstance', *Red Rag*, 9 (1975), 26–8 (p. 26).

56 See Samuel Solomon, *Lyric Pedagogy and Marxist-Feminism: Social Reproduction and the Institutions of Poetry* (London: Bloomsbury, 2019).

57 Denise Riley, *Marxism for Infants* (Cambridge: Street Editions, 1977).

6. Spilt Milk

1 Sinéad O'Connor, *Rememberings* (London: Penguin, 2021), pp. 204–5.

2 O'Connor, *Rememberings*, p. 205. See also Stuart Hall, Chas Critcher, Tony Jefferson, Brian Roberts and John Clarke, *Policing the Crisis: Mugging, the State, and Law and Order* (London: Macmillan, 1978).

3 Benjamin Zephaniah, 'Zephaniah Remembers Colin Roach' <https://
4wardevernewsvine.files.wordpress.com/2009/01/zephaniah-remembers-
colin-roach-final.pdf>.

4 Stuart Hall, *The Hard Road to Renewal* (London: Verso, 1988), p. 2. There is
contention as to whether or not Hall officially coined the term. See Richard Vinen, *Thatcher's Britain: The Politics and Social Upheaval of the Thatcher
Era* (London: Simon & Schuster, 2009), for a detailed summary.

5 See Lisa Downing, *Selfish Women* (Abingdon: Taylor & Francis, 2019).

6 Eileen Fairweather, 'Newshorts', *Spare Rib*, 83 (June 1979), p. 10.

7 See Campbell, *The Iron Ladies*, pp. 234–8.

8 See Downing, *Selfish* Women, and Campbell, 'Margaret Thatcher: To
be or not to be a woman', *British Politics*, 10 (2015), 41–51.

9 Campbell, 'Margaret Thatcher: To be or not to be a woman', p. 44.

10 *Making Margaret: A Very British Revolution*, dir. James House, written by
Katie Boxer, Polly Greetham, Rachel Kay-Williams (BBC, 2019).

11 *Making Margaret: A Very British Revolution*, dir. James House (BBC,
2019).

12 Margaret Thatcher, *The Path to Power* (London: Harper Collins, 1995), p. 65.

13 Zoe Williams, 'The accidental feminist', *Guardian*, 21 October 2004*.

14 *Maggie & Me*, Jon Snow (Channel 4, 2013).

15 Margaret Thatcher, Interview with John Negus, *Sixty Minutes*, 23 September 1981.

16 Marina Warner, *Monuments and Maidens: the Allegory of the Female Form*
(Berkeley, CA: University of California Press, 1985), p. 52.

17 *Maggie & Me*, Jon Snow (Channel 4, 2013).

18 Simon Jenkins, *Thatcher and Sons: A Revolution in Three Acts* (London:
Penguin, 2007), p. 3.

19 *Making Margaret: A Very British* Revolution, dir. James House (BBC,
2019).

20 See Emily Baughan, 'Bring Back National Milk', *Playgroup*, 22 May 2023*.
Despite the formation of the International Code of Marketing Breast-
Milk Substitutes in 1981, which aimed to prohibit such misleading
advertising strategies, formula milk remains a hugely profitable and
growing market for Nestlé and other companies. See Esther Leslie and
Melanie Jackson, 'Milk's Arrays', *Studies in the Maternal*, 10:1 (2018), 8.

21 Thatcher, *The Path to Power*, pp. 80–81.

22 *Woman to Woman*, Miriam Stoppard (ITV, 19 November 1985).

23 Thatcher, *The Path to Power*, p. 94.

24 Thatcher, *The Path to Power*, p. 82.

25 Lemn Sissay, 'A Child of the State' (*TED*, March 2014).

26 Douglas Keay, 'Interview with Margaret Thatcher', *Woman's Own*, 31 October 1987.

27 Thatcher, *The Path to Power*, pp. 544, 548.

28 Thatcher, *The Path to Power*, p. 553.

29 A. Sivananadan, *Communities of Resistance: Writings on Black Struggles for Socialism* (London: Verso, 1990), p. 92.

30 Thatcher, *The Path to Power*, pp. 561–3.

31 Campbell, *The Iron Ladies*, pp. 113, 119, 115.

32 Julie Burchill, 'Burchill on Burchill', *Face*, 2:9 (1989), p. 76.

33 Melissa Benn, *Madonna and Child* (London: Cape, 1998), p. 33.

34 Selma James, 'Hookers in the House of the Lord' (1983), *Sex, Race and Class: The Perspective of Winning: A Selection of Writings 1952–2011* (California: PM Press, 2012), pp.110–29 (p. 112). See also Judith R. Walkowitz, 'Feminism and the Politics of Prostitution in King's Cross in the 1980s', *Twentieth Century British History*, 30:2 (June 2019), 231–63.

35 James, 'Hookers in the House of the Lord', pp. 124–5.

36 In Europe the modern sex worker movement is generally considered to have begun in 1975, when sex workers in France occupied churches to protest against criminalization, poverty and police violence. See Mac and Smith, *Revolting Prostitutes*, p. 7.

37 *VIEWPOINT 87: Living on the Edge*, dir. Michael Grigsby (ITV, 1987).

38 Hall, *Hard Road to Renewal*, p. 47.

39 *Making Margaret: A Very British* Revolution.

7. The Enemies Within

1 This was something the WLM's night-cleaners campaign, centred around the Cleaners Action Group set up by May Hobbs, had drawn attention to the in the 70s.

2 Amrit Wilson in *Black British Feminism: A Reader*, ed. Heidi Safia Mirza (London: Routledge, 1997), pp. 32–4. See *Spare Rib*, 61 (August 1977). See Maya Amin-Smith, *Grunwick Changed Me* (BBC, 5 August 2016)*.

3 *Spare Rib*, 61 (August 1977).

4 Katrina Forrester, 'Feminist Demands and the Problem of Housework', *American Political Science Review* (2022), 1–15 (p. 3).

5 Adrian O'Dowd, 'A history of nursing in Britain: the 1980s', *Nursing Times*, 11 October 2021*.

6 Documents released in 2016 show that she remained committed to the project. See Alan Travis, 'Thatcher pushed for breakup of welfare state despite NHS pledge', *Guardian*, 25 November 2016*.

7 See Christopher Hart, *Behind the Mask: Nurses, Their Unions and Nursing Policy* (London: Ballière Tindall, 1994); Trevor Clay, Alison Dunn and Neil Stewart, *Nurses, Power and Politics* (Ann Arbor, MI: University of Michigan Press, 1987); Dale Evans, 'Nurses are Worth More': The 1982 Health Workers' Dispute', *Past Tense*, 22 September 2020*; Moya Crockett, 'The messy history of the nurses' strikes in 1988', *Huck*, 23 November 2021*; Stephen Williams and R. H. Fryer, *Leadership and Democracy* (London: Lawrence & Wishart, 2011); Tara Martin Lopez, *The Winter of Discontent* (Liverpool: Liverpool University Press, 2014); 'The Winter of Discontent in the NHS' <https://peopleshistorynhs.org/encyclopaedia/the-winter-of-discontent-in-the-nhs/>. See *Past Tense*, 'South London Women's Hospital occupation 1984–85', *libcom*, 6 February 2013*.

8 Andrew Rawnsley, 'Tapping into Tory store of rhetoric', *Guardian*, 3 February 1988. See also Sarah Hayward and Elizabeth Fee, 'More in Sorrow than in Anger: the British Nurses' Strike of 1988', *International Journal of Health Services*, 22:3 (1992), 397–415.

9 See Reevel Alderson, 'Lee Jeans women remember seven-month sit-in success', *BBC News*, 4 February 2011*; 'Episode 1 – The Lee Jeans Sit-in', Hedgie Films <https://www.youtube.com/watch?v=X_-oP1vsNhI>.

10 See Jonathan Moss, *Women, workplace protest and political identity in England, 1968–85* (Manchester, Manchester University Press, 2019); 'It's the pay off at VF . . .', *Greenock Telegraph*, 2 May 1981; 'Weeks without pay hit VF staff', *Greenock Telegraph*, 5 May 1981; 'Future looks dim for Jennifer and other 239', *Greenock Telegraph*, 5 March 1981.

11 Gordon Anderson, 'Tuck in for the Petticoat rebels', *Daily Record*, 7 February 1981

12 'Now it's the great knit-in!', *Greenock Telegraph*, 20 April 1981.

13 See 'Lee Jeans sit-in', Scottish Parliament debate 10 March 2011*.

14 See John Hill, 'A Working Class Hero is Something to be? Changing Representations of Class and Masculinity in British Cinema', *The Trouble with Men: Masculinities in European and Hollywood Cinema*, ed. Phil Powrie, Anne Davies and Bruce Babbington (London: Wallflower Press, 2004); Huw Beynon and Peter McMylor, 'Decisive Power: The New Tory State against the Miners', *Digging Deeper: Issues in the Miners' Strike*, ed. Huw Beynon (London: Verso, 1985); Raphael Samuel, Barbara Bloomfield and Guy Boanas (eds), *The Enemy Within: Pit Villages and the Miners' Strike of 1984–5* (London: Verso, 1986); Raymond Williams, 'Mining the Meaning: Key Words in the Miners' Strike', *Resources of Hope: Culture, Democracy, Socialism* (London: Verso, 1989).

15 *The Miners' Campaign Tapes Project*, Tape 6 (BFI, 1984).

16 See 'Marches and pickets', *Coalfield Women**.

17 Anne Scargill, Betty Cook and Ian Clayton, *Anne & Betty: United by the Struggle* (London: Route, 2020), p. 153.

18 Jean Stead, *Never the Same Again: Women and the Miners' Strike* (London: The Women's Press, 1987), p. 29.

19 Scargill, Cook and Clayton, *Anne & Betty: United by the Struggle*, p. 125.

20 Stead, *Never the Same Again*, p. 130; see also Florence Sutcliffe Braithwaite, 'Tesco and a motorway', *London Review of Books*, 43:17 (September 2021).

21 Stead, *Never the Same Again*, p. 11.

22 Stead, *Never the Same Again*, p. 26.

23 Ewan Gibbs, *Coal Country: The Meaning and Memory of Deindustrialization* (Edinburgh: Edinburgh University Press, 2020), pp. 94–8.

24 Scargill, Cook and Clayton, *Anne & Betty: United by the Struggle*, p. 66.

25 Stead, *Never the Same Again*, p. 10.

26 Vicky Seddon, *The Cutting Edge: Women and the Pit Strike* (London: Lawrence & Wishart, 1986), p. 45.

27 Dawn Foster, 'Margaret Thatcher didn't expect it, but miners' wives galvanised the 84 strike', *Guardian*, 12 March 2014*.

28 *The Miners' Campaign Tapes Project,* Tape 1 (BFI, 1984).

29 See 'Early Days', *Coalfield Women**.

30 'Miners' strike – 30 years since the pit crisis of 1984', *Channel 4 News,* 6 March 2014*.

31 Guthrie Hutton, *Coal Not Dole: Memories of the 1984/85 Miners' Strike* (Mauchline: Stenlake, 2005), p. 60; pp. 17–19.

32 Scargill, Cook and Clayton, *Anne & Betty: United by the Struggle,* p. 128.

33 Hutton, *Coal Not Dole,* pp. 17–19.

34 Stead, *Never the Same Again,* p. 107.

35 David Pittam, 'Miners' strike: The decades-old feud that still divides communities', *BBC News,* 6 March 2019*.

36 Scargill, Cook and Clayton, *Anne & Betty: United by the Struggle,* p. 133; Hutton, *Coal Not Dole,* p. 13.

37 Stead, *Never the Same Again,* pp. 34, 16.

38 Seddon, *The Cutting Edge,* p. 45.

39 Stead, *Never the Same Again,* p. 28.

40 Scargill, Cook and Clayton, *Anne & Betty: United by the Struggle,* p. 164.

41 'Making Ends Meet', *Coalfield Women**.

42 Scargill, Cook and Clayton, *Anne & Betty: United by the Struggle,* pp. 139, 134; see also Jackie Keating, *Counting the Cost: A Family in the Miners' Strike* (Barnsley: Wharncliffe Publishing, 1991).

43 Clive James Nwonka, ' "You're what's wrong with me": Fish Tank, The Selfish Giant and the Language for Contemporary Social Realism', *New Cinemas: Journal of Contemporary Film,* 12:3, p. 213.

44 'Margaret Thatcher death song goes ahead in Billy Elliott musical', *BBC News,* 9 April 2013*.

45 David Alderson, 'Making Electricity: Narrating Gender, Sexuality, and the Neoliberal Transition in Billy Elliot', *Camera Obscura,* 25:3 (2011), 1–27, p. 3.

46 See Diarmaid Kelliher, *Making Cultures of Solidarity: London and the 1984–5 Miners' Strike* (London: Routledge, 2021); Kate Kellaway, 'When miners and gay activists united: the real story of the film Pride', *Guardian,* 31 August 2014*; Jeff Cole, *All Out! Dancing in Dulais – Lesbians and Gays Support the Miners* (2013)*.

47 See Matt Cook, 'From Gay Reform to Gaydar, 1967–2006', *A Gay History of Britain: Love and Sex between Men since the Middle Ages,* ed. Matt

Cook, H. G. Cocks, Robert Mills and Randolph Trumbach (Oxford: Greenwood Press, 2007).

48 Kellaway, 'When miners and gay activists united: the real story of the film Pride'.

49 Seddon, *The Cutting Edge*, p. 147.

50 Kellaway, 'When miners and gay activists united: the real story of the film Pride'.

51 Amanda Powell, 'The day Margaret Thatcher was egged in Porthcawl – as told by the women who were there', *Wales Online*, 25 June 2019*.

52 Stead, *Never the Same Again*, pp. 7, 22–3.

53 Foster, 'Margaret Thatcher didn't expect it, but miners' wives galvanised the 84 strike'*.

54 Seddon, *The Cutting Edge*, pp. 26, 130–33; Stead, *Never the Same Again*, p. 89.

55 Interview with Scargill and Cook, 'We Can Win' (2014)*.

56 See Rob Evans, 'UK political groups spied on by undercover police – search the list', *Guardian*, 15 October 2018*.

57 Scargill, Cook and Clayton, *Anne & Betty: United by the Struggle*, pp. 121–2.

58 *Not by Bread Alone* programme, 1985, Heather Wood collection (2009–129), Beamish Museum Regional Resource Centre. See also Sutcliffe Braithwaite, 'Tesco and a motorway': 'The NCB took responsibility for pithead baths, medical facilities and canteens, and funded provision for convalescence, retirement, education and recreation, including events such as residential drama weekends for members of thespian societies in the coalfields.'

59 Ian Krause, *Not by Bread Alone* (1986), Yorkshire and North East Film Archive*.

60 Margaret Pine, *Not by Bread Alone*, Heather Wood Collection (2009-129), Beamish Museum Regional Resource Centre, p. 2.

61 Pine, *Not by Bread Alone*, p. 27.

62 Pine, *Not by Bread Alone*, p. 6.

63 Pine, *Not by Bread Alone*, p. 37.

64 Pine, *Not by Bread Alone*, p. 75.

65 Pine, *Not by Bread Alone*, pp. 77–85.

66 Stead, *Never the Same Again*, p. 89; Steve Duffy, 'Maerdy: Still fighting, 25 years after pit closure', *BBC News* (22 December 2015)*.

Notes

67 Foster, 'Margaret Thatcher didn't expect it, but miners' wives galvanised the 84 strike'.
68 Lisa Hutchinson, 'Tributes paid to County Durham community stalwart who cooked 800 meals a day for striking miners', *Chronicle Live*, 6 June 2019*.
69 Scargill, Cook and Clayton, *Anne & Betty: United by the Struggle*, p. 246.

8. Mother Earth and Mother Courage

1 See Winnicott, 'Hate in the Counter-transference', *International Journal of Psychoanalysis*, 30, 69–74.
2 Penny Rimbaud, Crass, 'How Does It Feel (To Be the Mother of 1000 Dead)?'.
3 Bertolt Brecht, *Mother Courage and Her Children*, trans. Lee Hall, *Plays 2* (London: Methuen), p. 111.
4 Roland Barthes and Hella Freud Bernays, 'Seven Photo Models of "Mother Courage"', *TDR*, 12:1 (1967), 44–55 (pp. 44–5).
5 Barthes and Bernays, 'Seven Photo Models of "Mother Courage"', p. 46.
6 Brecht, *Mother Courage*, pp. 111, 145.
7 Barthes and Bernays, 'Seven Photo Models of "Mother Courage"', p. 47.
8 Katie Baker, 'Brecht's Mercenary Mother Courage Turns 75', *Daily Beast*, 31 January 2018*.
9 Cecile Latham and Cricket Keating 'Mother Courage Peace Tour', *Off Our Backs*, 21:4 (April 1991), 1–2.
10 See 'Tony Kushner: Mother Courage is not just an anti-war play', *Guardian*, 8 September 2009*; Veronica Lee, 'Mummy dearest', *Guardian*, 21 March 2000*.
11 Peter Thomson, 'Brecht: *Mother Courage and Her Children*' (Cambridge: Cambridge University Press, 1997), p. 139.
12 In May 1982, at Theatre Space in London, the Internationalist Theatre group staged a production of the play that, although it did not go as far as Thomson suggests, made an 'attack on the practice of war [that] could not – with South Atlantic news filling the front pages – have

been more topical'. British Theatre Association, *Drama: The Quarterly Theatre Review* (1981), 139–54, p. 32.

13 Warner, *Monuments and Maidens*, p. 40.

14 Jacqueline Rose, 'Margaret Thatcher and Ruth Ellis', *New Formations*, 6:1 (Winter 1988), p. 3.

15 Rose, 'Margaret Thatcher and Ruth Ellis', p. 23.

16 Hall, *The Hard Road to Renewal*, pp. 27–8, 36–7.

17 Warner, *Monuments and Maidens*, p. 41.

18 Brian Bond, 'A military historian, Brian Bond, looks at the Falklands war', *London Review of Books*, 5:4 (March 1983).

19 Thatcher, *The Downing Street Years* (London: Harper Collins, 1993), p. 181.

20 *Falklands War: The Untold Story* (Channel 4, 2022)*.

21 *Falklands War: The Untold Story*.

22 Carol Thatcher, *Diary of an Election* (London: Sidgwick & Jackson, 1983), p. 109.

23 *Making Margaret: A Very British Revolution*, dir. James House (BBC, 2019).

24 See Thatcher, *Diary of an Election*.

25 See Carol Thatcher, *Mummy's War* (Channel 4, 2007); Vanessa Thorpe, 'My own Falklands mission', *Guardian*, 18 March 2007*; Thatcher, 'My Mother's War', *Daily Mail*, 24 March 2007*.

26 Raymond Briggs, *The Tin-Pot Foreign General and the Old Iron Woman* (London: Hamish Hamilton, 1984).

27 Briggs, *The Tin-Pot Foreign General and the Old Iron Woman*.

28 Jean Carr, *Another Story: Women and the Falklands War* (London: Hamish Hamilton, 1984), pp. 4–5.

29 Diana Gould, 'After the war', *London Review of Books*, 6:21 (November 1984).

30 Gould, 'After the war'.

31 Carr, *Another Story*, p. 69.

32 Carr, *Another Story*, pp. 15, 29, 41–4.

33 Carr, *Another Story*, pp. 45, 23–4, 30.

34 'Britain Honours the Fallen in Falklands', *New York Times*, 27 July 1982*.

35 Carr, *Another Story*, p. 67.

36 Carr, *Another Story*, p. 150.

37 Stead, *Never the Same Again*, p. 53

38 Beth Junor and Katrina Howse, *Greenham Common Women's Peace Camp: A History of Non-Violent Resistance 1984–1995* (London: Working Press, 1995), p. xiii.

39 Beth Junor and Katrina Howse, *Greenham Common Women's Peace Camp*, p. x.

40 Women for Life on Earth, *Women's Action for Disarmament*, Glamorgan Archives (1986)*.

41 See Anna Reading, 'Singing for My Life: Memory, Nonviolence and the Songs of Greenham Common Women's Peace Camp', *Cultural Memories of Nonviolent Struggles* , ed. Anna Reading and Tamar Katriel (London: Palgrave Macmillan, 2015).

42 'Second Peace Woman Expects Baby at Camp', *Newbury Weekly News*, 4 August 1983.

43 Suzanne Moore, Homa Khaleeli, Moya Sarner, Leah Harper and Justin McCurry, 'How the Greenham Common protest changed lives: "We danced on top of the nuclear silos" ', *Guardian*, 20 March 2017*.

44 Perminder Dhillon, 'They're killing us in here', *Spare Rib*, 84 (July 1979). The first national demonstration organized by Afro-Caribbean and Asian women was against police brutality and immigration harassment in the aftermath of the murder of Blair Peach in 1979, and in the 1980s a 'Women in Black' picket of Jewish feminists stood outside the Israeli airline office in London collecting signatures. See Sivanandan, *Communities of Resistance*, p. 55: 'It is a community of women again, predominantly middle-aged women, which has helped keep alive in Britain the issue of Israeli terror in the Occupied Territories.'

45 See Joram Ten Brink, *Born 1981 – Babies Against the Bomb* (Moonshine Community Arts Workshop, 1984).

46 Ruth Wallsgrove, 'Greenham Common Women's Peace Camp: So why am I still ambivalent?', *Trouble and Strife*, 1 (Winter 1983, p. 5).

47 Wallsgrove, 'Greenham Common Women's Peace Camp: So why am I still ambivalent?', p. 5. See also Sasha Roseneil, *Common Women: Uncommon Practices* (London: Cassell, 2000), p. 184 (note 6), and

Disarming Patriarchy: Feminism and Political Action at Greenham (Maidenhead: Open University Press, 1995); D.-M. Withers, 'Laboratories of gender: Women's liberation and the transfeminist present', *Radical Philosophy*, 2:44 (Spring 2019).

48 Campbell, *The Iron Ladies*, p. 128.

49 See Sue Finch, 'Socialist-Feminists and Greenham', *Feminist Review*, 23 (Summer 1986), 93–100.

50 Mary Midgley, 'Shouting across the gulf', *London Review of Books*, 6:19, 18 October 1984. One particularly vitriolic example from 1983 came from the *Daily Mail*. The journalist Ann Leslie, barely able to hide her disdain for her interviewee Eva, 'breast-feeding by the fire, a vague, amiable, ever-smiling lesbian mother from Islington', who was living at Greenham with her two children, notes that not only are Eva's children the offspring of two different fathers, but one of them is West Indian; she also heavily implies that social services should find her an unfit mother. Ann Leslie, 'The fantasy of Greenham Common', *Daily Mail*, 13 January 1983, pp. 16–17.

51 See Alexandra Kokoli, 'A Virtual Museum of Greenham Common: (Art) Histories of Feminism as Feminist Resistance' <https://amkokoli.wixsite.com/greenhamcommon/about>.

52 Ann Pettitt, *Walking to Greenham: How the Peace-Camp Began and the Cold War Ended* (Aberystwyth: Honno Press), pp. 75–6.

53 See Alice Cook and Gwyn Kirk (eds), *Greenham Women Everywhere* (Boston, MA: South End Press, 1983), p. 33.

54 See Caroline Blackwood, *On the Perimeter* (London: Heinemann, 1984); Sue Gorbing and Helen Parsonage, 'Reviewed Works: *Greenham Common: Women at the Wire* by Barbara Harford, Sarah Hopkins; *On the Perimeter* by Caroline Blackwood', *Feminist Review*, 20 (Summer 1985), 109–13; Christopher Moores, 'Opposition to the Greenham Women's Peace Camps in 1980s Britain: RAGE against the "Obscene"', *History Workshop Journal*, 78 (Autumn 2014), 204–27.

55 Sarah Hipperson (Oral history), Imperial War Museum <https://www.iwm.org.uk/collections/item/object/80019678>, and Cheryl Side, Mass Observation Archive <https://soundcloud.com/observing80s/slack-cheryl-side-03-00-00-08>.

56 Lucy Robinson, 'It did get tiring to welcome everyone: the fire, politics and spirituality at Greenham Common Peace Camp', *Observing the 80s*, 8 November 2013*.

57 See Moores, 'Opposition to the Greenham Women's Peace Camps in 1980s Britain: RAGE against the "Obscene"'.

58 MayDay Rooms, London, GC/GK/1/1982/1-37, document no. 7. With handwritten note on top 'Distributed at 12 December action at Greenham'.

59 *Spare Rib*, 142 (May 1984), pp. 6–8

60 Bryan, Dadzie and Scafe, *The Heart of the Race*, p. 175.

61 Wilmette Brown, *Black Women and the Peace Movement*, 2nd edn (Bristol: Falling Wall Press, 1986), p. 16.

62 *Shocking Pink*, in the collection of the Sparrows' Nest Library and Archive, Nottingham; see also Roseneil, *Uncommon Practices*, pp. 178–82.

63 Brown, *Black Women and the Peace Movement*, pp. 42, 24, 29.

64 Barbara Harford and Sarah Hopkins (eds), *Greenham Common: Women at the Wire* (London: The Women's Press, 1984).

65 Rose, 'Margaret Thatcher and Ruth Ellis', p. 19.

66 Daniel Finn, *One Man's Terrorist* (London: Verso, 2019), p. 159.

67 Beatrix Campbell, 'The legacy of Greenham Common has outlived Margaret Thatcher', *Guardian*, 17 April 2013*.

68 By the end of the decade, this was no longer possible: the Scottish Arts Council began to insist on 'impartiality' as a prerequisite for funding. Brian Logan, 'What did you do in the class war, Daddy?', *Guardian*, 15 May 2002*.

9. Mother Ireland

1 Patricia Malone, 'Measures of obliviousness and disarming obliqueness in Anna Burns' *Milkman*', *Textual Practice*, 36:7 (Spring 2022), 1143–74.

2 Bryonie Reid, 'Creating counterspaces: identity and the home in Ireland and Northern Ireland in Environment and Planning', *Society and Space*, 25 (2007), 933–50 (p. 943).

3 Eli Davies, ' "At Least We Can Lock the Door": Radical Domesticity in the Writing of Bernadette Devlin and Nell McCafferty', *Journal of War & Culture Studies*, 14:1, 70–88 (p. 75).

4 As recently as 2016, there was uproar within the Democratic Unionist Party upon the election of Arlene Foster, with her colleague Edwin Poots making a speech in the Northern Irish Assembly declaring that her 'most important job has been and will remain that of a wife, mother and daughter'.

5 See Miren Mohrenweiser, 'The Limitations of "Maternal" Activism in Troubles Narratives', *Writing the Troubles*, 19 April 2021*; Marie Hammond Callaghan, 'Bombings, Burnings and Borders: Remembering Women's Peace Groups under Internment', *Canadian Journal of Irish Studies*, 32:1 (Spring 2006), 32–45; Amanda E. Donahoe, *Peacebuilding through Women's Community Development: Wee Women's Work in Northern Ireland* (Basingstoke: Palgrave Macmillan, 2017); see Sharon Pickering, 'Engendering Resistance: Women and Policing in Northern Ireland', *Policing and Society*, 11 (2001), 337–58, and 'Women, the Home and Resistance in Northern Ireland', *Women and Criminal Justice*, 11:3 (2000), 49–82.

6 Mary McKay, 'Living with the Army in Your Front Garden', *Spare Rib*, 43 (February 1976), p. 521.

7 Melissa Thompson, 'Interview with Anne Crilly', *Sli na mBan* (1998–2006) <http://www.tallgirlshorts.net/marymary/anne.html>.

8 According to Margaret Dickinson, Anne Cottringer and Julian Petley who wrote about *Hush-a-Bye Baby* in *Vertigo*, 1:1 (Spring 1993).

9 Melissa Thompson, 'Interview with Anne Crilly'.

10 See Monica McWilliams, 'Struggling for Peace and Justice: Reflections on Women's Activism in Northern Ireland', *Journal of Women's History*, 6:4/7:1 (Winter/Spring 1995), 13–39.

11 Teresa O'Keefe, ' "Mother Ireland, Get Off Our Backs": Republican Feminist Resistance in the North of Ireland', *The Troubles in Northern Ireland and Theories of Social Movements*, ed. Lorenzo Bosi and Gianluca De Fazio (Amsterdam: Amsterdam University Press, 2017), pp. 165, 175.

12 Eileen Fairweather, Roisin McDonough and Melanie McFadyean, *Only the Rivers Run Free: Northern Ireland: The Women's War* (London: Pluto Press, 1984), p. 43.

13 O'Keefe, ' "Mother Ireland, Get Off Our Backs" ', Interview No. 18, p. 170; Nell McCafferty, *The Armagh Women* (Ann Arbor, MI: Co-op Books, 1981), p. 35.

14 According to Christina Loughran, by 1986 'more than two thousand strip-searches have been carried out; one woman held on supergrass evidence was strip-searched 240 times') – Christina Loughran, 'Armagh and Feminist Strategy: Campaigns around Republican Women Prisoners in Armagh Jail', *Feminist Review*, 23 (Summer 1986), 59–79 (p. 61).

15 Evelyn Brady, *In the Footsteps of Anne: Stories of Republican Women Ex-Prisoners* (Dublin: Connolly Books, 2011), pp. 210, 251.

16 O'Keefe, ' "Mother Ireland, Get Off Our Backs" ', p. 165.

17 Thompson, 'Interview with Anne Crilly'.

18 See Margaretta Jolly, 'The feelings behind the slogans: abortion campaigning and feminist mood-work circa 1979', *New Formations*, 82:1 (2014), 100–113.

19 Dolours Price, 'Review: Survivors of Religion, Marriage, and War', *Fortnight*, 208 (October 1984), 21–2 (p. 21).

20 Fairweather, McDonough and McFadyean, *Only the Rivers Run Free*, pp. 111, 128–32, 116.

21 Price, 'Review: Survivors of Religion, Marriage, and War', p. 21.

22 Fairweather, McDonough and McFadyean, *Only the Rivers Run Free*, pp. 3, 5, 148.

23 See Valerie Morgan, *Occasional Paper 3: Peacemakers? Peacekeepers? Women in Northern Ireland 1969–1995* (Derry: INCORE, 1996); see Eilish Rooney, 'Women, community and politics in Northern Ireland: -isms in action', *Journal of Gender Studies*, 1:4 (1992), 475–91 (p. 476).

24 Bernadette Devlin McAliskey, *The Price of My Soul* (London: Pan Books Ltd, 1969), p. 202.

25 Loughran, 'Armagh and Feminist Strategy', p. 61.

26 See Charitini (Hari) Ntini, ' "Where were the women?": Women active service members of the Provisional IRA in the Northern Ireland conflict', *Writing the Troubles*, 2 May 2022*.

27 Fairweather, McDonough and McFadyean, *Only the Rivers Run Free*, pp. 238–9.

28 O'Keefe, ' "Mother Ireland, Get Off Our Backs" ', p. 173.

29 Fairweather, McDonough and McFadyean, *Only the Rivers Run Free*, p. 264.

30 Fairweather, McDonough and McFadyean, *Only the Rivers Run Free*, p. 261.

31 Evelyn Brady, *In the Footsteps of Anne: Stories of Republican Women Ex-Prisoners* (Dublin: Connolly Books, 2011), p. 22.

32 Fairweather, McDonough and McFadyean, *Only the Rivers Run Free*, p. 270.

33 Sandra M. McEvoy, 'Protestant Paramilitary Mothering: Mothers and Daughters during the Northern Irish Troubles', *Troubling Motherhood*, ed. Lucy B. Hall, Anna L. Weissman and Laura J. Shepherd (Oxford: Oxford University Press, 2020), p. 36.

34 McEvoy, 'Protestant Paramilitary Mothering', p. 46.

35 Daniel Finn, *One Man's Terrorist* (London: Verso, 2019), p. 49.

36 Finn, *One Man's Terrorist*, p. 135. The five demands of political status were the right not to wear a prison uniform; the right not to do prison work; the right of free association with other prisoners, and to organize educational and recreational pursuits; the right to one visit, one letter and one parcel per week, and full restoration of remission lost through the protest.

37 Bobby Devlin, 'Preface', *An Interlude with Seagulls: Memories of a Long Kesh Internee* (London: Information on Ireland, 1985).

38 Fairweather, McDonough and McFadyean, *Only the Rivers Run Free*, pp. 92, 49.

39 Ronan Bennett, 'Life and death in Long Kesh', *Guardian*, 22 October 2008*.

40 Fairweather, McDonough and McFadyean, *Only the Rivers Run Free*, pp. 56, 62–3, 72, 90.

41 Brady, *In the Footsteps of Anne*, pp. 125, 147.

42 Fairweather, McDonough and McFadyean, *Only the Rivers Run Free*, pp. 50–51.

43 McCafferty, *The Armagh Women*, p. 52.

44 O'Keefe, ' "Mother Ireland, Get Off Our Backs" ', p. 170.

45 Brodie Nugent and Evan Smith, 'Intersectional solidarity? The Armagh women, the British left and women's liberation', *Contemporary British History*, 31:4 (2017), 611–35 (pp. 620–21).

46 McCafferty, *The Armagh Women*, p. 10.

47 Loughran, 'Armagh and Feminist Strategy', p. 64.

48 Martina Durac, *Mairéad Farrell: An Unfinished Conversation* (Loopline Films, 2014).

49 Nugent and Smith, 'Intersectional solidarity?', pp. 615, 619.

50 Nugent and Smith, 'Intersectional solidarity', p. 628.

51 It wasn't until the mid-90s that women prisoners' efforts began to be properly acknowledged. In the Winter 1996 issue of *The Captive Voice*, Mary McArdle reports on the events of Prisoners' Day 1995, the theme of which was 'Women in the Struggle'. The event, she writes, was a reminder of the fact that 'our contribution to the struggles has gone largely unnoticed and unrecorded', and marked hopes that this would begin to change. The events included a volleyball match, the exhibition of a quilt made by Irish Women's groups for the UN Women's Conference in Beijing, to which prisoners in Maghaderry – Armagh had closed ten years earlier – had contributed a panel, the unveiling of a memorial, and a colour parade for women who had fallen in the line of duty, Farrell among them. See Mary McArdle, 'Remembering – Women in the struggle', *An Glór Gafa/The Captive Voice*, 8:1 (Winter 1996), 6–7.

52 Brady, *In the Footsteps of Anne*, pp. 253–5.

53 McCafferty, *The Armagh Women*, p. 22.

54 Brady, *In the Footsteps of Anne*, p. 66.

55 O'Keefe, ' "Mother Ireland, Get Off Our Backs" ', p. 172.

56 O'Keefe, ' "Mother Ireland, Get Off Our Backs" ', p. 176. WAI was formed by working-class women from Belfast and Derry with links to People's Democracy, the Irish Republican Socialist Party and Sinn Féin: they organized demonstrations outside the prison on International Women's Day 1979 and 1980, with over 500 supporters in attendance at the latter. In October 1980, they published the results of their investigation into prison conditions that warned that women in Armagh were in 'grave danger' due to the ongoing intransigence of the British government. In London, meanwhile, the Armagh Co-ordinating Group organized pickets outside Downing Street, Whitehall and the General Medical Council offices. *Spare Rib* was an important ally to the Armagh

women's cause in Britain: it publicized the IWD demonstrations and other campaign events, and – unlike many feminist groups at the time – made the case for the links between feminism and republicanism. See Nugent and Smith, 'Intersectional solidarity?'.

57 Brady, *In the Footsteps of Anne*, pp. 253–5.
58 *The Falls Women's Centre 1982–2009*, ed. David Jardine and Jamie Finlay (Northern Visions Archive, 2009)*.
59 Paedar Whelan, 'Armagh women's prison struggle told in inspiring film', *An Phoblacht*, 7 March 2016*.
60 Fairweather, McDonough and McFadyean, *Only the Rivers Run Free*, p. 196.
61 Brady, *In the Footsteps of Anne*, p. 304.
62 McCafferty, *The Armagh Women*, pp. 38–41.
63 Fairweather, McDonough and McFadyean, *Only the Rivers Run Free*, pp. 205, 210.
64 Martina Durac, *Rose Dugdale – Mná an IRA* (Loopline Films, 2012).
65 Brady, *In the Footsteps of Anne*, p. 25.
66 Fairweather, McDonough and McFadyean, *Only the Rivers Run Free*, pp. 26–7.
67 Fairweather, McDonough and McFadyean, *Only the Rivers Run Free*, p. 29.
68 Finn, *One Man's Terrorist*, p. 134.
69 David McKittrick and David McVea, *Making Sense of the Troubles: A History of the Northern Ireland Conflict* (London: Penguin, 2012), p. 136.
70 'Eire and Graces', *Vox*, 50 (November 1994), 68–73 (p. 72).
71 See Devlin McAliskey, *The Price of My Soul*.
72 Cole Moreton, 'Bernadette McAliskey: Return of the Roaring Girl', *Independent on Sunday* (5 October 2008).
73 Moreton, 'Bernadette McAliskey: Return of the Roaring Girl'.
74 Ronan Burtenshaw, 'Left Behind by Good Friday: an Interview with Bernadette Devlin McAliskey', *Jacobin*, 25 April 2016*.
75 William D. Montalbano, 'Her Mother's Daughter – Jailed, a Symbol of Protest – Bernadette Devlin's Child Facing Charges', *Los Angeles Times* (23 March 1997).
76 Ros Wynne-Jones, 'The Devlin legacy that made her "guilty"', *Independent*, 10 March 1998; Éamon Phoenix, 'Roisin McAliskey case put British government under pressure', *Irish News*, 20 December 2020*.

77 Montalbano, 'Her Mother's Daughter'.

78 Heather Mills, 'Chaining women backed', *Independent*, 10 January 1996*.

79 Wynne-Jones, 'The Devlin legacy that made her "guilty"'.

10. *No Father*

1 According to the sociologists Karen Atkinson, Sarah Oerton and Diane Burns, 1993 was 'the year in which the pathologizing of single mothers reached its peak, strategically exploited to initially usher in the freezing of one-parent benefit by the Tories'. Karen Atkinson, Sarah Oerton and Diane Burns, ' "Happy Families?": Single Mothers, the Press and the Politicians', *Capital and Class*, 22:1 (Spring 1998), 1–11 (p. 1).

2 Will Hodgkinson, 'They fuck you up, your mum and dad', *Guardian*, 18 March 2005*.

3 Riley, 'The Force of Circumstance', p. 26.

4 Pat Thane, 'Unmarried Motherhood in Twentieth-Century England', *Women's History Review*, 20:1 (February 2011), 11–29 (pp. 11–12).

5 Kathleen Kiernan, Hilary Land and Jane Lewis, *Lone Motherhood in Twentieth-Century Britain* (Oxford: Oxford University Press, 1998), p. 21.

6 See Pat Thane and Tanya Evans, *Sinners, Scroungers, Saints: Unmarried Motherhood in Twentieth-Century England* (Oxford: Oxford University Press, 2012).

7 Steedman, *Landscape for a Good Woman*, pp. 6, 18.

8 Nelson, *The Argonauts*, p. 97.

9 Thane, 'Unmarried Motherhood in Twentieth-Century England', pp. 11–12.

10 Riley, 'The Force of Circumstance', p. 28.

11 Steedman, *Landscape for a Good Woman*, pp. 69–70.

12 See Thane, 'Unmarried Motherhood in Twentieth-Century England', pp. 11–12.

13 Atkinson, Oerton and Burns, ' "Happy Families?" ', p. 1. See also Angela McRobbie, 'Folk Devils Fight Back', *New Left Review*, January/February 1994, 203.

14 Benn, *Madonna and Child*, pp. 148–74.

15 Atkinson, Oerton and Burns, ' "Happy Families?" ', p. 2.

16 Thane, 'Unmarried Motherhood in Twentieth-Century England', p. 26.

17 See Dorothy E. Roberts, 'Punishing Drug Addicts Who Have Babies: Women of Color, Equality, and the Right of Privacy', *Harvard Law Review*, 104:7 (May 1991), 1419–1821.

18 Thane and Evans, *Sinners, Scroungers, Saints*, p. 149. 'Briefing – Lone parent benefits', *BBC News*, 10 December 1997*.

19 Thane and Evans, *Sinners, Scroungers, Saints*, pp. 188–9.

20 Gil McNeil (ed.), *Soul Providers: Writings by Single Parents* (London: Virago, 1994), pp. 100, ix.

21 McNeil (ed.), *Soul Providers*, pp. 100, ix.

22 See Richard Power Sayeed, *1997: The Future that Never Happened* (London: Zed Books, 2020), and David Stubbs, *1996 and the End of History* (London: Repeater Books, 2016).

23 Thane and Evans, *Sinners, Scroungers, Saints*, p. 169.

24 Jenkins, *Thatcher and Sons*, p. 205.

25 Tony Benn, *The Benn Diaries: The Definitive Collection*, ed. Ruth Winstone (London: Hutchinson, 2017), p. 448.

26 Tony Blair, 'The Strong Society: Rights, responsibilities and reform', *Guardian*, 30 May 2001*.

27 Jenkins, *Thatcher and Sons*, pp. 216–17.

28 See Miriam E. David, 'Home, work, families and children: New Labour, new directions and new dilemmas', *International Studies in Sociology of Education*, 9:2 (1999), 111–32 (p. 119).

29 Thane and Evans, *Sinners, Scroungers, Saints*, p. 198.

30 See 'Blair suffers in benefits revolt', *BBC News*, 11 December 1997*; see 'Briefing – Lone parent benefits', *BBC News*, 10 December 1997*.

31 Harriet Harman, *A Woman's Work* (London: Allen Lane, 2017), p. 204.

32 Thane, 'Unmarried Motherhood in Twentieth-Century England', p. 26; see also Jane Millar and Tess Ridge, 'Parents, children, families and New Labour: developing family policy?', *Evaluating New Labour's Welfare Reforms*, ed. Martin Powell (Bristol: Bristol University Press, 2002), pp. 85–106.

33 Harman, *A Woman's Work*, pp. 186–7.

34 See Thane, 'Unmarried Motherhood in Twentieth-Century England'.

35 Thane and Evans, *Sinners, Scroungers, Saints*, p. 197.

36 Gerry Mooney and Tricia McCafferty, ' "Only looking after the weans"? The Scottish nursery nurses' strike', *Critical Social Policy*, 25:2 (2005), 223–39 (p. 226).

37 In Tony Benn's diary from June 1992, he writes that 'The *Daily Mail* had a huge six-page extract from some book about Princess Diana's attempted suicide. It really is a sensational story in its impact on the monarchy' (Benn, *The Benn Diaries*, p. 390).

38 Mandy Merck (ed.), *After Diana: Irreverent Elegies* (London: Verso, 1998), pp. 63, 183, 17.

39 Helen McCarthy, *Double Lives: A History of Working Motherhood* (London: Bloomsbury, 2020), p. 360.

40 Melissa Denes, 'That's me in the picture: Cherie Blair, the morning after Labour's election victory, 2 May 1997', *Guardian*, 11 May 2015*.

41 'Nanny's mother attacks Blairs', *BBC News*, 29 March 2000*.

42 Paul Waugh, 'Cherie Blair is the "Lady Macbeth" of British politics', *Independent*, 8 August 2000*.

43 Cherie Booth, 'All women should have the chance to have a family and a career', *Guardian*, 20 October 2013*.

44 See Deborah Ross, 'Cherie Blair: "You can't please people who don't really know you" ', *Independent*, 2 August 2008*; Polly Toynbee, 'How could Cherie Blair do this without blushing?', *Guardian*, 8 June 2005*; Barbara Ellen, 'Days of whine and poses', *Observer*, 18 May 2008*.

45 Ross, 'Cherie Blair: "You can't please people who don't really know you" '.

46 Hilary Mantel, 'The princess myth: Hilary Mantel on Diana', *Guardian*, 26 August 2017*.

47 Thane and Evans observed in *Women's History Review* that families with lone parents constituted a quarter of all families in Britain, with nine out of ten of these single parents being women: 'lone mothers,' they write, 'are the poorest group within British society'. The article asserts that the state is no more successful than it has ever been (and is possibly less so) in getting fathers to pay child support, or in providing secure, well-paid employment opportunities for single parents, with many – especially teen mums – experiencing active stigmatization and

discrimination in the housing and job market. Thane and Evans, 'Lone Mothers', *Women's History Review*, 20:1 (February 2011), 1–9 (p. 8).

48 See Neil Armstrong, 'Our Friends in the North: One of the greatest ever TV dramas', *BBC Culture*, 13 January 2021*.

11. *Teen Mom UK*

1 Amelia Hill, 'How the UK halved its teenage pregnancy rate', *Guardian*, 18 July 2016*.

2 Health Protection Division, Public Health Wales, *Reducing Teenage Conception Rates in Wales: Project Report* (March 2016)*; Luke Sproule, 'Why are there fewer teenager mothers in Northern Ireland?', *BBC News NI*, 24 October 2021; Scottish Government, *Pregnancy and Parenthood in Young People Strategy 2016–2026* (March 2016)*.

3 Daniel Bentley, 'Labour attack Tories over "dodgy" pregnancy figures', *Independent*, 15 February 2010*.

4 Polly Toynbee, 'The drop in teenage pregnancies is the success story of our time', *Guardian*, 13 December 2013*.

5 Toynbee, 'The drop in teenage pregnancies is the success story of our time'.

6 Anne Enright, *Making Babies: Stumbling into Motherhood* (London: Vintage, 2004), pp. 112, 115, 116.

7 Sheila Wayman, 'What are the factors behind a 73% drop in teenage pregnancies in Ireland?', *Irish Times*, 25 January 2022*.

8 See Rhian E. Jones, *Clampdown: Pop-cultural wars on class and gender* (Winchester: Zero Books, 2013), pp. 17–20.

9 'Series Three, Episode Two', *Alan Davies: As Yet Untitled* (Dave, 2015).

10 Patrick Sproull, 'Melvin Burgess: "*Junk* was one of the first teen books: I invented the territory." ', *Guardian*, 14 August 2014*.

11 Sarah Lyell, 'On British Soaps, the Poor and the Jobless', *The New York Times*, 29 June 1997.

12 Jacqueline Rose and Sam Frears, 'You haven't got your sister pregnant, have you?', *London Review of Books*, 44:12 (23 June 2022).

13 Alice Azania-Jarvis, 'Last Night's Television: Kimberley: Young Mum Ten Years On, BBC4', *Independent*, 24 April 2009*.

14 Tim Teeman, 'Kimberley: Young Mum Ten Years On', *The Times*, 24 April 2009*.

15 Fairweather, McDonough and McFadyean, *Only the Rivers Run Free*, p. 148.

16 Bonnie Angelo and Toni Morrison, 'Toni Morrison: The Pain of being Black', *Time* (May 1998)*.

17 Benn, *Madonna and Child*, p. 151.

18 Urmee Kahn, 'Tracey Emin's new artwork inspired by teenage pregnancy', *Telegraph*, 13 June 2008*.

19 Tracey Emin, 'I felt that, in return for my children's souls, I had been given my success', *Independent*, 29 January 2009*.

20 World Health Organization, 'Adolescent Pregnancy', 2 June 2023*.

21 Sage, *Bad Blood*, pp. 277–8.

22 Emine Saner, 'Lorna Sage, my mum', *Guardian*, 9 October 2010*.

23 See Simon Duncan, Rosalind Edwards and Claire Alexander (eds), *Teenage Pregnancy: What's the Problem?* (London: Tufnell Press, 2010); Joanna Moorhead, 'We're glad we chose to be mothers in our teens', *Guardian*, 10 January 2015*.

24 Amelia Hill, 'Hope and ambition at the school for teenage mothers', *Guardian*, 19 April 2011*.

25 Amelia Hill, 'Hope and ambition at the school for teenage mothers'.

12. Austerity Parenting

1 'What is austerity and how has it affected British society?', *The New York Times*, 24 February 2019*.

2 See Derica Shields, *A Heavy Nonpresence* (London: Triple Canopy, 2021)*.

3 Thane and Evans, *Sinners, Scroungers, Saints*, p. 205.

4 Sophie Arie, 'UK's "austerity experiment" has forced millions into poverty and homelessness, says UN rapporteur', *BMJ*, May 2019*.

5 See Andrew Gregory, 'Austerity in England linked to more than 50,000 extra deaths in five years', *Guardian* 14 October 2021*; see Colin Leys, 'How a Decade of Austerity Brought the NHS to its Knees, *Tribune*, 1 July 2020*.

6 See John Osmond, 'Riot Reflections 1: Why Wales escaped', *Institute of Welsh Affairs*, 16 August 2011*; see Joey Simons, *The Fearful Part of It was the Absence*, Collective Gallery Edinburgh, 2022.

7 Raekha Prasad and Fiona Bawdon, 'Don't blame our parents, say rioters', *Guardian*, 6 December 2011*.

8 *London's Burning*, dir. Justin Hardy (Channel 4, December 2011).

9 Rebecca Camber, Nick Fagge, Katherine Faulkner, Nick McDermott and Laura Caroe, 'Rage of the girl rioters: Britain's students take to the streets again – and this time women are leading the charge', *Daily Mail*, 25 November 2010*.

10 'The women who rioted' in 'Reading the riots: A data-driven study into the causes and consequences of the August 2011 riots', *Guardian*, 9 December 2011*; Camber, Fagge, Faulkner, McDermott and Caroe, 'Rage of the girl rioters'*.

11 Debra Black, 'British mum distraught after turning in daughter over UK riots', *Star*, 17 August 2011*; and Ben Griffiths, 'Keep my daughter locked up for full sentence, urges Olympics ambassador rioter's dad', *Mirror*, 26 February 2012 <https://www.mirror.co.uk/news/uk-news/keep-my-daughter-locked-up-for-full-743606>.

12 Maya Oppenheim, 'How Strict Prison Sentences after the London Riots Have Caused a Cycle of Reoffending', *Buzzfeed*, 5 June 2015*.

13 Helen Carter and Owen Bowcott, 'Riots: mother jailed for handling looted shorts freed on appeal', *Guardian*, 19 August 2011*.

14 See Alexandra Topping and Patrick Wintour, 'London riots: Wandsworth council moves to evict mother of charged boy', *Guardian*, 12 August 2011*.

15 Nasrul Ismail, 'Impact of austerity on prison health in England: a qualitative study involving the national policymaker', *European Journal of Public Health*, 9:4 (November 2019), p. 274.

16 Maya Oppenheim, 'Austerity blamed for "troubling" incarceration rates gap as women in north four times likelier to be jailed', *Independent*, 30 April 2019*.

17 Dawn Foster, 'Whose recovery?: Gendered austerity in the UK', *Open-Democracy*, 4 August 2014*; Gillian MacNaull, 'The problem with women's prisons – and why they do more harm than good', *Conversation*, 30 July 2019*.

18 See 'Key Facts', *Women in Prison**.

19 See Rhiannon Lucy Coslett, 'Locking up pregnant women damages mothers and children – yet the UK does it', *Guardian*, 16 May 2022*; Jade Biggs, 'Should pregnant women really be sent to prison? How the criminal justice system is failing mums-to-be', *Cosmopolitan*, 10 November 2021*; 'My baby died during childbirth in my prison cell', *BBC Newsnight* (21 September 2021); Prisons and Probation Ombudsmen Independent Investigations, *Independent investigation into the death of Baby B at HMP&YOI Styal* (18 June 2020).

20 Nicola Kelly, ' "Cramped and unsafe" Glasgow housing unit forced to suspend mother and baby services', *Guardian*, 19 May 2022*.

21 Jamie Grierson, 'Shamima Begum's mother asks Home Office to show mercy', *Guardian*, 11 March 2019*.

22 Azadeh Moaveni, 'Shamima Begum's is a story of trafficking, betrayal and now, it seems, a state cover-up', *Guardian*, 2 September 2022*.

23 Andrew Norfolk, the Chief Investigative Reporter of *The Times*, who was rapidly promoted after his coverage of the Rotherham child sexual exploitation scandal and whose stories were found to be substantially fabricated. Ella Cockbain and Waqas Tufail, 'Failing victims, fuelling hate: challenging the harms of the "Muslim grooming gangs" narrative', *Race & Class*, 61:3 (2020), 3–32.

24 Sisters Uncut, 'Sisters Uncut Reclaim Holloway Prison: Addressing the legacy of state violence', *Verso* blog, 5 June 2017*.

25 Sisters Uncut, 'Sisters Uncut statement on the sale of Holloway Prison', 8 March 2019*.

26 'Occupy vs. Reclaim: what's in a name?', *Sisters Uncut*, 6 September 2016*.

27 In 1990, during Glasgow's tenure as the UK's City of Culture, the Easthall Theatre Group wrote and staged their play *Dampbusters*: McCormack and others dress up as different kinds of fungus, cultivating their homes inside council properties, and children perform a

pantomime of the very greedy city officials who are misappropriating the funds they need to improve their housing. See also Cathy McCormack and Marian Pallister, *The Wee Yellow Butterfly* (Glendaruel: Argyll Publishing, 2009).

28 Cathy McCormack, 'From the fourth to the third world – a common vision of health', *Community Development Journal*, 28:3 (1993), 206–17.

29 'Solar homes are cold comfort in Easterhouse', 22 October 1992, *Herald Scotland**.

30 Joey Simons, *Scheming* (Glasgow: Good Press, 2021), p. 7.

31 Amelia Gentleman, 'Is Britain broken?', *Guardian*, 31 March 2010*.

32 Cathy McCormack, *War without Bullets* (dir. Barbara Orton and Cassandra McGrogan), 1995.

33 Sandra Laville, 'Ella Kissi-Debrah: how a mother's fight for justice may help prevent other air pollution deaths', *Guardian*, 16 December 2020.

34 Dawn Foster, *Lean Out* (London: Repeater Books, 2016).

35 *Evening Standard*, 24 September 2014, p. 27.

36 Focus E15 archival material held in the Bishopsgate Institute, London. Transcript included in Emer Mary Morris and Nina Scott, *The Land of the Three Towers* (2016).

37 'East London artist paints UK's tallest mural to highlight crisis in affordable housing', *East End Review*, 27 November 2014.

38 For a discussion of the possible reorganization of the UK and its pitfalls, see Alex Niven, *New Model Island* (London: Repeater Books, 2019).

39 See Craig McAngus and Kirstein Rummery, 'Campaigning for the Female Vote in the Scottish Independence Referendum: Comparing Women for Independence and Women Together', *Scottish Affairs*, 27:2 (April 2018); Chris Bambery, *A People's History of Scotland* (Verso: London, 2014), p. 325.

40 Bambery, *A People's History*, p. 328.

41 Burtenshaw, 'Left Behind by Good Friday: an Interview with Bernadette Devlin McAliskey'.

42 Brian Coney, ' "We're not an army – we're three boys from Belfast": rap crew Kneecap laugh off their week of controversy', *Guardian*, 19 August 2022*.

Coda: Three Babies

1 Lauren Berlant, *The Female Complaint: The Unfinished Business of Sentimentality in American Culture* (Durham, NC: Duke University Press, 2008), p. 1.

2 Ernaux, *A Woman's Story*, trans. Tanya Leslie (New York, NY: Seven Stories Press, 1991), pp. 89, 31.

3 O'Connor, *Rememberings*, p. 205.

Bibliography

Books and Articles

Abusneineh, Bayan, 'Zionism, Anti-Black Racism and the Depo-Provera Affair', *Feminist Review*, 128, 96–113

Adelman, Janet, *Suffocating Mothers: Fantasies of Maternal Origin in Shakespeare's Plays*, Hamlet *to* The Tempest (Oxford: Routledge, 1991)

Agarwal, Pragya, *(M)otherhood: On the Choices of being a Woman* (Edinburgh: Canongate, 2021)

Ahmed, Sara, and Stacey, Jackie (eds), *Thinking through the Skin* (Abingdon: Routledge, 2001)

Alderson, David, 'Making Electricity: Narrating Gender, Sexuality, and the Neoliberal Transition in Billy Elliot', *Camera Obscura*, 25:3 (2011), 1–27

Alexander, Sally, *Becoming a Woman* (London: Virago, 1994)

Amos, Valerie, and Parmar, Pratibha, 'Challenging Imperial Feminism', *Feminist Review*, 17 (Autumn 1984)

Anderson, Gordon, 'Tuck in for the Petticoat rebels', *Daily Record*, Saturday 7 February 1981

Andrews, Kehinde, *Resisting Racism: Race, Inequality and the Black Supplementary School Movement* (London: Institute of Education Press, 2013)

Appignanesi, Lisa, *Mad, Bad and Sad: Women and the Mind Doctors* (London: Virago, 2008)

Appignanesi, Lisa, and Forrester, John, *Freud's Women* (London: Weidenfeld and Nicholson, 1992)

Apter, Emily K., ' "Women's Time" in Theory', *differences: A Journal of Feminist Cultural Studies*, 21:1 (2010), 1–18

Archer, Marilyn, 'Gay Wives and Mothers', *Spare Rib*, 31 (January 1975); 'Lesbian Mothers Unite', *Spare Rib*, 47 (June 1976)

Arnot, Margaret L., 'Infant death, child care and the state: The baby-farming scandal and the first infant life protection legislation of 1872', *Continuity and Change*, 9:2 (1994), 271–311

Aston, Elaine, and Clarke, Ian, 'Feminist theory and the matriarchal soap: *EastEnders*', *Critical Survey*, 6:2 (1994), 211–17

Atkinson, Karen, Oerton, Sarah, and Burns, Diane, ' "Happy Families"?: Single Mothers, the Press and the Politicians', *Capital and Class*, 22:1 (Spring 1998), 1–11

Austin, Arlen, and Federici, Silvia (eds), *Wages for Housework, The New York Committee 1972–1977: History, Theory, Documents* (Chicago, CA: AK Press, 2018)

Bambery, Chris, *A People's History of Scotland* (Verso: London, 2014)

Bar-Haim, Shaul, *The Maternalists: Psychoanalysis, Motherhood, and the British Welfare State* (Philadelphia, PA: University of Pennsylvania Press, 2021)

Baraitser, Lisa, *Enduring Time* (London: Bloomsbury, 2017)

— *Maternal Encounters: The Ethics of Interruption* (London: Routledge, 2009)

—, and Riley, Denise, 'Lisa Baraitser in Conversation with Denise Riley', *Studies in the Maternal*, 8:1 (2016), 5

—, and Tyler, Imogen, 'Private View, Public Birth: Making Feminist Sense of the New Visual Culture of Childbirth', *Studies in the Maternal*, 5:2 (July 2013), 1–27

Barker, Drucilla K., and Kuiper, Edith (eds), *Towards a Feminist Philosophy of Economics: Economics as Social Theory* (London: Routledge, 2003)

Barthes, Roland, *Camera Lucida*, trans. Richard Howard (New York, NY: Hill and Wang, 1981)

—, and Bernays, Hella Freud, 'Seven Photo Models of "Mother Courage"', *TDR*, 12:1 (1967) 44–55

Battersby, Christine, *The Phenomenal Woman: Feminist Metaphysics and the Patterns of Identity* (Cambridge: Polity Press, 1998)

de Beauvoir, Simone, *A Very Easy Death*, trans. Patrick O'Brien (London: André Deutsch Ltd and George Weidenfeld and Nicolson Ltd, 1965)

Benn, Melissa, *Madonna and Child* (London: Cape, 1998)

Benn, Tony, *The Benn Diaries: The Definitive Collection*, ed. Ruth Winstone (London: Hutchinson, 2017)

Berlant, Lauren, *Cruel Optimism* (Durham, NC: Duke University Press, 2011)

—— *The Female Complaint: The Unfinished Business of Sentimentality in American Culture* (Durham, NC: Duke University Press, 2008)

—— 'America, "Fat," the Fetus', *boundary 2*, 21:3 (Autumn 1994)

Bernstein, Sarah, 'After the good life: squatting and the politics of the commons in *The good terrorist*', *Studia Neophilologica*, 92:2 (May 2020), 209–21

Bertolino, Elisabetta, 'Predictable Medea', *Studies in the Maternal*, 2:1 (2010), 1–10

Betterton, Rosemary, *Maternal Bodies in the Visual Arts* (Manchester: Manchester University Press, 2014)

Beynon, Huw, and McMylor, Peter, 'Decisive Power: The New Tory State against the Miners', *Digging Deeper: Issues in the Miners' Strike* (London: Verso, 1985)

Bhattacharya, Tithi (ed.), *Social Reproduction Theory: Remapping Class, Recentring Oppression* (London: Pluto Press, 2017)

Biggs, Joanna, 'Diary: Abortion in Northern Ireland', *London Review of Books*, 39:16 (17 August 2017)

Blackwood, Caroline, *On the Perimeter* (London: Heinemann, 1984)

Bond, Brian, 'A military historian, Brian Bond, looks at the Falklands war', *London Review of Books*, 5:4 (March 1983)

Brady, Evelyn, *In the Footsteps of Anne: Stories of Republican Women Ex-Prisoners* (Dublin: Connolly Books, 2011)

Brathwaite, Candice, *I am Not Your Baby Mother* (London: Quercus, 2020)

Breathnach, Ciara, 'Handywomen and Birthing in Rural Ireland, 1851–1955', *Gender & History*, 28:1 (April 2016), 34–56

Brecht, Bertolt, *Mother Courage,* trans. Lee Hall, *Plays 2* (London: Methuen)

Brennan, Teresa, *The Interpretation of the Flesh: Freud and Femininity* (London: Routledge, 1992)

Briggs, Kate, *The Long Form* (London: Fitzcarraldo, 2023)

Briggs, Laura, 'Discourses of "Forced Sterilization" in Puerto Rico', *Differences*, 10:2 (1998), 30–66

Briggs, Raymond, *The Tin-Pot Foreign General and the Old Iron Woman* (London: Hamish Hamilton, 1984)

British Theatre Association, The, *Drama: The Quarterly Theatre Review* (1981), vols 139–54

Brooke, Stephen, *Sexual Politics: Sexuality, Family Planning, and the British Left from the 1880s to the Present Day* (Oxford: Oxford University Press, 2011)

Brooke, Stephen, ' "A New World for Women"? Abortion Law Reform in Britain during the 1930s', *American Historical Review*, 106:2 (April 2001), 431–59

Brookes, Barbara L., *Abortion in England 1900–1967* (London: Routledge, 1988)

Brown, Wilmette, *Black Women and the Peace Movement*, 2nd edn (Bristol: Falling Wall Press, 1986)

Browne, Victoria, *Pregnancy without Birth: A Feminist Philosophy of Miscarriage* (London: Bloomsbury, 2022)

— 'The politics of miscarriage', *Radical Philosophy*, 2:3 (December 2018), 62–72

Bryan, Beverley, Dadzie, Stella, and Scafe, Suzanne, *The Heart of the Race: Black Women's Lives in Britain* (London: Verso, 1985)

Burchill, Julie, 'Burchill on Burchill', *Face*, 2:9 (1989)

Burton, James, 'Reframing the 1950s: race and representation in recent British television', *Adjusting the Contrast: British Television and Constructs of Race*, ed. Sarita Malik and Darrell M. Newton (Manchester: Manchester University Press, 2017), pp. 71–89

Butler, Judith, *Gender Trouble* (New York, NY: Routledge, 1999)

Cain, Chelsea, *Wild Child: Girlhoods in the Counterculture* (Cypress, CA: Seal Press, 1999)

Callaghan, Marie Hammond, 'Bombings, Burnings and Borders: Remembering Women's Peace Groups under Internment', *Canadian Journal of Irish Studies*, 32:1 (Spring 2006), 32–45

Campbell, Beatrix, 'Margaret Thatcher: To be or not to be a woman', *British Politics*, 10 (2015), 41–51

— *The Iron Ladies: Why do women vote Tory?* (London: Virago, 1987)

Campion, Sarah, *National Baby* (London: Ernest Benn, Ltd, 1950)

Carby, Hazel, *Imperial Intimacies: A Tale of Two Islands* (London: Verso, 2019)

Carr, Jean, *Another Story: Women and the Falklands War* (London: Hamish Hamilton, 1984)

Cavarero, Adriana, *Inclinations: A Critique of Rectitude* (Stanford, CA: Stanford University Press, 2016)

Chodorow, Nancy, *The Reproduction of Mothering: Psychoanalysis and the Sociology of Gender* (Berkeley, CA: University of California Press, 1978)

Clark, Veronica, and Steel, Helen, *Deep Deception: The story of the spycop network, by the women who uncovered the shocking truth* (London: Penguin, 2022)

Clay, Trevor, Dunn, Alison, and Stewart, Neil, *Nurses, Power and Politics* (Ann Arbor, MI: University of Michigan Press, 1987)

Cockbain, Ella, and Tufail, Waqas, 'Failing victims, fuelling hate: challenging the harms of the "Muslim grooming gangs" narrative', *Race & Class*, 61:3 (2020), 3–32

Cohen, Deborah A., 'Private Lives in Public Spaces: Marie Stopes, the Mothers' Clinics and the Practice of Contraception', *History Workshop Journal*, 35:1 (Spring 1993), 95–116

Committee for Abortion Rights and Against Sterilization Abuse, The, *Women under Attack: Abortion, Sterilization Abuse and Reproductive Freedom* (New York, NY: Committee for Abortion Rights and Against Sterilization Abuse, 1979)

Cook, Alice, and Kirk, Gwyn (eds), *Greenham Women Everywhere* (Boston, MA: South End Press, 1983)

Cook, Hera, *The Long Sexual Revolution: English Women, Sex, and Contraception 1800–1975* (Oxford: Oxford University Press, 2004)

Cook, Matt, 'From Gay Reform to Gaydar, 1967–2006', *A Gay History of Britain: Love and Sex between Men since the Middle Ages*, ed. Matt Cook, H.G. Cocks, Robert Mills, and Randolph Trumbach (Oxford: Greenwood Press, 2007)

Cornell, Drucilla, *The Imaginary Domain: Abortion, Pornography and Sexual Harassment* (London: Routledge, 1995), p. 35

de Costa, Caroline M., 'The king versus Aleck Bourne: the case that established the lawfulness of terminating pregnancy to preserve women's health', *Medical Journal of Australia*, 191:4 (2009), 230–31

Cusk, Rachel, *A Life's Work* (London: Picador, 2021)

Dain, Marion, 'Society for the Protection of the Unwanted Child', *Red Rag*, 7 (August 1974), 12–13

David, Miriam E., 'Home, work, families and children: New labour, new directions and new dilemmas', *International Studies in the Sociology of Education*, 9:2 (1999), 111–32

Davies, Eli, ' "At Least We Can Lock the Door": Radical Domesticity in the Writing of Bernadette Devlin and Nell McCafferty', *Journal of War & Culture Studies*, 14:1 (2021), 70–88

Davis, Angela, *Modern Motherhood: Women and Family in England 1945–2012* (Manchester: Manchester University Press, 2014)

Davis, Angela Y., *Women, Race and Class* (New York, NY: Random House, 1981)

Davis, Jude, 'Albany Midwifery Practice', *AIMs Journal*, 26:3 (September 2014)

Delap, Lucy, 'Feminist Bookshops, Reading Cultures and the Women's Liberation Movement in Great Britain, c. 1974–2000', *History Workshop Journal*, 81:1 (2016), 171–96

— ' "For ever and ever": Child-raising, domestic workers and emotional labour in twentieth century Britain studies', *Studies in the Maternal*, 3:2 (2011), 1–10

Delphy, Christine, *Close to Home: A Material Analysis of Women's Oppression*, trans. Diana Leonard (London: Verso, 2016)

Dever, Carolyn, *Death and the Mother from Dickens to Freud: Victorian Fiction and the Anxiety of Origins* (Cambridge: Cambridge University Press, 1998)

Devlin McAliskey, Bernadette, *The Price of My Soul* (London: Pan Books Ltd, 1969)

Devlin, Bobby, 'Preface', *An Interlude with Seagulls: Memories of a Long Kesh Internee* (London: Information on Ireland, 1985)

Dhillon, Perminder, 'They're killing us in here' *Spare Rib*, 84 (July 1979)

Diamond, Elin, 'Realism and Hysteria: Toward a Feminist Mimesis', *Discourse*, 13:1 (Fall–Winter 1990–91), 59–92

Dickinson, Margaret, Cottringer, Anne, and Petley, Julian, 'Hush-a-Bye Baby', *Vertigo*, 1:1 (Spring 1993)

Doherty, Maggie, *The Equivalents: A Story of Art, Female Friendship, and Liberation in the 1960s* (New York, NY: Penguin Random House USA, 2020)

Dolby, Norma, *Norma Dolby's Diary: An Account of the Great Miners' Strike* (London: Verso, 1987)

Donahoe, Amanda E., *Peacebuilding through Women's Community Development: Wee Women's Work in Northern Ireland* (Basingstoke: Palgrave Macmillan, 2017)

Dow, Katharine, ' "The men who made the breakthrough": How the British press represented Patrick Steptoe and Robert Edwards in 1978', *Reproductive BioMedicine and Society Online*, 4 (2017), 59–67

Downing, Lisa, *Selfish Women* (Abingdon: Taylor & Francis, 2019)

Duncan, Simon, Edwards, Rosalind, and Alexander, Claire (eds), *Teenage Pregnancy: What's the Problem?* (London: Tufnell Press, 2010)

Dunn, Nell, *Talking to Women* (London: Silver Press, 2018)

— *Living Like I Do* (London: Futura Publications, 1977)

Duschinksy, Robbie, and Walker, Susan (eds), *Juliet Mitchell and the Lateral Axis: Twenty-First-Century Psychoanalysis and Feminism* (New York, NY: Palgrave Macmillan, 2015)

Edwards, Robert, and Steptoe, Patrick, *A Matter of Life: The Story of a Medical Breakthrough* (London: Hutchinson, 1980)

'Eire and Graces', *Vox*, 50 (November 1994), 68–73

Elliott, Ruth, 'How Far Have We Come? Women's Organization in the Unions in the United Kingdom', *Feminist Review*, 16:1, 64–73

Emejulu, Akwugo, and Bassel, Leah, 'Minority Women, Austerity and Activism', *Race & Class*, 57:2 (October 2015), 86–95

Enright, Anne, *Making Babies: Stumbling into Motherhood* (London: Vintage, 2004)

Epstein, Helen, *Children of the Holocaust: Conversations with Sons and Daughters of Survivors* (London: Penguin, 1979)

Evening Standard, 24 September 2014

Ernaux, Annie, *Happening*, trans. Tanya Leslie (London: Fitzcarraldo Editions, 2019)

— *A Woman's Story*, trans. Tanya Leslie (New York: Seven Stories Press, 1991)

Fairweather, Eileen, 'Newshorts', *Spare Rib*, 83 (June 1979)

Fairweather, Eileen, McDonough, Roisin, and McFadyean, Melanie, *Only the Rivers Run Free: Northern Ireland: The Women's War* (London: Pluto Press, 1984)

Federici, Silvia, *Caliban and the Witch: Women, the Body and Primitive Accumulation* (New York, NY: Autonomedia, 2004)

Feminist Social Policy Group, The, 'Rest in Pieces', *Red Rag*, 9 (August 1980), 34

Ferber, Alona, 'Judith Butler on the culture wars, JK Rowling and living in "anti-intellectual times"', *New Statesman* (22 September 2020)

Fildes, Valerie, *Wet Nursing: A History from Antiquity to the Present* (Oxford: Wiley Blackwell, 1988)

—, Marks, Lara, and Marland, Hilary (eds), *Women and Children First: International Maternal and Infant Welfare 1870–1945* (London: Routledge, 1992)

Finch, Sue, 'Socialist-Feminists and Greenham', *Feminist Review*, 23 (Summer 1986), 93–100

Finn, Daniel, *One Man's Terrorist* (London: Verso, 2019)

Firestone, Shulamith, *The Dialectic of Sex* (New York, NY: William Morrow and Company, Inc., 1970)

—, and Koedt, Anne (eds), *Notes from the Second Year: Women's Liberation* (New York, NY: Radical Feminism, 1970)

Fitzgerald, Louise, 'Taking a pregnant pause: Interrogating the feminist potential of *Call the Midwife*', *Upstairs and Downstairs: British Costume Drama Television from the Forsyte Saga to Downton Abbey*, ed. James Leggott and Julie Anne Taddeo (Lanham: Rowman and Littlefield, 2015), pp. 249–63

Forrester, Katrina, 'Feminist Demands and the Problem of Housework', *American Political Science Review* (2022), 1–15

Foster, Dawn, *Lean Out* (London: Repeater Books, 2016)

Fraiman, Susan, *Extreme Domesticity: A View from the Margins* (New York, NY: Columbia University Press, 2017)

Franklin, Sarah, *Biological Relatives: IVF, Stem Cells, and the Future of Kinship* (Durham, NC: Duke University Press, 2013)

Freeman, Barbara Claire, *The Feminine Sublime: Gender and Excess in Women's Fiction* (Berkeley, CA: University of California Press, 1995)

Freud, Sigmund, *Three Essays on the Theory of Sexuality: The 1905 Edition*, trans. Ulrike Kistner, ed. Philippe Van Haute and Herman Westerink (London: Verso, 2016)

—, and Breuer, Josef, *The Standard Edition of the Complete Psychological Works of Sigmund Freud, Volume II (1893–1895): Studies on Hysteria*, ed. and trans. James Strachey (London: Vintage, 2001)

Gaskin, Ina May, *Ina May's Guide to Childbirth* (New York, NY: Bantam Books, 2012)

— *Spiritual Midwifery* (Summertown, TN: Book Publishing Co., 1976)

Gibbs, Ewan, *Coal Country: The Meaning and Memory of Deindustrialization* (Edinburgh: Edinburgh University Press, 2020)

Gildea, Robert, *Backbone of the Nation: Mining Communities and the Great Strike of 1984–85* (New Haven, CT: Yale University Press, 2023)

Giles, Mary, and Hutt, Jane, 'Life on Social Security', *Spare Rib*, 85 (August 1979)

Gillick, Victoria, *Dear Mrs Gillick* (Basingstoke: Marshalls, 1985)

Golden, Janet, 'From Commodity to Gift: Gender, Class, and the Meaning of Breast Milk in the Twentieth Century', *Historian* 59:1 (1996), 75–87

Gorbing, Sue, and Parsonage, Helen, 'Reviewed Works: *Greenham Common: Women at the Wire* by Barbara Harford, Sarah Hopkins; *On the Perimeter* by Caroline Blackwood', *Feminist Review*, 20 (Summer 1985), 109–13

Gordon, Linda, *Woman's Body, Woman's Right: A Social History of Birth Control in America* (New York, NY: Grossman Publishers, 1976)

Gotby, Alva, *They Call It Love: The Politics of Emotional Life* (London; Verso, 2023)

Greenock Telegraph, 'It's the pay off at VF . . . ', 2 May 1981

— 'Weeks without pay hit VF staff', 5 May 1981

— 'Future looks dim for Jennifer and other 239', 5 March 1981

— 'Now it's the great knit-in!', 20 April 1981

Gulley, Lois, 'Letters', *Spare Rib*, 68 (March 1978)

Hall, Stuart, *The Hard Road to Renewal* (London: Verso, 1988)

Hall, Stuart, Critcher, Chas, Jefferson, Tony, Roberts, Brian, and Clarke, John, *Policing the Crisis: Mugging, the State, and Law and Order* (London: Macmillan, 1978)

Hanley, Lynsey, *Estates* (London: Granta, 2007)

Hannity, Mary, 'Two-Year-Olds are Often Cruel', *London Review of Books*, 45:3 (2 February 2023)

Hanscombe, Gillian E., and Forster, Jackie, *Rocking the Cradle: Lesbian Mothers: A Challenge in Family Living* (London: Sheba, 1982)

Harford, Barbara, and Hopkins, Sarah (eds), *Greenham Common: women at the wire* (London: The Women's Press, 1984)

Harman, Harriet, *A Woman's Work* (London: Allen Lane, 2017)

Harne, Lynne, 'Lesbian Mothers' Custody Conference', *Spare Rib*, 129 (April 1983), 22–3

— *Valued Families: Lesbian Mother's Legal Handbook* (London: The Women's Press, 1977)

Hart, Christopher, *Behind the Mask: Nurses, Their Unions and Nursing Policy* (London: Ballière Tindall, 1994)

Hay, Kristin, ' "More than a defence against bills": feminism and national identity in the Scottish abortion campaign, c. 1975–1990', *Women's History Review*, 30:4 (July 2020), 594–612

Hayward, Sarah, and Fee, Elizabeth, 'More in Sorrow than in Anger: the British Nurses' Strike of 1988', *International Journal of Health Services*, 22:3 (1992), 397–415

Hemmings, Susan, 'Horrific Practices: How Lesbians were Presented in the Newspapers of 1978', *Homosexuality: Power and Politics*, ed. Gay Left Collective (London: Verso, 2018)

— 'In the best interests of the children', *Spare Rib*, 74 (September 1978)

Heron, Liz, ed., *Truth, Dare or Promise: Girls Growing up in the 50s* (London: Virago, 1985)

Heti, Sheila, *Motherhood* (London: Harvill Secker, 2018)

Hewitt, Margaret, *Wives and Mothers in Victorian Industry* (London: Rockcliff, 1958)

Hill, John, 'A Working Class Hero Is Something To Be? Changing Representations of Class and Masculinity in British Cinema', *The Trouble with Men: Masculinities in European and Hollywood Cinema*, ed. Phil Powrie, Anne Davies, and Bruce Babbington (London: Wallflower Press, 2004)

Hunter, Billie, and Leap, Nicky, *The Midwife's Tale: An Oral History from Handywoman to Professional Midwife* (London: Scarlet Press, 1993)

Hutton, Guthrie, *Coal Not Dole: Memories of the 1984/85 Miners' Strike* (Mauchline: Stenlake, 2005)

Ismail, Nasrul, 'Impact of austerity on prison health in England: a qualitative study involving the national policymaker', *European Journal of Public Health*, 9:4 (November 2019)

Jacobs, Bethany, 'Mothering herself: manifesto of the erotic mother in Audre Lorde's *Zami: A New Spelling of My Name*', *MELUS*, 40:4 (Winter 2015), 113–14

James, Selma, *Sex, Race and Class: The Perspective of Winning: A Selection of Writings 1952–2011* (California: PM Press, 2012)

Jenkins, Simon, *Thatcher and Sons: A Revolution in Three Acts* (London: Penguin, 2007)

Jennings, Rebecca, 'Lesbian Motherhood and the Artificial Insemination by Donor Scandal of 1978', *Twentieth Century British History*, 28:4 (2017), 570–94

Jolly, Margaretta, 'The feelings behind the slogans: abortion campaigning and feminist mood-work circa 1979', *New Formations*, 82:1 (2014), 100–113

— (ed.), *Sisterhood and After: An Oral History of the UK Women's Liberation Movement, 1968–present* (Oxford: Oxford University Press, 2019)

Jones, Rhian E., *Clampdown: Pop-cultural wars on class and gender* (Winchester: Zero Books, 2013)

Junor, Beth, and Howse, Katrina, *Greenham Common Women's Peace Camp: A History of Non-Violent Resistance 1984–1995* (London: Working Press, 1995)

Keating, Jackie, *Counting the Cost: A Family in the Miners' Strike* (Barnsley: Wharncliffe Publishing, 1991)

Keay, Douglas, 'Interview with Margaret Thatcher', *Woman's Own*, 31 October 1987

Kelliher, Diarmaid, *Making Cultures of Solidarity: London and the 1984–5 Miners' Strike* (London: Routledge, 2021)

Keown, John, *Abortion, Doctors and the Law: some aspects of the legal regulation of abortion in England from 1803 to 1982* (Cambridge: Cambridge University Press, 1998)

Kiernan, Kathleen, Land, Hilary, and Lewis, Jane, *Lone Motherhood in Twentieth-Century Britain* (Oxford: Oxford University Press, 1998)

Kindo, Yann, and Darmangeat, Christophe, 'Caliban and the Witch: A critical analysis', *Intransigence*, 5 (2019)

Kitzinger, Sheila, *The Experience of Childbirth* (London: Victor Gollancz Ltd, 1962)

— (ed.), *Episiotomy and the Second Stage of Labour* (Coventry, Penny Press, 1984)

Knott, Sarah, *Mother: An Unconventional History* (London: Penguin, 2020)

—, and Griffin, Emma (eds), 'Mothering's Many Labours', *Past & Present*, Supplement 15 (January 2021)

Kristeva, Julia, *Powers of Horror: An Essay on Abjection*, trans. Leon S. Roudiez (New York: Columbia University Press, 1982)

— 'Women's Time', trans. Alice A. Jardine and Harry Blake, *Signs*, 7:1 (Autumn 1981), 13–35

Kühl, Steffan, *For the Betterment of the Race: The Rise and Fall of the International Movement for Eugenics and Racial Hygiene*, trans. Lawrence Schofer (New York, NY: Palgrave Macmillan, 2013)

Latham, Cecile, and Keating, Cricket, 'Mother Courage Peace Tour', *Off Our Backs*, 21:4 (April 1991), 1–2

Leslie, Ann, 'The fantasy of Greenham Common', *Daily Mail*, 13 January 1983, 16–17

Leslie, Esther, and Jackson, Melanie, 'Milk's Arrays', *Studies in the Maternal*, 10:1 (2018), 8

Lessing, Doris, *Walking in the Shade: The Growing Point* (London, HarperCollins, 2009)

— *The Good Terrorist* (London: Cape, 1985)

Lewis, Gail, 'Whose movement is it anyway? Intergenerationality and the problem of political alliance', *Radical Philosophy*, 2:14 (April 2023), 64–74

— 'Birthing Racial Difference: Conversations with My Mother and Others', *Studies in the Maternal*, 1:1 (2009), 1–21

Lewis, Sophie, 'Free Anthrogenesis: Antiwork Abortion', *Salvage*, 12 (1 June 2022)

— *Full Surrogacy Now* (London: Verso, 2019)

— 'International Solidarity in reproductive justice: surrogacy and gender-inclusive polymaternalism', *Gender, Place & Culture: A Journal of Feminist Geography*, 25:2 (2018), 207–27

Lintott, Sheila, 'The Sublimity of Gestating and Giving Birth', in *Philosophical Inquiries into Pregnancy, Childbirth, and Mothering*, ed. Sheila Lintott and Maureen Sander-Staudt (Abingdon: Routledge, 2012), pp. 237–50

— 'Lonely among the Feminists', *Spare Rib*, 132 (July 1983)

Lopez, Iris Ofelia, 'Agency and Constraint: Sterilization and Reproductive Freedom among Puerto Rican Women in New York City', *Urban Anthropology and Studies of Cultural Systems*, 22:3/4 (Fall 1993), 299–323

Lopez, Tara Martin, *The Winter of Discontent* (Liverpool: Liverpool University Press, 2014)

Lorde, Audre, *Zami: A New Spelling of My Name* (Watertown, MA: Persephone Press, 1982)

— 'Uses of the Erotic', *The Selected Works of Audre Lorde*, ed. Roxane Gay (New York, NY: 2020)

Loudon, Irvine, *Death in Childbirth: An International Study of Maternal Care and Maternal Mortality 1800–1950* (Oxford: Clarendon Press, 1992)

Loughran, Christina, 'Armagh and Feminist Strategy: Campaigns around Republican Women Prisoners in Armagh Jail', *Feminist Review*, 23 (Summer 1986), 59–79

Lyell, Sarah, 'On British Soaps, the Poor and the Jobless', *The New York Times*, 29 June 1997

Mac, Juno, and Smith, Molly, *Revolting Prostitutes: The Fight for Sex Workers' Rights* (London: Verso, 2018)

Malone, Patricia, 'Measures of obliviousness and disarming obliqueness in Anna Burns' *Milkman*', *Textual Practice*, 36:7 (Spring 2022), 1143–74

Marder, Elissa, *The Mother in the Age of Mechanical Reproduction: Psychoanalysis, Photography, Deconstruction* (New York, NY: Fordham University Press, 2012)

Martin, Emily, *The Woman in the Body: A Cultural Analysis of Reproduction* (Boston, MA: Beacon Press, 2001 edn)

Mayberry, Lorel, and Daniel, Jacqueline, ' "Birthgasm": A Literary Review of Orgasm as an Alternative Mode of Pain Relief in Childbirth', *Journal of Holistic Nursing*, 34:4 (December 2016), 331–42

Mayo, Rosalind, and Moutsou, Christina (eds), *The Mother in Psychoanalysis and Beyond: Matricide and Maternal Subjectivity* (London: Routledge, 2017)

McAngus, Craig, and Rummery, Kirstein, 'Campaigning for the Female Vote in the Scottish Independence Referendum: Comparing Women for Independence and Women Together', *Scottish Affairs*, 27:2 (April 2018)

McArdle, Mary, 'Remembering – Women in the struggle', *An Glór Gafa/ The Captive Voice*, 8–1 (Winter 1996), 6–7

McCafferty, Nell, *The Armagh Women* (Ann Arbor, MI: Co-op Books, 1981)

McCarthy, Helen, *Double Lives: A History of Working Motherhood* (London: Bloomsbury, 2020)

McCormack, Cathy, 'From the fourth to the third world – A common vision of health', *Community Development Journal*, 28:3 (1993), 206–17

McCormack, Cathy, and Pallister, Marian, *The Wee Yellow Butterfly* (Glendaruel: Argyll Publishing, 2009)

McCrindle, Jean, and Rowbotham, Sheila (eds), *Dutiful Daughters: Women Talk about their Lives* (London: Pelican Books, 1979)

McEneaney, Sinead, 'Home Sweet Home? Housing Activism and Political Commemoration in Sixties Ireland', *History Workshop Journal*, 87 (Spring 2019), 5–26

McEvoy, Sandra M., 'Protestant Paramilitary Mothering: Mothers and Daughters during the Northern Irish Troubles', *Troubling Motherhood*, ed. Lucy B. Hall, Anna L. Weissman, and Laura J. Shepherd (Oxford: Oxford University Press, 2020)

McIntosh, Tania, *A Social History of Maternity and Childbirth: Key Themes in Maternity Care* (Abingdon: Routledge, 2012)

McKittrick, David, and McVea, David, *Making Sense of the Troubles: A History of the Northern Ireland Conflict* (London: Penguin, 2012)

McLean, Donna, *Small Town Girl: Love, Lies and the Undercover Police* (London: Hodder Studio, 2022)

McNeil, Gil (ed.), *Soul Providers: Writings by Single Parents* (London: Virago, 1994)

McKay, Mary, 'Living with the Army in Your Front Garden', *Spare Rib*, 43 (February 1976)

McRobbie, Angela, 'Inside the socialist nursery: welfare maternity and the writing of Denise Riley', *Feminist Review*, 23:1 (2020), 287–96

— 'Feminism, the Family, and the new "Mediated" Maternalism', *New Formations*, 80/81 (2014)

— 'Folk Devils Fight Back', *New Left Review*, 203 (January/February 1994).

McWilliams, Monica, 'Struggling for Peace and Justice: Reflections on Women's Activism in Northern Ireland', *Journal of Women's History*, 6:4 and 7:1 (Winter–Spring 1995)

Merck, Mandy (ed.), *After Diana: Irreverent Elegies* (London: Verso, 1998)

Midgley, Mary, 'Shouting across the gulf', *London Review of Books*, 6:19 (18 October 1984)

Millar, Erica, *Happy Abortions: Our Bodies in the Era of Choice* (London: Zed Books, 2017)

Millar, Jane, and Ridge, Tess, 'Parents, children, families and New Labour: developing family policy?', *Evaluating New Labour's Welfare Reforms*, ed. Martin Powell (Bristol: Bristol University Press, 2002)

Miller, Milo (ed.), *Speak Out!: The Brixton Black Women's Group* (London: Verso, 2023)

Miller, Nancy K., 'Mothers, Daughters, and Autobiography: Maternal Legacies and Cultural Criticism', *Mothers in Law: Feminist Theory and the Legal Regulation of Motherhood*, ed. Martha Albertson Fineman and Isabel Karpin (New York, NY: Columbia University Press, 1995)

Milligan, Rowan, 'The politics of the crowbar: Squatting in London, 1968–1977', *Anarchist Studies*, 24:2 (2016), 8–32

Mirza, Heidi Safia (ed.), *Black British Feminism: A Reader* (London: Routledge, 1997)

Mitchell, Juliet, *Woman's Estate* (London: Verso, 2015)

— *The Longest Revolution: Essays on Feminism, Literature and Psychoanalysis* (London: Virago, 1984)

— *Psychoanalysis and Feminism: A Radical Reassessment of Freudian Psychoanalysis* (London: Allen Lane, 1974)

Moan, Pat, 'Learning to Learn', *The Squatter* (1976), 182

Montalbano, William D., 'Her Mother's Daughter – Jailed, a Symbol of Protest – Bernadette Devlin's Child Facing Charges', *Los Angeles Times*, 23 March 1997

Mooney, Gerry, and McCafferty, Tricia, ' "Only looking after the weans"? The Scottish nursery nurses' strike', *Critical Social Policy*, 25:2 (2005), 223–39

Moores, Christopher, 'Opposition to the Greenham Women's Peace Camps in 1980s Britain: RAGE against the "Obscene" ', *History Workshop Journal*, 78 (Autumn 2014), 204–27

Moreton, Cole, 'Bernadette McAliskey: Return of the Roaring Girl', *Independent on Sunday* (5 October 2008)

Morgan, Valerie, *Occasional Paper 3: Peacemakers? Peacekeepers? Women in Northern Ireland 1969–1995* (Derry: INCORE, 1996)

Moss, Jonathan, *Women, Workplace Protest and Political Identity in England, 1968–85* (Manchester: Manchester University Press, 2019)

Munday, Diane, Francome, Colin, and Savage, Wendy, 'Twenty-One Years Of Legal Abortion', *British Medical Journal*, 298:6682 (May 1989), 1231–4

National Federation of Claimants Unions, *The Fight to Live* (Birmingham: 1977)

— *Women and Social Security* (London: 1977)

— *Claimants Union Guidebook* (Birmingham: 1978)

Nelson, Maggie, *The Argonauts* (London: Melville House, 2016)

— *The Art of Cruelty: A Reckoning* (New York, NY: W. W. Norton, 2011)

Nicholls, Jill, 'Going Back to the Beginning', *Spare Rib*, 47 (June 1976)

Niven, Alex, *New Model Island* (London: Repeater Books, 2019)

Nochlin, Linda, 'Why Have There been No Great Women Artists?', *Art News*, January 1971

Notley, Alice, 'A Baby is Born Out of a White Owl's Forehead – 1972', *Mysteries of Small Houses* (New York, NY: Penguin, 1998)

Nugent, Brodie, and Smith, Evan, 'Intersectional solidarity? The Armagh women, the British left and women's liberation', *Contemporary British History*, 31:4 (2017), 611–35

Nwonka, Clive James, ' "You're what's wrong with me": *Fish Tank*, *The Selfish Giant* and the Language for Contemporary Social Realism' *New Cinemas: Journal of Contemporary Film*, 12:3 (2014), 205–23

O'Brien, M. E., *Family Abolition: Capitalism and the Communizing of Care* (London: Pluto Press, 2023)

O'Brien, Mary, *The Politics of Reproduction* (London: Unwin Hyman, 1981)

O'Connor, Sinéad, *Rememberings* (London: Penguin, 2021)

O'Keefe, Teresa, ' "Mother Ireland, Get Off Our Backs": Republican Feminist Resistance in the North of Ireland', *The Troubles in Northern Ireland and Theories of Social Movements*, ed. Lorenzo Bosi and Gianluca De Fazio (Amsterdam: Amsterdam University Press, 2017)

Ogden, Emily, *On Not Knowing: How to Love and Other Essays* (London: Peninsula Press, 2022)

Olsen, Tillie, *Silences* (London: Virago Modern Classics, 1994)

Olszynko-Gryn, Jesse, 'The feminist appropriation of pregnancy testing in 1970s Britain', *Women's History Review*, 28:6 (2019), 869–94

— *A Woman's Right to Know: Pregnancy Testing in Twentieth-Century Britain* (Cambridge, MA: The MIT Press, 2023)

Olufemi, Lola, *Experiments in Imagining Otherwise* (London: Hajar Press, 2021)

— *Feminism, Interrupted* (London: Pluto Press, 2019)

Parker, Clare, 'From Immorality to Public Health: Thalidomide and the Debate for Legal Abortion in Australia', *Social History of Medicine*, 25:4 (2012), 863–80

Parmar, Sandeep, 'An Uncommon Language', *Poetry* (April 2019)

Perry, Ruth, 'Colonizing the Breast: Sexuality and Maternity in Eighteenth-Century England', *Journal of the History of Sexuality*, 2:2 (October 1991), 204–34

Pester, Holly, 'Songs of Rest: An Intervention in the Complex Genre of the Lullaby', *The Restless Compendium: Interdisciplinary Investigations of Rest and Its Opposites*, ed. Felicity Callard, Kimberley Staines, and James Wilkes (London: Palgrave Macmillan, 2016)

Pettitt, Ann, *Walking to Greenham: How the Peace-Camp Began and the Cold War Ended* (Aberystwyth: Honno Press)

Phillips, Adam, *Winnicott* (Cambridge, MA: Harvard University Press, 1988)

— *The Beast in the Nursery: On Curiosity and Other Appetites* (London: Faber & Faber, 1998)

Pickering, Sharon, 'Engendering Resistance: Women and Policing in Northern Ireland', *Policing and Society*, 11 (2001), 337–58

— 'Women, the Home and Resistance in Northern Ireland', *Women and Criminal Justice*, 11:3 (2000), 49–82

Pine, Margaret, *Not by Bread Alone*, Heather Wood Collection (2009-129), Beamish Museum Regional Resource Centre

Poovey, Mary, *Uneven Developments: The Ideological Work of Gender in Mid-Victorian England* (Chicago, IL: University of Chicago Press, 1988)

— ' "Scenes of an Indelicate Character": The Medical "Treatment" of Victorian Women', *The Making of the Modern Body: Sexuality and Society in the Nineteenth Century*, ed. Catherine Gallagher and Thomas Laqueur (Berkeley, CA: University of California Press, 1987), pp. 137–68

Postel, Thierry, 'Childbirth climax: The revealing of obstetrical orgasm', *Sexologies*, 22:4 (2013), 89–92

Price, Dolours, 'Review: Survivors of Religion, Marriage, and War', *Fortnight*, 208 (October 1984), 21–2

Prisons and Probation Ombudsmen Independent Investigations, The, *Independent investigation into the death of Baby B at HMP&YOI Styal* (18 June 2020)

Rada, Michelle, 'Overdetermined: Psychoanalysis and Solidarity', *differences*, 33:2/3 (2022), 1–32

Radcliffe, Walter, *Milestones in Midwifery and the Secret Instrument: The Birth of the Midwifery Forceps* (San Francisco, CA: Jeremy Norman & Co., 1989)

Ragoné, Helena, *Surrogate Motherhood: Conception in the Heart* (London: Taylor & Francis, 1994)

Rawnsley, Andrew, 'Tapping into Tory store of rhetoric', *Guardian*, 3 Feb 1988

Reading, Anna, 'Singing for My Life: Memory, Nonviolence and the Songs of Greenham Common Women's Peace Camp', *Cultural Memories of Nonviolent Struggles*, ed. Anna Reading and Tamar Katriel (London: Palgrave Macmillan, 2015)

— 'Squatting in Britain 1945–1955: housing, politics and direct action', *Housing Studies*, 33:1 (October 2017), 141–3

— 'The UK Squatters Movement 1968–1980', *Jaarboek voor socialistische Discussie en Analyse*, ed. Leendert van Hoogenhuijze (Amsterdam, NL: Kritiek, 2009), 137–59

Reeve, Kesia, 'Squatting since 1945: the enduring relevance of material need', *Housing and Social Policy: Contemporary Themes and Critical Perspectives*, ed. Peter Somerville and Nigel Springings (London: Routledge, 2005), 197–217

Reid, Bryonie, 'Creating counterspaces: identity and the home in Ireland and Northern Ireland in Environment and Planning', *Society and Space*, 25 (2007), 933–50

Reynolds, Tracey, 'Studies of the Maternal: Black Mothering 10 Years On', *Studies in the Maternal* 13.1 (2020)

Rich, Adrienne, *Of Woman Born: Motherhood as Experience and Institution* (London: Virago, 1977)

Riley, Denise, *Time Lived, without Its Flow* (London: Picador, 2019)

— *The Words of Selves: Identification, Solidarity, Irony* (Stanford, NY: Stanford University Press, 2000)

— *'Am I That Name?': Feminism and the Category of 'Women' in History* (London: Macmillan, 1988)

— *War in the Nursery: Theories of the Child and Mother* (London: Virago, 1983)

— ' "The Free Mothers": Pronatalism and Working Women in Industry at the End of the Last War in Britain', *History Workshop*, 11 (Spring 1981), 58–118

— *Marxism for Infants* (Cambridge: Street Editions, 1977)

— 'The Force of Circumstance', *Red Rag*, 9 (1975), 26–8

Roberts, Dorothy E., 'Punishing Drug Addicts Who Have Babies: Women of Color, Equality, and the Right of Privacy', *Harvard Law Review*, 104:7 (May 1991), 1419–1821

Roberts, Michèle, *Paper Houses: A Memoir of the 70s and Beyond* (London: Virago, 2007)

Rooney, Eilish, 'Women, community and politics in Northern Ireland: -isms in action', *Journal of Gender Studies*, 1:4 (1992), 475–91

Rooney, Sally, 'An Irish Problem', *London Review of Books*, 40:10 (May 2018)

Rose, Jacqueline, 'The Analyst', *New York Review of Books* (21 September 2023)

— *On Violence and On Violence against Women* (London: Faber and Faber, 2021)

— *Mothers: An Essay on Love and Cruelty* (London: Faber and Faber, 2018)

— *Women in Dark Times* (London: Bloomsbury, 2014)

— 'Julia Kristeva – Take Two', in *Ethics, Politics, and Difference in Julia Kristeva's Writing*, ed. Kelly Oliver (London: Routledge, 1993), pp. 41–61

— 'Margaret Thatcher and Ruth Ellis', *New Formations*, 6:1 (Winter 1988)

— *Sexuality in the Field of Vision* (London: Verso, 1986)

Rose, Jacqueline, and Frears, Sam, 'You haven't got your sister pregnant, have you?', *London Review of Books*, 44:12 (23 June 2022)

Roseneil, Sasha, *Common Women: Uncommon Practices* (London: Cassell, 2000)

— *Disarming Patriarchy: Feminism and Political Action at Greenham* (Maidenhead: Open University Press, 1995)

Rothman, Barbara Katz, *The Tentative Pregnancy: How Amniocentesis Changes the Experience of Motherhood* (New York: W. W. Norton & Company, 1986)

Rowbotham, Sheila, *Beyond the Fragments: Feminism and the Making of Socialism* (Newcastle upon Tyne: Newcastle Socialist Centre, 1979)

— *The Past is Before Us: Feminism in Action since the 1960s* (London: Penguin, 1990)

—, Segal, Lynne, and Wainwright, Hilary, *Beyond the Fragments: Feminism and the Making of Socialism* (London: Islington Community Press, 1979)

Rowe, Marsha (ed.), *Spare Rib Reader: 100 Issues of Women's Liberation* (London: Penguin, 1982)

— 'What happened at Heywood', *Spare Rib*, 31 (January 1974)

Ryan, Frances, *Crippled: Austerity and the Demonisation of Disabled People* (London: Verso, 2018)

Sage, Lorna, *Bad Blood* (London: Fourth Estate, 2000)

Samuel, Raphael, *The Lost World of British Communism* (London: Verso, 2017)

—, Bloomfield, Barbara, and Boanas, Guy (eds), *The Enemy Within: Pit Villages and the Miners' Strike of 1984–5* (London: Verso, 1986)

Sandford, Stella, 'What is Maternal Labour?', *Studies in the Maternal*, 3:2 (2011), 1–11

Sanger, Margaret, 'The Eugenic Value of Birth Control Propaganda', *Birth Control Review* (October 1921)

Sayeed, Richard Power, *1997: The Future that Never Happened* (London: Zed Books, 2020)

Sayers, Janet, *Mothering Psychoanalysis* (London: Penguin, 1992)

Scargill, Anne, Cook, Betty, and Clayton, Ian, *Anne & Betty: United by the Struggle* (London: Route, 2020)

'Second Peace Woman Expects Baby at Camp', *Newbury Weekly News*, 4 August 1983

Seddon, Vicky, *The Cutting Edge: Women and the Pit Strike* (London: Lawrence & Wishart, 1986)

Segal, Lynne, *Making Trouble: Life and Politics* (London: Verso, 2017)

— 'Subject to Suspicion: Feminism and Antistatism in Britain', *Social Text*, 18:1 (Spring 2000), 143–51

Sheldon, Sally, O'Neill, Jane, Parker, Clare, and Davis, Gayle, ' "Too Much, too Indigestible, too Fast"? The Decades of Struggle for Abortion Law Reform in Northern Ireland', *Modern Law Review*, 83:4 (23 April 2020), 761–96

Shelter, 'Shelter', *The Times*, 12 January 1967

Shiels, P., 'Letter', *Red Rag*, 8 (February 1975)

Showalter, Elaine, *Hysteria beyond Freud* (Berkeley, CA: University of California Press, 1993)

Simons, Joey, *Scheming* (Glasgow: Good Press, 2021)

Sivanandan, A., *Communities of Resistance: Writings on Black Struggles for Socialism* (London: Verso, 1990)

Smith, Zadie, 'Joy', *New York Review of Books* (10 January 2013)

Snow, Julian, 'How We are Helping Cathy to Come Home', *Labour Woman*, 56:3 (1967)

Solnit, Rebecca, *The Mother of All Questions* (London: Granta, 2017)

Solomon, Samuel, *Lyric Pedagogy and Marxist-Feminism: Social Reproduction and the Institutions of Poetry* (London: Bloomsbury, 2019)

Spare Rib, 61 (August 1977)

— 142 (May 1984)

Spielrein, Sabina, *The Essential Writings of Sabina Spielrein: Pioneer of Psychoanalysis*, ed. Ruth I. Cape and Raymond Burt (Abingdon: Taylor & Francis, 2018)

Spillers, Hortense J., 'Mama's Baby, Papa's Maybe: An American Grammar Book', *Diacritics*, 17:2 (Summer 1987), 64–81

Springer, Kimberley, 'Third wave black feminism?', *Signs*, 27:4 (Summer 2002), 1059–82

Srinivasan, Amia, 'Who Lost the Sex Wars?', *New Yorker* (6 September 2021)

Stead, Jean, *Never the Same Again: Women and the Miners' Strike* (London: The Women's Press, 1987)

Steedman, Carolyn, 'Middle-Class Hair', *London Review of Books*, 39:20 (19 October 2017)

— *Past Tenses: Essays on Writing, Autobiography and History* (London: Rivers Oram Press, 1992)

— *Landscape for a Good Woman* (London: Virago, 1986)

— *The Tidy House: Little Girls Writing* (London: Virago, 1983)

Stone, Alison, *Feminism, Psychoanalysis, and Maternal Subjectivity* (London: Routledge, 2012)

Stubbs, David, *1996 and the End of History* (London: Repeater Books, 2016)

Sutcliffe Braithwaite, Florence, 'Tesco and a motorway', *London Review of Books*, 43:17 (September 2021)

—, and Thomlinson, Natalie, *Women and the Miners' Strike, 1984–1985* (Oxford: Oxford University Press, 2023)

Tew, Marjorie, *Safer Childbirth? A Critical History of Maternity Care* (London: Chapman & Hall, 1995)

Thane, Pat, 'Lone Mothers', *Women's History Review*, 20:1 (February 2011), 1–9

— 'Unmarried Motherhood in Twentieth-Century England', *Women's History Review*, 20:1 (February 2011), 11–29

—, and Evans, Tanya, *Sinners? Scroungers? Saints?: Unmarried Motherhood in Twentieth-Century England* (Oxford: Oxford University Press, 2012)

Thatcher, Carol, *Diary of an Election* (London: Sidgwick & Jackson, 1983)

Thatcher, Margaret, *The Path to Power* (London: Harper Collins, 1995)

— *The Downing Street Years* (London: Harper Collins, 1993)

Thompson, Charis, *Making Parents: The Ontological Choreography of Reproductive Technologies* (Berkeley, CA: MIT Press, 2005)

Thompson, E. P., 'The Peculiarities of the English', *Socialist Register 1965*, 311–62

Thompson, Mary, 'Misconceived Metaphors: Irene Vilar's *Impossible Motherhood: Testimony of an Abortion Addict*', *Frontiers: A Journal of Women's Studies*, 35:1 (2014), 132–59

Thomson, Peter, 'Brecht: *Mother Courage and Her Children*' (Cambridge: Cambridge University Press, 1997)

Turner, Jenny, 'Dark Emotions', *London Review of Books*, 42:18 (24 September 2020)

— 'As Many Pairs of Shoes as She Likes', *London Review of Books*, 33:24 (15 December 2011)

Tyler, Imogen, 'Introduction: Birth', *Feminist Review*, 93:1 (November 2009) 1–7

Valenze, Deborah, *Milk: A Local and Global History* (New Haven, CT: Yale University Press, 2011)

Vasudevan, Alexander, *The Autonomous City: A History of Urban Squatting* (London: Verso, 2017)

Vilar, Irene, *Impossible Motherhood: Testimony of an Abortion Addict* (New York, NY: Other Press, 2009)

Vinen, Richard, *Thatcher's Britain: The Politics and Social Upheaval of the Thatcher Era* (London: Simon & Schuster, 2009)

Wall, Christine, 'Sisterhood and Squatting in the 1970s: Feminism, Housing and Urban Change in Hackney', *History Workshop Journal*, 83:1 (Spring 2017), 79–97

Wallsgrove, Ruth, 'Greenham Common Women's Peace Camp: So why am I still ambivalent?', *Trouble and Strife*, 1 (Winter 1983)

Walkowitz, Judith R., 'Feminism and the Politics of Prostitution in King's Cross in the 1980s', *Twentieth Century British History*, 30:2 (June 2019), 231–63

— *Prostitution and Victorian Society – Women, Class, and the State* (Cambridge: Cambridge University Press, 1980)

Wandor, Michelene (ed.),*The Body Politic: Women's Liberation in Britain* (London: Stage 1, 1972)

Warner, Marina, *Monuments and Maidens: the Allegory of the Female Form* (Berkeley, CA: University of California Press, 1985)

Wates, Nick, and Wolmer, Christian (eds), *Squatting: The Real Story* (London: Bay Leaf Books, 1980)

Webber, Howard, 'A Domestic Rebellion: The Squatters' Movement of 1946', *Ex Historia*, 4 (2012), 125–46

Weir, Allison, 'Identification with the Divided Mother: Kristeva's Ambivalence', in *Ethics, Politics, and Difference in Julia Kristeva's Writing*, ed. Kelly Oliver (London: Routledge, 1993), pp. 79–91

White, Simone, *Dear Angel of Death* (New York, NY: Ugly Duckling Press, 2018)

van de Wiel, Lucy, *Freezing Fertility: Oocyte Cryopreservation and the Gender Politics of Aging* (New York, NY: NYU Press, 2020)

Williams, Raymond, 'Mining the Meaning: Key Words in the Miners' Strike', *Resources of Hope: Culture, Democracy, Socialism* (London: Verso, 1989)

409

— *Culture and Society 1780–1950* (London: Chatto & Windus, 1959)

Williams, Stephen, and Fryer, R. H., *Leadership and Democracy* (London: Lawrence & Wishart, 2011)

Wilson, Adrian, *The Making of Man-Midwifer: Childbirth in England 1660–1770* (Cambridge, MA: Harvard University Press, 1995)

Wilson, Elizabeth, *Women and the Welfare State* (Abingdon: Routledge, 1974)

—, and Weir, Angela, *Hidden Agendas: Theory, Politics, and Experiences in the Women's Movement* (London: Tavistock Publications, 1986)

Winnicott, D. W., 'This Feminism', *Home is Where We Start From: Essays by a Psychoanalyst*, ed. Clare Winnicott, Ray Shepherd, and Madeleine Davis (New York, NY: Norton, 1986), pp. 183–94.

— *Playing and Reality* (London: Penguin, 1971)

— *The Child, the Family, and the Outside World* (London: Pelican, 1964)

— 'Hate in the counter-transference', *International Journal of Psychoanalysis*, 30 (1949), 69–74

Withers, D.-M., 'Laboratories of gender: Women's liberation and the transfeminist present', *Radical Philosophy*, 2:4 (Spring 2019)

Wollen, Peter, 'Alphabet of Cinema', *Paris Hollywood: Writings on Film* (London: Verso, 2002)

'Women and the National Front', *Red Rag*, 14 (undated), 28–31

'Women in Co-ops', *Undercurrents*, 46 (June–July 1981)

'Women take the space they need', *Spare Rib*, 46 (May 1976)

Woolf, Virginia, 'Professions for Women', in *Collected Essays*, ed. Andrew McNeillie and Stuart N. Clarke, 6 vols (London: The Hogarth Press, 1986–2011), vol. 5: 1929–1932

— *A Room of One's Own* (London: The Hogarth Press, 1929)

Yamamori, Toru, 'A Feminist Way to Unconditional Basic Income: Claimants Unions and Women's Liberation Movements in 1970s Britain', *Basic Income Studies*, 9:1/2 (2014), 1–24 <https://www.researchgate.net/publication/276248577_A_Feminist_Way_to_Unconditional_Basic_Income_Claimants_Unions_and_Women%27s_Liberation_Movements_in_1970s_Britain>

Archival Resources

Bishopsgate Institute, London:
Denise Riley Archive
Focus E15 Campaign
National Women Against Pit Closures
Women's Liberation Conferences 1974–1986
CAIN archive, Ulster University <https://cain.ulster.ac.uk/>
Coalfield Women, National Coalmining Museum of England / University
    College London / University of Reading
Glasgow Women's Library:
Scottish Abortion Campaign
National Abortion Campaign
Women's Liberation Newsletters
Greenham Common Peace Camp Oral Histories, Imperial War Museum
    London Sound Archive
Heather Wood collection (2009-129), Beamish Museum Regional Resource
    Centre, County Durham
Observing the 80s, Mass Observation Archive, University of Sussex
MayDay Rooms, London:
Big Flame
Dissenting Ephemera, 1970s – Women's Movement
East London Big Flame
Greenham Common Women's Peace Camp
Housing Struggles
Squatting
The Midwife's Tale Oral History Collection, Royal College of Midwives,
    London
Safe and Legal Project, Casgliad Y Werin Cymru / People's Collection Wales
Shocking Pink, Sparrows' Nest Library and Archive, Nottingham
Sisterhood and After: The Women's Liberation Oral History Project, Brit-
    ish Library, London
Women for Life on Earth, Archifau Morgannwg / Glamorgan Archives

Online and Broadcast Resources

Adewole, Oluwatayo, 'Remembering Pearl Alcock, the Black bisexual she-been queen of Brixton', *gal-dem*, 2 February 2021 <https://gal-dem.com/remembering-pearl-alcock-black-bisexual-shebeen-queen-of-brixton/>

Alderson, Reevel, 'Lee Jeans women remember seven-month sit-in success', *BBC*, 4 February 2011 <https://www.bbc.co.uk/news/uk-scotland-12366211>

Amin-Smith, Maya, *Grunwick Changed Me* (BBC, 5 August 2016) <https://www.bbc.co.uk/sounds/play/b07npvfh>

Andrews, Kehinde, 'The Black Supplementary School Movement is as Essential as It's Ever Been', *Black Ballad*, 13 December 2020 <https://blackballad.co.uk/views-voices/saturday-schools--black-supplementary-schools-movement>

Angelo, Bonnie, and Morrison, Toni, 'Toni Morrison: The Pain of being Black', *Time* (May 1998) <http://content.time.com/time/subscriber/article/0,33009,957724-4,00.html>

Anon, '"Redevelopment" Housing & Squatting – Bengali Housing Action Group', *maydayrooms* <https://maydayrooms.omeka.net/items/show/289>

Arie, Sophie, 'UK's "austerity experiment" has forced millions into poverty and homelessness, says UN rapporteur', *BMJ* <https://doi.org/10.1136/bmj.l2321>

Armstrong, Neil, 'Our Friends in the North: One of the greatest ever TV dramas', *BBC Culture*, 13 January 2021<https://www.bbc.com/culture/article/20210112-our-friends-in-the-north-one-of-the-greatest-ever-tv-dramas>

Arnold, Andrea, dir., 'Cowboys and Nomads', *I Love Dick*, written by Sarah Gubbins and Heidi Schreck, Amazon Prime Video, 2017

Asthana, Anushka, 'Take care of your elderly mothers and fathers, says Tory minister', *Guardian*, 31 January 2017 <https://www.theguardian.com/society/2017/jan/31/take-care-of-your-elderly-mothers-and-fathers-says-tory-minister>

Atkins, Lucy, 'A happy birthday every day', *Guardian*, 24 July 2007 <https://www.theguardian.com/society/2007/jul/24/1>

— 'Austerity blamed for "troubling" incarceration rates gap as women in north four times likelier to be jailed', *Independent*, 30 April 2019 <https://www.independent.co.uk/news/uk/home-news/prison-women-north-south-prison-reform-trust-a8891811.html>

Azania-Jarvis, Alice, 'Last Night's Television: Kimberley: Young Mum Ten Years On, BBC4', *Independent*, 24 April 2009 <https://www.independent.co.uk/arts-entertainment/tv/reviews/last-night-s-television-kimberley-young-mum-ten-years-on-who-killed-the-honey-bee-bbc4-1673305.html>

Badshah, Nadeem, 'Shropshire maternity scandal: 300 babies died or left brain-damaged, says report', *Guardian*, 26 March 2022 <https://www.theguardian.com/society/2022/mar/26/shropshire-maternity-scandal-300-babies-died-or-left-brain-damaged-says-report>

Baker, Katie, 'Brecht's Mercenary Mother Courage Turns 75', *Daily Beast*, 31 January 2018 <https://www.thedailybeast.com/brechts-mercenary-mother-courage-turns-75>

Baughan, Emily, 'Bring Back National Milk', *Playgroup*, 22 May 2023 <https://emilybaughan.substack.com/p/bring-back-national-milk>

Beers, Laura, 'Amy Coney Barrett, Enoch Powell and IVF politics', *History Workshop*, 30 October 2020 < https://www.historyworkshop.org.uk/amy-coney-barrett-enoch-powell-and-ivf-politics/>

Bennett, Ronan, 'Life and death in Long Kesh', *Guardian*, 22 October 2008 <https://www.theguardian.com/politics/2008/oct/22/maze-prison-film-northernireland-hunger>

Bentley, Daniel, 'Labour attack Tories over "dodgy" pregnancy figures', *Independent*, 15 February 2010 <https://www.independent.co.uk/news/uk/politics/labour-attack-tories-over-dodgy-pregnancy-figures-1899727.html>

Berlant, Lauren, 'For Example', *supervalent thought*, 16 May 2012 <https://supervalentthought.wordpress.com/2012/05/16/for-example/>

Biggs, Jade, 'Should pregnant women really be sent to prison? How the criminal justice system is failing mums-to-be', *Cosmopolitan*, 10 November 2021 <https://www.cosmopolitan.com/uk/reports/a37988401/pregnant-prison/>

Black, Debra, 'British mum distraught after turning in daughter over UK riots', *Star*, 17 August 2011 <https://www.thestar.com/news/world/

2011/08/17/british_mom_distraught_after_turning_in_daughter_ over_uk_riots.html>

'Blair suffers in benefits revolt', *BBC News*, 11 December 1997 <http:// news.bbc.co.uk/1/hi/uk/38656.stm >

Blair, Tony, 'The Strong Society: Rights, responsibilities and reform', *Guardian*, 30 May 2001 <https://www.theguardian.com/politics/2001/ may/30/election2001.tonyblair>

Booth, Cherie, 'All women should have the chance to have a family and a career', *Guardian*, 20 October 2013 <https://www.theguardian.com/ politics/2013/oct/20/cherie-booth-women-family-career>

Brian, Kate, 'The amazing story of IVF: 35 years and five million babies later', *Guardian*, 12 July 2013 <https://www.theguardian.com/soci ety/2013/jul/12/story-ivf-five-million-babies>

'Briefing – Lone parent benefits', *BBC News*, 10 December, 1997 <http:// news.bbc.co.uk/1/hi/special_report/1997/uk_politics/38371.stm>

Brink, Joram Ten, *Born 1981 – Babies Against the Bomb* (Moonshine Community Arts Workshop, 1984).

'Britain Honors the Fallen in Falklands', *The New York Times*, 27 July 1982 <https://www.nytimes.com/1982/07/27/world/britain-honors-the- fallen-in-falklands.html>

British Medical Association, 'The law and ethics of abortion', September 2020<https://www.bma.org.uk/media/3307/bma-view-on-the-law-and- ethics-of-abortion-sept-2020.pdf>

Brown, Annie, 'From illiterate hippy kid to boss of major Scottish arts festival, Gwilym Gibbons talks of his amazing journey', *Daily Record*, 29 March 2011 <https://www.dailyrecord.co.uk/news/real-life/from- illiterate-hippy-kid-to-boss-of-major-1098818>

Burgum, Sam, 'The 1946 Squatters', *Squatting London*, 18 July 2017 <https:// squattinglondon.wordpress.com/2017/07/18/the-1946-squatters/>

Burtenshaw, Ronan, 'Left Behind by Good Friday: an Interview with Berna- dette Devlin McAliskey', *Jacobin*, 25 April 2016 <https://www.jacobinmag. com/2016/04/bernadette-devlin-interview-derry-civil-rights-troubles- good-friday >

Camber, Rebecca, Fagge, Nick, Faulkner, Katherine, McDermott, Nick, and Caroe, Laura, 'Rage of the girl rioters', *Daily Mail*, 25 November

2010 <https://www.dailymail.co.uk/news/article-1332811/TUITION-FEES-PROTEST-Students-streets-girls-leading-charge.html>

Cammock, Helen, *The Long Note* (2018) <https://lux.org.uk/work/the-long-note/>

Campaign for Social Justice Northern Ireland, The, *Northern Ireland: Why Justice Cannot be Done* (1964) <http://cain.ulst.ac.uk/events/crights/pdfs/csj85.pdf>

Campbell, Beatrix, 'The legacy of Greenham Common has outlived Margaret Thatcher', *Guardian*, 17 April 2013 <https://www.theguardian.com/politics/shortcuts/2013/apr/17/greenham-common-outlived-margaret-thatcher>

Campbell, Denis, 'Concerns over birthing options as NHS shuts midwife-led centre', *Guardian*, 11 February 2019 <https://www.theguardian.com/society/2019/feb/11/concerns-over-birthing-options-as-nhs-shuts-midwife-led-centres-england>

Campbell, Denis, and Doward, Jamie, 'British women treat abortion as the easy option, claims angry Archbishop', *Guardian*, 21 October 2007 <https://www.theguardian.com/uk/2007/oct/21/religion.health>

Campbell, Denis, and Duncan, Pamela, 'Is "incessant increase" in caesarean births putting first-time mothers' health at risk?', 31 January 2016 <https://www.theguardian.com/society/2016/jan/31/caesarean-health-risks-c-section-first-time-mothers>

Care Collective, The, 'COVID-19 pandemic: A Crisis of Care', *Verso* blog, 26 March 2020 <https://www.versobooks.com/blogs/4617-covid-19-pandemic-a-crisis-of-care?fbclid=IwAR3JowRRXnW1x3NoHuSSdZW_Aeule_OmFAOLzTCxd59UbR79us-XXorOH30>

Carter, Helen, and Bowcott, Owen, 'Riots: mother jailed for handling looted shorts freed on appeal', *Guardian*, 19 August 2011 <https://www.theguardian.com/uk/2011/aug/19/riots-mother-looted-shorts-freed>

— 'We fought the law and the law changed', *Utopia Britannica*, 28 February 2021 <http://blog.utopia-britannica.org.uk/1310>

— 'A wonderful anarchic-jumble-sale-of-a-disorganisation', *Utopia Britannica*, 13 June 2020 <http://blog.utopia-britannica.org.uk/2245>

— 'Your Children are Not Your Children', *Utopia Britannica*, 30 May 2020 <http://blog.utopia-britannica.org.uk/1630>

— 'The Price of Free Love', *Utopia Britannica*, 16 May 2020 <http://blog.utopia-britannica.org.uk/1622>

— 'Communal Family Trees (Part 2)', *Utopia Britannica*, 27 April 2013 <http://blog.utopia-britannica.org.uk/117>

Coates, Chris, 'The Basis of Communal Living', *Utopia Britannica*, 20 March 2013 <http://blog.utopia-britannica.org.uk/48>.

Cole, Jeff, *All Out! Dancing in Dulais – Lesbians and Gays Support the Miners* (2013) <https://vimeo.com/22972867>

Coney, Brian, ' "We're not an army – we're three boys from Belfast": rap crew Kneecap laugh off their week of controversy', *Guardian*, 19 August 2022<https://www.theguardian.com/music/2022/aug/19/rap-kneecap-belfast-interview>

Coslett, Rhiannon Lucy, 'Locking up pregnant women damages mothers and children – yet the UK does it', *Guardian*, 16 May 2022 <https://www.theguardian.com/commentisfree/2022/may/16/locking-up-pregnant-women-mothers-children-uk-trauma>

Crockett, Moya, 'The messy history of the nurses' strikes in 1988', *Huck*, 23 November 2021 <https://www.huckmag.com/perspectives/the-messy-history-of-the-nurses-strikes-in-1988/>

Crowbar: Squatting News, 44, 6 August 1985 <https://files.libcom.org/files/Crowbar44.pdf >

Daldry, Stephen, dir., *Billy Elliot* (2000)

Davies, Alan, 'Series Three, Episode Two', *Alan Davies: As Yet Untitled* (Dave, 2015)

Davies, Sarah, 'Albany midwives exonerated – ARM demands apology', *Association of Radical Midwives* (7 March 2017) <https://www.midwifery.org.uk/news/maternity-care/albany-midwives-exonerated-arm-demands-apology/>

Denes, Melissa, 'That's me in the picture: Cherie Blair, the morning after Labour's election victory, 2 May 1997', *Guardian*, 11 May 2015 <https://www.theguardian.com/artanddesign/2015/may/08/cherie-blair-nightie-downing-street-thats-me-in-the-picture>.

Department of Health and Social Care, 'Abortion Statistics, England and Wales: 2019', 11 June 2020 <https://assets.publishing.service.gov.uk/

government/uploads/system/uploads/attachment_data/file/891405/
abortion-statistics-commentary-2019.pdf>

Duffy, Steve, 'Maerdy: Still fighting, 25 years after pit closure', *BBC News* (22 December 2015) <https://www.bbc.com/news/uk-wales-35063090>

Durac, Martina, dir., *Mairéad Farrell: An Unfinished Conversation* (Loopline Films, 2014)

— *Rose Dugdale – Mná an IRA* (Loopline Films, 2012)

'Early Days', *Coalfield Women* <https://www.coalfield-women.org/early-days>

'East London artist paints UK's tallest mural to highlight crisis in affordable housing', *East End Review*, 27 November 2014 <http://www.eastendreview.co.uk/2014/11/27/stik-big-mother-mural/>

Ellen, Barbara, 'Days of whine and poses', *Observer*, 18 May 2008 <https://www.theguardian.com/books/2008/may/18/biography.politics>

Emin, Tracey, 'I felt that, in return for my children's souls, I had been given my success', *Independent*, 29 January 2009 <https://www.independent.co.uk/voices/columnists/tracey-emin/tracey-emin-i-felt-that-in-return-for-my-children-s-souls-i-had-been-given-my-success-1518934.html>

Evans, Dale, '"Nurses are Worth More": The 1982 Health Workers' Dispute', *Past Tense*, 22 September 2020 <https://pasttenseblog.wordpress.com/2020/09/22/today-in-radical-history-1982-a-day-of-action-during-the-nurses-strike/>

Evans, Rob, 'UK political groups spied on by undercover police – search the list', *Guardian*, 15 October 2018 <https://www.theguardian.com/uk-news/ng-interactive/2018/oct/15/uk-political-groups-spied-on-undercover-police-list>

Falklands War: the Untold Story (Channel 4, 2022)

Finney, Clare, 'A group of midwives like no other', *East London Lines*, 25 January 2010 <https://www.eastlondonlines.co.uk/2010/01/a-group-of-midwives-like-no-other/>

Forrester, Katrina, '"In and against the state": revolutionary feminism during deindustrialisation', lecture delivered on 9 June 2023, University of Cambridge

Foster, Dawn, 'Margaret Thatcher didn't expect it, but miners' wives galvanised the 84 strike', *Guardian*, 12 March 2014 <https://www.theguardian.com/commentisfree/2014/mar/12/margaret-thatcher-miners-wives-politicised-strike>

— 'Whose recovery?: Gendered austerity in the UK', *OpenDemocracy*, 4 August 2014 <https://www.opendemocracy.net/en/5050/whose-recovery-gendered-austerity-in-uk/>

Frampton, Ben, 'Escapee pregnancy test frogs colonised Wales for 50 years', *BBC News*, 29 June 2019 <https://www.bbc.co.uk/news/uk-wales-44886585>

Garratt, Hilary, 'Call the Midwife sends out a poignant message', *NHS England blog*, 27 February 2017 <https://www.england.nhs.uk/blog/hilary-garratt-4/>

Gentleman, Amelia, 'Is Britain broken?', *Guardian*, 31 March 2010 <https://www.theguardian.com/society/2010/mar/31/is-britain-broken >

Gregory, Andrew, 'Austerity in England linked to more than 50,000 extra deaths in five years', *Guardian*, 14 October 2021 <https://www.theguardian.com/society/2021/oct/14/austerity-in-england-linked-to-more-than-50000-extra-deaths-in-five-years>

Grierson, Jamie, 'Shamima Begum's mother asks Home Office to show mercy', *Guardian*, 11 March 2019 <https://www.theguardian.com/uk-news/2019/mar/11/shamima-begum-mother-asks-home-office-to-show-mercy>

Grieve, Lucy, 'The Scottish Government is failing women when it comes to abortion', *Scotsman*, 5 June 2022 <https://www.scotsman.com/health/the-scottish-government-is-failing-women-when-it-comes-to-abortion-lucy-grieve-3720095>

Griffiths, Ben, 'Keep my daughter locked up for full sentence, urges Olympics ambassador rioter's dad', *Mirror*, 26 February 2012 <https://www.mirror.co.uk/news/uk-news/keep-my-daughter-locked-up-for-full-743606>

Grigsby, Michael, dir., *VIEWPOINT 87: Living on the Edge* (ITV, 1987)

Hardy, Justin (dir.), *London's Burning* (Channel 4, December 2011)

Hartman, Saidiya, 'A conversation between Hazel Carby and Saidiya Hartman', *Paris Review*, 21 January 2020 <https://www.theparisreview.org/

blog/2020/01/21/errant-daughters-a-conversation-between-saidiya-hartman-and-hazel-carby/>

Health Protection Division, Public Health Wales, *Reducing Teenage Conception Rates in Wales: Project Report* (March 2016) <http://www.wales.nhs.uk/sitesplus/documents/888/Teenage%20conceptions%20in%20Wales%20%20FINALv1.pdf>

Heaney, Emma, 'Is a Cervix Cis? My Year in the Stirrups', *Asterix Journal*, 18 February 2021 <https://asterixjournal.com/is-a-cervix-cis/>.

Hedgie Films, 'Episode 1 – The Lee Jeans Sit-in' <https://www.youtube.com/watch?v=X_-oP1vsNhI>

Helm, Toby, and Savage, Michael, 'More nurses, better care – Tories' 10-year pledge on maternity services', *Guardian*, 29 December 2018 <https://www.theguardian.com/society/2018/dec/29/more-nurses-better-care-tory-10-year-pledge-maternity-services>

Herbstein, Winnie, *Dampbusters*, CCA Glasgow, 2021

Hill, Amelia, 'How the UK halved its teenage pregnancy rate', *Guardian*, 18July2016<https://www.theguardian.com/society/2016/jul/18/how-uk-halved-teenage-pregnancy-rate-public-health-strategy>

— 'Hope and ambition at the school for teenage mothers', *Guardian*, 19 April 2011 <https://www.theguardian.com/society/2011/apr/19/young people-schools >

Hill, Myrtle, Walker, Lynda, and Ward, Margaret, 'A Century of Women – 1970s', *A Century of Women* <https://www.acenturyofwomen.com/1970s/>

Hodgkinson, Will, 'They fuck you up, your mum and dad', *Guardian*, 18 March 2005 <https://www.theguardian.com/music/2005/mar/18/marthawainwright.popandrock >.

House, James, dir., *Making Margaret: A Very British* Revolution (BBC, 2019)

— 'How Strict Prison Sentences after the London Riots Have Caused a Cycle Of Reoffending', *Buzzfeed*, 5 June 2015 <https://www.buzzfeed.com/mayaruthoppenheim/reoffending-rates-amongst-the-august-2011-rioters-is-ris>

Howard, Sally, 'Is the boom in communal living really the good life?', *Guardian*, 17 January 2021 <https://www.theguardian.com/society/2021/jan/17/is-the-boom-in-communal-living-really-the-good-life>

Hutchinson, Lisa, 'Tributes paid to County Durham community stalwart who cooked 800 meals a day for striking miners', *Chronicle Live*, 6 June 2019 <https://www.chroniclelive.co.uk/news/north-east-news/tributes-paid-county-durham-community-16387591>

'I prayed, "Just let my baby see her first birthday"', *You* magazine, 13 December 2020 <https://www.you.co.uk/primodos-scandal-and-the-women-still-fighting-for-justice/>

Interview with Anne Scargill and Betty Cook, 'We Can Win' (2014) <https://www.youtube.com/watch?v=jhRwxBkllDg&t=14s>

Jardine, Lisa, 'A Point of View: IVF and the marketing of hope', *BBC News*, 25 October 2013 <https://www.bbc.com/news/magazine-24652639>

Jardine, David, and Finlay, Jamie (ed.), *The Falls Women's Centre 1982–2009* (Northern Visions Archive, 2009) <http://archive.northernvisions.org/specialcollections/ogfeatures/falls-womens-centre/>

Joseph Rowntree Foundation, 'UK Poverty 2022', 18 January 2022 <https://www.jrf.org.uk/report/uk-poverty-2022>

Jeffries, Dinah, 'My children grew up in a commune', *Guardian*, 14 June 2014 <https://www.theguardian.com/lifeandstyle/2014/jun/14/my-children-grew-up-in-commune>

Kahn, Urmee, 'Tracey Emin's new artwork inspired by teenage pregnancy', *Telegraph*, 13 June 2008 <https://www.telegraph.co.uk/news/celebritynews/2122965/Tracey-Emins-new-artwork-inspired-by-teenage-pregnancy.html

Kellaway, Kate, 'When miners and gay activists united: the real story of the film Pride', *Guardian*, 31 August 2014 <https://www.theguardian.com/film/2014/aug/31/pride-film-gay-activists-miners-strike-interview>

Kelly, Nicola, ' "Cramped and unsafe" Glasgow housing unit forced to suspend mother and baby services', *Guardian*, 19 May 2022 <https://www.theguardian.com/global-development/2022/may/19/cramped-and-unsafe-glasgow-mother-and-baby-housing-unit-is-suspended>

Kennedy, Gerry, 'Wild side of life', *Guardian*, 27 April 2005 <https://www.theguardian.com/society/2005/apr/27/guardiansocietysupplement4>

Kinga Papp, Réka, 'Decriminalizing childbirth', *Eurozine*, 28 June 2017 <https://www.eurozine.com/decriminalising-childbirth-power-dynamics-in-hungarian-birthing-care/>

Kinsella, Ana, 'Anything Else Would Not be Good Enough', *n+1*, 15 June 2018 <https://nplusonemag.com/online-only/online-only/anything-else-would-not-be-good-enough/>

Kokoli, Alexandra, 'A Virtual Museum of Greenham Common: (Art) Histories of Feminism as Feminist Resistance' <https://amkokoli.wixsite.com/greenhamcommon/about>

Krause, Ian, dir., *Not by Bread Alone* (1986), Yorkshire and North East Film Archive <https://www.yfanefa.com/record/27214>

Kushner, Tony, 'Tony Kushner: Mother Courage is not just an anti-war play', *Guardian*, 8 September 2009 <https://www.theguardian.com/stage/2009/sep/08/tony-kushner-mother-courage>

Laville, Sandra, 'Ella Kissi-Debrah: how a mother's fight for justice may help prevent other air pollution deaths', *Guardian*, 16 December 2020 <https://www.theguardian.com/environment/2020/dec/16/ella-kissi-debrah-mother-fight-justice-air-pollution-death>

'Lee Jeans sit-in', Scottish Parliament debate, 10 March 2011 <https://www.theyworkforyou.com/sp/?id=2011-03-10.18.0#g18.6>

Lee, Veronica, 'Mummy dearest', *Guardian*, 21 March 2000 <https://www.theguardian.com/culture/2000/mar/21/artsfeatures>

Leys, Colin, 'How a Decade of Austerity Brought the NHS to Its Knees', *Tribune*, 1 July 2020 <https://tribunemag.co.uk/2020/07/how-a-decade-of-austerity-brought-the-nhs-to-its-knees>

Lloyd, Kate, 'Meet the lesbian punks who've been written out of London's history', *Time Out*, 25 April 2017 <https://www.timeout.com/london/blog/meet-the-lesbian-punks-whove-been-written-out-of-londons-history-042517#:~:text=Brixton%20in%20the%20'80s%20was,by%20its%20diversity%20and%20experimentation>

Logan, Brian, 'What did you do in the class war, Daddy?', *Guardian*, 15 May 2002 <https://www.theguardian.com/culture/2002/may/15/artsfeatures>

Logan, Rob, 'Crossroads Women's Centre', 2014 <http://crossroads-women.net/watch-our-film>

MacNaull, Gillian, 'The problem with women's prisons – and why they do more harm than good', *The Conversation*, 30 July 2019 <https://theconversation.com/the-problem-with-womens-prisons-and-why-they-do-more-harm-than-good-120922>

Mahase, Elizabeth, 'Doctors question NICE recommendation to induce labour at 39 weeks in ethnic minority women', *BMJ*, 6 July 2021 <https://www.bmj.com/content/374/bmj.n1711.full>

'Making Ends Meet', *Coalfield Women* <https://www.coalfield-women.org/making-ends-meet>

Malone, Ray, 'Gay Sweatshop Theatre Company', *Unfinished Histories* (November 2013) <http://www.unfinishedhistories.com/history/companies/gay-sweatshop/care-and-control/>

Mantel, Hilary, 'The princess myth: Hilary Mantel on Diana', *Guardian*, 26 August 2017 <https://amp.theguardian.com/books/2017/aug/26/the-princess-myth-hilary-mantel-on-diana>

'Marches and pickets', *Coalfield Women* <https://www.coalfield-women.org/marches-and-pickets>

'Margaret Thatcher death song goes ahead in Billy Elliott musical', *BBC News*, 9 April 2013 <https://www.bbc.co.uk/news/entertainment-arts-22076220>

McCormack, Cathy, *War without Bullets*, dir. Barbara Orton and Cassandra McGrogan, 1995

McGrath, John, *Blood Red Roses* (Freeway Films, 1986)

McKay, Susan, 'Northern Ireland's women won abortion rights but its politicians won't accept that', *Guardian*, 20 March 2021 <https://www.theguardian.com/commentisfree/2021/mar/20/northern-ireland-women-abortion-rights-stormont-westminster>

Mills, Heather, 'Chaining women backed', *Independent*, 10 January 1996 <https://www.independent.co.uk/news/uk/politics/chaining-women-backed-1323238.html>

Miners' Campaign Tapes Project, The (BFI, 1984)

'Miners' strike – 30 years since the pit crisis of 1984', *Channel 4 News*, 6 March 2014 <Miners' strike – 30 years since the pit crisis of 1984 (youtube.com)>

Moaveni, Azadeh, 'Shamima Begum's is a story of trafficking, betrayal and now, it seems, a state cover-up', *Guardian*, 2 September 2022 <https://www.theguardian.com/commentisfree/2022/sep/02/shamima-begum-trafficking-spy-home-office-citizenship>

Mohrenweiser, Miren, 'The Limitations of "Maternal" Activism in Troubles Narratives', *Writing the Troubles*, 19 April 2021 <https://writingthe

troublesweb.wordpress.com/2021/04/19/the-limitations-of-maternal-activism-in-troubles-narratives/#more-1011>

Moore, Suzanne, Khaleeli, Homa, Sarner, Moya, Harper, Leah, and McCurry, Justin, 'How the Greenham Common protest changed lives: "We danced on top of the nuclear silos" ', *Guardian*, 20 March 2017 <https://www.theguardian.com/uk-news/2017/mar/20/greenham-common-nuclear-silos-women-protest-peace-camp>

Moorhead, Joanna, 'We're glad we chose to be mothers in our teens', *Guardian*, 10 January 2015 <https://www.theguardian.com/lifeandstyle/2015/jan/10/were-glad-we-chose-to-be-mothers-in-our-teens>

Moran, Caitlin, 'Call the Radical Feminist', *Sunday Times*, 26 January 2013 <http://www.thetimes.co.uk/>

Moss, Rachel, 'Two Women in UK are Facing Criminal Charges for Abortion. Here's Why', *Huffington Post*, 18 July 2022 <https://www.huffingtonpost.co.uk/entry/why-women-in-uk-face-criminal-charges-for-abortion_uk_62d5689ee4b0116f21be6fe1>

'My baby died during childbirth in my prison cell', *BBC Newsnight* (21 September 2021) <HMP Styal: My baby died due to errors in prison, says former inmate – BBC News>

'Nanny's mother attacks Blairs', *BBC News*, 29 March 2000 <http://news.bbc.co.uk/1/hi/uk/694446.stm>

Negus, John, Interview with Margaret Thatcher, *Sixty Minutes*, Australia, 23 September 1981

Ntini, Charitini (Hari), ' "Where were the women?": Women active service members of the Provisional IRA in the Northern Ireland conflict', *Writing the Troubles*, 2 May 2022 <https://writingthetroublesweb.wordpress.com/2022/05/02/women-active-service-members-of-the-pira/>

Nugent, Ciara, 'What It was Like to Grow Up as the World's First "Test-Tube Baby" ', *Time*, 25 July 2018 <https://time.com/5344145/louise-brown-test-tube-baby/>

O'Dowd, Adrian, 'A history of nursing in Britain: the 1980s', *Nursing Times*, 11 October 2021 <https://www.nursingtimes.net/news/history-of-nursing/a-history-of-nursing-in-britain-the-1980s-11-10-2021/>

O'Kelly, Ciarán, Hackett, Ciara, Hopkins, Samantha, and Patton, Clare, 'Businesses, Remedy and Vaccine Trials', *Cambridge Core*, 14 April 2021 <https://www.cambridge.org/core/blog/2021/04/14/businesses-remedy-and-vaccine-trials-reflections-on-the-business-and-human-rights-issues-in-the-irish-mother-and-baby-homes-report/>

Oppenheim, Maya, 'Maternity services at risk as midwives plan to quit over pandemic stress', *Independent*, 31 March 2021 <https://www.independent.co.uk/independentpremium/uk-news/nhs-maternity-nurses-leaving-pandemic-b1824570.html>

Osmond, John, 'Riot Reflections 1: Why Wales escaped', *Institute of Welsh Affairs*, 16 August 2011 <https://www.iwa.wales/agenda/2011/08/riot-reflections-1-why-wales-escaped-the-riots/>

Pascali-Bonarro, Deborah, dir., *Orgasmic Birth: The Best-Kept Secret* (2008)

Petersen, Sara, 'Victorian Era-Inspired Momfluencers are Taking Over Instagram', *InStyle*, 25 March 2021 <https://www.instyle.com/lifestyle/momfluencers-nostalgia-instagram>

Pittam, David, 'Miners' strike: The decades-old feud that still divides communities', *BBC News*, 6 March 2019 <https://www.bbc.co.uk/news/uk-england-nottinghamshire-47401859>

Powell, Amanda, 'The day Margaret Thatcher was egged in Porthcawl – as told by the women who were there', *Wales Online*, 25 June 2019 <https://www.walesonline.co.uk/news/wales-news/day-margaret-thatcher-egged-porthcawl-16447852>

Prasad, Raekha, 'I didn't have to have a man', *Guardian*, 4 June 2011 <https://www.theguardian.com/lifeandstyle/2011/jun/04/britains-first-lesbian-child-artificial-insemination>

—, and Bawdon, Fiona, 'Don't blame our parents, say rioters', *Guardian*, 6 December 2011 <https://www.theguardian.com/uk/2011/dec/06/dont-blame-parents-say-rioters>

Reeve, Kesia, '"Decent housing for all!" The UK Squatters Movement 1968–1980', *Explosive Politics* (19 December 2016) <http://explosivepolitics.com/blog/decent-housing-for-all-the-uk-squatters-movement-1968-1980/>

Robinson, Lucy, 'It did get tiring to welcome everyone: the fire, politics and spirituality at Greenham Common Peace Camp', *Observing the 80s*, 8 November 2013 <https://blogs.sussex.ac.uk/observingthe80s/2013/11/08/it-did-get-tiring-to-welcome-everyone-to-the-fire-politics-and-spirituality-at-greenham-common-peace-camp/>

Rogers, Simon, 'The women who rioted' in 'Reading the riots: A data-driven study into the causes and consequences of the August 2011 riots', *Guardian*, 9 December 2011 <https://www.theguardian.com/news/datablog/2011/dec/09/data-journalism-reading-riots>

Romm, Cari, 'Before There were Home Pregnancy Tests', *Atlantic*, 17 June 2015 <https://www.theatlantic.com/health/archive/2015/06/history-home-pregnancy-test/396077/>

Ross, Deborah, 'Cherie Blair: "You can't please people who don't really know you"', *Independent*, 2 August 2008 <https://www.independent.co.uk/news/people/profiles/cherie-blair-you-can-t-please-people-who-don-t-really-know-you-882383.html>

Roxborough, Scott, 'Toronto: Hungarian Filmmakers on the Personal Trauma behind "Pieces of a Woman"', *Hollywood Reporter*, 16 September 2020 <https://www.hollywoodreporter.com/news/toronto-hungarian-filmmakers-on-the-personal-trauma-behind-pieces-of-a-woman>

RTÉ, *Eye Witness*, 1979 <https://www.rte.ie/archives/exhibitions/1031-civil-rights-movement-1968-9/1032-caledon-protest/319335-caledon-civil-rights-campaign/>

— 'Austin Currie in Housing Protest', 1968 <https://www.rte.ie/archives/exhibitions/1031-civil-rights-movement-1968-9/1032-caledon-protest/>

— '"I Have No Confidence in Dungannon Urban Council Whatsoever"', 1968 <https://www.rte.ie/archives/exhibitions/1031-civil-rights-movement-1968-9/1032-caledon-protest/319306-interview-with-mrs-mccrystal/>

Rustin, Susanna, 'All British women have the right to a caesarean – they're not "too posh to push"', *Guardian*, 29 March 2016 <https://www.theguardian.com/commentisfree/2016/mar/29/british-women-right-caesarean-too-posh-to-push>

Saner, Emine, 'Lorna Sage, my mum', *Guardian*, 9 October 2010 <https://www.theguardian.com/lifeandstyle/2010/oct/09/lorna-sage-bad-blood>

Scottish Government, *Pregnancy and Parenthood in Young People Strategy 2016–2026* (March 2016) <https://www.lanarkshiresexualhealth.org/wp-content/uploads/sites/18/2019/06/pregnancyparenthoodinyp.pdf>

Shanahan, Harri, and Williams, Sian A., *Rebel Dykes* (2021)

Shapiro, Samantha May, 'Mommy Wars: The prequel', *The New York Times* magazine, 27 May 2012 <https://www.nytimes.com/2012/05/27/magazine/ina-may-gaskin-and-the-battle-for-at-home-births.html>

Sherwood, Harriet, 'Left in the lurch: mothers-to-be devastated as maternity scheme ends', *Guardian*, 2 February 2019 <https://www.theguardian.com/society/2019/feb/02/nhs-axes-personal-midwife-project>

Shields, Derica, *A Heavy Nonpresence* (London: Triple Canopy, 2021) <https://canopycanopycanopy.com/contents/a-heavy-nonpresence>

Simons, Joey, *The Fearful Part of It was the Absence*, Collective Gallery Edinburgh, 2022

Sissay, Lemn, 'A Child of the State' (*TED*, March 2014)

Sisters Uncut, 'Sisters Uncut Reclaim Holloway Prison: Addressing the legacy of state violence', *Verso* blog, 5 June 2017 <https://www.verso-books.com/blogs/3243-sisters-uncut-reclaim-holloway-prison-addressing-the-legacy-of-state-violence>

— 'Sisters Uncut statement on the sale of Holloway Prison', 8 March 2019 <https://www.sistersuncut.org/2019/03/08/sisters-uncut-statement-on-the-sale-of-holloway-prison/>

— 'Occupy vs. Reclaim: what's in a name?', 6 September 2016 <https://www.sistersuncut.org/2016/09/06/occupy-vs-reclaim-whats-in-a-name/>

Snow, Jon, *Maggie & Me* (Channel 4, 2013)

'Solar homes are cold comfort in Easterhouse', 22 October 1992, *Herald Scotland* <https://www.heraldscotland.com/news/12584759.solar-homes-are-cold-comfort-in-easterhouse/>

'South London Women's Hospital occupation 1984–85', *libcom*, 6 February 2013 <https://libcom.org/library/south-london-womens-hospital-occupation-1984-85>

Sowemimo, Annabel, 'Learning the African history of caesarean sections will help us better challenge stigma', *gal-dem*, 27 August 2020 <https://gal-dem.com/learning-the-african-history-of-caesarean-sections-will-help-us-to-better-challenge-stigma/>

Sparrow, Josie, 'A commitment to care . . . and to disobedience', *New Socialist*, 15 April 2020 <https://newsocialist.org.uk/commitment-to-care-lola-olufemi/>

Sproule, Luke, 'Why are there fewer teenager mothers in Northern Ireland?', *BBC News NI*, 24 October 2021 <https://www.bbc.co.uk/news/uk-northern-ireland-59001641>

Sproull, Patrick, 'Melvin Burgess: "Junk was one of the first teen books: I invented the territory"', *Guardian*, 14 August 2014 <https://www.theguardian.com/childrens-books-site/2014/aug/14/melvin-burgess-junk-first-teen-book>

Steel, Peta, 'Terry Marsland: Union leader who devoted her career to fighting for women's rights', *Independent*, 25 June 2011 <https://www.independent.co.uk/news/obituaries/terry-marsland-union-leader-who-devoted-her-career-to-fighting-for-women-s-rights-2302593.html>

Steiner, Susie, 'Natural birth: "I felt brilliant. I was in utter ecstasy"', *Guardian*, 1 June 2013 <https://www.theguardian.com/lifeandstyle/2013/jun/01/natural-birth-childbirth-midwife-ecstasy>

Stoppard, Miriam, Interview with Margaret Thatcher, *Woman to Woman*, ITV (19 November 1985)

Summers, Hannah, 'Black women in the UK four times more likely to die in pregnancy or childbirth', *Guardian*, 15 January 2021 <https://www.theguardian.com/global-development/2021/jan/15/black-women-in-the-uk-four-times-more-likely-to-die-in-pregnancy-or-childbirth>

Teeman, Tim, 'Kimberley: Young Mum Ten Years On', *The Times*, 24 April 2009 <https://www.thetimes.co.uk/article/kimberley-young-mum-ten-years-on-coronation-street-5rk59kxhjxk>

Thatcher, Carol, *Mummy's War* (Channel 4, 2007)

— 'My Mother's War', *Daily Mail*, 24 March 2007 <https://www.dailymail.co.uk/femail/article-444389/Carol-Thatcher-My-Mothers-War.html>

'This is the real Brixton Challenge', *Past Tense*, 18 April 2021 <https://past-tenseblog.wordpress.com/2021/04/18/this-is-the-real-brixton-challenge/>

Thomas, Tobi, and Elgot, Jessica, 'Women from poorer backgrounds three times more likely to have abortions', *Guardian*, 23 March 2021 <https://www.theguardian.com/world/2021/mar/23/women-from-poorer-backgrounds-three-times-more-likely-to-have-abortions>

Thompson, Melissa, 'Interview with Anne Crilly', *Slí na mBan* (1998–2006) <http://www.tallgirlshorts.net/marymary/anne.html>

Thorpe, Vanessa, 'My own Falklands mission', *Guardian*, 18 March 2007 <https://www.theguardian.com/uk/2007/mar/18/politics.military1>

Topping, Alexandra, and Wintour, Patrick, 'London riots: Wandsworth council moves to evict mother of charged boy', *Guardian*, 12 August 2011 <https://www.theguardian.com/uk/2011/aug/12/london-riots-wandsworth-council-eviction>

Toynbee, Polly, 'The drop in teenage pregnancies is the success story of our time', *Guardian*, 13 December 2013 <https://www.theguardian.com/commentisfree/2013/dec/13/drop-teenage-pregnancies-success-story-children>

— 'How could Cherie Blair do this without blushing?', *Guardian*, 8 June 2005 <https://www.theguardian.com/politics/2005/jun/08/labour.cherieblair>

Travis, Alan, 'Thatcher pushed for breakup of welfare state despite NHS pledge', *Guardian*, 25 November 2016 <https://www.theguardian.com/politics/2016/nov/25/margaret-thatcher-pushed-for-breakup-of-welfare-state-despite-nhs-pledge>

Turley, Miriam, 'Squatting Belfast', originally published in *The Vacuum*, 11 <https://en.squat.net/2015/01/11/a-squatters-guide-to-belfast/>

Veach, Nicole, 'Our trauma, by baby death couple', *Observer*, 16 May 1999 <https://www.theguardian.com/uk/1999/may/16/nicoleveash.theobserver1>

Walden, Brian, Margaret Thatcher Interview for London Weekend Television, *Weekend World* ('Victorian Values'), 16 January 1983

Ward, Lucy, and Butt, Riazat, 'Too many abortions: Lord Steel', *Guardian*, 24 October 2007 <https://www.theguardian.com/uk/2007/oct/24/politics.topstories3>

Waugh, Paul, 'Cherie Blair is the "Lady Macbeth" of British politics', *Independent*, 8 August 2000 <https://www.independent.co.uk/news/uk/politics/cherie-blair-is-the-lady-macbeth-of-british-politics-711023.html>

Wayman, Sheila, 'What are the factors behind a 73% drop in teenage pregnancies in Ireland?', *Irish Times*, 25 January 2022 <https://www.irishtimes.com/life-and-style/health-family/parenting/what-are-the-factors-behind-a-73-drop-in-teenage-pregnancies-in-ireland-1.4779434>

'What is austerity and how has it affected British society?', *The New York Times*, 24 February 2019 <https://www.nytimes.com/2019/02/24/world/europe/britain-austerity-may-budget.html>

Whelan, Paedar, 'Armagh women's prison struggle told in inspiring film', *An Phoblacht*, 7 March 2016 <https://www.anphoblacht.com/contents/25797>

Whyte, Michael, dir., *Scream Quietly or the Neighbours Will Hear*, 1974 (London Screen Archives)

Williams, Sally, 'My four mums', *Guardian*, 4 July 2009 <https://www.theguardian.com/lifeandstyle/2009/jul/04/feminism-communes-children>

Williams, Zoe, 'Where's all that grief going?', *Guardian*, 27 September 2013 <https://www.theguardian.com/society/2013/sep/27/ivf-where-all-grief-going>

— 'The accidental feminist', *Guardian*, 21 October 2004 <https://www.theguardian.com/world/2004/oct/21/gender.uk>

Women in Prison, 'Key Facts' <https://womeninprison.org.uk/about/key-facts>

World Health Organization, 'Adolescent Pregnancy', 2 June 2023 <https://www.who.int/news-room/fact-sheets/detail/adolescent-pregnancy>

Wynne-Jones, Ros, 'The Devlin legacy that made her "guilty"', *Independent*, 10 March 1998; Éamon Phoenix, *Irish News*, 20 December 2020 <https://www.irishnews.com/news/northernirelandnews/2020/

12/30/news/roisin-mcaliskey-case-put-british-government-under-pressure-2172602/>

Zephaniah, Benjamin, 'Zephaniah Remembers Colin Roach' <https://4wardevernewsvine.files.wordpress.com/2009/01/zephaniah-remembers-colin-roach-final.pdf>

Index

HC indicates Helen Charman.

New Deal for Lone Parents (1998)
270–72
New Labour xi, xii, 175, 216, 257–8,
263, 268–81, 297
New York Times 292
New Zealand ix, x
Newbury Weekly News 207
Newham Council 319–22
Newsnight 312
Newsom, Joanna: 'Divers' 25
NHS. *See* Natioonal Health Service
Nochlin, Linda: 'Why Have There Been
No Great Women Artists?' 33
non-monogamous relationships 123
nonviolent resistance 207, 212
normative families, prioritization of
270–73
Northern Ireland xix, xxvi, 5
abortion in 36–7, 45–6, 227–8,
230–31, 246
age of consent in 300
blanket-men 237
Brexit and 223
British soldiers in, mothers of
253–4
Cumann na mBan 226, 229, 234, 255
domestic abuse in 223–4, 231, 246
feminism and 224–30, 242–3, 244–6,
254
gendered violence 223–4, 227
Good Friday Agreement 45, 223, 253
hunger strikes 230, 237, 239,
243–5, 250
industrial action in 160, 163, 178
IRA, women and 215, 225, 227–8,
229, 230–34, 237, 238, 246, 248, 249,
251, 252, 255
Irish unification referendum, Sinn
Féin intention to hold 323, 324
jails *see individual jail name*

loyalist communities 194–5, 222,
232, 235–6, 252, 254, 325–6
maternal impulse to defend and
protect and 232–3
McAliskey on *see* McAliskey,
Bernadette Devlin
Mother Ireland (documentary) 221,
225–30
Only the Rivers Run Free 230–32, 234,
239, 299
Peace '93 251–2
Peace People 250–52
prisoners, pregnant 246–9, 255–6
prisoners, mothers as 241–9,
255–6
prisoners, mothers of 236–41
prisons *see individual prison name*
republican communities 106, 222,
224–35, 236, 243, 246, 249, 250,
252, 256
sexual harassment 227, 228
Special Category Status 236–7
squatting in 104–5, 106, 107–8
strip-searching of women 225, 228
teenage pregnancy rates in 286
Thatcher and 194–5, 215
Troubles, maternal involvement in
the 221–56
Warrington bombing, IRA 251–3
'Zombie' and 252–3
Northern Ireland Abortion
Campaign 45
Northern Ireland Abortion Law
Reform Association 45
Northern Ireland Civil Rights
Association 106, 107
Northern Ireland Housing Executive
107–8
Northern Ireland Women's Coalition
(NIWC) 226